MILEPOST I-80

San Francisco To New York

by

Mary Lu Kost

© COPYRIGHT 1993, MILEPOST PUBLICATIONS

ISBN 0-9633489-0-6
Library of Congress Catalog Card Number: 92-90985

Title page and above photo credit: San Francisco Convention & Visitors Bureau Photo

D edicated to all those bored travelers who
stare out at endless miles of sagebrush, sand and corn
without a flicker of interest in anything that flashes by,
while secrets of the past, the present and the joys
that can be, lay hidden over the hill or across the river.

1906 CLIFFHOUSE, SAN FRANCISCO
Photo credit: Dunn Family Heirloom

INTRODUCTION TO MILEPOST TRAVELING

Interstate I-80 is the longest and the most direct East-West interstate in the United States. It extends from San Francisco 2899 miles to almost the gates of New York City. This highway was completed in 1975 cutting days off cross-country travel. In "On The Road With Charles Kuralt", he says: "Thanks to the Interstate Highway System, it is now possible to travel across the country from coast to coast without seeing anything." "MILEPOST I-80" challenges this concept! With this as your guide, you can see EVERYTHING!

"Mileposts" are short green signs that line I-80 marking EVERY mile from the western Nevada border to New York city. Each state begins with "zero" at its Western Border. The Exits are then numbered according to the nearest milepost sign. At the end of each chapter of this book there is a line map with Exit diamonds giving the milepost numbers for every Exit. Intersecting highway numbers are noted. The key will direct you to Campgrounds, Reststops, Parking areas, Malls and Information centers. Eastbound you can compute the distance to any exit by noting a milepost sign nearest you and subtracting that number from the exit number you desire.

"Milepost I-80" is written West to East as that is the sequence of the green Mileposts signs. California is the only state that does not have mileposts, so we have had to implement them. Information on city "sights" are listed at one of the Western entrances of those cities.

With relatives on both coasts, the Kost family has traversed this country on US 30, 40, 6 and I-80 dozens of times. On each trip a log was kept of campgrounds, service stations, cafes, etc. As we have traveled on a budget by car, trailer, camper and motor home we especially noted the less expensive fuel, food, and camping prices. We preferred buffets where we would not have to wait to be served and where we could readily see the quality of the food. We have had to find an emergency hospital, garage, dentist, a quiet campground, a grocery store, and place for the children to run. So our log grew. The computer enabled us to pull the logs together into one Milepost Book. Now it includes museums, art galleries, historical sights and some unusual places for people with special interests.

We are retired teachers who enjoy learning and have always been interested in the geography and geology of our country, and the Western Movement of our pioneers. We hope you enjoy some of the stories of our heritage from those who traveled before us and paved the way for I-80 today.

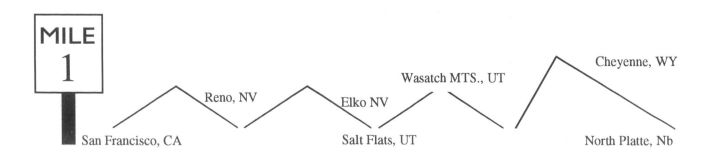

Services change yearly and gas stations and motels may be under new management. Restaurants get new cooks or close and museum hours and prices vary seasonally. New exits are under construction. But in spite of all that, we hope you will be able to find the services you need. When you find errors/changes, we would appreciate your dropping a card to inform us for the next edition. You will notice that fuel prices may be as much as 10 cents less per gallon in town than on I-80. Nebraska and Iowa service stations sell Ethanol/Gasohol which is 10% alcohol and 90% gasoline. In the summer heat, it caused vapor-lock on our Chrysler and the engine would cut out. Read the small print on the pumps.

Campgrounds can be an adventure all their own. Included are all that we could find. Some have scant information so you'll have to check them out. No guarantees! Distances from the freeway are noted to help you choose. Those close to the freeway are designated "NEAR I-80." Included are some more primitive or more distant ones FOR THE ADVENTURESOME. Although a State Park may have a "full" sign, it may have room for an overnighter in the "overflow area", so ask. Expect a $1-$4 increase in campground prices each year. A tip for showering in public places is to wear plastic "flip-flops" while ladies need a loose cover-up with big pockets for toiletries. (Restrooms rarely have enough hooks or dry seats.) Most state parks now are well-equipped. County and municipal parks may not have as high a quality of facility, but are less expensive ($6-$8) than the private ones ($14 to $25). Public parks in some areas subject to freezing have pit toilets, but if you want the beautiful scenery you have no choice. (Carry paper seat-covers.)

Many restaurants are listed, but again you're on your own. The best rule is to ask locally. Don't be afraid to walk away after seeing the food or the menu; we have walked out of the finest. Lunch prices are usually $3-$5 less than dinner prices, so eat before 4 pm. Carry snacks, especially fruit and nuts and check food markets for barbecued chicken, ribs and salad bars.

The Budget motel chains seem to be Motel 6, Motel 8, Western Super Budget, Western, Rodeway, Shilo Inn, Red Roof and Econo Lodge. But they vary so ask the price and if it's too much, walk away. If they have been listed somewhere as "Budget", there will be an "*"after the name. Undoubtedly there are many more than are so designated but the information is absent. Often the locally owned motels are less expensive but sometimes less reliable too. Inspect a room and turn on the heat or air-conditioning BEFORE you register.

Stop at State Visitor Centers for maps and other information. These information centers are noted on the maps with an "I". Be sure to get a STATE MAP for each state. If you want to see the sights in a city ask for a CITY MAP so you won't become lost. "Woodall", "Trailer Life", AAA's "Tour" and "Camping" books are handy if you are going off I-80. Area maps like "Western States" lack the detail you will need.

Read this book BEFORE you go on your trip and highlight the sights you prefer. Mark your total trip on a U.S. map so that you'll have "The Big Picture". This book attempts to give you the opportunity to know what is out there beyond the concrete, sagebrush and corn fields.

WE ARE BLESSED WITH A BEAUTIFUL COUNTRY!
ENJOY IT!

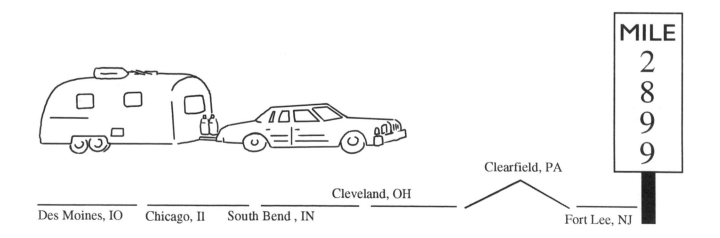

MILE
2
8
9
9

Clearfield, PA

Cleveland, OH

Des Moines, IO   Chicago, Il   South Bend , IN

Fort Lee, NJ

CONTENTS

California

The Golden State!

California has been "The Golden State", "The Eldorado" for millions of dreamers and emigrants! For the Spanish explorers and the gold-crazed miners it was for that shiny gold metal. But since those early years it was the vision of golden opportunity of the first settlers, the European and Asian immigrants, the dust-bowl migrants of the 1930's, the post World War II vets, the Vietnamese, and today's Russian and Ukrainian immigrants. They all came to "See the elephant!" and most found it favorable and stayed.

In the gold rush days, writers equated the massive Westward Movement with the old East Indian story of "The Ten Blind Men And The Elephant". One blind man felt the tail and said that the elephant was like a rope. Another felt his side and said that he resembled a wall. One felt his trunk and pronounced him, a snake. And so on. Thus each person sees California according to individual values and dreams. If the reality matches the dream, they stay.

California's population has doubled every 20 years since 1852. Sacramento County had just 170,000 people in 1941, mostly within Sacramento city limits. The state had 7 million. The post war influx multiplied it. Now Sacramento County has over one million, most outside the city limits. California is not only the third largest state in SIZE with 158,000 square miles, but today it has the largest population in the nation, 30 million. California is a cosmopolitan state with citizens of all nations, all tongues. It's an Ethnic Potpourri!

State symbols are also "Golden". The State Flower is the Golden Poppy that used to cover whole hillsides. California's golden Grizzly bear was such a problem for the Native Indians but now it is extinct except for its place on the state flag. But the state's motto, "Eureka, I've found it!" still holds true for many today.

The topography is more varied and more dramatic than that of any other state. From the ocean, the Coast Range rises sharply. Then the land slides into the largest valley in the U.S., the Great Valley of California. It's 60 miles wide and 475 miles long with deep transported soil that makes it some of the richest agricultural land in the world. To the East are the Sierra Nevada Mountains, with a ridge of high peaks over 300 miles long which include the highest peak in the continental U.S., Mount Whitney at 14,494 feet. (Few know it yet but new measurements of a peak in the White Mountains of California challenge Whitney's supremacy.) The lowest point in the U.S., not far from either of these mountains, is Death Valley, 282 feet below sea level. The oldest trees in the world, the Bristle Cone Pine grows in the White Mountains. The tallest living trees are the Pacific Coast Redwoods, over 300 feet tall. The largest in total size are the Giant Sequoias protected in parks from the Placer County Grove, near Forest Hill, to Sequoia National Park. Yosemite has the highest waterfall. Death Valley is the hottest spot, up to 136 degrees in the summer. California boasted of the only active volcano in the U.S., Mount Lassen, until Oregon's Mount St. Helens blew its top. The California coast winds 1264 miles, equal to the distance from Maine to Georgia. It is dramatic and spectacular with high cliffs and a pounding surf! The gem of California is Lake Tahoe, the largest alpine lake in the nation, 22 miles long and 12 miles wide.

The varied terrain also makes for varied weather. Though the deserts and the valley have hot weather in the summer, San Francisco's mean temperature only varies from 60-70 degrees winter to summer. In winter the high Sierras can have below zero temperatures and some of the deepest snows in the nation while the Great Valley rarely goes below 30 degrees and has NO snow. High Sierra snowpack can range from 10 to 25 feet. Rainfall is 100" in the Northwest and 2" in the desert. Fog may sit in the valley in dreary January and keep the temperatures there in the 40's while it is lovely, mild and sunny in the foothills. San Francisco may be foggy and cold in one part of town and sunny

Poppy

and warm in another. In California, if you don't like the weather, either just wait awhile or go to another part. In one winter day you can ski at 7,000 feet and then surf in the ocean.

While you are here in California you should see some of its highlights. Four of the National Parks: Lassen, Redwood, Yosemite, and Sequoia are MUST STOPS. The Redwoods, in groves along the coast, are the tallest trees in the world with tiny flat needles like yew or hemlock. The Giant Sequoias, the largest trees in the world, are in the Sierras with needles that are jointed like cedar. Their tiny cones are filled with thousands of seeds and their thick spongy bark protects them from fires. "Discovery Tree", in "Calavaras Big Trees" was 1300 years old when it was felled in 1852 to make a bowling alley. The giant stump was used for a 4th of July Dance Cotillion in 1854. You can still dance on the stump today. You have to walk through these groves to feel their splendor. The only other trees in the redwood family in the WORLD are the Dawn Redwoods in China .

Interstate I-80 in California was marked in tragedy by the Donner Party who starved and froze by Donner Lake in 1846. The first road through there was the "Donner Lake Wagon Road". After the turn of the century it became part of the transcontinental highway from San Francisco to New York and was named the "Abraham Lincoln Memorial Highway". In 1926 it became US 40. The "Blue Star Memorial Highway" was added in 1947. The highway climbs 7,000 feet in 75 miles, so in the 1950's, long lines of cars slowly snaked up US 40, radiators boiling, stuck behind growling trucks. It was also difficult to keep this highway open due to the deep snows. Cars traveling through a trough of snow ten feet high on either side would be stopped by snow and rock slides. Changing this twisty 2-lane road into Interstate I-80 was an engineering achievement. It required 2.5 million pounds of explosives and several summers to break through the solid granite of the Sierras. When it was finally completed in 1964 it won a "Civil Engineering Achievement of Merit" and a National award for outstanding scenic beauty.

CALIFORNIA HISTORY

The Native American tribes migrated here some 4,000 to 10,000 years ago from across the Bering Straits and Alaska. California had the densest Native population in the nation estimated at 180,000 to 250,000. They had no need for farming as the Eastern Indians did. They lived in harmony with nature with a sea rich in food and land rich in antelope, deer, elk, nuts and seeds. The narrow Pacific Flyway and the mild climate provided them with thousands of ducks and geese each fall through spring. The migrating salmon and trout were bountiful. California Indians were a peaceful people. They had no horses or tipis. They lived mostly along the coast, just as today when Los Angeles and San Francisco are the most densely populated.

California's name came from Cortez who called Mexico, "Bajo California", Lower California. He never traveled further North but declared all the land North of Mexico all the way to Alaska as "Alta California", Upper California. Cortez' terms included the land from the Continental Divide to the Pacific.

European explorers began dropping in from Cabrillo in 1542, Sir Francis Drake in 1579, Vizcaino in 1602, to Portola in 1768. The latter brought Fr. Serra and other Franciscan monks from 1769 to 1823 who eventually built 22 Missions up and down the coast, and taught the Native Californians to plant fruit trees, grapes and field crops. But the Europeans also brought small pox, malaria and venereal diseases that killed the natives. They rebelled from the rigid conformity and attacked and burned the missions. After the Natives had been instructed as farmers, they were supposed to get rights to the lands they had tilled. But then the Mexicans won their independence from Spain. Mexico took the Missions from the church in 1834 and sold the lands, the cattle, horses and other stock to white settlers. By this time two generations of Indians had lived in the missions and had lost the knowledge of their ancestors to survive on the land. Many became virtual slaves to the new owners. By the time of the gold rush there were only 100,000 Native Americans left. The valley tribelets had been little affected by the Spanish or Mexicans who had stayed along the coast. Their mainstay was the mush made from acorns from the foothill oak trees. The miners came with their contempt and fear of ALL Native tribes fired by generations of warfare with Native Americans in the midwest and along the Oregon Trail. The gentle California tribelets, having never known war, were helpless against them. By 1900 there were only about 15,000 Natives left. One of our priceless heritages from these first Californians is their basketry which is of the finest in the world. You can see it displayed in the "Indian Museum" in Sacramento.

In 1741 Russia's Vitus Bering was ship-wrecked on a North Pacific island. He and his crew wrapped themselves in sea otter skins to keep from freezing. They built a boat from the wreckage of their ship and returned to Siberia to find that these furs were very valuable to Russian and Asian princes. Thereafter Russian ships sailed through the Bering Sea and the coast of Alaska to Northern California enjoining and even forcing the natives to hunt sea otters by the thousands. The Russians would buy the furs for a few scraps of iron and sell them in Siberia for $40 to even $1,000 a pelt. Over 5,000 pelts a year were taken from Sitka alone. Spanish law protected the sea otters along the California coast, so when Europeans and Americans joined the trade, they became smugglers.

Sea otters, made almost extinct by this mass slaughter, have recovered and are now seen in Monterey Bay floating on their backs feeding on sea urchins and abalone. Visit the excellent Aquarium in Monterey.

The Russians established a colony at Ft. Russ (Ft. Ross) North of San Francisco in 1812 and built the first Orthodox Christian Church in the continental U.S. (Since 1794 Orthodox Christian Missions had been established among the Alaskans.) The purpose of Fort Russ was to grow crops and supply their Alaskan trade. The project was unsuccessful so the Fort was abandoned in 1841. Today it is a State Historic Park, a lovely place to visit!

SUTTER'S FORT
Photo Credit: Sacramento Convention and Visitors Bureau

Spain had made only 25 land grants in Southern California, but after the revolution Mexico made some 800 land grants to affluent citizens. Receiving one in 1839 was Swiss-born Captain John Sutter. He had 44,000 acres encompassing the Sacramento and the American Rivers North from Sacramento to the Sutter Buttes. With his Hawaiian and American natives he built a fort of sun-dried adobe blocks on a rise of land a mile from the Sacramento River and 1/4 mile from the American River. Here it was safe from the frequent flooding of the two rivers. He also built an irrigation system, a distillery, a flour mill and a salmon fishery. He sold hides and tallow for export. Sutter called his Fort, New Helvetia, where trappers, adventurers and emigrants stopped to replenish their supplies. When the Russians left in 1841, Sutter bought some of their equipment and brought it to his fort. The Donner Party found refuge here after their long ordeal. Visit Sutter's Fort in Sacramento, Milepost 90.

The combined forces of Commodore Stockton, Colonel Stephen Kearny with the Mormon Battalian, and John C. Fremont with his unruly Bear Flaggers defeated Mexico at Los Angeles in January 1847. The next month Washington appointed Kearny as Governor of the new California Republic.

In January 1848 James Marshall was building a sawmill for Sutter at Coloma on the South Fork of the American River. He picked out some shiny nuggets from the mill-race and took them to Sutter who declared it to be gold. He asked Marshall to keep it quiet as he didn't want his farming and trading empire disturbed. As the story goes, Marshall told his fellow Mormon, Sam Brannon about it. Sam hurried back to San Francisco, bought up all the shovels, picks and pans and printed his newspaper. Then he rode through the streets of San Francisco proclaiming, "Gold at Sutter's Mill!" William Tecumseh Sherman was in the U.S. Army at the Presidio in San Francisco and reported to Washington D. C., on the desertions of his men to the gold fields.

Word filtered out via ship and before the year was out, 14,000 men arrived from Oregon, Hawaii, Australia, Mexico, Chile and Peru. Back in the "States" (as they called East of the Mississippi) the people were skeptical until December when President Polk announced to Congress that he had information from the army that gold had been discovered in quantity. The rush was on! The greatest migration in history began! Close to 100,000 men, professional men to jailbirds came in 1849 alone all aiming to get rich quickly. Old sailing ships were hauled out of storage in Eastern Ports to make the voyage. Arriving ships were abandoned by sailors heading for the "diggin's", until over 600 ships were left to rot in San Francisco Bay and the Sacramento River. Owners would have liked to sail them out, but they could not get sailors to leave California. Ships were soon stripped of their canvas, which was used to build the first shelters in San Francisco, Sacramento and along the '49er trail. In both San Francisco and Sacramento the ships were used as residences, hotels, warehouses, restaurants and even a jail and an insane asylum.

With 100,000 people in California by the end of 1849 an orderly government was desperately needed. With an election in August and a convention in September, the "Constitution of Monterey" was drawn up. They elected state officials and declared themselves a "Free State" (no slavery). They did this not for moral convictions but because they did not want one miner with a slave to have unfair competition at the diggin's. (There were already 1,000 blacks here and some were slaves.) The "Compromise of 1850" allowed California to enter the Union as a free state.

CALIFORNIA MILEPOSTS

California does not have the green Milepost signs as do the rest of the states. The Highway Department debated using Mileposts but California has so many freeways running parallel and criss-crossing (in the Los Angeles area particularly) that they felt the task would be impossible. There are some small white mileposts, county by county, that have to be added together to arrive at the milepost numbers. To complicate things further, California has many more freeway exits than any other state. To simplify this chapter, some Milepost exits that are within just blocks of each other have been combined. California Highway signs will NOT be numbered! Read the NAMES of exits and the Highway numbers (e.g. US 101).

EMERGENCY: DIAL 911!
ROAD CONDITIONS: PHONE NUMBERS VARY IN EACH AREA SO ARE SHOWN THROUGHOUT.
STATE DEPARTMENT OF TOURISM: 1-800-862-2543.

MILEPOSTS:

0   **MAJOR INTERCHANGE!**
US 101 SOUTH TO SAN JOSE. NORTH TO FELL STREET.
        CAMPGROUNDS: "Pacific Park RV Resort": Private. (All campgrounds are either privately or publicly owned.) About 18 miles. South on US 101 to South on I-280 to South on CA 1 to the town of Pacifica. On the Pacific ocean with all modern facilities including pool and spa. Tents/RVs. About 15 minutes from San Francisco via bus. Call for prices: Out-of-state, 800-822-1250; in state, 800 992-0554.
        "Candlestick RV Park": Private. Good Sam. South 6 miles on US 101 to Candlestick Park. RV Park is on the East side of the stadium. Follow blue & white trailer signs. RVs only. All modern facilities. $32. Jog in the park. $5 shuttle to China Town, San Francisco or take public bus to town. Call for prices and reservations 800-888-2267.
        HIGHWAY CHANGES! The elevated connections with US 101 North were damaged during the 1989 earthquake and are closed. San Francisco has been very reluctant to destroy any of the city by extending the elevated system through the city. Therefore US 101 NEVER WAS completed to the Golden Gate Bridge. Now with the damage, both US 101 North and I-480 are closed. In fact, I-480 has now been removed. Check your map and eliminate those routes.

4   **WESTBOUND EXIT FOR 9TH STREET/US 101:**
        Keep to your right as you exit and you will come out on Harrison & 8th (which is one way going South). Go straight ahead one block on Harrison to 9th Street and turn Right. You will cross Market Street, the main street of San Francisco.
        OPERA HOUSE/CIVIC CENTER: From 9th Street, an immediate Left on Hayes Street takes you two blocks to Van Ness which is US 101. Turn right on Van Ness. Symphony Hall, the Opera House (where the United Nations was born), and the Veterans' War Memorial (with the Museum of Modern Art) will be on your Left. The domed City Hall on your Right is higher than the U.S. Capitol. Continue out Van Ness to Lombard Street, the Golden Gate Bridge and US 101 North.
        LOMBARD STREET/GOLDEN GATE BRIDGE/US 101: Keep to your Right after crossing Market and you will be on Larkin Street. It is one-way North. Make a Left turn in 7-8 blocks onto Ellis or Geary. Go two blocks to Van Ness and turn Right to be on US 101 going North to Lombard Street and the Golden Gate Bridge.
        MOTELS: San Francisco hotels brag about $76 prices and most are over $100. On Lombard Street you'll find motels closer to the $40 range. City public transportation is good and eliminates parking problems that are enormous. Besides, San Francisco is an invigorating place to walk!

5   **WESTBOUND, 5TH STREET:**
        EASTBOUND, 4TH STREET/DOWNTOWN/MARKET STREET:
        CAMPGROUND: "San Francisco RV Park": Private. 250 King Street. Exit EASTBOUND 4th Street or WESTBOUND 5th Street and go South to Townsend and 4th Street. South to King Street. Left

4

to the park. All modern conveniences. RVs only. $32. Public transportation available. Call for prices and reservations 800-548-2425.

5A   FIRST STREET ENTRANCE TO I-80 EAST:
EASTBOUND LEAVING SAN FRANCISCO: First have your car full of San Francisco Sour Dough Bread! To get onto the San Francisco-Oakland Bay Bridge from the Embarcadero, go up Harrison to First Street. Watch for the sign to take you Left onto the Bridge.

6   WESTBOUND TO MAIN STREET/ EMBARCADERO/FISHERMAN'S WHARF:
GET INTO THE FAR LEFT LANE ON THE BRIDGE AND EXIT AT THE "MAIN STREET" SIGN. THIS IS THE FIRST EXIT INTO SAN FRANCISCO. Follow the signs to a Right on Harrison to the waterfront, the Embarcadero. Turn Left and follow it around to Pier 39, Fisherman's Wharf, Hyde Street Pier Park, Marina, etc. Read "DRIVING TOUR OF SAN FRANCISCO" below.

SAN FRANCISCO

SAN FRANCISCO RADIO FOR WEATHER, ROAD CONDITIONS AND NEWS: 810 AM.
ROAD CONDITIONS PHONE: 557-3755. PUNCH "80" AND "#" FOR I-80. "#" is the bottom-Right button on the telephone.

San Francisco is expensive so expect to pay twice as much as in other cities for motels, hotels, campgrounds, and restaurant food. This is the nation's fourth largest metropolitan area with a population of 6 million. It's the most cosmopolitan city in the nation with its International Harbor. First settled by the Spanish, Mexicans and Russians, then attracting the Chinese, Portuguese, French, Italians, Japanese, Irish, and other Europeans. It has the largest Chinese population of any city outside of Asia.

Whether you're staying at a hotel or campground or just driving in, the same basic route will orient you around the city. Be sure to get a MAP OF SAN FRANCISCO at your first stop! Also ask for a SAN FRANCISCO GUIDE that gives you details of transportation and the city's attractions. Their newest book is SAN FRANCISCO BOOK a 96 page guide. To get your guide by mail send $1 to: "Visitor Information Center, PO Box 429097, San Francisco, 94142-9097". It's best to come to San Francisco prepared. Your hotel or campground can tell you how to use public transportation to get to the various parts of the city. DO NOT ATTEMPT TO DRIVE A MOTOR HOME OR PULL A TRAILER AROUND THE CITY! USE PUBLIC TRANSPORTATION!

DRIVING TOUR OF SAN FRANCISCO:
You are on the Embarcadero (docks) going West. The famous 1895 **FERRY BUILDING** with the clock tower will be on your Right. It was fashioned after the Giralda Bell Tower in Seville Spain and has survived all of the earthquakes. In the 1930's this was the hub of activity in the city. Hundreds of commuters arrived in ferries, crossed the walkway above the street and walked up Market Street to the large department stores or to the business and financial district. Some of the ferries carried passenger trains that connected with Eastbay Trains. The docks were alive with thousands of people! Today this is the "World Trade Center" and the "Port of San Francisco". Boats sail to Sausalito (the art colony) from here.

If you turn Left here on Washington Street you run into **GRANT AVENUE**, the center of **CHINATOWN**. A MUST STOP! You'll enjoy the shops selling brocade and jade and displaying intricate carvings of ivory. Park in the garage at Washington and Kearny. This is a good area to visit in the evening. Note the green and ochre gateway over Grant Avenue at Bush Street.

Further down Grant Avenue you'll come to Lombard Street. Turn Right and circle up **TELEGRAPH HILL** to **COIT TOWER** (It looks like a fire-hose nozzle.) Great murals on the ground floor and view of the bay and bridges from the top. When you're back on the Embarcadero, you'll note how Telegraph Hill was eaten away by early seamen to get the ballast for their sailing ships. They brought supplies to San Francisco but when California had nothing to export they had to load stone for ballast to keep the ship from capsizing as it sailed back "around the horn" (Cape Horn of South America.) Thus part of Telegraph Hill traveled to Europe. In 1992 you saw pictures on TV of a large apartment complex sliding down this hill, made unstable by the 1989 earthquake.

From the Embarcadero if you turn Left onto Broadway you'll go through what used to be the "Barbary Coast", a Night-life area today. Continue on to a Right on Columbus and it's the **NORTH BEACH** area. First this was the old Portuguese district, then Italian with many Italian restaurants here today.

BACK ON THE EMBARCADERO: You will come to "PIER 39". This has become a festival of novelty shops and restaurants. On your Left watch for a square-block, parking-rise at Powell & Jefferson. Park here for Pier

39, the Cable car ride into downtown, a bay cruise, or to take a "Motorized Cable Car Tour" (from Pier 39 or 41 or Sabella's restaurant). Walk a couple blocks over to Bay and Taylor for the cable car. This will take you by the **CABLE CAR MUSEUM**, downtown **UNION SQUARE** (the main downtown shopping area), and to Market Street, the center of the city. Adult $2. Senior 15 cents.

    CABLE CAR MUSEUM: Mason & Washington. Absolutely NO car parking here. The Cable Car conductor will tell you where to get off. First you'll go down into the basement to see the "Sheaves", the giant wheels and cables that wind through to draw the cable cars. Upstairs are old cable cars and parts, old photos, a video film describing the construction and working of the cars, and views of the machinery that runs the cables. The first cable car was built in 1873 by Andrew Hallidie, who manufactured wire rope. Previous transportation had been horse-drawn cars that could not climb the high hills and left the problem of tons of manure. The cable cars used to go all the way to the Cliff House on the ocean. A few years ago the whole system was in such disrepair that it was about to be abandoned. But San Franciscans would not part with their unique history and raised the money to restore the system.

BACK ON THE EMBARCADERO: You can easily pass up shopping at "Pier 39" and continue ahead to the parking to your Left between two streets. Do stop here and walk around **FISHERMAN'S WHARF.** A MUST STOP! Treat yourself to a "Sidewalk Cocktail". Find the walkway between the restaurants to get to the wharf to see the fishermen unload their catches. Street musicians roaming through this whole area, range from an excellent violinist to a one-man band. People put money in their hats to show their appreciation. There is a World War II submarine you might board. Take a Red & White Fleet boat to **ALCATRAZ PRISON**, now a National Monument. Or take a **BAY CRUISE** here or back at Pier 39. You can also sail to **ANGEL ISLAND**, (the Ellis Island of the West) to spend the day. It is a park today with 200 deer plus bike and hiking trails and a beach. The Park Service has elephant-train tours in the summer.

    Drive or walk West on Beach Street to many more shops at **THE CANNERY** or on to **GHIRARDELLI SQUARE**. The Square used to be a chocolate factory. The Cannery was Del Monte's. Comics, jugglers, mimes, magicians and puppeteers perform in the patio of the Cannery and often along the streets. There are many restaurants throughout this whole area. At Hyde Street in the park you can board the **HYDE STREET CABLE CAR** for a trip downtown. It joins Powell Street for the same trip past the Cable Car Museum to downtown. There is inside parking to the Left near the Cannery and also under Ghirardelli Square. You'll be glad if your car is small! At the bottom of Van Ness Street by the Square there is more street-parking.

    HYDE STREET PIER: National Park Service Museum of ships. A MUST STOP! Several old ships are tied up at the pier including the 1886 sailing ship, the Balclutha, that traveled 15 times "Around the Horn", and the Ferry that used to cross the bay to connect US 101 here to US 101 in Sausalito. Also there are a Family Lumber Schooner, a Side-wheeler from the River Wear in England, a Bay Scow, and an old houseboat. All of this and more for $3 for Adults. Senior & Child free. 9-5pm. Don't miss it! From here go to the **NATIONAL MARITIME MUSEUM** on Beach Street with ship models and the history of shipping on the West coast. On up Hyde Street to a Left on top of **RUSSIAN HILL** and go down the famous **LOMBARD STREET**, the crookedest street in the world. SMALL cars only!

NOW BACK ON BAY STREET: Notice that you are following the blue signs **"49-MILE SCENIC DRIVE"**. Continuing your tour, keep to the Right on Bay Street to stay by the bay. Turn Right at the light just past Fort Mason to get onto the famous **MARINA**. This was a marshland in the early years. It was filled-in to house the 1915 Fair. First it was the home of the early Italian immigrant fishermen. Now it has some of the most expensive homes in the city. It was devastated by the earthquake of 1989. The homes in that section to your Left are the ones that were damaged. You know the Biblical story of the house built on sand? The rest of San Francisco is on rock and withstood the pressure. The Yacht Harbor is on your Right. San Franciscans enjoy kite flying and other sports here.

    When you see the pink dome and pillars of the PALACE OF FINE ARTS on your Left, take a Left at Broderick or Baker and go around the building to the parking on its West side. (Or see if you may park in "Crissy Field".) This building is all that is left of the 1915 Panama-Pacific International Exposition. It celebrated the completion of the Panama Canal and the redevelopment after the 1906 Earthquake. It was a marvel of colors and lights! The building was restored in 1967 at a cost of $8 million.

    EXPLORATORIUM: A MUST STOP for science buffs and older

PALACE of FINE ARTS
Photo Credit: San Francisco
Convention & Visitors Bureau

children. Housed in the old "Palace" is a fantastic hands-on science museum. Levers and signs encourage you to explore light, sound, heat, vision, hearing, etc. The whole family will love it. It will take 2 hours before you'll be able to get them to leave. Wed-Sun 10-5pm. Adult $6. Senior $3. Child $2. Wed evenings 5-9:30pm, free.

If you did not stop at "The Palace" you'll find yourself on US 101 passing through **THE PRESIDIO**, a Spanish fort in 1776, then Mexican, then a U.S. Army post until 1991. Follow US 101 out to the **GOLDEN GATE BRIDGE**. This has the highest bridge towers in the world and is one of the longest single-span suspension bridges. It is constantly being painted that brilliant orange/red. You might want to drive across the bridge (or take a 50 minute walk across) to a Right at a VIEWPOINT on the other side. Then follow signs under the highway and back to San Francisco. (You'll have to pay the $3 bridge toll to return.) Either way you'll want to get off US 101 at the toll plaza. **NORTHBOUND** it will be a quick Right just before the toll plaza. **SOUTHBOUND** it will be the first Right. There is a tunnel under the toll booths for cars to pass under. Lovely gardens and great viewpoint here North of the toll-booths. John C. Fremont named this beautiful bay entrance, "Golden Gate".

FORT POINT: Leave the toll-booth parking and go Left onto Lincoln Blvd for a few blocks until you see a sign and Left turn to "Fort Point". Go to the end of the road. There was a Spanish Fort here in 1794. The present fort was built by the U.S. Government in 1853 for fear of the Mexicans coming to reclaim their land. It was designed like Ft. Sumter. Walls were 5-12 feet thick. There were 126 cannons on three floors. It cost $3.2 million to build. (That would be closer to a billion today!) By the time it was completed in 1861 it was obsolete. Rifled artillary (no longer iron balls) was now in use and could destroy it easily. Interesting historical displays are in the rooms. 10-5pm. Free.

To get onto Lincoln Way going toward the ocean, go back to the Toll Plaza Parking lot. Go Under the Plaza/Toll area through the little tunnel from the parking lot. Turn Left immediately and then Right to Lincoln Way. This is a lovely drive past some beautiful homes with great ocean views ending at Lincoln Park and another "Palace", the **PALACE OF THE LEGION OF HONOR** One of the GREAT art galleries! (Closed in 1992-93 for remodeling.) Many European Masters in oils and in sculpture with an extensive collection of Rodin. Exhibits are changed and special ones may feature anything from fans and laces to jade and Renoir. You will need a couple hours here. Adult $4. Senior & Child $2. Wed-Sun 10-5pm.

Continue your tour on down the hill through the golf course and the stop sign, straight ahead to Geary Street. Right on Geary to the **SEAL ROCKS**. A MUST STOP! The park above the **CLIFF HOUSE** was the home of Adolph Sutro who built the Virginia City Tunnel to drain the hot water from the silver mines. He built a grand 8-story Cliff House, and public **SUTRO BATHS** with 7 swimming pools (different water temperatures) down by the ocean. If you park in the big lot on the hill and look down over, you'll see the remnants. (This may be the only parking space you'll find anywhere near the SEAL ROCKS.) The pools were covered with glass domes. Besides the usual diving boards, the pools had water slides, trapezes and rings. There was a train to the beach and you could enjoy all of this including an art gallery for just "two bits", 25 cents. When the fabulous Cliff House burned down in 1907, Sutro's daughter constructed the present building. Go out on the deck behind the buildings to see the sea lions on the rocks below. Feel the power of the wind and the waves! You might like a snack at the Cliff House Restaurant. See the picture of that amazing "Cliff House" that used to be here! Look down along the ocean to watch the surfers in their wet suits ride the pounding waves. Not for amateurs! A half mile further down the beach is a good place for the kids to wade and look for sea life. For a swimming beach you'll need to go further South down the coast to Santa Cruz for a more protected beach.

Riding down the beach highway, the Esplanade, the area to your Left was only large sand dunes before San Francisco housing spread out to the ocean and John McLaren took on the job of transforming four miles of sand into a park. He began in 1887 and by 1894 **GOLDEN GATE PARK** had lakes, waterfalls, woods and rolling lawns. It is a work of art and a joy to all San Franciscans. A MUST STOP! It has miles of hiking, biking and bridle trails. When you come to a Dutch Windmill on your Left, turn Left into Golden Gate Park and John F. Kennedy Drive. Keep Left at the intersection with South Drive. You'll pass the **BUFFALO PADDOCK**, possibly seeing elk also. After **SPRECKLES LAKE** on your left you'll pass **PORTALS OF THE PAST**, the last remains of a mansion after the 1906 earthquake. When you come to the **MUSIC CONCOURSE** and signs to the museums and art gallery, turn Right. Then a quick Left and drive down the Left side of the Concourse to the parking areas. If you have found a space you can spend all day here!

CALIFORNIA ACADEMY OF SCIENCES: A complex of several science museums in one. Open 10-5pm. Adult $4. Senior & Child $2. Food in the basement.

STEINHART AQUARIUM: A MUST STOP! It's in the back of the building. Fantastic collection of sea life from all over the world! Watch the feeding of the seals and dolphins in a large tank. It occurs every 2 hours beginning at 10:30am. Experience the ocean by picking up a sea star or crab from the round **TIDE POOL.** Walk up into a **FISH ROUND-ABOUT** where the fish are swimming in a circle all around you. Hope you have time to see the rest of the Academy:

THE MORRISON PLANETARIUM: Far Left of the building. Scheduled shows for a fee.

HALL OF GEMS AND MINERALS: Right side. Beautiful stones of all kinds.

SIMSON AFRICAN HALL: Left side. Mounted African animals in dioramas.

WILD CALIFORNIA HALL: Right front. California animals in their natural settings.

WATTIS HALL OF HUMAN CULTURES: Far rear of building. The story of man.

EARTH AND SCIENCE HALL: Left rear. Stand on a platform where you can sense how an earthquake feels while watching scenes of buildings falling.

CROSS THE CONCOURSE TO THE MUSEUM:

M.H. DE YOUNG MEMORIAL MUSEUM: Yes another MUST! Rockerfeller collection of paintings by American artists plus furniture, costumes, rugs, arts of Africa and the Americas, Egypt, Rome & Greece. Special visiting exhibits are here regularly. They have a garden for outdoor dining. Wed-Sun 10-5pm. Adult $4. Senior & Child $2.

ASIAN ART MUSEUM: Left side of the Museum. Sculptures, jade, paintings, miniatures, bronzes.

JAPANESE TEA GARDEN: A MUST STOP! Just past the Museum. Walk through this lovely garden of bonsais, pagodas, bridges, and steps. It is a re-creation of the famous gardens in Kyoto, Japan. In the Tea House be served by a lady in a kimono.

CONSERVATORY OF FLOWERS: Back out to Kennedy Drive just past the Concourse. A Victorian greenhouse modeled after the Kew Gardens in London. Seasonal decorative plantings outside and masses of flowers inside. 9-5pm. Adult $1.50. Senior & Child $.75.

STRYBING ARBORETUM: 9th & Lincoln. 70 acres of 7,000 plants. Several gardens in one. Mon-Fri. 8-4:30pm. Guided tours at 1:30pm.

Hungry? From the park try Geary Blvd (a few blocks North of and parallel to the Park). There is food from all nations in San Francisco and you'll pass many wherever you go. There are many Chinese restaurants in China Town (Grant Avenue) and Japanese food at "The Japanese Trade Center" at Geary and Fillmore with shops and art too.

OTHER SAN FRANCISCO SIGHTS:

MISSION DOLORES: Just off Mission at 16th & Dolores Streets. It's San Francisco's oldest building. Built in 1776 with 4-foot-thick adobe walls and hand-hewn timbers tied with leather, it has withstood many earthquakes. Named "Mission San Francisco de Assisi" it gave the city its name.

Ride the **CALIFORNIA STREET CABLE CAR** to the top of "**NOB HILL**" where the early railroad and silver millionaires lived. Grace Cathedral (Episcopalian) is here. The ride back down is one you won't soon forget.

SAN FRANCISCO ZOO: South of the Park on Sloat Blvd near the ocean. Entrance near 45th Street. An outstanding collection of over 1,000 animals in naturally landscaped habitats. Their Gorilla World views the animals from 3 levels. Includes a children's petting zoo. 10-5pm. Adult $6. Senior & teens $3. Child $1.

SAN FRANCISCO-OAKLAND BAY BRIDGE

WESTBOUND VIEW OF SAN FRANCISCO: Eastbound has NO view (unless you're in a motor home) as there is a high wall on the Eastbound lower level of the bridge. Westbound has a great view of the San Francisco skyline! To the West and North is Angel Island, San Francisco's Ellis Island. South of that is Alcatraz, the former prison. Ahead is the San Francisco skyline punctuated by the Transamerica Building with the pointed tower. The small tower on the hill toward the bay shaped like a hose nozzle is Coit Tower.

The Oakland-San Francisco Bay Bridge is an 8.5 mile engineering marvel founded on bedrock 250 feet below the

BAY BRIDGE and SKYLINE from YERBA BUENA
Photo Credit: San Francisco Convention & Visitors Bureau
Photo By: Craig Buchanan

water. It is built to have some "sway" and on a windy day you might feel it. When first built it had passenger cars on the upper level going both ways. The lower level had two lanes for trucks to go both ways and two railroad tracks. The Bay Area had an excellent train system that served the towns on both sides of the bay and continued on down the peninsula. General Motors and Shell Oil Company purchased the system, tore up the tracks and put in buses. The need for those trains is all too evident today with "grid-lock" imprisoning the population.

9   **YERBA BUENA/TREASURE ISLAND:** Treasure Island Naval Base site of the 1939 Fair.
        TREASURE ISLAND MUSEUM: Follow signs. Depicts the history of Yerba Buena and of Treasure Island that was built on a sandbar and housed the 1939-40 Golden Gate International Exposition. This was also the base of the Pan American clippers that provided air service between U.S. and China in the 1930's-40's. Artifacts tell the history of the U.S. Navy, Marines, and Coast Guard in the Pacific clear back to Commodore Perry in 1853.

11   **WESTBOUND TOLL PLAZA:**
        $1 FOR CARS. All tollbooths are on the "inbound" side toward San Francisco, to prevent more traffic jams within the city. Westbound bridge toll pays for both directions. EASTBOUND: Free direction.

12   **M A J O R   I N T E R C H A N G E !**
        OAKLAND/I-980/I-580/MACARTHUR FREEWAY/TO CA 24:
        EASTBOUND I-80: Keep in the Left lanes for a Left curve.
        EASTBOUND EXIT TO I-580/TO CA 24/EAST OAKLAND/MACARTHUR BLVD: Stay in the middle.
        WESTBOUND I-80: Keep Right on I-80 to the Bay Bridge.
        WESTBOUND EXIT TO I-580: Keep left. **EXIT TO I-880: WATCH SIGNS!**
                I-880 was the two-tiered freeway that collapsed with the 1989 earthquake. You saw it on TV. Watch for detours! You've certainly heard of San Francisco earthquakes. The Famous San Andreas Fault is Southwest of the city. It moved 14-21 feet during the 1906 quake. A great part of the damage of that quake was the fire that followed and the dynamiting used, probably erroneously, to stop the fire. The experts are still discussing the cause of the more recent 1989 earthquake. Tectonic plates of the earth are shifting so that the land to the West of the San Andreas fault is slowly moving Northward.

13   **POWELL STREET, EMERYVILLE:**
        FUEL: North to Shell. South to BP.
        FOOD: North to Charlie Brown's. South to Dennys.
        MOTEL: North to Holiday Inn. South to Days Inn.

        SAN FRANCISCO BAY: Eastbound has just crossed San Francisco Bay on the San Francisco-Oakland Bay Bridge. The bay was formed in fairly recent geological, Pliocene Epoch. Look to the West here and you'll see the Golden Gate Bridge spanning the narrow exit to the ocean. At that point the "gate" is 340 feet deep. But the San Francisco Bay only averages 10 feet deep. Channels have been dug to 30 feet to allow ocean going vessels to pass. The island you see framed under the Golden Gate Bridge is infamous Alcatraz, a former federal prison. Two other bays are North of you now, San Pablo Bay and Suisun Bay. You will be crossing a bridge at a narrow passage between those two bays called "Carquinez Straits". Draining into this chain of bays are the Sacramento River that drains all of the Great Valley to the North, and the San Joaquin River that drains all of the Great Valley to the South. This tremendous volume of water all flows out the Golden Gate via the shallow bays. Since the Deep Water Channel has been dredged to Sacramento, ocean ships can go up river to both Sacramento and Stockton. This area used to be the tidelands of the bay. Bay tidelands have been filled for homes, Candlestick Park, and those tall hotels you see along the shore, so that it has decreased the size of the Bay from 700 square miles to less than 400 square miles.
        The tide flows through all three bays and into the rivers. With a shift in the tide from high to low, a massive volume of water from this chain of rivers and bays rushes out the Golden Gate. It carries fresh water and debris miles out into the ocean. The velocity of the tide is so great that it has washed out the deep channel at the gate.

During the Big Flood of 1862 fresh water elevated the bay 18-24 inches, reached the Farallon Islands 15 miles West of San Francisco and resulted in no tides for 4 days. No prisoner ever escaped from Alcatraz Prison and lived. Depending on the tide, the man would have no control and his body would swiftly wash out to sea or way up river. The three islands you see, Alcatraz, Yerba Buena (you tunneled through it on the bridge) and Angel Island are all composed of Jurassic rocks.

14   **ASHBY AVENUE, BERKELEY/CA 13:** NO NEAR SERVICES!

15   **UNIVERSITY AVENUE, BERKELEY:**
West to BERKELEY MARINA. East to U. C. BERKELEY.
FUEL: South to Beacon.
FOOD: "Spenger's Fish Grotto". Turn Southeast/In-land toward the University. Spenger's is on your Left, but Left turns are very difficult from University Avenue. Go Right at the first light, Right at next corner, 2 blocks and Right again. Straight ahead to Spenger's parking lot. This has been the site of delicious fish since Johann Spenger settled here in 1865 and built the first structure. It's a 4-generation family enterprise. Decor is old relics from dismantled vessels with thousands of corks on the ceilings and the "Star of Denmark" diamond in the bar. Dad still fishes in the bay for that fresh catch, and tends the oyster and mussel beds. Their sourdough bread is the best!
MORE FOOD: China Station, Brennan's Restaurant, Celia's Mexican Food, Mermaid Cambodian Seafood. Go toward the Marina on the bay for more nice restaurants.

UNIVERSITY OF CALIFORNIA, BERKELEY: Straight up University Ave. Note the "Campanile", the 1914 tower modeled from the St Mark's Campanile in Venice. It chimes on the hour and plays music at noon and 6pm. **The UNIVERSITY ART MUSEUM** is on Bancroft near Bowditch. Works by Cezanne and Rubens plus Asian and Contemporary art. Wed-Sun 11-5pm. Adult $4. Senior $3. **LOWIE MUSEUM OF ANTHROPOLOGY** is in Kroeber Hall on Bancroft Way. Includes archeology and ethnology. Mon-Tues & Thurs-Fri 10- 4:30pm. Sat noon-4:30pm. Adult $1.50. Senior $.50.
    LAWRENCE HALL OF SCIENCE: In Berkeley Hills. No trailers or large RVs up here. Five miles East on University. Left on Oxford. Right on Hearst. Right on Gayley Road. Left on Rim Way. Left on Centennial. Lawrence's original cyclotron is here with a replica of nose section of the Challenger Space Craft, and hands-on science exhibits. Mon-Fri 10-4:30pm. Sat-Sun noon-4pm. Adult $4. Senior & Students $3.

16   **GILMAN STREET/GOLDEN GATE FIELDS:** NO NEAR SERVICES!
BUCHANNAN/PIERCE STREET, ALBANY: NO NEAR SERVICES!

17   **CENTRAL AVENUE, EL CERRITO:** BART STATION, TRAIN TO SAN FRANCISCO.
    FUEL: South to Exxon & Shell.

18   **CARLSON BLVD., RICHMOND:** FUEL: North to '76.
EASTBOUND ONLY: POTRERO AVENUE, EL CERRITO.

19   M A J O R   I N T E R C H A N G E !
EASTBOUND I-580 WEST TO SAN RAFAEL BRIDGE: Keep to Left.
EASTBOUND I-80: Keep in Right 2 lanes.
    CAMPGROUND: "Marin RV Park Inc": Private. 2130 Redwood Highway, San Rafael. Take I-580 across the San Rafael Bridge to South on US 101, and Lucky Drive exit from US 101. On Frontage road. All modern facilities including pool, sauna, deli. Gravel sites for Tents/RVs. $25 day, $110 week. Walk to hourly bus and Ferry to San Francisco (a lovely way to see S.F.) or car rental. Sightseeing information. Call for reservations and prices: 415-461-5199.

20   **EASTBOUND ONLY MACDONALD AVENUE, RICHMOND.**
SAN PABLO AVENUE, CENTRAL RICHMOND:

BART STATION: Train to San Francisco.
EASTBOUND ONLY: SOLANO AVENUE, RICHMOND.

21 **SAN PABLO DAM ROAD:** HOSPITAL.
North to LUCKY FOOD, PAYLESS DRUG. "CAMPERLAND" has services.
FUEL: North to BP.
FOOD: North to Dennys.

22 **EL PORTAL DRIVE, SAN PABLO:** CONTRA COSTA COLLEGE.

23 **HILLTOP DRIVE, RICHMOND:**
MOTEL: North to Days Hotel.
I-80 is now rolling over the hills of the Coast Range Mountains. These are comprised of sedimentary rocks of the Pliocene period that were laid down in ancient waters. You are also crossing the "Hayward Fault" that caused the Livermore jolt of a few years ago. Easterners get skittery about the earthquakes here but in this area they usually just shake a few glasses off the shelves and cause little damage. Some of the largest quakes in the U.S. occurred in South Carolina and Missouri.

24 **APPIAN WAY, PINOLE:** HOSPITAL.
North to SAFEWAY & LONGS. South to LUCKY FOOD & K-MART.
FOOD: South to Taco Bell & Sizzler.
MOTEL: South to Motel 6*.

25 **PINOLE VALLEY ROAD, PINOLE:**
FUEL: South to Shell, Chevron.
FOOD: Zip's Restaurant. South to Jack in the Box.

27 **HERCULES/EASTBOUND CA 4 EAST TO CONCORD.**

28 **WILLOW AVENUE, RODEO:**
VIEW: Past the refinery toward San Pablo Bay. This is the second Bay of the chain. You'll often see a tanker here unloading oil at the refinery.

29 **WESTBOUND CA 4 TO MARTINEZ/CONCORD:** NO NEAR SERVICES!
EASTBOUND: CUMMINGS SKYWAY: NO NEAR SERVICES!
JOHN MUIR HOME: East on CA 4 to Martinez. Left on Alhambra Road. The home of the founder of the Sierra Club. It was his influence on Teddy Roosevelt that brought about the National Park System. John Muir was able to save Yosemite Valley for us but he lost the battle for the "Grand Canyon of the Toulumne", when the Hetch Hetchy Dam was built. This may have contributed to his death the next year.

31 **CROCKETT:**
FOOD: Nantucket Seafood down under the bridge on the water, just West of the bridge.
Crossing over the "Carquinez Straits" connecting San Pablo Bay on the West with Suisun Bay on the East. **EASTBOUND: $1 TOLL. WESTBOUND: FREE!**

32 **EASTBOUND SONOMA BOULEVARD & SEQUOIA STREET:**
CA 29 NORTH TO SONOMA:
WESTBOUND MARITIME ACADEMY DRIVE/CA 29 NORTH:
FUEL: North to Chevron, Arco.
MOTELS: North to Motel 6,* All Star Inn.

32A **MAGAZINE STREET, VALLEJO/LINCOLN ROAD WEST:**
FUEL: North to Shell.

FOOD: North to Hickory Pit.
MOTELS: North to Golden Penny Inn, Curtola Motel, El Rancho, Budget Inn, Lincoln. South to Travel Lodge.
CAMPGROUND: "Tradewinds RV Park": Private. Good Sam. Exit to North of I-80 and under the overpass onto Lincoln Road West. All facilities. Call for prices and reservations: 707-643-4000. Around $19.

33 **BENICIA/MARTINEZ/I-780 TO I-680:** NO NEAR SERVICES!
    BENICIA CAPITOL STATE PARK: South on I-780 to Benicia. Right on Military Street. Left on First Street. This was the State Capitol for 13 months. There is a 100 year old garden here also.

33A **GEORGIA STREET, CENTRAL VALLEJO:** North to SAFEWAY GROCERIES.

34 **SOLANO AVENUE, VALLEJO/SPRINGS ROAD, VALLEJO:**
MALL: North to Payless, Lucky Food, Hitch World. South to Auto Bros.
FUEL: South to Beacon.
FOOD: South to Smorga Bob's, Bud's Burgers. North to Taco Bell, Church's Chicken.
MOTELS: South to Islander. North to Gateway.

34A **TENNESEE STREET, VALLEJO/MARE ISLAND NAVAL BASE:**
    This was a busy place during World War II building ships and repairing those damaged in the Pacific Theater.
FUEL: South to '76, Exxon.
MOTELS: South to Bell, Royal Inn.

35 **REDWOOD STREET, VALLEJO:**
MALL to North.
FUEL: EASTBOUND ONLY: South to Cheaper Gas, Chief Auto Parts.
FOOD: North to Dennys, Kim Wah, Hong Kong. South to Perkins.
MOTELS: North to Motel 6*, Value Inn.
    WESTBOUND: From here into San Francisco it is a congested area. It's better not to travel during commute-hours. Fuel up here and go straight through. There are few service stations in San Francisco. Some exits are Eastbound or Westbound only.

36 **COLUMBUS PARKWAY/CA 37 TO SAN RAFAEL:**
    MARINE WORLD-AFRICA USA: This is a theme park with both sea and land animals to pet, ride and watch perform. Children and adults enjoy it. Here a butterfly lands on your shoulder and killer whales leap and splash. Spend the day to see it all. Summers daily 9:30-6:30pm. Rest of year Wed-Sun 9:30-5pm.
    MILEPOST 37 WESTBOUND HUNTER HILL REST AREA/VISTA POINT: Step out and enjoy the view. Here is a ridge of serpentine, "Green Stone" (related to asbestos) that was squeezed up from deep in the earth. It is greenish in color and slippery when wet. There are outcroppings up and down the Sierras.

39 **AMERICAN CANYON ROAD:** NO NEAR SERVICES!

42 **RED TOP ROAD:** FUEL: North to '76.

43 **CA 12 WEST TO NAPA/SONOMA:** NO NEAR SERVICES!

44 **GREEN VALLEY ROAD/I-680 SOUTH TO WALNUT CREEK:**
FUEL: Cordelia Junction Truck Stop, Chevron.
FOOD: Old San Francisco Express (restaurant in trains).

45 **SUISUN VALLEY ROAD:** SOLANO COMMUNITY COLLEGE.

CAMPING WORLD: South & East 2 blocks. RV supplies, repairs, dump station, LP gas.
SCANDIA, Miniature Golf.
FUEL: North to BP Truck Stop. South to Chevron, Shell.
FOOD: South to Carls Jr. Wendys, Burger King, Dennys, Taco Bell, Arbys, Old San Francisco Express.
MOTELS: South to Economy Inn, Best Western, Hampton Inn.

48   CHADBOURNE ROAD/ABERNATHY ROAD/CA 12 EAST TO RIO VISTA:
NO NEAR SERVICES! ANHEUSER BUSCH BREWERY.

48A   WEST TEXAS STREET/ROCKVILLE ROAD, FAIRFIELD:
FUEL: North to Shell.
FOOD: North to Gordidos, Chuck E Cheese.
MOTEL: South to Motel 6*.

49   TRAVIS BLVD., FAIRFIELD: HOSPITAL. North to HIGHWAY PATROL.
MALL: South to Sears, Macy's. North to Raley food.
FUEL: North to Arco, Standard, Shell.
FOOD: North to Burger King, Dennys.
MOTELS: North to Motel 6*, Holiday Inn.

50   AIR BASE PARKWAY/TRAVIS A F B/WATERMAN BLVD, FAIRFIELD.

52   NORTH TEXAS STREET, FAIRFIELD:
FUEL: South to Arco, Shell, BP.
FOOD: South to Muffin Treat.
MOTELS: South to Howard Johnson, EZ 8 Motel.

55   PENA ADOBE/LAGOON VALLEY/CHERRY GLEN ROAD: NO NEAR SERVICES!

56   MERCHANT STREET/ALAMO DRIVE, VACAVILLE:
MALL: North to Alamo Food, Bakery, Thrifty, Hardware, Yogurt.
MALL: South to Food For Less.
FUEL: North to Chevron, Shell.
FOOD: North to Baker's Square, McDonalds, Lyons, Burger King, A & W.
MOTELS: North to Travel Lodge, Monte Vista Motel, Quality Inn.
　　You are now traveling across the "Great Valley of California". It is a level plain formed from millions of years of deposits from the streams that flow into it. The valley is an enormous deep trough 475 miles long and 60 miles wide, full of sediments on its deepest Western side up to 12 miles deep. The valley is only a few feet above sea level. The Sacramento River has deposited sediments on either side that form natural levees, but more levees have been built to protect towns and fields from flooding.

57   DAVIS STREET/ELMIRA ROAD/PEABODY ROAD, VACAVILLE.
MASON STREET/TRAVIS AIR FORCE BASE.

58   NUT TREE ROAD/MONTE VISTA/ SHARP ROAD, VACAVILLE:
South to FACTORY OUTLET STORES, Walmart, Safeway Food.
(WESTBOUND: To go South of I-80, exit and go Northeast to the overpass.)
MALL: North to K Mart, Donuts, Grand Auto, Firestone.
FUEL: North to Chevron, Shell, BP, Beacon. South to Arco.
FOOD: North to Brigadoon, Sizzler, Dennys, Murillos, El Charro, Wendys, Arbys, McDonalds, Long Johns, Pelayos, Burger King. South to Buttercup Pantry, Black Oak, Coffee Tree.
　　North to **NUT TREE**, restaurant, shops, ice cream. This is an old California institution. The Nut Tree started selling walnuts at a roadside stand and grew to be a very attractive and popular

place to rest, relax, and browse through the speciality shop. The restaurant is excellent. Prices are moderate to high.

MOTELS: South to Motel 6*. North to Brigadoon, Best Western.

59   **M A J O R   I N T E R C H A N G E !**

I-505 NORTH TO REDDING:
    CAMPGROUND: "Gandy Dancer RV Park": Private. Good Sam. North 3 miles on I-505 to Midway Road. East .2 mile. Pool, playground. $16.

61   **LEISURE TOWN ROAD, VACAVILLE:**
    FUEL: South to BP.
    FOOD: South to Joe's Seafood, Wendys, Hickory Pit, Jack in the Box.
    MOTEL: South to Quality Inn.
    CAMPGROUND: "Neil's Vineyard RV park": Private. North 2 miles to Midway Road. Pool, playground. LP Gas. $16.

62   **MERIDIAN ROAD/WEBER ROAD, DIXON:** NO NEAR SERVICES!

64   **MIDWAY ROAD/LEWIS ROAD, DIXON:**
    CAMPGROUNDS: "Gandy Dancer RV Park": West on Midway Rd almost to I-505. Read above.
    "Neil's Vineyard RV Park": West on Midway Road at Leisure Town Road. Read above.

66   **DIXON AVENUE, DIXON:**
    FUEL: North to Cheaper Mini Mart.

67   **PITT SCHOOL ROAD, DIXON:**
    FUEL: South to Chevron.
    FOOD: South to Chevy's Mexican Restaurant, Dennys, Burger King, McDonalds, Taco Bell, Arbys, IHOP Restaurant.

69   **CURREY ROAD/ FIRST STREET, DIXON/CA 113 SOUTH TO RIO VISTA:**
    FOOD: Cattlemen's Restaurant, good steak house.

70   **MILK FARM ROAD, DIXON:** NO NEAR SERVICES!

71   **PEDRICK ROAD:** **FUEL:** North to BP gas and Left at BP to Produce stand.

75   **HUTCHISON DRIVE, UC DAVIS/CA 113 NORTH TO WOODLAND:**
    FOOD: North to Buckhorn Restaurant.

76   **OLD DAVIS ROAD/ UNIVERSITY OF CALIFORNIA, DAVIS:**
    The University of California has 9 campuses. This branch began as the Agricultural College of the University System. Now it includes Schools of Medicine, Law, and Veterinary Medicine as well as Arts and Sciences.
    DAVIS BOTANICAL GARDEN: Exit to North. Get map at entrance and park in Lot 5. Walk North toward the redwood trees. Native plants and shrubs.

77   **OLIVE DRIVE, CENTRAL DAVIS.**

78   **MACE BLVD. & EL MACERO, DAVIS:**
    VILLAGE RV: Parts & Service. South of I-80 on Chiles Road.
    FUEL: South to Chevron, Shell.
    FOOD: South to McDonalds, Cindys.
    MOTELS: South to Motel 6*, Hotel El Rancho.

MILEPOST 82-85 CROSSING YOLO BYPASS: This is a flood-control basin. Originally the Sacramento River flowed naturally through this basin every winter when the water level was high. In 1862 this whole valley flooded! An area that today is lucky to get 15" of rain a year was deluged with 45"! The snow was 18 feet deep in the mountains covering the telegraph wires. It had a very high water content. Then warm rains in January sent down 105" of rain in the mountains that melted the snowpack. As a result the valley became a lake 20-60 miles wide by 300 miles long. The wind blew up heavy waves. A steamboat could sail 50 miles up the valley to the Sutter Buttes that you see to the North. (They are California's smallest mountain range.) The government has raised the natural levees formed by the river and built more plus a "Wier" which can be opened to let the water into the basin when the river is too high and might endanger properties. No buildings may be constructed in the basin, but the rich river-bottom land is leased out for farming. The soil all along the river is peat like you use for potting soil. Formed from the rotting of fast-growing marsh plants, it is so rich that if a fire starts, it can smolder for weeks.

This is the narrowest section of the **PACIFIC FLYWAY**. Ducks, geese and monarch butterflies from as far North as Alaska and the Arctic Circle pass through a narrow funnel in this area and fan-out South of here. During Fall and Spring you may see 12 flocks at one time stretched across the sky. Some water-fowl winter here so you'll see occasional flocks flying from a feeding field to a safe resting place. There are many bird-observation areas within 50 miles. Call the Audubon society in Sacramento for information on them: 916-448-2473 or 481-5332. You'll probably see a Kite, a large white bird with black markings hovering in one spot looking for his dinner below.

85 **WEST CAPITOL AVE. WEST SACRAMENTO/ENTERPRIZE & INDUSTRIAL BLVDS:**
FUEL: North to Shell, Exxon Truck Stop, Chevron. South to Arco.
FOOD: North to Eppie's. Right at stop sign.
MOTEL: North to Granada Inn. Right at stop sign.
CAMPGROUND: "Sacramento Metropolitan KOA": Private. South of I-80.
Eastbound: Go straight ahead through the light. Westbound: Go left under I-80 & left at the light (Lake Road). Pool, fish, playground. Tents/RVs. $23-$25.

86 **MAJOR INTERCHANGE!**
EASTBOUND I-80 NORTH TO BYPASS SACRAMENTO:
EASTBOUND BUS 80 THROUGH DOWNTOWN: Connections with US 50 East, I-5 and US 99 South.
WESTBOUND STAY ON I-80 WEST.

87 **REED AVENUE, BRYTE/WEST SACRAMENTO:** NO NEAR SERVICES!
MILEPOST 88 CROSSING THE SACRAMENTO RIVER: This river drains ALL of the Northern California Valley.

89 **WEST EL CAMINO AVENUE:**
FUEL/FOOD: North to '76 Auto/Truck Stop, & Restaurant.

90 **MAJOR INTERCHANGE!**
I-5 NORTH TO THE AIRPORT/ WOODLAND/REDDING.
US 99 NORTH TO MARYSVILLE/YUBA CITY.
I-5 SOUTH TO OLD SACRAMENTO AND STOCKTON.
RADIO STATIONS FOR WEATHER, ROAD CONDITIONS AND NEWS:
1530 AM/92.5 FM. 1320 AM/96.1 FM. 1140 AM/105 FM.
ROAD CONDITIONS PHONE: 653-7623. ADD: "80" and "#" for I-80.

SIDETRIP INTO SACRAMENTO!

This exit is the fastest way into downtown Sacramento and Old Town. Exit I-5 South on J Street. Follow the signs to **OLD SACRAMENTO & STATE HISTORIC PARK.** There is a parking lot on your Left as you enter Old Town. Many excellent motels, hotels and restaurants in downtown Sacramento. All Star Inn and Days Inn are just off I-5. You can return to I-80 by going North on I-5 again, or by going East on any street to Left on 16th

Street/CA 160, or driving further East to Bus 80 at 30th Street. You'll have to cross under Bus 80 to enter it Eastbound.

SACRAMENTO

Captain John Sutter landed at this Embarcadero in Old Sacramento in 1839 and built his fort a mile inland. With his fort operating, in 1846 he laid out his town of "Sutterville" also inland but South of his fort. The river had already been named for the Sacraments by Jose Moraga, comandante of the presidio of San Jose. Sam Brannan, a Mormon pioneer who had arrived by ship in 1846, saw more opportunity by choosing to build his store down on the Embarcadero. Gold was discovered and sailing ships came up the river. Everyone raced to the gold fields leaving ships stranded. With the canvas from the sailing ships, sprang the tent city of Sacramento. Sutter's son came but instead of helping his father with his plans for the inland town of Sutterville, he joined Sam Brannan in development of the waterfront. Lieutenant William Tecumseh Sherman surveyed the area and called it Sacramento City after the river. Sutterville and Sacramento vied to sell lots but the action was all at the waterfront. By 1850 Sutter had lost his Fort to bad debts. He died in Washington D.C. still trying to regain control of his land.

In 1850 the inevitable happened and Sacramento was flooded. Levees were built for several miles for protection, but in 1852 these were breached and the town was flooded again. They proposed raising the buildings on jack screws and raising the level of the streets. The plan lost support until 1862 when the biggest flood of all time engulfed them. (Read Milepost 82.) Some owners just wrote off their ground floors, and the streets were just built up to their second floors. Others jacked-up their buildings. Wagons brought in thousands of yards of earth and the work of elevating the streets continued for several years. Today you can still see evidence of the construction used to accomplish this. The cobblestone streets are paved with stones from Folsom Prison, dubbed "Folsom Potatoes". You can stroll the old plank sidewalks, visit the restored buildings and museums and see the brick arches used to support the buildings and streets.

The **OLD EAGLE THEATER** here cost $75,000 to build in October 1849. The roof was sheet iron, the sides canvas, the floor was the ground. The stage was made from crates and scraps while the audience sat on rough boards. The balcony was reached by ladder on the outside with canvas underneath to shield the underside of a lady's skirts. The flood of January 1850 carried the theater away.

Old Sacramento was also the beginning of the Transcontinental Railroad and the terminus of the Pony Express. Collis P. Huntington and Mark Hopkins had a hardware store here. Leland Stanford was a grocer and Charles Crocker was a blacksmith who sold dry goods. Their gold was in merchandising until they combined into "The Big Four" to build the Central Pacific Railroad. They wanted the silver trade and also thought to capture the Orient-to-Europe trade that took four weeks from San Francisco to New York by sailing ship and by crossing the Isthmus of Panama. A train could make it in 7 days argued the determined engineer, Theodore Judah, who had treked through the mountains and found the route. So they backed him to survey the route to Virginia City's silver. They broke ground for the Central Pacific RR at the foot of K Street in Old Town in January 1863. But they had already pushed Judah out of his own company and he died before the year was out. He never saw his dream accomplished. The first 40 miles of track weren't laid until 1865. Sacramento has restored the old buildings into museums, restaurants and shops. The Dixieland Jazz Jubilee is held here with 100 bands coming from all over the world.

CALIFORNIA STATE RAILROAD MUSEUM: 2nd & I Streets. This is A MUST STOP for all visitors to Sacramento. The most comprehensive and largest railroad museum in the U.S. You'll need at least 2 hours. It is in the large brick building across from the parking lot and houses 21 restored "rolling stock". You start with a film history, walk through a "moving car", see how the "Fruit Express" was iced, and examine engines from the first and smallest to the big steam "malley" that weighs in at more than a million pounds. Then you'll cross the square to experience the Passenger station on Front Street, the terminal of the Central Pacific. More trains to see. 10-5pm. Adult $3. Child $1.

STEAM TRAIN RIDE: Summer weekends only. A 6-mile 45-minute ride on the banks of the Sacramento River. On the hour 10-5pm.

RIVER CITY QUEEN: On Front Street. Summer

OLD TOWN SACRAMENTO
Photo credit: Sacramento Convention & Visitors Bureau

river cruises.

BIG FOUR BUILDING: Near the Railroad Museum. This was moved here when I-5 was built. It was Huntington & Hopkin's Hardware Store where plans for the Central Pacific Railroad took shape. Today the building is a replica of the 1880s store. Upstairs the "Board Room" has been recreated. Tues-Sat 10-5pm. Free.

OLD SACRAMENTO SCHOOL HOUSE: Front & L Streets.

SACRAMENTO HISTORY CENTER: In the same block. Between 1840-1860, 253,397 emigrants passed through the Sacramento area. You'll see displays on life in early California and a $2 million gold collection. Tues-Sun 10-5pm. Adult $2.50. Senior $1.50. Child $1.

B.F. HASTINGS BUILDING: 2nd & J Streets. Built in 1852 this was the terminus of the Pony Express. It was also the Wells Fargo Express Office, the Telegraph Company and the State Supreme Court. There is a communications museum downstairs and the restored court upstairs. The life-size bronze of the Pony Express Rider is across the street. The mail came up the river from San Francisco to be carried East by the Ponies.

OTHER SIGHTS IN SACRAMENTO:

TOWE FORD MUSEUM: South to Front and V Streets. Displayed are 170 Fords from 1903 to 1953. Tours 10-6pm. Fee.

CROCKER ART GALLERY: 216 O St. Victorian home of Charles Crocker of the Big Four that built the Central Pacific. Also the oldest art museum in the West. Paintings and sculpture of old European, western, contemporary and Asian artists. Tues-Sun 10-5pm. Adult $3. Child $1.50.

STATE CAPITOL: Exit Old Town and go East. Then South on 9th Street to the Capitol. You can travel East on N Street and West on L Street. The large shrubs around the capitol are the famous "Camelias". They look like roses blooming in February and March. The capitol was renovated in 1982 to its original 1890 splendor. A tour is best but you can just wander the halls here enjoying the murals, the pastel & gold rotunda, the tiled mosaic floors, massive staircases, the crystal chandeliers and the Isabella statue. There are historical displays in seven of the rooms. Free Tours on every hour 9-4pm.

STATE INDIAN MUSUEM: East from the Capitol on K Street. Wonderful displays of Indian artifacts and hands-on experience of the old culture. Daily 10-5pm. Adult $1. Child $.50.

SUTTER'S FORT: Behind the Indian Museum with the entrance on L Street. This was the center of Sutter's kingdom. With a talking "Magic Wand" experience life in the fort in 1848. Traveling men slept on the floor of the attic of the central building, a 3 X 7 foot space for $1. There might be 250 men here at one time, the air dense with the smell of sweat, tobacco and boots.

GOVERNOR'S MANSION: 16th & H Streets. Take a charming docent tour through this old 1877 Victorian with its mohogany staircase and marble fireplaces. The last governor here was Edmond Brown. Weekdays 10-4pm. Tours every hour from the carriage house. Weekends 10-4:30pm. Tours every half hour. Adult $1. Child $.50.

WILLIAM LAND PARK:

LAND PARK ZOO: Sutterville Road & Land Park Drive. Go South on 9th Street to Land Park Drive. Or go South on I-5 to Sutterville Road and then Left to the park. A well-developed zoo with animals in their natural habitats. Weekdays 9-4pm. Weekends 9-5pm. Adult $2. Child $.50.

FAIRYTALE TOWN: Across the street from the zoo. The children love this storytown where they can walk the Crooked Mile, slide down a shoe or a rabbit hole and visit the Three Pigs and Mary's Lamb. Tues-Sun 10-5pm. Adult $1. Child $.50. Across another street there is a children's play land with pony rides, Merry-go-round, etc.

93   **NORTHGATE BLVD./ARCO ARENA**
    FUEL: South to Shell.
    FOOD: South to McDonalds, Taco Bell, Finnegans, Kentucky Fried, Carls Jr.
    MOTEL: South to Travel Inn.

94   **NORWOOD AVENUE:**
    FUEL: North to Arco.
    FOOD: North to Jim Denny's Burgers.

95   **MARYSVILLE BOULEVARD/RALEY BOULEVARD:** ELEVATION: 56 FEET.
    DEL PASO HEIGHTS TO SOUTH/RIO LINDA TO NORTH:
    GROCERY: South to Market Basket.

FUEL: North to Chevron, Gas N Diesel, Arco. South to Hooten, & Parish Tires.

97 **WINTERS STREET:** NO NEAR SERVICES!

97A **LONGVIEW DRIVE: FUEL:** North to Chevron.

98 **WATT AVENUE, SACRAMENTO/AUBURN BLVD.:**
McCLELLAND AIR FORCE BASE/NORTH HIGHLANDS:
    FUEL: North to '76, Arco, Firestone tires.
    FOOD: North to Carrows, Golden Egg Cafe, Carls Jr, Pizza Hut. Dennys on the overpass. South to Burger King.
    MOTELS: South to Inncal*. North & left to Rodeway Inn behind Carrows.

99 **M A J O R   I N T E R C H A N G E !**
WESTBOUND I-80 MOVE INTO LEFT LANES.
WESTBOUND BUS 80 GET INTO THE RIGHT TWO LANES. This is a good route for a sidetrip through Sacramento to visit the INDIAN MUSEUM and SUTTER'S FORT. Exit Bus 80 on J Street for 2-3 blocks. You'll run into it. Read Milepost 90 for descriptions of Sacramento sights.
    CAMPGROUND: "Stillman RV Park": Private. Adults only. Good Sam. South on Bus 80 to US 99 South. Exit on 47th Avenue. West one block to light. Right a block. No tents. Pool. $22. Good Sam Member $19.80.
    RV SUPPLIES, REPAIRS, SERVICES OFF BUS 80 LOOP: All South on Bus 80 to exit at El Camino Avenue. Groceries/gas here too.
        "KW RV Center": West on El Camino on Northwest corner. Supplies.
        "Happy Daze RV's: West .7 mile, on right. Supplies, repairs, LP gas.
        "McColloch's RV Repair": West on El Camino for couple blocks to light. Right on Van Ness, Left on Auburn Blvd, under underpass it becomes Harvard. 1 block on Right. Good repairs.
        Linville Bros Tires: East on El Camino a couple blocks.
    ARCADE CREEK: The BIG FOUR railroad builders received $48,000 a mile for mountain construction and $16,000 for valley construction. The government surveyor said that the Sierra Nevada mountains started 50 miles East of Sacramento. That would be at Auburn or Placerville and most accurate. When it came to Court, the verdict was Newcastle, just below Auburn. But Crocker, with his usual duplicity, managed to convince the Congress that the Sierras started right here at Arcade Creek, elevation 60 feet.
        EASTBOUND WINTER TRAVEL WARNING! Before you head for Nevada, be sure that I-80 is open and clear of snow. Call Road Conditions at 653-7623. Then dial "80#" and you'll get I-80 conditions.

100 **MADISON AVENUE:**
    CALIFORNIA STATE AAA to South. Left at First light. Right to AAA.
    AMERICAN RIVER COLLEGE: South to College Oak. Right to college.
    HIGHWAY PATROL to South. Ford Garage South and left. South to Target Stores.
    FUEL: South to Exxon, '76, Arco, BP. Goodyear tires. North to Shell, Beacon Gas.
    FOOD: South to Eppie's, Carls Jr. A & W, Jack in the Box. North to Brookfield Family Restaurant, Foster Freeze, Pizza, Fish & Chips, Dennys.
    MOTELS: South to Holiday Inn, going Left at first light. North to Super 8.

102 **ELKHORN BLVD./GREENBACK LANE, CITRUS HEIGHTS:**
    KW RV CENTER: South on Greenback .5 mile. Right on Auburn Blvd.
    Repairs, parts, LP gas, dump station.
    MALL: North to Elkhorn Plaza with Safeway, Longs Drugs.
    FUEL: North to '76.
    FOOD: North to McDonalds, Rico Pizza, Yogurt, China Deluxe, Baskin-Robbins Ice Cream.

104 **ANTELOPE ROAD, CITRUS HEIGHTS:**

MALL: North to Payless drug, Raley food, Hardware, Albertson food.
FUEL: North to '76.
FOOD: North to Kentucky Fried, McDonalds, Carls Jr, Wendys, Taco Bell, Yogurt, Pizza.

105 RIVERSIDE AVENUE, ROSEVILLE:
AUTO DEALERSHIPS to North.
MALL: South to K Mart, Thrifty.
FUEL: South to Shell, Exxon.
FOOD: South to Jimboys Tacos, Roseville Junction.

107 DOUGLAS BOULEVARD, ROSEVILLE/FOLSOM LAKE: HOSPITAL to South.
MALLS: South to Placer Center Plaza: Auto Parts, Payless, Lucky food and Auto Dealers. North to Roseville Square: Raley food.
FUEL: South to Chevron, Shell, Auto Care, Arco. North to Arco, '76, Big O Tires.
FOOD: South to Dennys, Carrows, Carls Jr, Del Taco, Togos. North to McDonalds, Burger King, Jack in the Box.
MOTELS: North to Best Western, Heritage Inn.

109 ATLANTIC STREET/EUREKA ROAD, ROSEVILLE: NO NEAR SERVICES!
WESTBOUND: EUREKA ROAD & TAYLOR ROAD:
ART CONSTRUCTION ON SOUTH SIDE OF I-80 AT INTERSECTION.
Here is the boundary of the California Valley where the land starts its rise up the "tilted block" of the Sierras. On this Western side, the rise is gradual. Rest your arm on your lap and then slowly raise your hand without moving your elbow. This Western edge of the Sierras is at your elbow. The Eastern edge of the Sierras at your fingertips. It is sharply uplifted and forms a steep escarpment that I-80 will descend rapidly into Nevada. These Sierras are masses of "Granite", a salt & pepper looking stone, that was formed under the earth and pushed up through the metamorphosed Paleozoic & Mesozoic rocks. It is from the latter older rocks that the gold originated and was deposited in the river gravels.

109A TAYLOR ROAD, ROSEVILLE: ELEVATION: 250 FEET.
VENTURE OUT RV CENTER: RV parts & repairs, LP gas.
FOOD: Cattlemens, specializing in beef.

110 LINCOLN/MARYSVILLE/CA 65: NO NEAR SERVICES!

111 ROCKLIN ROAD, ROCKLIN:
MALL: North to Payless Drug, Auto Parts. Camping world to North & Right.
FUEL: North to Exxon, BP. South to Arco.
FOOD: North to Dennys, Jack in the Box, Arbys, Taco Bell, Kentucky Fried, Carls Jr, Safeway, Rosie's (interesting food combinations).
MOTELS: North to First Choice Inn, Ramada Inn.
See those rocks sticking up out of the ground? These are the granite mentioned above. The stone quarried in these foothills were used to build the California State buildings.

113 SIERRA COLLEGE BLVD.: RADIO: 950 AND 1140 AM.
SIERRA COLLEGE to South. LP GAS: North .5 mile to East on Taylor Road 2.5 mile.
MALL: South.
FUEL: North to '76, Chevron.
CAMPGROUND: "Loomis KOA": Private. North .5 mile on Sierra College Blvd to Taylor Road. East one block. Pool, spa, campfires, playground. $19-$23.

115 LOOMIS/HORSESHOE BAR ROAD: NO NEAR SERVICES!

116 PENRYN: TRAFFIC ALERT: RADIO: 1610 AM.

FUEL: North to Beacon.
FOOD: North to Penryn Restaurant.

    GRIFFITH QUARRY PARK: North one mile. Right on Taylor Road for one mile. Picnic and walk the 1/4 mile trail to the Quarry. Walk around the quarry where the granite has been cut out in big chunks.

    LIFE ZONES: As you ascend or descend the Sierras, you pass through different "Life-zones", elevations at which certain trees and shrubs flourish. It's similar to going North where the climate becomes wetter and colder. The valley floor has some oak trees that multiply into an Oak Woodland in these foothills. Soon you'll be in the "Mixed Conifer Forest". Higher up it will be the "Red Fir Forest". At the pass you'll be in a "Sub-alpine Forest". If you hiked to the tops of peaks you'd be in the "Alpine Zone" where there are NO trees.

    Here now you see the first pine, the "Digger Pine" that grows at this low elevation. It is a lightly foliaged tree with thin twigs and sparse needles 7-13" long, three in a bundle. It isn't good for much! Poor shade, firewood, but the cones are interesting, large and heavy. They're usually thick with pitch, so watch out. Read Milepost 155 for precautions with pitch.

    In the Spring you'll see big bushes of "Buckbrush" with spears of white flowers, and on the ground blue "Lupines", flowers on a stem like snapdragons. If you're lucky you'll see the beautiful golden poppies, the state flower. In the 1930's-1950's they covered the hills and the levees, some planted by the railroads. But with the tremendous migrations of people, who loved to pick them instead of letting them go to seed, they started disappearing. CAUTION, DO NOT PICK! There is a hefty fine.

    The California Valley and foothills have several resident birds you will probably see. The large blue bird is the Scrub Jay, the larger black and white bird with the yellow bill is the Yellow-Billed Magpie (only found in the Sacramento Valley), and the large hawk perched on a pole or circling overhead is the Red-Tailed Hawk. The soaring large black bird looking for carrion is the Vulture.

119   **NEWCASTLE:** HIGHWAY PATROL. ELEVATION: 1,000 FEET.
        FUEL: South to Arco, Exxon.
        FOOD: South to Dennys.

120   **NEWCASTLE/LINCOLN/CA 193:** NO NEAR SERVICES!

123   **EASTBOUND: MAPLE STREET/OLDTOWN.**
        WESTBOUND: NEVADA STREET, AUBURN/OPHIR ROAD: Go Right and across the overpass toward the domed Placer County Courthouse to get to Old Town.
        RADIO STATIONS FOR WEATHER, ROAD CONDITIONS AND NEWS: 900 AM, 101.1 FM.
        ROAD CONDITIONS PHONE: 885-3786. ADD: "80#" for info on I-80.

AUBURN

    Auburn was born in the Gold Rush. Many of the earliest dwellings were part canvas from the hundreds of sailing vessels left on the Sacramento River. The town burned down several times. The old fire house was built in 1852 and is the oldest volunteer fire department West of the Mississippi. Next to the Firehouse is a statue of a miner, an iron barrel used to bring ore from the mine, and a mine car. The stage coach would come down the hill behind the fire house. The brick buildings you see here in old town have iron shutters, steel doors, and a tin roof with dirt in the ceilings to protect them from fire. From here $10-$15,000 in gold at $16 an ounce was shipped out twice a week for 1.5 years. The son of Sacajawea, of the Lewis and Clark Expedition, lived here.

    Up the street from the Firehouse is the Shanghai Restaurant. It's a 4th generation family business. Locals say the food is good. Walk or at least drive by the newly renovated County Courthouse. They hope to have a museum inside soon.

    BERNHARD MUSEUM: .5 mile South on Sacramento Street, from the firehouse. Restored Victorian house showing old skills. Tues-Fri 11-3pm. Sat-Sun noon-4pm. Adult $1. Child $.50.

123A   **AUBURN/GRASS VALLEY/PLACERVILLE/CA 49:** TRAFFIC ALERT: 1610 AM.
        SOUTH TO COLOMA GOLD DISCOVERY SITE: HOSPITAL to North. THRIFTY DRUG.
        FUEL: North to Shell.
        FOOD: North to Foster Freeze.

CAMPGROUND: "Auburn KOA": Private. Exit to North of I-80 for 2 miles on CA 49. 35-foot Max RV. Pool, spa, Pond fish, playground. $14-19.

SIDETRIPS TO GOLD MINING SITES

CA 49 IS THE FAMOUS TRAIL OF THE 49ERS AS THEY SEARCHED THESE MOUNTAINS LOOKING FOR GOLD.

SOUTH TO COLOMA GOLD DISCOVERY SITE: Go South about 17 miles on CA 49, a curvy road, across the American River where men panned for gold, past Cool, to Coloma. "Placer gold", consisting of nuggets and flakes that had washed down from above, was first found in the American River. Gold is heavy so it would be found caught behind large stones, especially after the Spring rains had washed the heavier gold down.

MARSHALL GOLD DISCOVERY STATE HISTORIC PARK: The Visitor Center is on your Right. Open 10-5pm. This museum is excellent with displays concerning gold discovery and mining. Park fee: Adult $3. Senior $2. James Marshall discovered gold in the millrace in January 1848. This structure has been restored down by the river. Picnic here, skip rocks across the American River, and walk or drive up the hill to the Marshall monument and cabin. Several other buildings have been restored. Delta Kappa Gamma, a Women Educators' Society has restored the school house.

NORTH TO GRASS VALLEY AND NEVADA CITY North about 24 miles on CA 49 to Grass Valley, 4 miles more to Nevada City and ten miles more again to Malakoff Diggins. (If you are Westbound on I-80, a shorter route to this area will be from Milepost 138, but that road is narrow and twisty.)

EMPIRE MINE STATE HISTORIC PARK: East Empire Street, Grass Valley. From CA 49, turn Right on Empire Street for about a mile. Follow signs. In 1850 a lumberman discovered an outcropping of quartz (a milk-white stone) imbedded with gold. Men rushed in to stake claims and dig their "coyote holes". However the quartz had to be blasted out and the ore crushed so it became a corporation hard-rock underground mining operation. Tin miners were imported from Cornwall, England to work the mines. This mine shaft is more than a mile down, with some 367 miles of underground tunnels that connected the various veins. Deep mining continued here, except during World War II, until 1950. Over $100 million in gold was produced by the Empire mine. Tour the engineering office and machine shops. The Visitor Center has gold samples, a film, and mining machinery. They have tours of the owner's home and garden on summer weekends. Summers 9-6pm. Rest of year 10-5pm. Adult $2. Child $1. The Cornish miners are known for their male chorus, their Christmas celebration and their food. While you're in town try their Cornish Pasties and saffron buns.

LOLA MONTEZ' HOME AND CHAMBER OF COMMERCE: South on Mill Street, Grass Valley's "old town".

NEVADA CITY: Four miles further North on the CA 49/CA 20 freeway. Exit on Broad Street and cross the freeway. Right on Coyote Street to the CHAMBER OF COMMERCE next to "Ott's Assay Office". Walk the streets of Nevada City and see the Monitors, the big "water cannons" that washed out the gravel to get at the placer gold in ancient riverbeds. Also see the **AMERICAN VICTORIAN MUSEUM** and the **NEVADA COUNTY HISTORICAL MUSEUM** with relics from the Donner Party and a California Indian basket collection. There's a Joss House altar from the once large Chinese population.

MALAKOFF DIGGINS HISTORIC STATE PARK: Ten miles North of Nevada City off of CA 49 take the North Bloomfield Road. Follow signs. This was the world's largest hydraulic gold mine. High-powered streams from the "monitors" blasted away whole hillsides. Visitor Center has film and exhibits about hydraulic mining and the life of the miners. Includes a restored church, store, stable. Summers 10-4:30pm. Rest of year weekends 10-4:30pm. $4 per Vehicle. Camping, picnicking. Campground reservations: 800-444-PARK.

124 **ELM AVENUE, AUBURN:**
    MALL: North to Longs Drugs, Lucky Food.
    FUEL: North to Shell. South to Arco, Exxon.
    MOTEL: South to Elmwood Motel.

125 **LINCOLN WAY, AUBURN: FUEL:** South to BP, Exxon, Arco.

126 **FORESTHILL ROAD:**
    MALL: Raley Food.
    FUEL: South to Arco, Chevron, '76, Shell. North to Exxon, Thrifty, One-Stop Gas.

FOOD: South to Burger King, Ikeda's (good hamburgers), Kentucky Fried, Pizza Factory, Lyons, Baker's Square (pies), Country Inn, Lou La Bonte's, Sizzler, Jack in the Box, McDonalds, Dairy Queen, Country Waffles. North to Dennys, Taco Bell, Arbys, Wendys, Sams, Wienershnitzal, Sweet Peas.

MOTELS: South to Best Western, Country Squire Inn. North to Auburn Inn, Super 8, Foothills.

126A **BOWMAN:** TRAFFIC ALERT RADIO: 1610 AM. LP GAS: North to Frontage Road.
YOU ARE RIDING ALONG THE TOP OF THE RIDGE WITH A GREAT VIEW OF THE CREST OF THE SIERRAS TO THE EAST.
WESTBOUND CAMPGROUND: "Bowman Mobile Home & RV Park": Private. A Senior Citizen park. North of I-80 and Left. No tents or children. 35 foot max RV length. Cable TV. $15.

127 **BELL ROAD, BOWMAN:**
FOOD: Drive to South side of I-80. Then go East along the freeway to "Headquarters House Restaurant". This is a gourmet stop for a special lunch or dinner. Sunday Brunch too. Moderate prices.
CAMPGROUND: "Auburn KOA": Private. North of I-80. Three miles West on Bell Rd to CA 49. One block North. 35 foot Max RV. Pool, spa, Pond fish, playground. $17-24.

128 **DRY CREEK ROAD:** NO NEAR SERVICES!

129 **CLIPPER GAP/MEADOW VISTA:** NO NEAR SERVICES!

132 **APPLEGATE:** North to Applegate Station, El Patio Cafe, Firehouse Motel.

133 **HEATHER GLEN:** NO NEAR SERVICES! ELEVATION: 2,000 FEET.
Note the Pondersoa Pines with the long needles, three in a bundle. The mature trees produce nice fat cones about 6" long that are prickly. May to July the high bushes of Scotch Broom are masses of yellow flowers.

134 **WEST PAOLI LANE, WEIMAR:** Mini Mart, Propane. **FOOD:** Jimmy Inn.

135 **WEIMAR CROSS ROAD:** NO NEAR SERVICES! POST OFFICE.
VIEW OF CREST OF SIERRAS TO SOUTHEAST. Watch for a wall of green-colored rock, called soapstone or greenstone.

137 **CANYON WAY/PLACER HILLS ROAD:**
FOOD: Dingus McGees. THE place to eat according to locals! Unusual food. The prices are moderate to high.
You're into a Mixed Conifer Forest with fir trees with the short little needles.

138 **COLFAX/CA 174 NORTH TO GRASS VALLEY:** ELEVATION: 2500 FEET.
LP GAS: Southeast to 210 Canyon Way.
VISITOR INFORMATION: North to Chamber of Commerce in a railroad car to your Left just before the railroad tracks, as you go down the hill into town.
FUEL: South to Exxon, Beacon, Chevron. North & Left to Arco. North & Right to Chevron, Auto Parts.
FOOD: South to A & W, Subway, Burgers. North & Left to Rosies (interesting dishes), Pizza, Market. North & Right into town to D & M Market, corner Cafe, Madonnas Classic Kitchen. Left on Oak to building by railroad to The Fruit Exchange & Trackside Grill.
CAMPGROUNDS: "Bear River CG: Three miles North through Colfax, follow signs to "Milk Ranch Road" and/or Bear River CG. Small county park. It may be full.
"Rollins Lake: 7 miles. Private. North into Colfax on CA 174. Then follow signs. Four sites. One has showers, store, hookups.

WESTBOUND ALTERNATE ROUTE

TO GRASS VALLEY AND THE EMPIRE MINE: Go Northwest on CA 174, to Grass Valley and Nevada City sights. (Left onto Empire Street to the Empire Mine.) Return to I-80 via CA 49. Read Milepost 123A.

MILEPOST 139 CAPE HORN: This is a steep grade for the train. It climbs the Sierras on the North side of I-80. Then it crosses I-80 on a high trestle and makes a hairpin turn to the South and skirts the hill on the South side of I-80, traveling high on the edge of the deep American River Canyon. In the early days, the trains stopped on the curve of this cliff, "Cape Horn", for the passengers to look down 1,000 feet into the canyon.

143 **MAGRA ROAD/ROLLINS LAKE:**
CAMPGROUNDS: "Rollins Lake Campgrounds": Three miles North down a steep canyon. If you don't like this canyon entrance, go to Colfax, Milepost 138, and enter via that route. Read above.

144 **SECRET TOWN ROAD/MAGRA ROAD:** ELEVATION: 3,000 FEET.
Note the "Douglas Fir" now at this elevation. These have soft, droopy limbs. The needles are short, flat, blunt-ended sticking out in all directions. In the Spring you'll notice the lighter green tips of new growth. It has soft little 2"-long cones with thin "fingers" sticking out of them. It's a beautiful tree that grows in both the Sierras and the Cascade Ranges. Canyon Live Oaks are also interspersed.

147 **GOLD RUN ROAD:** **FUEL:** South to '76 Mini Mart.
MILEPOST 147A REST AREAS: Trailer dump.
HYDRAULIC MINING FOR GOLD
Stop and read the description of hydraulic mining on the West bound side of the hill by the old "Monitor" hose that was used to tear down this mountain. The peak of river mining was in 1855-1856. By 1859 most of the placer gold in the streams had been mined-out and the claims were left to the Chinese who were charged exorbitant fees to mine. Now the scene changed. They found gold deposits in ancient dry Tertiary streambeds that had been deposited there before the rivers had changed their courses. How to get water there to process the sand and gravel? Now instead of individual miners each coveting his own "claim", they had to cooperate to either haul the soil to the river or channel the water to the claim. To get the water they built ditches, canals and flumes. In 1857 there were 4,405 miles of waterways and two years later there were 5,726 miles.

Experimentation with a hydraulic process began in 1853. It was a gigantic operation! They had big "fire" hoses that channeled water out of the rivers or canals and fired it at the hillsides to wash them down. You are in the head of one of these operations at this Rest Area. The dirt was funneled into "sluice" boxes where the heavier gold would be caught at the rate of $50,000 - $100,000 a day. A man with a single sluice box could only process one cubic yard of dirt a day while with this hydraulic system he could sluice 50-100 cubic yards. This whole mountainside was washed away yielding $6,000,000. To the South of I-80 you'll see some of the debris that was washed down. The hydraulic mining was stopped here not because they ran out of gold, but because the railroad is up on that cliff. In fact they also washed out the OTHER side of this hill and left the railroad sitting on top.

By 1870 there were 425 companies with this type of operation. The rivers filled with silt and resulted in floods in the valley. Marysville, on the Yuba River, had been 19 feet ABOVE the river. By 1878, 30 feet of silt had come down the river so that Marysville was then, and is now, BELOW the level of the river. Levees were built around towns like Marysville and Sacramento to protect them from flooding. In 1883 legislation was finally passed that effectively stopped the hydraulic mining. On the high bank on the North side of I-80 you'll see the history of the river. This bank was laid down in layers by the river over hundreds of years of erosion activity. When the water flowed slowly the silt left behind was sandy and fine. Then during a flood year larger rocks were washed down. Check it out! Can you identify the flood years?

149 **DUTCH FLAT/GOLD RUN ROAD:** Highway Patrol to South.
FUEL: South to BP.
FOOD: Monte Vista Inn.
CAMPGROUND: "Canyon Creek RV Resort". No further information.

150   ALTA: NO NEAR SERVICES!

   THE BIRTHPLACE OF SIERRA SKIING: There used to be a town here called "Towle" with a sawmill, homes, canals, etc. It had been deserted for some time when an Auburn group ordered some wooden skiis through a catalog, began skiing and formed the "Auburn Ski Club". They built the first ski jump at Towle. In later years they got the highway department to plow the snow off the roads in the winter. Then they moved their operation to Cisco Grove where they held the first Slalom races. By 1939 the World Championships were held at Cisco. Today skiing is very popular in California and the Sierras are dotted with ski resorts. You'll pass several above Kingvale.

152   CRYSTAL SPRINGS: NO NEAR SERVICES!

152A   BAXTER: ELEVATION: 4,000 FEET.
   FOOD: North to Old Baxter Cafe.

   BAXTER SPRINGS: This is the source of 60% of the bottled water in Northern California. Bottles carry the "Crystal Springs" label. The springs have been owned by the same family since 1860.

   In the Winter the **CHAIN CONTROLS** are at Baxter. The Highway Department controls the vehicles passing over the Sierras. WHEN YOU ARE TRAVELING OVER THE SIERRAS DURING THE WINTER YOU MUST CARRY CHAINS FOR YOUR TIRES. Men line the road here ready to put them on or take them off for a fee. Sometimes when snows are especially heavy, the Highway Patrol leads lines of vehicles through. In 1992 California has been in a drought phase for several years with the snowfall and the snowpack very light. Other years the snowpack has been around 12 feet and cabin owners had to use ladders to get up the snowbanks and enter by the second floor. In 1862 the snow was 18 feet deep.

155   DRUM FOREBAY ROAD: HIGHWAY ADVISORY RADIO 1610 AM.

   SUGAR PINES: California's most dramatic pine!. This tree grows very big and tall and towers over the other trees. But it has an irregular scraggley top, not neat and pointed like the conifers. So look up at the skyline for the tallest trees with wide horizontal branches near the top. You'll see 12"-15" long cones hanging from them. Then search around the ground underneath to find one to take home. They are the freshest in the fall. Great to decorate for Christmas! Handle them carefully for they have sticky "pitch". It is removable only with a grease-removing hand cleaner such as mechanics use. Remember to put the cones into paper or plastic bags or you'll have pitch all over your car. The dark green trees with feathery red bark are Incense-Cedar with jointed flat leaves. A beautiful tree! The spruce trees may resemble firs from a distance, but touch them and you'll find their needles sharp. To remember the difference between them think "sharp/ spruce". Note that this forest is mostly a mixture of several different conifers including a few oaks and dogwood. The latter has big white blossoms in the Spring and red round leaves in the fall. The Sierras don't have the masses of fall colors of the deciduous trees of the Appalachians, but instead have green trees all year!

159   BLUE CANYON: ELEVATION: 5,273 FEET. NO NEAR SERVICES!

   I-80 has been following up a ridge Eastbound from Auburn to this point. Now you're at the top of the ridge with a great view North down into Bear Valley! Now the road will begin dropping off the ridge to the South Fork of the Yuba River. Blue Canyon got its name in the early years from the smoke rising from the many sawmills along the railroad. Putts Lake is to your right.

160   NYACK ROAD: **FUEL/FOOD/GARAGE:** South to Nyack.

   MILEPOST 161 WESTBOUND VIEWPOINT: Looking down from Emigrant Gap across Bear Valley, you'll see US 20 angling up the hill on the other side. These hills show some Pliocene volcanic activity in mudflows. Pioneers lowered their wagon parts down over the Emigrant Gap cliff into Bear Valley and then followed the Bear River down to the Sacramento Valley. Pioneer, Nicholas Carreger's wife had a baby girl in Bear Valley. His father & sister-in-law died within the same hour. While he buried his dead, his oxen ate poisoned weeds and died. He reached Johnson's Ranch, the first home on the Bear River, and bought oxen to finish the trip.

The first rescue party heading for Donner Lake to rescue the Donner-Reed Party in the winter of 1846-47, stopped at the Johnson Ranch, bought several cattle and "jerked" the meat to take to the stranded survivors. When James Reed was coming up with his rescue party, he met his wife and two children coming out with the first rescue team. Their food cache in Summit Valley had been eaten by animals, so Reed gave them some of his food and then went on up to Donner lake to get his other two children. He said that the snow was 15 feet deep on the Yuba River, up I-80 a few miles, and 30 feet deep in Summit Valley/Norden.

Another more recent story at this site is about the Westbound "City of San Francisco" passenger train that was marooned near here for 3 days in 1952. The snows were so deep that the snow-plows and a 40-man section crew could not reach the train. It was running out of fuel and food while the one doctor on the train was busy caring for ill passengers. Power went out, and with no heat and they were in danger of freezing to death. The Donner Summit Ski Patrol was sent in, coal was brought in to fire the cook stoves and a doctor came by snowsled with medical supplies. A contingent of men including some prison Trustees walked in from US 40/I-80 to trample the snow down to make a 1.5 mile trail. Then they walked the passengers out to the big Nyack Lodge that used to be at this Vista Point before I-80 was built.

162 EMIGRANT GAP:
　　EASTBOUND TO THE VISTA POINT: Exit here, go through the underpass and West on I-80.
　　CAMPGROUND: "North Fork CG": National Forest. FOR THE ADVENTURESOME! Exit to South of I-80. Turn right at the intersection. Six miles Southeast on Texas Hill Road. Vault toilets/piped water. 16-foot max RV Length. Enquire locally. Limited parking. Elevation: 4400 feet.
　　In Pioneer days this area was called **CARPENTER FLAT**. Here in the meadow the pioneers dismantled their wagons again. (They had just done so at Donner Pass.) Then they hauled the parts up to where the Vista Point is today and lowered them down the cliff.

163 LAING ROAD: NO NEAR SERVICES! EASTBOUND ONLY. NO REENTRY.

164 YUBA GAP: NO NEAR SERVICES!
　　CAMPGROUND: "Lodgepole PGE CG": Utility Company public CG. Four miles. Turn South toward "Lake Valley Reservoir" for 1.2 miles. Then take the Right fork 1.5 miles to the campground. Max length 30 feet. Pit toilets. Swim/boat. $9. Elevation: 5800 feet.
　　EASTBOUND: Views are spectacular now with snow-capped peaks ahead much of the year. "Old Man Mountain" is to the Left and then "Red Peak". Note the massive granite hills and the short trees growing out of solid rock. The lake North of I-80 nestled at the base of the mountains is Lake Spaulding, one of the first reservoirs built here. It is on the South Fork of the Yuba River. Watch the railroad tracks through this area. Eastbound the trains will go through 13 tunnels to get to the summit. There are lodgepole pines and red firs here. The red firs have a lacey appearance as you look up through their branches. They are often used for Christmas trees.

165 US 20 WEST:
　　Highway 20 is a beautiful drive to the Sacramento Valley and then across the state to US 101 near the Pacific coast. If you're headed for anywhere along the NORTH COAST, this might be your choice. Check your map.
　　CAMPGROUND: "Lake Spaulding PGE CG": Utility Company Public CG. West 2.3 miles on US 20. Turn Right for a half mile to the campground. Pit toilets. Swim/boat. $9. Max RV length 30 feet. Elevation: 5000 feet.

167 INDIAN SPRINGS/EAGLE LAKES ROAD: NO NEAR SERVICES!
　　CAMPGROUND: "Indian Springs CG": National Forest. North for one mile. 22-foot Max RV length. Piped water, vault toilets, fish, swim, hike. Elevation: 5600 feet. $8. Near the river with lots of rocks for the kids to climb!
　　I-80 has dropped down into the granite of the main part of the Sierras. Dancing along by I-80 now is the South Fork of the Yuba River. The Pioneer Trail pioneers had no easy passage here. It was an engineering challenge to construct this portion of I-80 through the granite of this narrow

canyon. One winter one of the bridges and the highway washed out and had to be rebuilt. In the Winter and Spring this is a beautiful sight as the river splashes over snowcovered granite boulders and icicles hang down over the water.

169 CISCO GROVE: ELEVATION: 5650 FEET.
FUEL/FOOD: Chevron & Cafe.
CAMPGROUND: "Woodchuck CG": National Forest. FOR THE ADVENTURESOME!
Three miles. Exit North, Left onto Frontage Road, Right just before "Thousand Trails" onto "Rattlesnake Rd." Tents only. Bring your own water or boil it. Pit toilets. Elevation: 6300 feet.

170 BIG BEND/RAINBOW ROAD:
FORESTRY SERVICE VISITOR CENTER AT BIG BEND: East 1/4 mile. Stop for information on campgrounds and hiking trails along I-80. Wagon tracks of the old Pioneer Trail are still visible in the rocks. Go Left of the Historical Marker at Big Bend toward the campground. Just before the bridge, go to the Right down a trail. The wagon tracks are near a big Jeffrey Pine by the riverbank. The first wagon train through here was the Stephen-Murphy-Townsend party in 1844. They had hauled their wagons up 10-foot sheer vertical walls of Donner Pass with chains and windlass. Just ten miles beyond the pass, Martin Murphy's wife had a baby. She named her child, Elizabeth Yuba Murphy for the river. The men built a cabin for the women and children, left two men with them while the strongest went to Sacramento for help. It was three months before they could get back to their women. By that time they were surviving on hides, but unlike the later Donner Party, they all lived.
CAMPGROUND: "Big Bend CG": National Forest. Go East 1/4 mile. Tents/RVs. 16-foot Max RV length. Vault toilets/piped water. Fish, swim, hike. Pets allowed. Elevation: 5900 feet. $8.
EASTBOUND: Exit here and take Old US 40 for awhile. It's a beautiful drive through the woods to Kingvale or Soda Springs. The South Fork of the Yuba River is a clear mountain stream with bright green poplars along it. In the fall these are a bright yellow. Notice the "glacial erratic" rocks left by an ancient glacier as it receded. It's as if a giant just pitched rocks around and left them where they landed. Get out, feel the air, smell the flowers, and walk in this paradise. You might see a Red-Headed Woodpecker or a Stellar's Jay, bright blue with a crest.

172 HAMPSHIRE ROCKS/RAINBOW ROAD/BIG BEND:
FOOD: RAINBOW TAVERN: Just North of Hampshire Rocks. This lodge has been a landmark here since 1920. The stone structure inside is impressive. Try a meal here. Sometimes they have a "Buffet". In 1935 a card shark was killed for cheating at the card tables here.
CAMPGROUNDS: "Hampshire Rocks": National Forest. South of I-80 off Frontage Road. Vault toilets, piped water, campfires. Hike, fish, swim. 22-foot Max RV. Elevation: 5800 feet. $8.
Big Bend CG: WESTBOUND: 1.5 miles West. Read Milepost 170.

175 KINGVALE: ELEVATION: 6,118 FEET.
FUEL: Arco.
FOOD: Cafe.
CAMPGROUND: To North. No information.
EASTBOUND: You can see 9103 foot Castle Peak now at the summit. It's on the North side of I-80 with turrets like a castle. Alpine Zone, NO trees up there!
WESTBOUND: This is a 60-mile downhill grade to the valley. Take note of the yellow signs that are instructions for truckers, as their advice will help you also. When brakes get too hot from overuse, they burn out and you have NO brakes. Take it easy and use your brakes sparingly. Slow your vehicle by downshifting to a lower gear.

178 SODA SPRINGS/NORDEN SKI RESORTS: ELEVATION: 6766 FEET.
WESTBOUND: If you exit here onto old US 40 you can enjoy a wonderful drive through the woods and along the Yuba River. You can return to I-80 at Big Bend and Milepost 170.
FUEL: Exxon and LP gas.
FOOD: Tinkers Station Bar & Grill, Fred's Hof Brau.

MOTELS: Donner Summit Lodge, Soda Springs Station.
SKI RESORTS: Four Alpine ski resorts and Cross Country skiing.

EASTBOUND ALTERNATE ROUTE:

OLD DONNER PASS! THE OLD PIONEER TRAIL: Exit to the South to take old US 40 just 12 miles down to Donner Lake and back onto I-80. This is A MUST ROUTE for visitors! Have your camera ready! The view from the summit is unsurpassed! In the Winter, this pass is closed just East of the last ski resort. The "Sugar Bowl" is an old favorite where you take a tram across the valley to the lifts on the far hillside. You will pass Lake Norden which can still be frozen-over in June with several feet of snow on top. Before refrigeration, large chunks of ice were cut from this lake and stored to "ice" the "Fruit Express" railroad cars. The homes, resorts, and railroad facilities all had tunnels to get from the highway to and between the buildings. Only the snowsheds for the tracks remain.

On the emigrant trail Norden was called "Summit Valley". When the first team of rescuers for the Donner-Reed Party reached here, they cached some food for their return trip by tying it in bundles and hanging it in the trees. But when they arrived back up the hill with the 21 starving people, the food was gone. Animals had gnawed the ropes and devoured the food. John Denton, one of the victims, could go no further. They built a fire for him and left him a bit of food. When the 2nd rescue party led by James Reed arrived they found a notebook and pencil beside his body. In his dying days he had written a poem about his youth. In early March when Reed's rescue party struggled back up from Donner Lake with 17 survivors, including his children, Patty and Tommy Reed, they were stopped by a weeklong snowstorm. A third rescue party reached them just in time.

Now you're getting up closer to the summit. Watch the railroad tracks and see when they disappear into the tunnel ahead through the solid granite of this pass. At the top of the pass pull off to the Right and park near the Mountaineer building. Find the dirt road to the Left behind the building between two iron poles. This is the old "Donner Lake to Dutch Flat Toll Road". Note the very old juniper growing in the solid rock. Go on through the willows and find a large rock on the Right with a bronze plaque. It notes the Stevens Party who pulled their wagons up here in November 1844. About 10 feet downhill they forced their oxen through a crack in the rocks. Then they put chains from them to the wagons, and with the animals pulling and the men pushing, they got the wagons up the hill. You can go down further to pass through a tunnel under the railroad. Then turn around and look back at a wall of stone that was built with no mortar by the Chinese.

DONNER SUMMIT from OLD U.S. 40
Donner Lake and I-80 in distance
Photo Credit: John A. Kost

Now over the pass! Just after you cross the bridge make an immediate Left turn into the viewing area. You'll want a picture of this jewel of a lake. Donner Lake is three miles long and 600 feet deep at one point. Before I-80 was built, this view from the turnout was one of the most photographed scenes in the U.S.! Look at the railroad dodging in and out of tunnels with snow sheds between tunnels. Those sheds are cement now but they used to be made of wood. See all that lumber discarded on the tallus slope below each snowshed. If you have a AAA "Lake Tahoe Region" map look at how the railroad tracks have to snake around the mountains above the lake. At the Eastern end of the lake, the trains make a 2-mile loop up a canyon and back in order to make it up this steep grade. Now down the hill. At the West end of the lake is a swimming beach, playground, fishing, boating and a small RV park. Drive slowly by the lake as this is a resort area.

180 CASTLE PEAK/BOREAL RIDGE SKI AREA:

Boreal Ridge is a busy Winter resort area, but in the summer you can still ride a sled down a chute. **THE AUBURN SKI CLUB MUSEUM** displays the history of skiing. **SNOWSHOE THOMPSON** was the famous Sierra mailman from 1856-1876. He carried the Virginia City mail across the Sierras. His unusual skis are part of the exhibit.

PACIFIC CREST TRAIL HEAD: As the East Coast has the Appalachian Trail, the West has the "Pacific Crest Trail". Following the crest of the Sierras and the Cascades, backpackers can travel between Mexico and Canada.

Note the trees in this area. Lots of tall 2-needle Lodgepole Pines. Many have twisted trunks since their sapling days when the heavy snows bent them. Also the branches have been broken off quite high up the trunks by the blasting action of the snowplows. This is a sub-alpine life area and includes red and white firs.

MILEPOST 181 REST AREAS: DONNER SUMMIT. ELEVATION: 7239 FEET.

In the Rest Area walk around the giant boulders that were glaciated in Pleistocene time. Glaciers carved out many small lakes like the one on the South East edge of the summit and I-80. Rest and picnic and enjoy the Hemlock with its soft tiny needles, its buggy-whip top and droopy branches. **EASTBOUND:** Steep downgrade as you drop 1200 feet in 7 miles. Shift to a lower gear as you'll be using your trailer brakes.

MILEPOST 182 VIEWPOINTS

You are privileged here with spectacular scenery! The Sierras are solid granite pushed up from underneath. Note the railroad tunnels and snowsheds high up on Schallenberger Ridge to the South. In 1868 it took 10,000 Chinese digging, handdrilling, chipping and blasting to dig the tunnels just 7" a day. To build the tracks around the hills, Chinese would be lowered in baskets out over the sheer cliffs to drill holes in the rock and place explosive charges. If a rope broke or a blast went off too soon, the man was killed. Their lives were expendable to the railroad. Only the Chinese would do this work and for the lowest pay too. Next up the economic ladder were the track-layers, the Irish, who had just arrived from famine-ridden Ireland. Visit the Railroad Museum in Sacramento and see photos of the building of the railroad through the Sierras.

The Chinese had come during the Gold Rush, mostly from the Southern Provinces of China. Rich Chinese paid the passage of many of these peasants and then sold their labor to mining and manufacturing companies. In the Census of 1860 there were 35,000 Chinese in California. By the time railroad construction began, the mines had closed and there was little other work for them.

Even after the railroad was completed the Chinese were treated horrendously. Townspeople in Truckee burned down the Chinese part of town four times and forced them to leave. In the town of Volcano, men used the powerful hydraulic hoses to wash the Chinese houses down the canyons laughing when women and children ran out screaming. An 1852 "Foreign Miners' Tax" was forced on the Chinese. The Sheriff was allowed to collect $3 per month (later $4) from each Chinese miner. He got 20% for

RAILROAD TUNNELS through SIERRA GRANITE
Photo credit: John A. Kost

himself, the County and the State each received 40%. This tax paid 25% of the State budget and 100% of County budgets. The Sheriffs were the highest paid officers in the state. The law was repealed in 1870.

To the Southwest you'll see old US 40 switchbacking down over a 1000 foot granite cliff. The Stephens Party of 1844 had winched some of their wagons up this cliff before they gave up and left the rest of the wagons for the winter in the care of three 17-year old boys. They built a cabin of pine boughs and hides. Then they made snowshoes and tried to walk out. But Moses Schallenberger was too weak and couldn't make it. So he said "Goodby" to his two friends and struggled back to the cabin. He killed a coyote and a couple foxes. The foxes were delicious but he couldn't make the coyote palatable. Dr. Townsend had left his books so Moses read aloud to himself to break the silence. He was finally rescued in the spring. In 1846 when the Donner party was caught at the lake in deep snows, they used Moses' cabin.

Donner Lake was named "Mountain Lake" by Captain Stephens of the first wagon train. When the Donners arrived in 1846 it was called "Truckee Lake" for Chief Trokay who led the Stephens party to the Truckee River. After the Donner Party tragedy, pioneers avoided this trail for some time and Carson Pass was preferred.

As you look South out across the lake, you'll see the light granite of the hills, but also note further East some dark rocks that are Pliocene volcanic. The lake was carved out by a glacier that extended Eastward down the Truckee River. This is the typical "U-shaped" valley that a glacier leaves. "V-shaped valleys" have been carved by rivers. Spruces and fir trees here. Feel the needles; remember spruce has sharp needles. Manzanita, so plentiful in the Sierras, is the red-barked bush with the tiny green leaves. It has pink blossoms from which bees make delicious honey. Turn around and look at the ridge behind you North of I-80. This ridge was devastated by a terrible forest fire in 1960 that lasted for 7 days. With no seed-producing trees left, it will not recover unless replanted.

185 DONNER LAKE ROAD:

This is a very steep road switchbacking down to Donner Lake. Trailers and large motorhomes not advised. Are your ears closing? It's the change in elevation and air pressure. Open your mouth and throat as for a big yawn and your ears will pop open.

188 TRUCKEE/DONNER LAKE STATE PARK: ELEVATION: 5980 FEET.
FUEL: Shell, '76 with garage, Chevron.
CAMPGROUND: DONNER MEMORIAL STATE PARK: Open May-Sept. South a few blocks toward Donner Lake. Follow signs. 24-foot Max RV length. Showers, campfires, fish, swim in lake. $14. Senior $12. Call 1-800-444-PARK for reservations. Open May-Oct.

EMIGRANT TRAIL MUSEUM, DONNER LAKE STATE PARK: Exit I-80 and go South and West following signs to the park. This is A MUST STOP for everyone. The film at the Visitor Center tells you the tragic story of the Donner-Reed Party. The Donners were prosperous Illinois farmers, James Reed owned a saw-mill. But they were not wise in the ways of frontier travel, took the wrong routes, made the wrong decisions. The party of 81, half children, arrived at Donner Lake in late October weak from their arduous journey. When they saw the sheer cliffs of the pass they tried to find another route. George and Jacob Donner were left behind when they stopped by Alder Creek, several miles up CA 89, to fix a broken axle.

DONNER MONUMENT
Photo credit: John A. Kost

It began to snow and by the time it stopped there was four feet of snow. Since it was only October, they expected this snow to melt so that they could get over the pass. But it began to snow again trapping them right where they were. They constructed makeshift cabins, lean-tos and tent structures. Six times members of the party tried to get out. Once 15 made snowshoes and tried to cross the mountains. Seven made it! Most of the party had to stay the winter. The base of the monument at 22 feet shows you the depth of the snow that year. As the snow kept falling, the people had to climb up from their makeshift cabins of pine branches and tarps to get to the top of the snow bank. Then they struggled through the soft snow, often up to their waists, to find wood for their fires.

The first rescue party came on Feb 18th. They took 23 of the strongest out including Mrs. Reed and her 4 children. Little Patty and Tommy Reed only made it 2 miles before they were sent back to the cabins to be taken in by the Breens. James Reed brought the next rescue party the 1st of March. He found his daughter Patty sitting on top of the snowbank above the Breen cabin. Reed took 17 out but it was the end of April before the last man was rescued. Gen. Stephen Kearny stopped here a few weeks later to find dismembered bodies and stripped bones. Cannabalism plagued the survivors and most denied it. But the last man to be rescued was haunted by it. Only 47 members survived to Sutter's Fort and only the Reed and Breen families survived intact. Adult $2. Ch $1. Summers 10-5pm. Rest of year, 10-4pm with time out for lunch. You can buy one of the books to read the whole fascinating story.

WESTBOUND ALTERNATE ROUTE
UP OLD US 40, DONNER SUMMIT: As you are leaving Donner Lake State Park, turn Left and you

are on Old US 40. You'll ride around the North side of the lake and then climb to the summit. Be sure to stop at the viewpoint just this side of the bridge. It's a steep hard climb so you might not want to pull a trailer up this grade. Read Milepost 178 for description of this route.

189   SQUAW VALLEY/TAHOE CITY/CA 89 SOUTH:

MALLS: North to Gateway Mall with Safeway food, Payless drug, Sizzler. South to Truckee Crossroads Mall with Longs Drugs, Lucky Food, Burger King, China Garden, Subway, Ice Cream and Yogurt.

MOTELS: Star Hotel, Sunset Inn, Richards, Alpine Village. Super 8 (South 3 miles). Moderate-high in this resort area. Many resorts have rooms.

CAMPGROUNDS: "Granite Flat": National Forest. South on CA 89 .5 mile. 22-foot Max RV length. Piped water/vault toilets. Campfires, river fish, swim. Elevation: 5800 feet. Limited parking. $8.

"Goose Meadow CG": National Forest. South on CA 89 four miles. Hand-pump water, vault toilets, 22-foot Max RV length. River fish, swim. Elevation: 5800 feet.

"Silver Creek CG": National Forest. Six miles South of Truckee. Elevation: 5800 feet. Hand pump wells, vault toilets. $8.

ALTERNATE ROUTES:

SOUTH TO SQUAW VALLEY AND LAKE TAHOE: You have several alternatives here but if you are a visitor you MUST SEE Lake Tahoe! So get out your map and see the possibilities.

CHOICE #1: EASTBOUND FROM MILEPOST 190 or WESTBOUND FROM MILEPOST 192 take CA 267 to the North Shore of Lake Tahoe and continue either way around the lake. (Descriptions of sights below under Choice #2.)

CHOICE #2: South on US 89 to Squaw Valley, 10 miles. Site of 1960 Winter Olympics. Hike, bike, horseback ride, ice skate winter, swim in the summer; snow sports in the winter; ride the cable car all year. Following the Truckee River up to the lake you'll see some lava rocks tumbling down a hillside evidence of OLD volcanic activity. No active volcanos in this area today. On to Lake Tahoe, four miles more. When you get to the intersection at Tahoe City, go right for just one block to the bridge. Get out and view the large fish under the bridge. This is the beginning of the Truckee River. Now you have several choices. Here are a couple.

FROM TAHOE CITY, EASTBOUND: When you get to Tahoe City go Left/North on CA 28 around the North end of the lake. Beautiful views here! At the Northeast corner take NV 431 up over twisty Mount Rose Highway to US 395 (trailers and large rigs not advised) and go North to I-80 at Reno. Or continue on NV 28 to US 50 and over Spooner Summit to US 395 and Carson City and North to I-80 in Reno. (A good route for large rigs.)

FROM TAHOE CITY, WESTBOUND: You can continue South on CA 89 along the West side of the lake to US 50 and West to Sacramento and I-80.

Lake Tahoe is the jewel in the necklace of the Sierras. It's colors vary with the sky's and the depth of the water, from deep green at Emerald Bay to bright blue. It's greatest depth on the West shore is 1600 feet, the deepest lake in North America. The mountains rise over 4,000 feet above the shore. Tahoe was formed by a "fault" and was filled by snow runoff.

A ride around the lake is an experience you'll never forget! Beautiful views from all sides! Winter snow pack here can be from 5 to 15 feet. You'll find restaurants, campgrounds and hotels all around the lake, and casinos on the Nevada borders. There are 19 downhill ski resorts around the lake plus cross-country skiing.

NORTHSHORE: Views, casinos, vacation homes and **PONDEROSA RANCH.** This is the "Cartwright House" set for "Bonanza" in a Western Theme Park on the Northeast corner of the lake. Summers daily 10-4pm. Adult $6.50. Child $5.50. The Eastshore road runs close to the lake and if you can find a parking space you can sit on a beach or the rocks and enjoy yourself.

WESTSHORE: The highway runs along the beach for awhile and then higher on the hills. Highlights are:

VIKINGSHOLM: A Norse style building on Emerald Bay. Park at lot on West side of road to "Eagle Falls". Hike down to the Lodge with the flower garden on the roof. The small island on the bay used to be the owner's "Teahouse". Coming back up the hill is tougher but you can do it. Summers daily 10-4pm. Adult $1. Child $.50.

TRAIL TO EAGLE FALLS: From the same parking lot. First walk the short distance to the falls, then on up the trail over the granite to a small glacial lake nestled in the rocks. This is a great experience and takes only an hour or so. Don't try to hurry at this elevation, take many rests. If you have not yet hiked in the Sierras, this will give you a first experience of the granite interior.

CAMPGROUNDS: Westshore's "Sugar Pine Point", "Emerald Bay", "DL Bliss" State Parks have GREAT campgrounds along the lakeshore. You'll need reservations at all these so call as far ahead as possible: 1-800-444-7275.

South shore has the largest casinos with big shows nightly. Many hotels, restaurants. Take the Chair Lift up "Heavenly Valley" Ski Resort.

TAHOE QUEEN: Have a refreshing ride on a paddlewheeler to Emerald Bay, Cave Rock, etc. Includes glass-bottomed viewing area. Food served. June-Sept daily 11am, 1:30pm and 3:55pm. Oct-May daily 12:30pm.

READ MORE INFORMATION ABOUT LAKE TAHOE IN NEVADA MILEPOST 15.

190 CENTRAL TRUCKEE/CA 267 SOUTH TO NORTH SHORE OF LAKE TAHOE:

This is the Western entrance into the old town of Truckee. Exit South and East. You will connect with CA 267 South in the middle of town. This is a beautiful route to Lake Tahoe. Truckee was a bustling ice harvesting and lumbering town when the Central Pacific Railroad arrived here in 1868. Today it is a fun town with good cafes and ice cream shops.

VISITOR INFORMATION CENTER: At the railroad station. "Zina's Creative Cuisine" is in "The White House" an historical Register house on your Left. The old Truckee jail is up Spring Street and the log Waystation is up Bridge Street. Drive through town and check them out.

Look up on the hill from town for a yellow quonset-hut Veterans' Hall. (While on I-80, you can see it just South of the highway.) Right beside it is a Gazebo over **INDIAN ROCKING STONE.** This is a natural phenomenon of a large rock sitting on top of a giant boulder. From town you can drive up the hill to see it. The local Tribes had a legend about how the smaller stone got on top of the large one. Today we know about "glacial radicals" wherein glaciers left stones in strange positions as they receded. The smaller stone was so balanced on the larger that when touched by a finger it would rock. It even rocked in the wind! The Natives felt that as long as it did so, they would have plenty of food and would be able to live in peace with their neighbors. They revered it so it may have been used as a kind of altar. C. F. McGlashan, author of "History of the Donner Party", built the gazebo in 1895 to protect it and to house his Donner Party artifacts. The Olympic Torch of 1960 made an overnight stop here. The stone rocks no more. The city fathers cemented it for fear it would be dislodged during an earthquake and descend on the town.

EASTBOUND: You can continue on through town to get back on I-80 at Milepost 192.

**192 CENTRAL TRUCKEE/CA 89 NORTH TO SIERRAVILLE.
CA 267 SOUTH TO NORTH SHORE TAHOE:**

South on CA 267 is a great route to the Northeastern shore of Lake Tahoe. Check your map and read Milepost 189 for descriptions of the sights around the lake. You can turn this into an alternate route.

CAMPGROUNDS: "Annie McCloud CG": National Forest. North on CA 89 for .5 mile. Right on "Prosser Dam Road" for 4.5 miles. Vault/Chemical toilets. Bring your own water or boil the water before drinking. $8.

"Prosser CG": National Forest. North on US 89 for 3 miles. Piped water/vault toilets. Elevation: 5800 feet. $8.

"Lakeside CG: National Forest. 4 miles North on CA 89. Vault toilets/bring water or boil it. Boat landing. Elevation: 5700 feet. $8.

"Coachland Camper Park": Private. Good Sam. No tents. North on CA 89. Spa. $17.

"Lakeside": National Forest. North 4.3 miles on CA 89. East .4 mile on Forest Road 18N47. 22-foot Max RV length. Cable TV. Campfires, lake fish, swim.

"Village Green Mobile Park: Private. Good Sam. South 1.3 miles on CA 267. No pets or tents. Cable TV, playground. $18.

"Martis Creek Lake": Corp of Engineers. 5 miles South off Ca 267. Tents/RVs. No showers. Chemical toilets. Swim, fish.

You are passing through Martis Valley that was filled in by landslides and glacial debris.

ALDER CREEK SITE OF DONNER CAMP: North on US 89 for three miles to Forestry Service Picnic Ground. Read the sign and walk the trail. A broken axle and a cut hand stranded the Jacob and George Donner families here while the rest of the party had gone ahead to Donner Lake. Jacob had 7 children and George and Tamsen had five. Their teamsters helped to construct makeshift shelters from the canvas. Their cattle were lost in a storm. Jacob was dead when rescuers arrived and George barely alive. Rescuers took the children but Tamsen would not leave George. Later his body was found but no trace of Tamsen. She was a lady of intelligence, grace and compassion, an artist and botanist. She cared for a stray young man who died in her arms at Grantsville, Utah.

194 **PROSSER VILLAGE ROAD:** NO NEAR SERVICES!
    MILEPOST 195 WESTBOUND: You will go through the California State Inspection Station. You must stop and answer their questions. They will ask about your having particular fruits, vegetables and plants. They are trying to protect agriculture by keeping certain insect pests out of California.
    EASTBOUND: You are now coming into the canyon of the Truckee River that flows out of Lake Tahoe. As you come to the East end of this valley there is a brown cinder cone on the side of the Gorge at a sharp bend of the river. Look above high on the hill and you'll see a layer of basalt that has the sides sliced off like you might trim a loaf of bread. It is called "columnar", like columns.
    CROSSING THE TRUCKEE: Note the outcroppings of volcanic flow here and the talus slopes/rock slides. This was an active volcanic area in Cenozoic time. Along the Truckee River Canyon here you might pick out the cones of ancient volcanos. The highest one to the South is Bald Mountain.

198 **HIRSCHDALE ROAD/BOCA DAM:** EASTBOUND RESTSTOP. ELEVATION: 5523 FEET.
    Notice how the old landslides have formed rolling bumpy hills.
    CAMPGROUNDS: "Boca CG": National Forest. Exit North to the dam. Go Left to the Southwest shore. Portable toilets. Bring own water or boil it. Tenters. Limited space for trailers. Elevation: 5600 feet. Boat ramp. $8.
    "Boca Rest CG": National Forest. North 2 miles North of dam. Piped water/vault toilets. Boat ramp. Fish, swim, hike. Elevation: 5700 feet. $8.
    EASTBOUND: SLOW DOWN. STEEP DOWNGRADE HERE FOR 5 MILES. This is the sharp Eastern "scarp" of the Sierras. It requires three diesel engines to get a train up this grade, one at each end and one in the middle. The Sierras were pushed up very sharply on this side, whereas the Western slope is just a gradual uplift from the valley. The first wagon party over this route had 10 river crossings in one mile because of the steep canyon walls of the Truckee. One account has the Donners crossing this river 49 times in 80 miles.

203 **TRUCKEE RIVER/FLORISTON:** ELEVATION: 5301 FEET. NO NEAR SERVICES!
    Watch the canyon walls. The Pliocene agglomerate here is most interesting with volcanic rocks in little towers while water and weather cause landslides below them. Have you been noticing the trees getting smaller and fewer as you go downhill. The Sierras behind you took all the rain and snow and left little for this desert side of the mountains. These slopes were also victim of the need for timber for The Virginia City Mines in the 1860's.

205 **FARAD:** NO NEAR SERVICES!
    Note the "flumes" beside the road. The first thing that settlers had to do was to get water to their homes, mines and farms. Wood was plentiful in the Sierras, so they built these wooden flumes to transport the water from a higher source. There were large "V-shaped" ones used to float logs from the Sierras over to the Virginia City mines. There used to be flumes all over the Sierras but today few are left.

209 **NEVADA STATE LINE:**
    EASTBOUND: Say "Goodby" to the Golden State and prepare for the basin/range.
    WESTBOUND: Greet the Golden State and the spectacular Sierra Nevada Mountains! Today, in just a few hours, you may travel from the 7,000 foot mountain pass in front of you, to sea level on the Pacific Ocean.

CALIFORNIA I 80 MILEPOSTS

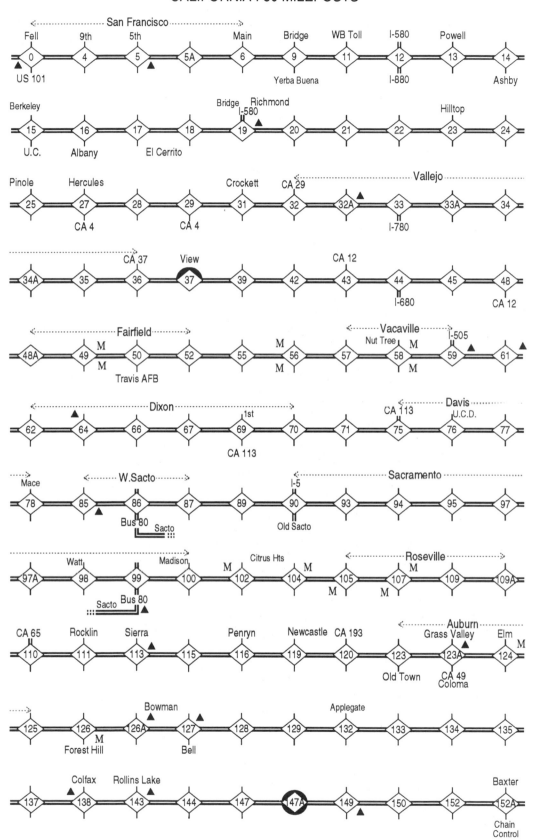

CALIFORNIA I 80 MILEPOSTS - CONTINUED

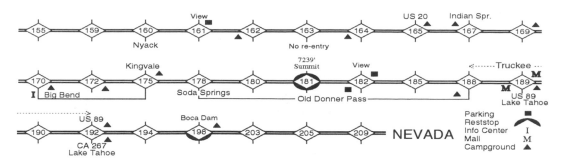

On I-80 In the Sierras, Mother Nature is in Command.
Photo credit: California Department of Transportation

Nevada

The Silver State

In its early years Nevada was but a great desert that pioneers crossed as quickly as possible. It was part of the "Utah Territory" in 1850, but by 1858 became the "Sierra Nevada Territory", Nevada meaning "snow-capped". Then in 1859 silver was discovered on Sun Mountain and the character of two states was dramatically changed forever. The resultant millions of dollars in silver and gold that was mined, rushed the Civil War government into giving the state an explosive birth in 1864. The smallest state capitol in the U.S. is Carson City, and the smallest capitol building sports a shiny silver dome. The flag waving above it wears the blue of the wide sky and the silver of the mineral that made Nevada rocket into importance. Even the state flower is the lowly but silvery-spiked sage-brush.

The Mountain Bluebird is the state bird and their animal is the magnificent Bighorn Sheep that lives in the mountains on grass, pinenuts, yucca, joshua and cactus plants. Both male and female have curving horns but the male's are larger. The Pinon Pine, a short gnarled pine growing in the rocky soil of the mountains, is the state tree. You'll notice it as the greenest green growing on the western slopes as you climb over the mountain passes. The Indians used the sweet pine nuts as one of their staples. The Bristlecone pine tree, that Nevada shares with California, is the oldest living tree, some being more than 3,500 years old. Although Nevada is our 7th largest state with 110,540 square miles, it has one of the smallest populations, 1,201,833, among the states (43rd).

Nevada is a gambling, ranching and mining state leading the nation in production of gold, mercury and magnesite. Barite, silver, copper, diatomite, fluorspar, iron ore, lithium, molybdenum and perlite are also mined, with the total industry generating more than $2 billion in 1986 alone.

Nevada is a basin/range state as first described by the Army surveyor and topographer, John C. Fremont. Actually it is one gigantic basin encompassing most of state with many mountain ranges pushing up out of the desert all lined in a North-South orientation. From the air they have been equated to an army of caterpillars all wriggling South-ward. Nevada's basin actually rests on a 4000 foot plateau, so that it is not as low as would be expected from its desert climate. The lowest point is 470 feet on the Colorado River. Many of its rivers are trapped between ranges and do not flow to the sea. The Truckee River that you will follow Eastward into Nevada flows into Pyramid Lake North of I-80. The dancing Carson River that the first mountain men followed upstream to the Sierras, flows into a basin just South of I-80. The Humboldt River that led the emigrants across the deserts to Lovelock, also sinks into a basin you'll see to the South of I-80 just five miles from the Carson Sink. The 14,000 foot Sierra Nevada Mountains claim most of the moisture from the clouds blowing Eastward, leaving very little for Nevada. Yet Nevada has its own snowcapped mountains as high as 13,000 feet that catch snow and save it for the ranches below. On these ranges roam deer, wild mustang, desert big-horn sheep, squirrel and chipmunk. Along the brooks dashing down from the peaks are the busy beaver working amongst the aspen and colorful wildflowers, while cool mountain breezes blow even in the hottest summer on the desert. Temperatures

Sagebrush

may vary 20-30 degrees from the basins to the hills.

The federal government controls 85% of the state with bombing ranges, munitions storage facilities, and the "Nevada Test Site" for nuclear weapons. Two-thirds of the state lands are managed by the U.S. Bureau of Land Management. Some of this is in grazing land and mining.

NEVADA'S SILVER-DOMED CAPITOL
Photo credit: Carson City Convention & Visitor's Bureau

NEVADA HISTORY

Nevada's very first inhabitants hunted mammoth, giant ground sloth and camel. The 19th Century Natives were mainly the Northern and Southern Paiutes in the basins, with the Washoe in the Sierra Nevada / Carson City area, and the Shoshoni East of the Tuscarora Mountains. They were mostly nomadic tribes depending on bison, antelope and rabbits, fishing and roots, seeds and berries. Once part of Mexico and then Utah Territory, Nevada was first viewed by a white man, Jedediah Smith, in 1826 in the Southern part of the state. He returned East the next year across Central Nevada. In 1826 Peter Skene Ogden of Hudson's Bay Company began trapping beaver in the North state and subsequently explored all along the Humboldt River. He named it Mary's River but others called it Ogden River. In 1833 explorer, Joseph Walker, followed the Humboldt to the sink and later crossed the Sierra up the Walker River. Eastbound again he found Walker Lake and then went back up the Humboldt to Utah. Walker's explorations helped fill out the empty spaces in the maps of the West. Then came other trappers and Mountain men, including Kit Carson.

In 1843-1844, John C. Fremont came down from his Oregon trip into Nevada, named Pyramid Lake and Lake Bonpland, which later became Lake Tahoe. Then he went across the Sierras South of Carson Pass. Later in 1845 Fremont, with Kit Carson & Walker guiding him, came on a Surveying and Mapping Expedition from the Arkansas River across the Basin-range of Utah and Nevada. Fremont's expedition was running out of water on the Salt Flats when Carson found the springs on Pilot Peak, NV and set up a smoke signal to guide the expedition there. Fremont then split his party and sent Walker down the Humboldt River while he took a more Southwesterly course to meet him at Walker Lake. They split again and Walker proceeded West up the Walker River and down to Sonora while Fremont followed the Truckee River to Donner Pass. Being the official map-maker, he had the privilege of naming everything he drew on his maps. He used his two guides names for the Carson River and Pass and the Walker River and Lake. It was Fremont who named the "Humboldt River" after a German geographer whom he admired. He also named the area between the Wasatch Mountains in Utah and the Sierras, the "Great Basin". He noted that the streams here do not flow to the sea but form lakes and evaporate. Therefore he equated the area with a great "bowl" or "basin". His name stuck although it is not totally accurate. The area is not "basin-shaped" but has irregular dimensions.

In 1850, when Nevada was part of the "Utah Territory", the Mormons established the first permanent settlement in Nevada just South of Carson City. It was known as "Mormon Station". Today it is historic Genoa just off US 50. Brigham Young was having problems with the Federal Government, so in 1857 he recalled the Mormons to Salt Lake City.

By 1859 most placer gold in the Sierras had been panned out. Now men roamed over the Nevada hills digging their "coyote holes" searching for gold. Two Irishmen found some gold on Gold Hill, but there was a lot of "blue stuff" in the way. Wiley old Henry Comstock saw the "color", the gold, in their diggin's and announced that they were on his ranching claim of 160 acres and were using water from his spring. He bullied them into giving him shares. A local rancher and a trader were intrigued by "the blue stuff" and took 2 bags of it to Grass Valley, CA for assay. It assayed at $3,100 a ton in silver and $1500 a ton in gold. They hurried back to buy up interests and stake their claims. As did the assayer! Word got out and the rush was on. The original owners were happy to sell out for from $3500 to $8500 while Comstock managed to get $11,000. They all felt themselves rich! Old Comstock left only his name on the "Comstock Lode". "Old Virginny", an old miner, tripped over a stone breaking his bottle of whiskey. In his inebriated state he turned it into a christening and the miners' camp on Sun Mountain became "Virginia City".

When Virginia City was first claimed by gold miners, they stripped the hills of the pinon pines for their firewood. One source says that the miners "bought" the pinon orchards from the Paiutes. Mostly the miners just appropriated the land. Now when the underground silver mines required wood for timbering and for charcoal, they logged off the trees up the Sierras and reached over them for more, denuding the hills for 100 miles. First they hauled the logs on wagons. Then an ingenious man invented the "V Flume" that could float the timbers and the firewood for miles down from the Sierras. The mines became so honeycombed with logs that someone dubbed them "The Tomb of the Forest". No mature trees were left to drop seeds for new growth! And the trees were never replanted. That is why there are so few trees in the area today.

It took money to mine the silver, so the bankers came from San Francisco to make their deals. Virginia City was sitting on a nest of millions! The mines produced $1 million in gold & silver in 1860, $16 million in 1864, and $38 million in 1876 when the richest part of the "Big Bonanza" was struck. Silver made millionaires, built Carson City, Sacramento and San Francisco and helped the North fight the Civil War. There are many fascinating stories on Virginia City and its rags-to-riches-to-rags citizens. Do visit the town and Bower's Mansion in Washoe Valley and read more about this fascinating era. Read Milepost 15, "Sidetrip to Virginia City" and "Alternate Returning Routes". Since Lincoln needed the silver to fight the Civil War, he accelerated the statehood process and in 1864 he welcomed "Nevada" as the 36th state in the Union. This was before Nebraska, Wyoming or Utah became states.

The riches of Sun Mountain/Mt. Davidson were protected by heat surging up from its innards. At 1500 feet it was 100 degrees, at 2,000 feet it was 120 degrees. Miners could only work 15 to 30 minutes at a time. They were allotted 95 pounds of ice a man per day. They chewed it and carried it in their hands and on their backs . Finally it was impossible to mine due to the hot water and steam. Then came Adolph Sutro who proposed building a tunnel from the desert on the East side of the mountain into the very heart of the mines to drain out the hot water. His detractors called it "Sutro's Folly". He began digging in 1871 and completed it in 1878. But by that time the mines were 1500 feet deeper than the tunnel. He charged a royalty of $2 a ton on all ore produced thereafter. It solved their hot water problem, but didn't help get the ore out. Just two years later, he wisely sold his stock and went to San Francisco. With his million dollars he built himself a mansion, and for the public, an 8-story Cliff House and seven temperature-controlled swimming pools. (Read San Francisco's Tour of the Cliff House area.)

Congress passed the "Coinage Act of 1873". It demonetized silver and made gold the sole monetary standard. Nevada was frantic! They had fought it for years and called it the "Crime of 1873". As long as the silver and gold mines were producing well, Nevada prospered until its high in 1880. The Virginia City mines began to fade, but new ones sprang up further South in Tonopah and Goldfield. Then the silver mines closed, gold mining dropped off and people left the state by the thousands. Nevada's population dropped to 44,000 and never got back to 1880's 62,000 level until after World War I. The Federal Government even talked about withdrawing statehood for lack of population and a tax base to support the state. But little by little ranching became a way of life in Nevada and famous movie stars like Bing Crosby had "spreads" there.

The famous "Ghost Dance" that worried the army so much in 1890 when the Sioux took it up, originated here at Walker Lake by Wovoka, a Shaman/medicine man. It was a religious revival to find meaning to their lives with whites destroying their habitat and their food supply. It's precepts were a life of virtue, reincarnation, and the disappearance of the whites. The concept spread Eastward to the other tribes, put the Sioux and the army on edge, and ended with the massacre of 200 Indians at Wounded Knee.

Gambling has been off and on in Nevada. It was born into gambling, then became illegal until 1869. In

1910 it was prohibited again. In 1931 Nevada legalized gambling which today provides a significant portion of the state budget. There are thriving Casino towns at each of Nevada's gates to other states including Reno, Las Vegas, Wendover, Jackpot and Laughlin. They have added flamboyant floor shows, convention centers, and big name stars. Tourists prefer Reno to "Vegas" because of its relaxed friendliness and its better odds. So Reno flourishes today with ever bigger and more garish casinos. Call the Reno Visitor Center 702-348-7788 for information and a behind-the-scenes tour of casinos. Milepost 13 takes you into Downtown Reno and the casino area.

Nevada also thrived in the Wedding/Divorce business, especially after 1920 when Mary Pickford's Reno divorce got national publicity. You could get a divorce in six weeks (instead of months) if you could prove that you had been a "resident" of Nevada for that period. So "Divorce Motels" and "Ranches" had a lucrative business housing prospective divorcees from the East and testifying as to their clients' "residence" with them for the legal period. Although this received a lot of notoriety in the news media and movies, there were always more marriages performed in Nevada than divorces. Nevada required no blood tests, no "wait" between applying for a marriage license and the wedding ceremony. The depression was on and money was tight. Parents did not have the money for a big wedding. So thousands of Californians bypassed blood tests, parental approval, and expensive family weddings and "eloped" to Nevada. Even today California families choose big Reno and Las Vegas hotels to celebrate a marriage and avoid that big social-status wedding at home.

NEVADA MILEPOSTS

MEDICAL EMERGENCIES: DIAL 911.
OTHER EMERGENCIES: DIAL OPERATOR AND ASK FOR ZENITH 1-2000.
ROAD CONDITIONS: 702-793-1313.
COMMISSION ON TOURISM, 1-800-NEVADA 8.
RENO-SPARKS VISITORS' AUTHORITY: 800-FOR-RENO.
ALL OF NEVADA HAS THE SAME AREA CODE: 702.

MILEPOSTS:

2 **WEST VERDI:** ELEVATION: 4893 FEET.
CAMPGROUND: "Gold Ranch Casino RV Park": Private. Exit to North. Pull-through spaces, Cable TV, propane, gas, restaurant, playground, volleyball, horseshoes, bar-b-ques. $16.
EASTBOUND: You have been following the canyon of the Truckee River down from the town of Truckee. Now I-80 crosses the river.
WESTBOUND: You are now ascending the Eastern scarp of the Sierras. I-80 follows the Truckee back up as did the Donner Trail. The canyon is so steep and narrow that the emigrants had to cross the river many times and sometimes just stay in the middle. Men and animal feet became cut and bruised and bleeding. In later years men avoided the river and cut a trail up from Verdi to Boca. It is possible to see wagon ruts near the old Verdi Crystal Peak Cemetery. You have to go into Verdi, turn left on Bridge Street and a Right just after the "Donner Trail Dinner House". The tracks are diagonally across the other side of the Cemetery.

3 **VERDI:**
The Transcontinental Railroad had just been completed in 1869 when temptation got the best of some heretofore respectable citizens. Five City Council Members of the town of Verdi led by the Sunday School Superintendent, A.J. Davis, heard that a large shipment of gold was coming through from California. So on November 4, 1870 they boarded the Eastbound Central Pacific Overland Express at Verdi and disconnected the engine and the express car containing the gold. The train continued .5 mile towards Reno and a barricade they had put on the tracks. They forced the messenger to "open up" the locked strong box and made off with $41,600 in gold coin. Their joy didn't last long. Within 2 years they were all behind bars and 90% of the gold was recovered. This is considered the first train robbery of the new Transcontinental Railroad. Jessie James committed another along the I-80 corridor in Adair, IA on July 21, 1873. Sam Bass committed the third train robbery along I-80 at Big Springs, NE in 1877.

4 **BOOMTOWN, GARSON ROAD:**
BOOMTOWN CASINO, HOTEL, RESTAURANT, GAS AND TRUCK STOP:

CAMPGROUND: "Boomtown RV Park": Private. Exit and follow the signs North past the casino and down the hill to the campground. The hill protects it from the noises of the highway and the casino. It has a pool, 2 spas, connections for Cable TV, and 200 RV spaces. No tents. Free shuttle to Casino. $13. Reservations: 1-800-648-3790.

WESTBOUND: This is your last big casino stop before entering California.

5 EAST VERDI:

Crossing the Truckee River again. It flows out of Lake Tahoe, down through the Reno-Sparks area, and then East 38 miles to turn North to Pyramid Lake.

MILEPOST 6 VIEWPOINT: Parking only. You might be able to see the yellow historical marker and emigrant wagon tracks down the hill from here.

7 MOGOL: NO NEAR SERVICES!

8 WEST 4TH STREET: NO NEAR SERVICES!

Just homes here now, but there used to be a great Mineral Spa next to the Truckee River. Many Californians liked to rest and refresh in the mineral baths.

10 MC CARRAN BOULEVARD WEST: NO NEAR SERVICES!

12 KEYSTONE AVENUE: ROAD CONDITIONS: RADIO 530 AM.

MALLS: Both North and South. North to Osco.
FUEL: North to Shell. South to Auto Parts.
FOOD: North to Raleys Food. South to Albertsons Food.
MOTELS: Travel Lodge. North to Motel 6, Gateway Inn.
CAMPGROUNDS: "Keystone RV Park": Private. South one block. West one block. Near Truckee River. Max length 35 feet.

"Chism Trailer Park": Private. South .5 mile to 2nd Street. West 4 blocks. Max length 35 feet. $12.

13 VIRGINIA STREET/SIERRA STREET, RENO/BUS US 395: ELEVATION: 4490 FEET. UNIVERSITY OF NEVADA.

FUEL: EASTBOUND: Chevron.

RENO
THE BIGGEST LITTLE CITY IN THE WORLD

If you have not visited Reno before, and especially if you have not experienced a gambling center, this is a MUST STOP! When you exit for downtown Reno either EASTBOUND or WESTBOUND go to the 2nd light to Virginia Street/Bus 395, a Southbound street. Turn South to downtown casinos, hotels, restaurants. Center Street is Northbound only! There is casino parking and many parking lots plus 3 RV lots just North of Harrah's. To get to the Center Street lot, go South on Virginia Street under the "Biggest Little" sign. Turn Left at the next corner for one block and Left again on Center. Keep in the Right lane as it's just past the railroad tracks. For trailer parking: Go down Virginia Street, Left/East 2 blocks to Lake Street and turn Left. It will be on your Right opposite the Center Street lot. As you turn South toward downtown, you'll see the large Casino-Hotels looming ahead: Hilton, Harrah's, Harold's Club, Circus-Circus and many more. They operate 24 hours a day with a variety of types of gambling, floor shows, cabaret entertainment and restaurants. Harrah's has a big dinner-show room with performances by nationally known entertainers at 6 p.m. and midnight. The food is most often good in the Casinos because they want to be sure you'll stay there and gamble. You'll also pass many small motels and coffee shops. Harold's Club on Virginia Street was one of the earliest casinos designed for recreational gambling and at one time they had over 2300 large billboards across 41 states with "Only ... miles to Harold's Club". They developed a Western theme and added an unusual antique gun collection on the second floor. Today the guns are in lighted cases with descriptive labels. They show the history and development of firearms from 1500 to the 20th Century. Open 24 hours a day. Free. They also have displays of pioneer trappings, music boxes, slot machines, and carriages.

Also on Virginia Street is the "Liberty Belle" casino with antique slot machines and player pianos. Circus-

Circus has circus acts intermittently all day and night and an Arcade for the children. The Arcade eats money almost faster than the slots. Most of the casinos have some kind of entertainment such as video games for the children who are barred from the casinos. If you have never been here, you'll want to at least look into a few casinos. Nowhere except Las Vegas has as much neon-flashing and bell-ringing as Reno. You have to experience it to believe it. If mother and the kids need some exercise there's a nice walk on a tree-shaded path along the Truckee river. (Before the price of gold went up, the divorcees used to toss their wedding rings into this river. The biggest problem is getting Grandma out of the Casino! Reno is the second largest city in Nevada. Virginia Street used to be the main highway through Reno where today as before you still ride under the big sign saying: "THE BIGGEST LITTLE CITY IN THE WORLD". Reno has a mild dry climate as the Sierras capture the rain and snow. It has some interesting annual events from Balloon and Air Races to a Rodeo and a Basque festival.

RENO'S HISTORIC ARCH
Photo credit: Lonnie Peck, Reno News Bureau

In 1844 the Stevens-Murphy-Townsend Party brought the first wagon on the California Trail. When they got to Idaho, they followed the trail of Mountain Man Joe Walker down to the Humboldt and on to the Humboldt Sink. Not sure of Walkers trail to the Carson River and over Carson Pass, they asked a Paiute named "Trokay" to show them the way. The latter led them to the Truckee River instead of the Carson, and on upstream to "Truckee Meadows" which today is Reno. Trokay was Chief of the Paiutes, the father of Chief Winnemucca. In 1846 the stressed Donner Party also came this way. Here they made their final mistake by resting the animals several days. If they had left right away, they would have made it over the pass before it started to snow.

In 1852 Jamison built a way-station here. Then in 1860 Myron C. Lake built an Inn and a bridge over the Truckee River. So this became known as "Lake's Crossing". During the years of the "Great Westward Migration" until 1867, the pioneers gratefully rested here from their long desert trek and readied their equipment for the haul over the Sierras. Opportunists often brought food and other supplies from California to sell at Truckee Meadows. But their prices were exorbitant and the destitute pioneers often had to do without! One hungry emigrant noted that a trader wanted a mule for just 10 pounds of flour.

Reno was named for a Union officer of the Civil War, General Jesse Lee Reno. As part of the "incentive" the Congress allocated for the building of the railroad, was a bonus of 20 square miles for every mile of railroad. In practice this amounted to alternate quarter-sections of land either side of the railroad. With all of this land to sell in 1868, a railroad agent gave explosive birth to the town of Reno by selling lots for homes and businesses. The town sprang up almost overnight. It grew as a rail center for the mining camps to the South at Virginia City and later Goldfield and Tonopah.

THE HARRAH FOUNDATION NATIONAL AUTOMOBILE MUSEUM: Mill and Lake Streets. A MUST STOP! South on Virginia Street, across the river, Left on Mill Street. Parking East of the building. You might find it easier to walk there from the casino area. Ask! There are 200 vintage and classic cars with other antiques and a automotive research library. This is a fabulous collection of reconditioned vehicles that you won't want to miss! Dad can take the kids to see it while Grandma and Mom gamble. William Fisk Harrah purchased and restored these cars for over 40 years. First you watch a film and then an "Acoustiguide Audio System" guides you through the exhibits with music, stories and sound effects. Adult $7.50. Senior $6.50. Child $2.50. There is food at the "Wheel's Roadhouse Cafe" by the river.

UNIVERSITY OF NEVADA: North of I-80 on Virginia Street.

FLEISCHMANN ATMOSPHERIUM-PLANETARIUM: 1650 North Virginia Street. In an upswept building behind the Lawlor Events Center at the North end of the campus. The planetarium has evening shows as well as astronomy and earth science exhibits. To see planets in action, you put a coin in a machine and watch it disappear into a "Black Hole". Telescope viewing also. Mon-Thurs 8-5pm and 7-9pm. Fri 8-10pm. Sat 10:30-

10pm. Sunday 10:30-5pm and 7-9pm. Museum and telescope viewing free. Shows: Adult $5. Senior and Child $3.50.

NEVADA STATE HISTORICAL SOCIETY MUSEUM: 1650 North Virginia Street. Across the parking lot from the Planetarium. This excellent museum depicts how the Indians lived before the Europeans came and then their transition with the new influence. Shows Pioneers from the first explorers through the silver miners to the Nevada Divorces and gambling. Also Washoe Indian Basketry that are works of art. Mon-Sat 10-5pm. Donation.

WILBOR D. MAY MUSEUM AND ARBORETUM: In San Rafael Park at 1502 Washington Street. Accessible from Sierra Street. From the planetarium above, go North and Left at the first intersection/Sierra Street. Then South a block or so to a Right into the Museum area. Follow signs. May was the founder of "May Company", the department store chain. The museum is a replica of May's "Double Diamond Ranch" and contains objects which he collected on his world-wide trips. Exhibits include souvenirs of African safaris, 18th Century sterling silver, and Tang Dynasty horse sculptures. The Arboretum includes twelve gardens representing plant habitats of the Eastern Sierras. Summers Tues-Sun 10-5pm. Rest of year Wed-Sun. Includes "Great Basin Adventure" for the under-12 year olds. Adult $2. Senior and Child $1. Picnicking permitted, parking ample.

MACKAY SCHOOL OF MINES: (Say it,"Mackie".) North of I-80. One block East of Virginia Street to Center Street and North into the campus. Parking is a problem so ask at the gate. They are presently renovating the museum which will have geological, metallurgical, and mineralogical collections and mining history exhibits. It should be ready by 1993 or 1994.

14   **WELLS AVENUE, RENO:**
>   **FOOD:** South to Dennys, Carrows.
>   **MOTELS:** North to Motel 6*. South to Days Inn, Holiday Inn.

15   **M A J O R   I N T E R C H A N G E !**
US 395 NORTH TO SUSANVILLE AND HONEY LAKE, CA: Beautiful country!
US 395 SOUTH TO CARSON CITY, NV:
>   **CAMPGROUNDS:** "Shamrock RV Park": Private. Three miles North on US 395 to Parr Boulevard. West one mile. Pool.
>   "Reno RV Park": Private. South on US 395 past Bally's to Mill Street. West one mile. $15.
>   "Bally's RV Park": South on US 395 to Glendale, behind the casino. $14.
>   **BALLY'S CASINO:** South on US 395 to Glendale. East .5 mile. Lots of parking here for large vehicles. You can just stay overnight here in the parking lot as you can with most casinos. However, they also have a nice campground on the East side of the lot. The casino has a spectacular floor show on one of the largest stages anywhere. A well-known celebrity usually headlines the show.

WESTBOUND ALTERNATE ROUTES
VARIOUS ROUTES OVER THE SIERRAS, VIA LAKE TAHOE, OR VIRGINIA CITY: Check your map! All of the passes through the Sierras are very beautiful!

CHOICE #1: I-80 is 4 to 6 lanes, has fast streams, granite hills and boulders, lakes, and Donner Lake State Park. If you have already been on this section of I-80, you might want to choose another route. You MUST see Lake Tahoe and there are several routes for this. Read CA Milepost 189 as it might be the Alternate Route of your choice to get from I-80 to Lake Tahoe, US 50, Sacramento and I-80 again.

CHOICE #2: South on US 395 to NV 431 and the steep, twisty "Mount Rose Highway" to the Northeast end of Lake Tahoe. It's quite a climb to 8900 feet! Not for trailers! Spectacular views of the lake and a lovely ride around it. Again read CA Milepost 189 for descriptions of sights.

CHOICE #3: South on US 395 past Carson City to US 50 and "Spooner Summit". Then either way around the lake. Casinos both North and South. The South Tahoe ones are bigger. US 50 becomes just 2-lanes around the lake and over Echo Summit before it spreads out into a freeway again and takes you to I-80 at Sacramento. US 50 at Echo Pass climbs up a sheer cliff. Views are great! It is too magnificent to destroy with a super highway. The West side of the pass has domes of solid granite. Read California Milepost 189 and Alternate Routes below. Read "Carson City" below and "Choices #2 and #3."

VIRGINIA CITY
Photo credit: Reno News Bureau

SIDETRIP TO VIRGINIA CITY

This is a fabulous trip if you have a day or even a few hours to spare. Journey back in time to the silver mining days of Virginia City. Go 23 miles South on US 395 and NV 341 to Virginia City. There's a lovely Viewpoint over Washoe Valley from the top of the hill on NV 341. Look across the valley to Mount Rose and Slide Mountain Ski Resorts. The rock walls here are of andesite, a volcanic material.

VIRGINIA CITY

Back in the 1870's Virginia City had a population of 30,000, 4 churches, 100 saloons, an Opera House that attracted national performers, and Julia Bulette of "Sporting Row". Millions in gold and silver lay inside Sun Mountain right under the town. Mark Twain said that the vein of ore was 50 to 80 feet thick and that there were 30 miles of streets and 5,000 men working under the town when he was there. (Read "Roughing It" by Mark Twain.) Julia Bulette got her share of the pot at the rate of $1,000 a night. But what made her famous was her raising money for the "Sanitary Commission" (like the Red Cross) during the Civil War, and turning her house into a hospital to nurse sick miners. When she was killed, her accused was one of the rare persons hanged for murder in Virginia City. His picture and a fragment of the rope reside in the State Capitol in Carson City. Murders were committed openly in front of crowds but the culprits were rarely prosecuted or even charged.

Virginia City is open for tourists all year, but a few of the tours are only available May to September. You will enter the city on the main street which is C Street. First see the continuous 20-minute video by the VISITOR BUREAU on C Street between Taylor and Union, and get your map. Open Summers 9-7pm. Winters 9-5pm. Donation. Then amble along the wooden sidewalks and through the restored saloons. Or begin down the hill at the Freight Depot with the train ride.

TRAIN RIDE TO GOLD HILL: On E Street, two blocks down the hill. Four-mile .5 hour narrated ride on the Virginia and Truckee Railroad. In 1870, 45 trains a day were hauling passengers, merchandise and ore to Carson City. Adult $4. Child $2. Or take a narrated Trolley Ride through the streets with descriptions of the buildings. Either of these rides will give you some background on Virginia City.

VIRGINIA AND TRUCKEE RAILROAD VISITOR CENTER: A railroad car on the East side of C Street. They have brochures and other information on the area.

FACE ON THE BARROOM FLOOR: Free.

BUCKET OF BLOOD SALOON: Free.

TERRITORIAL ENTERPRISE: Where both Mark Twain and Bret Harte got their starts. **MARK TWAIN MUSEUM OF MEMORIES:** In the same building. Rare nickelodeons, radios, telephones and ladies fashions from the 19th century. "Mark Twain" recites his works here. Donation.

CHOLLAR MINE: Tours on summer afternoons. Fee.

THE CASTLE: Up one block to the South end of B Street. See how the new silver millionaires lived with crystal chandeliers and Italian marble fireplaces. Fee.

MACKAY MANSION: On C Street. Tour of building includes an old Chinese laundry.

FIREMEN'S MUSEUM: Antique fire engines.

PIPER'S OPERA HOUSE: Where Lotta Crabtree performed.

VIRGINIA CITY
Photo credit: Gary Elam, Virginia City Chamber of Commerce

FOURTH WARD SCHOOL: South end of C Street. Tours.

CAMPGROUNDS: "The RV Park": In Virginia City, turn East/left at Carson Street (downhill) for three blocks.

FROM VIRGINIA CITY CONTINUE SOUTH DRIVING SLOWLY THROUGH HISTORIC "GOLD HILL" AND "SILVER CITY". "Comstock RV Park": South of Silver City, where NV 341 joins US 50. When you reach US 50, turn Right/West 14 miles to Carson City.

CARSON CITY

Carson City, at 4697 feet elevation, is 30 miles South of Reno on US 395. John C. Fremont named the Carson River and Pass for his scout, Kit Carson, who had accompanied him on his 1843-44 trip when they had used this pass to get to Sutter's Fort in California. Eagle Valley here got its name when, in 1851, a trader fastened an eagle stuffed with straw over the door of his post. There was little here until the silver boom exploded the little village into a trade center between the mines and California supplies. Nevada's silver-domed capitol still holds all the state offices, but they have new legislative, court and archive buildings. From US 50 turn South/Left onto US 395/Carson Street into downtown.

NEVADA STATE MUSEUM: On your Right as you go South. A MUST STOP! It's in the old U.S. Mint Building where machinery stamped out $50 million in silver and gold

NEVADA STATE MUSEUM, CARSON CITY
Photo credit: Carson City Convention and Visitor's Bureau

coins. The "Carson City Silver Dollars" are famous. This is an excellent modern museum! There are great silver, mineral, and gun exhibits, a ghost town, and archeological, anthropological, and Natural History sections. There is the beautiful Washoe Indian basketry of DatSoLaLee and a walk through a Devonian Seascape, (When Nevada was under the sea.) You end your tour by walking through a replica of an old gold mine in the basement. Allow at least 2 hours for the museum. Daily 8:30-4:30pm. Adult $2. Child free.

Notice the blue lines on the sidewalks. These guide you on a walking tour of Carson City's old buildings. Within a few blocks of the Museum are Orrum Clemens home (Mark Twain's brother) and the Governor's Mansion. Ask in the Museum gift shop. Also ask for a "Kit Carson Trail Map" and have it stamped. When stamped at 3 attractions, the Visitor Bureau, South of town will give you a Sheriff's badge and casino coupons.

NUGGET CASINO: Across the street from the Mint/Museum. Just inside the entrance is a Rare Gold Exhibit. On display is gold in its natural state from the fine crumbs of "Placer gold", tumbled smooth nuggets from the streams, and gold embedded in quartz, to delicate leaf, ribbon, wire and thread gold.

NEVADA STATE CAPITOL: Just four blocks South of the museum on your left. The capitol was built in 1870-71 with stone from the Nevada Prison Quarry. The hallways are of lovely grey Alaskan marble arranged in a striking pattern. Take the elevator to the second floor to the "History of the Nevada Capitol", the old governor's office, and across from the elevator, the old Supreme Court. All very interesting. Daily 8-5pm.

HUMANE ALLIANCE FOUNTAIN: A block South and across the street from the Capitol. Donated in 1909 by the Humane Alliance to provide water for horses and pets.

NATIONAL FORESTRY SERVICE: Continue South to signs. It's on your right. Stop here for information on campgrounds and trails throughout the Sierras.

CARSON CITY VISITOR BUREAU: At the old train station. Turn Right at the light at Fairview Dr. Get maps and information there.

NEVADA STATE RAILROAD MUSEUM: Just the next building South of the Visitor Bureau. See 26 pieces of rolling stock of the "Virginia and Truckee Railroad". They carried gold and silver and many famous dignitaries from Virginia City. These trains were later used in Hollywood movies. Summers daily 8:30-4:30pm. Winters Wed-Sun. Adult $1. Child free.

STEWART INDIAN MUSEUM: South past the next light and left onto Snyder Avenue for one mile to the sign. (Snyder is just .5 mile North of the intersection where US 50 climbs up the Sierras.) Photos of

Native Americans, basketry, paintings, and crafts. Gift shop of authentic Native crafts. This was a school for Native children from 1890 to 1980. Western and Southwestern children were brought here to educate them, but more deliberately to separate them from their culture. They were not allowed to go home for the whole year. They were trained as house maids and farm laborers. They had just 1/2 day of classes and then worked on the buildings and in the fields. In the 1960's the school was devoid of any Indian decor. Even in arts and crafts classes their innate culture, designs and skills were discouraged. Daily 9-4pm. Donation.

CAMPGROUNDS: "Camp 'n Town": Private. North of Carson City, .5 mile North of junction of US 50 and US 395. Pool.

"Oasis Trailer Haven": Private. Two miles South of Carson City on US 395.

"Comstock Country RV Resort": Private. South of town. Junction of US 395 & US 50. Pool and spa.

For PUBLIC campgrounds North of Carson City, read "Alternate Return Routes" below.

ALTERNATE RETURN ROUTES

CHOICE #1: From Carson City you can go back up US 395 past BOWER'S MANSION COUNTY PARK to Reno and I-80.

BOWER'S MANSION COUNTY PARK: Ten miles North of Carson City, West of Washoe Lake on Old US 395/NV 429. (20 miles South of Reno). The mansion was built in 1864 by Sam Bower, Nevada's first mining millionaire, at a cost of $200,000. By 1868 he was dead followed by his only daughter. His wife, Eilley, was left in poverty. In the summer there are 30-minute tours through the building, 11-4:30pm, and a great story! Open weekends in the Winter. Adult $3. Child and Senior $2. You can also relax at the picnic ground, playground, and swimming pool.

CAMPGROUNDS: "Washoe Lake State Park": From US 395 South of Washoe Lake go 3 miles East on NV 428. Max length 30 feet.

"Davis Creek County Park": 2 miles North of Bower's Mansion on Old US 395. Max length 25 feet.

WARNING! BE SURE TO OBSERVE THE VEHICLE SIZE LIMITATIONS THROUGHOUT THE SIERRAS OR YOU MAY FIND YOURSELF BETWEEN ROCKS AND TREES, UNABLE TO MANEUVER!

CHOICE #2: On over the Sierras just 14 miles on US 50 to beautiful Lake Tahoe. Again another decision to be made. North around the lake on NV 28 with beautiful views at every turn of the road to swim at "SAND HARBOR BEACH" or "INCLINE BEACH" or visit TV's "PONDEROSA RANCH". Then to North Shore and Crystal Bay Casinos and North on CA 267 to Truckee and I-80. OR go to Tahoe City and take CA 89 to "SQUAW VALLEY" ski resort and home of the 1960 Winter Olympics. Then North to I-80 at Truckee.

CHOICE #3: Or Southward at the lake to "CAVE ROCK VIEW POINT", "Zephyr Cove Forestry Campground" (Max length 32 feet) and a ride on the stern-wheeler "M.S. DIXIE" or a timaran "WOODWIND". Then there's "Round Hill Pines Beach", "Nevada Beach and Campground", past the "Edgewood Golf Course" (the former site of "Friday Station Pony Express Station"), and the famous big casinos at "STATELINE". Ride the glass-bottomed "TAHOE QUEEN". Take the "HEAVENLY VALLEY TRAM" up the mountain for a gorgeous view of Lake Tahoe, swim at "South Lake Tahoe" beaches, or stay in one of the Forestry Campgrounds along the Southshore or at Meyers. On the Southwest end of the lake at TIMBER COVE, rent anything from jet skis to mountain bikes. Finally over Echo Summit on US 50 114 miles to Sacramento and I-80 again. (The pass itself is still in its natural beauty, just 2 lanes up a sheer cliff.) All of these routes are very beautiful! You could take one route traveling West and another going East.

CHOICE #4: Take US 50 to US 89 and North up the West side of Lake Tahoe past Emerald Bay to Squaw Valley and I-80 at Truckee. Read choice #3 at California Milepost 189.

16 RENO, EAST 4TH STREET/B STREET:

EASTBOUND: Exit North to a Right on B Street and you are on the main street through Sparks. Many motels, restaurants, casinos here including the Nugget.

FUEL: South to Chevron.

MOTELS: North to Motel 6*.

17 SPARKS: SOUTH ROCK ROAD/ROCK BOULEVARD/NUGGET AVENUE:

You've crossed into Sparks, NV now with no discernible difference. Exit North and turn Right/ East to Nugget, Mint, Silver Club, Treasury Club, Gambling Hall, etc. Many motels and restaurants also. Parking provided for RVs behind and East of the Nugget.

FUEL: North to Exxon, Arco. **Grand Auto + Garage:** 2 blocks North.

MOTELS: Emerald, Blue Fountain Inn, and many more.

CAMPGROUND: "River's Edge RV Park": Private. South on Rock Road for one mile. Pool and fishing. $14-$15.

18 SPARKS, PYRAMID WAY/NV 445:

WESTBOUND: Exit to the North to Left on B Street. This is the main street of Sparks and "Victorian Square". Here you'll find restaurants, casinos, including the Nugget, hotels and "HERITAGE MUSEUM" (free). Sparks grew from railroad buildings that were transported here from Wadsworth in 1904 by the Southern Pacific Railroad. There is a railroad exhibit on B Street just East of the Nugget. Chamber of Commerce Tourist information at the train station. RV PARKING SOUTH OF THE RAILROAD TRACKS JUST EAST OF THE NUGGET.

EASTBOUND SIDETRIP

PYRAMID LAKE
Photo credit: Nevada Commission on tourism

TO PYRAMID LAKE: 36 miles to the North on NV 445. Several miles up is the "Wild Horse and Burro Placement Center". These animals await adoption. Pyramid is Nevada's largest natural lake and one of the last remnants of ancient Lake Lahontan that once covered Nevada's basins. The Truckee River ends its life in this lake surrounded by red and brown sandstone mountains and joined by 8,000 white pelicans that nest on the islands. There are "tufa" (tower-like formations) which are calcium carbonate deposits left when ancient Lake Lahonton was drying up. Don't expect greenery and trees as it's quite barren here, but this lake has its own palate of colors. The shape of "ANAHOE ISLAND" inspired John C. Fremont, the first white man to view it, to name the lake in 1844. Fishermen like to challenge the trout here that can be as large as 40 pounds. They have a peculiar fish here called the Cuiui (quee-wee) that does not exist anywhere else. It has an extra fin and swims up the Truckee in April to spawn.

The lake is a Paiute Indian Reservation so you'll have to get permission to fish from the Tribal Council on the Westside of the lake at Sutcliffe. They boat, water ski and swim here but it is not developed well so expect primitive conditions. The Paiutes fought dearly for this lake when they were being forced off their lands. Their game was disappearing and the rabble that came with the silver rush attacked their women. When the Paiutes retaliated by killing four white men, an impromptu army was formed, and entered a narrow canyon along the Truckee where the Paiutes killed seventy. Then the U.S. Army came augmented by settlers, overwhelming the Paiutes and forcing Chief Winnemucca's surrender. From the lake, take NV 446 and NV 447 to Wadsworth and I-80 at Milepost 43.

19 SPARKS, EAST McCARRAN BOULEVARD:

MALLS: North a few blocks to Safeway Food and Osco Drug. One block more to a Left on East Prater Way to McCarran Plaza on the right with Albertsons, Longs Drugs and Pep Boys (auto parts and garage). Another Mall is across the street to the South with Kragen, Midas and Sizzler.
FUEL: North to Exxon on West corner, '76 Truck Plaza on East corner.
FOOD: Lyons, Sid's, Burger King.
MOTELS: North to Best Inn, Nendels. South to McCarran House. There are others along B Street, which is the main street North of I-80.

20 SPARKS BOULEVARD: NO NEAR SERVICES!

FACTORY OUTLETS: North on Sparks Blvd 1/4 mile. Outlets on the Left.
WILD ISLAND: North on Sparks Blvd. Follow signs. There are 8 water rides, wave pool, picnic area, rafting, Adventure golf, fast food.

21 **GREG STREET/VISTA:** NO NEAR SERVICES!
Nice view of Reno/Sparks and the Sierras. Those tall buildings are all hotels and casinos.

22 **LOCKWOOD:** NO NEAR SERVICES!.
We are following the Truckee again to her last hurrah. How grateful the pioneers were to be traveling along this cool river after their ordeal in the "40-mile desert" just East of here. What used to be lovely pastoral farms along the Truckee have been turned into sub-divisions. For flood control, in 1959 the Truckee River was dredged deeper by the US Army Engineers.

23 **MUSTANG RANCH:**
No, no horses here and only one service. You'll not be impressed by the series of mobile homes, but note, they all have air-conditioners. This is THE famous "House of Ill Repute". Nevada does not allow street prostitution, but instead has licensed facilities usually some distance outside each major town. Hang on to your husbands, girls! Note the old landslide of rocks and the terraces from old Lake Lahontan.

28 **PATRICK:** NO NEAR SERVICES!

32 **TRACY CLARK STATION:** NO NEAR SERVICES!
TRACY POWER PLANT: Opening in 1963, this plant uses natural gas to produce electricity for Reno. The gas comes in a pipeline from New Mexico via Salt Lake city.
MILEPOST 33 EAGLE-PICHER DIATOMITE PLANT: Here they process the diatomatious earth from the mine at Milepost 38. It is used for insulation and for filtering impurities from liquids, e.g. swimming pools.
MILEPOST 35: Note the red and black cinder outcropping on the hills all along this canyon. The remnants of ancient volcanos.

36 **THISBE-DERBY DAM:** NO NEAR SERVICES!
This dam takes water from the Truckee and sends it South to the Lahontan Reservoir and Lahontan Valley on the Carson River. Note the red rock hills on the North side of the highway and the small lake next to the road formed when US 40 was built. You are traveling through the Virginia Range that was uplifted after the Truckee was formed. The latter just continued eroding on through. Here the Pliocene volcanic flows are lighter in color.

38 **ORCHARD:** NO NEAR SERVICES!.
STONE PILLARS: Pull off here to see the two unusual stone pillars of many colors. It's all volcanic except for the quartz and iron pyrite (Fool's Gold). Some of the rock has been altered by hot solutions as at Painted Rock.
CALATOM DIATOMITE MINE: Note the mining on the hills to the South. This mineral is formed by ancient lake deposits. It is fossilized diatoms which were ancient microscopic organisms.

40 **PAINTED ROCK:** NO NEAR SERVICES!
These volcanic rocks are altered by hot water forces deep in the earth. Iron oxide in this process colors the rocks red. Colors of rocks are enhanced by the sun in the AM. If you see level white layers back North of the road, these were deposited by ancient Lake Lahontan.
NEVADA CEMENT COMPANY PLANT: Opening in 1964 this plant produces 3,000 barrels of cement a day. The limestone and the clay are quarried nearby but the gypsum is brought from 72 miles to the North.
MILEPOST 42 WESTBOUND REST AREA: Fall colors brighten this spot.

43 **WADSWORTH/PYRAMID LAKE/NV 447:**
CAMPGROUND: "I-80 Smokeshop/RV Park": Paiute Indian Reservation facility just to the North. NEAR I-80.
The Truckee River crosses from South of I-80 and flows North 16 miles into Pyramid Lake.

This is an endangered nesting ground for the White Pelican. It is a barren lake with no trees except right where the Truckee flows into the lake. Along the Truckee River here, pioneers who had crossed "The 40-Mile Desert" reached their first drinkable water since the Humboldt River. Can you visualize their relief? Falling into the river face first! Splashing the water all over themselves! Washing themselves and their clothes! Many walked-in, their wagons left behind in the desert, their stock dead. One traveler called this "The River of Life". The Donner Party not only found water here but FOOD! C.T. Stanton met them here with seven mules packed with flour and dried beef provided by Captain John Sutter.

46 **FERNLEY, WEST MAIN STREET/US 50/US 95:** NO NEAR SERVICES!
1.5 miles to the following services on Bus 80 in Fernley.
FUEL: Chevron, Jackpot.
MOTELS: Ranchotel, Lahontan Motel.
CAMPGROUND: "Kornegay's RV Park": Private. No further information.

WESTBOUND ALTERNATE ROUTE

TO PYRAMID LAKE: You can travel North here on NV 447 to Pyramid Lake and then NV 446 and NV 445 back to Sparks and I-80 again. It's about 32 or more miles out of your way. If you're a bird-watcher and would like to see the White Pelicans this will be especially interesting to you. Read Milepost 18.

48 **EAST MAIN STREET, EAST FERNLEY/ALT US 50:** WEATHER RADIO: 980 AM
SOUTH ON US 50 TO FALLON.
FUEL: North to Truck Inn Chevron, Exxon Truck Stop.
FOOD: South to Warehouse Market and Laundramat.
MOTEL: South to Super 8.
One mile to Bus 80 services in Fernley listed in Milepost 46.
CAMPGROUND: "Truck Inn": Private. Chevron Truck Stop. NEAR I-80.

40-MILE DESERT

Eastbound you are starting out across the infamous "40-Mile Desert". This actually is the lakebed of an ancient sea of the Pleistocene Epoch called **LAKE LAHONTAN**. It covered most of Northwestern Nevada when the Sierras were covered with glaciers that streamed down the valleys. The lake was up to 500 feet deep and covered 8400 miles. Pyramid, Walker, Winnemucca and Honey lakes are its last remnants. Watch for horizontal terraces on the hills carved by high waves.

The ancient lake-bed sand is thick, the dust, fine. It was so drying to the face and lips of immigrants that they used camphorice and glycerine to sooth the skin. But by the time the pioneers got here their lips were blistered and their feet bruised and bleeding from the hot sand. Their shoes were long gone. Most of them made it, but they lost many of their animals and their wagons and goods littering the desert with their throw-aways. One blacksmith went back out onto the desert some time later to retrieve his tools. He found someone else's before he found his and settled for them. Actually if they were using the Donner Trail, the distance is closer to 62 miles that the pioneers had to traverse between the Humboldt River and the Truckee. Not a tree anywhere! Only the shade of the wagon if the animals were still capable of pulling it. One emigrant said that dead animals lined the way and their stench was horrific! Someone counted 900 graves in the 40 miles but that contradicts other testimony that most of the pioneers made it.

Have you seen any dust-devils yet? Or maybe you call them whirlwinds? How many do you see at any one time? The dust is so fine and the winds so constant that the two elements seem to be playing a constant tag game across Nevada. Do you see any ancient terraces?

When the Donner party struggled by here, they were already in dire straights. The Eddys had lost all their cattle to the Paiutes. They left their goods and walked across this desert carrying their children. (It was James Reed and William Eddy who had rescued the party when they were dying of thirst on the Salt Flats.) When they requested water for their children from the Breens, they were refused. Eddy took it at gunpoint. One old Belgium man named "Hardcoop" had walked until his legs could carry him no longer. He sat down to die in the desert. No one could help him.

MILEPOSTS 53-58: Note the salt marshes North and South of the highway. You'll often see long-legged avocets and other water-birds feeding on the brine- sustained life in the pools. What is the source of this water?

No rivers! Nevada, a basin/range state, has no outlet to the sea for the rivers and rains. So the water just flows to the lowest point and sinks into the ground. But it does come bubbling up again in various mineral springs and this was one of the Pioneer springs. The water of some hot springs was drinkable after it had cooled. Note the mounds in the sand due to the Arrowplants that gather the blowing sand under them and just keep growing higher over it. The Mopung Hills are beyond.

65 **NIGHTINGALE HOT SPRINGS:** NO NEAR SERVICES! WEATHER RADIO: AM 980.

To the South note the many wisps of steam rising from the ground. There is a hot spring just above where that plant is today, where the water gushed out too hot to use. The emigrants built channels to spread out the hot water to cool it. These are still visible today from behind the plant. The taste of the water was still not that acceptable so they tried all kinds of things to make it palatable. Mark Twain tried adding pickles and molasses. Look to the South and you may be able to see the yellow California Trail sign. Fifty years ago the springs were channeled for hot mineral baths. Thirty years ago the area was deserted and if you walked out cross the flats the ground sounded like a great hive of bees! You could feel vibrations from the ground through your shoes as if it were ready to erupt. Now this energy has been harnessed to dehydrate onions! This is the "Geothermal Food Processors" plant.

MILEPOST 69 Kitty Litter Plant: Note the piles of material between the East and West bound lanes. Diatomatious earth from old Lake Lahontan is processed into Kitty Litter.

MILEPOST 75: Tufa pillars to the Southeast formed by the ancient lake.

78 **JESSUP:** To the North. NO NEAR SERVICES!

83 **US 95: SOUTH TO FALLON:**

FUEL AND TIRE REPAIR SERVICE to the North.

REST AREA: There is no water here but there are "Composting toilets". To the Southeast note the red cinder cone. In the fall the grey sage may be in bloom along the road with greyish tufts, hardly noticeable. The green "rabbit brush" is more flamboyant with its bright yellow blossoms.

MILEPOST 88: Look South out across Alkali flat. Beyond is a gravel bar from ancient Lake Lahontan separating the Humboldt Sink from the Southern Carson Sink. The Carson River flows out of the Sierras past Carson City and Fallon, and sinks into the ground in a vast basin five miles to the South of I-80 and the Humboldt Sink. The trails of the early trapper/mountain men went from the Humboldt River and Sink to the Carson Sink and River and then followed it up over Carson Pass. Or they could transfer to the Walker River and go over Sonora Pass. The first wagons through here were the Stevens-Murphy-Townsend train in 1844. Chief Trokay guided them to the Truckee River so they were the first up that route. The Donner party also used the Truckee Route in 1846. After that tragedy most of the wagon trains were afraid of the Truckee and Donner Pass and used this route over the gravel bar to the Carson River.

MILEPOST 90: The Humboldt Sink to the South is where Nevada's longest river ends. The Humboldt is also the only river in the U.S. that begins and ends in the same state. I-80 follows the Humboldt, as did the California Trail, for 300 miles. Look past the sink to the West Humboldt Range. On the lower slopes can you see the terraces of Lake Lahontan? Feel like getting out and walking? This trek across the desert from Lovelock to the Carson River took the pioneers 6 to 8 days.

93 **TOULON:** NO NEAR SERVICES! TOULON MILL processed tungsten here until 1957.

SIDETRIP!

TO GIANT TUFA: FOR THE ADVENTURESOME! About six miles on a dirt road. Check locally before taking a large vehicle in. Go North and West on the dirt road. Make a Right at the first big gravel road and go about 3.5 miles. Go past two gravel pits about .25 mile and turn Left for 1.5 to 2 miles and you are heading for the hill where the tufa begin. They are on your left as you drive along the road. These are calcium carbonate deposits left by ancient Lake Lahontan as it was drying up. There are dozens of these "Calcareous tufa" formations over a hundred acres. They are 10 to 20 feet tall with colorful lichens on them. Hawks light on top to search for prey.

MILEPOST 98 GRANITE POINT: Opposite the Lovelock airport. So named because Northwest of I-80 Cretaceous granite has intruded through Jurassic limestone.

105 **WEST LOVELOCK:** ELEVATION: 3,975 FEET. WEATHER RADIO: 880 AM.
EASTBOUND BUS I-80 INTO LOVELOCK/OLD US 40:
   TIRES: Cooper.
   FUEL: Jack Pot, Shell, '76, Sinclair, 2 Stiffs.
   FOOD: Andy's Cafe. Safeway food to North.
   MOTELS: Brookwood, Lovelock Inn, Cadillac Inn, Sierra, Lafons.
   CAMPGROUND: Brookwood Motel & Mobile Park. West end of Bus 80.
   The Humboldt Range to the Southeast is 8900 feet. The Trinity and Seven Troughs Ranges to the Northwest are 7000 feet. The latter are known for their agate, jasper, opal and petrified wood. Lone Mountain, Northwest of Lovelock, is intruded granite with rhyolite over it.

L O V E L O C K

Lovelock was originally called "Big Meadows" with the water of the Humboldt disappearing about 2 miles Southeast of the present town. It was one of the last important stops on the California Trail. Here the pioneers rested from their long hot journey along the Humboldt. They replenished their supplies of water and cut the native blue hay for the stock before crossing the "40-Mile Desert". By the time the Donner Party reached here they had only 15 wagons left. An 1849 pioneer described this area as a 3-mile marsh with 250 wagons there at one time, some arriving, some leaving to cross the "40-mile". No wonder it seemed so far to the Donners! It was more like 62 miles to the Truckee River.

Some of the pioneers through here returned in the 1860's to settle along the Humboldt. At first they grew the native hay to sell to immigrants. They built irrigation ditches to get more water and increase production. Today the field crops are alfalfa, wheat, barley and oats along with "Hearts of Gold" cantaloupe. They specialize in alfalfa seed culture, crossing strains. Lovelock has had its water problems with springs that dried up. They tried to dig wells but the water was so hard! They said if you threw it you'd kill someone. So they hauled water in from Sparks in Tank Cars. Now they have five wells drilled in the mountains and piped into town.

A real adventurer, George Lovelock, came from Wales via Australia and Hawaii. He had already tried several businesses when in 1866 he bought 320 acres at Big Meadows. He paid $2250 and bought the first water rights on the Humboldt River. In 1867 he donated 85 acres for a townsite, depot and right-of-way for the train for which he was promised a block in town and a lifetime pass on the railroad. As usual the railroad defrauded him and he had to pay $500 for a half-block of his own land. He got one free ride!

   MARZEN HOUSE MUSEUM: Turn North/Left at the first light just East of the underpass on West Bus 80. It's in a big white frame house to the Northwest. This Pershing County Museum displays minerals, an assay office, pioneer history, and Indian artifacts. It was the home of a German immigrant, Joseph Marzen who started farming here in 1876 on 3,480 acre "Big Meadow Ranch". He grew grain and hay, started a creamery, and raised prize Shorthorn and Hereford cattle, Percheron, Clydesdale, and English Shire horses. Tues-Sun 1:30-4pm. Donation.

   EAGLE-PICHER DIATOMITE MINE: To the West. The diatomite is processed in Coal Canyon, Milepost 112.

106 **MAIN STREET, LOVELOCK:** EXIT TO DOWNTOWN LOVELOCK. HOSPITAL.
   FUEL: Chevron.
   FOOD: Davins, Sturgeon's Restaurant.
   MOTELS: Best Western, Covered Wagon, Desert Haven, Windmill, Brenda's.
   ROUND PERSHING COUNTY COURTHOUSE": Straight up Main Street until you run into it. Built in 1921 residents wanted something completely new. They got a classical look with six ionic columns in the front. There are only two such courthouses in the nation. The **POST OFFICE** is across the street from the courthouse.

S I D E T R I P !
TO LEANORD'S ROCK SHELTER AND LOVELOCK INDIAN CAVE: 20 miles. Archeological sites FOR THE ADVENTURESOME! Enquire locally before you go. Exit onto Main and go to the North of I-80. Then a quick left near I-80 onto Amherst which becomes South Meridian. In 17 miles South you are on the Old

California Trail. Leanord Rock Shelter is a vertical rock dyke protruding from the Humboldt Range. There are petroglyphs by ancient peoples on the North face of the dike. A human infant and a basket here were carbon dated as 4,000 B.C. Other artifacts from 2,000 B.C.

About 3 miles further to the Indian Cave. This 160' X 40'cave was created by the waters of ancient Lake Lahontan. It was a shelter in 2,000 B.C. Artifacts have been found here for three different groups of primitive peoples. The cave was discovered in 1886, and mined for its bat guano deposits in 1911. University of California, Berkeley obtained hundreds of artifacts from this cave which now reside in museums nationwide including University of Nevada, Carson City and Winnemucca. The extreme dryness of the cave preserved the artifacts well. Red-haired 6.5 to 7 foot mummies were found here. The Paiutes were not surprised because they have passed down stories of cannibalistic red-headed giants living in caves in the area. Sarah Winnemucca Hopkins described the cave and ancient tribes in her book published in 1883, before the mummies were found! She said that tribe would eat their own dead and dig up Paiute dead after they were buried. She told of how the Paiutes fought these "red heads" for three years and forced their retreat into their cave. Then the Paiutes built a large fire at the mouth of the cave and all the giants were killed. Whether they were cannibals or not has not been established in archeological fact. Scientists believe that the red hair could be due to chemical action. To deepen the mystery a calendar stone was found with 52 dots on the inside and 365 dots on the outside.

107   EAST LOVELOCK/WESTBOUND EXIT FOR BUS 80:
Read MILEPOST 105-6 for services.
CAMPGROUND: "KOA": On East side of Bus 80. $18-$25.
Crossing the Humboldt as it heads for its death in the Humboldt Sink to the Southwest.

112   COAL CANYON: NO NEAR SERVICES!
EAGLE PICHER MINERALS, COLATO PLANT: To the North. With a multi-million dollar diatomaceous earth processing plant. The source of the earth is 15 miles West of Lovelock. U.S.Gypsum Company has two "perlite" mines near here.

119   OREANA-ROCHESTER: NO NEAR SERVICES!
OREANA: This is a Railroad siding where few people live today. But in 1863 there was a silver-mining camp up scenic Buena Vista Canyon/NV 50. Read Milepost 149. ROCHESTER: A ghost town left by an old silver mine.

COEUR-ROCHESTER GOLD MINE: Ore was deposited in rocks that were folded and faulted. During the Cretaceous Era, 90 million years ago, the molten rock boiled up out through these cracks dissolving some minerals in the rocks as it passed and forming the coveted ores. When the early miners came prospecting, they found gold and silver and built mills North at Mill City, Milepost 149, to get the minerals out of the rocks. The Nenzel Mine, about 14 miles South of here, closed in 1929 as it was no longer profitable considering the price of gold, $35 an ounce, and the low grade of the ore.

Ralph Roberts, a geologist, noted a major fault across Northcentral Nevada where the rocks from the West had moved Eastward up over the Eastern rocks. Exploring this concept, the Carlin Mine was found that produced 3.2 million ounces of gold. Today ore is again being mined at Nenzel Mountain with larger machinery, modern technology, the higher price of gold and the new leaching process which recovers minute flecks from low grade ore. A rancher called it "No see-Um Gold". With 190-ton trucks and an electric shovel that holds 40 cubic yards, they move 60,000 to 70,000 tons of rock a day to produce 5 to 6 million ounces of silver and 60,000 ounces of gold a year. First the ore is crushed to 3/8 inch or less. The ore is hard and doesn't compact so it is layered onto 80 mil high-density polyethylene, a thick sheet of plastic. A weak cyanide solution, 0.1%, is applied through drip lines. The gold leaches out and is collected with a carbon process. The chemicals circulate around and are recycled. The resulting gold is in a round shape like a bowl.

129   RYE PATCH DAM:
FUEL: South to Burns Bros Truck Stop.
CAMPGROUND: RYE PATCH STATE PARK: Public. North .5 mile. Cross the dam and take a Left to the campground below the dam. Small. Flush toilets and showers. $5. If this campground is full drive back up to the dam and turn Left to go to a parking area on the upper North side. No trees and primitive there, but good for self-contained vehicles. Hunting, fishing, boating, swimming and picnicking. You'll notice that even though the daytime temperature may rise to

90-100 degrees, it may drop to 50 to 60 degrees at night.

RYE PATCH DAM: Use your imagination to envision Lake Lahonton receding. The Humboldt River brought down sediments from all the lands through which it passed including the Humboldt and Ruby Ranges. This became a giant delta as far upstream as Winnemucca. Bones 23,000 years old have been found here of bison, camels and elephants. Now the river has cut a 100-foot channel through these sediments. Thus the river is hidden from view below the level of the land and you only see the water when it is high in the channel behind the dam. One-half mile West of this exit is RYE PATCH DAM, completed in 1936 providing water for the farms around Lovelock that only get six inches of rain a year. In the reservoir and river they fish for walleye, large mouth bass, white bass, crappie, perch, sunfish and catfish. A record walleye and a 31-pound channel catfish were caught here. Star Peak, 9835 feet, is just East of I-80 which is running North-South at this point.

MILEPOSTS 137: PEGASUS GOLD MINE, FLORIDA CANYON PROJECT:

Note the big mountain of red earth on the Southeast side of I-80. Now check out the shiny border at the base of the red pile. This is the plastic base for a "heap-leaching" process to extract fine gold and silver from rock. This process is 10% of the cost of a mill. The Pegasus operation is one of the lowest-grade operations in the country, processing ore that is 0.010 to 0.018 ounces per ton. (Compare this with the Comstock Lode's $3,000 a ton in silver and $1500 a ton in gold.) They began mining in 1986, subcontracting the mining end to Degerstrom who moves 15.4 million tons of rock a year. The rock is crushed and then placed on a conveyer where lime, cement and cyanide are added. It is taken to the "stacker" which loads the ore evenly over the pile. Drip emitters drop more cyanide over the ore. The leach solution goes into a pond and then a recovery plant. (The ponds are netted over with wire to protect wildlife.) Gold and a small amount of silver are recovered. This process gives them a 55% to 70% recovery of the metals present. (Milling would obtain more but would not be cost-effective.) This process uses 200 employees and costs $282 to recover an ounce of gold, but with gold at $349 an ounce they can still make a profit.

138 HUMBOLDT: NO NEAR SERVICES! ELEVATION: 4500 FEET.

Train travelers in 1877 described Humboldt as a green oasis with willows, poplars and antelope. Sulphur, gold and silver mining was in progress.

145 IMLAY: NO NEAR SERVICES! RADIO WEATHER INFORMATION: 1400 AM. 92.7 FM.

THE APPLEGATE TRAIL

Nor were there any services here 146 years ago when the California Trail was full of pioneers. This was the "Turnoff of Death" from 1846 to the 1860's. It began with Jesse Applegate, a surveyor, who was in the "Big Migration" to Oregon with the missionary doctor, Marcus Whitman, in 1843. Jesse lost his son and other party members going down the Columbia gorge of the Oregon Trail in 1843. The British had become difficult after they saw all the new American settlers arriving. Jesse thought to avoid the dangerous Columbia route AND the British by building a new road to Oregon by connecting with the California Trail on the Humboldt. So he went South from Oregon across the Northeastern tip of California and the Blackrock Desert of Nevada to Imlay. It was a very difficult and dangerous trip. Yet all his effort was really for naught because by the time he had finished the trail, it was not needed. As of 1847 the U.S. and Great Britain had settled their border dispute at the 49th Parallel, where it is today. Also Samuel Barlow had found a route over Mount Hood avoiding that dangerous stretch of the Columbia gorge.

The Applegate Road left the Humboldt at Imlay and headed Northwest across the flat level plain of the notorious **BLACKROCK DESERT**. This too was part of the Lahontan Lake bed. It was, and is today, 100 miles of searing desert, with NO forage for the stock. The fine white silt rose in clouds as the wagons rode over it and the pioneers could hardly see where they were walking. They would see mirages of lakes and trees but come upon only hot, and sometimes boiling springs, 140 to 200 degrees. They could cook their meat and heat their coffee in the springs. Double Hot Springs had steep banks down which the stock would slide to their deaths. Carcasses of dead animals lined the trail. One historian counted 511 dead oxen in 50 miles. If the emigrants made it past this they still had High Rock Canyon, vicious Paiute attacks, Fandango Pass through the Cascades and a couple hundred miles to the Willamette Valley in Oregon. Wagons used this trail in 1847 and 1848.

At this point, **PETER LASSEN** comes into the story. He had a Mexican Land Grant near Corning, Northern

California and he wanted to lure settlers there. He half-forged a trail from the Applegate Road in Northern California past Lake Almanor and onto his Sacramento Valley land. He got lost himself for 2 months in the process and had to be rescued. Lassen sent a glowing report of his new trail to Eastern newspapers claiming that coupled with the Applegate it would outflank the Sierras and save 200 miles to the goldfields. Easterners had a great fear of the Sierras, so this new trail sounded great! Actually it ADDED 200 - 300 miles.

In 1849 pioneers followed the tracks leading off the Humboldt at Imlay and hundreds followed them. Someone put up a sign, "Only 110 miles to the diggins." It's believed that a third of the California emigrants followed this trail. Those who survived the desert were trapped by early winter snow in the Sierras. The governor of California realized what had happened and sent out relief parties. Thereafter this trail was dubbed "The Greenhorn's Cutoff" or the "Death Route". As word got around fewer emigrants dared it. The Black Rock Desert is still a dangerous place to be as some mysterious killer is leaving dead bodies of trespassers around.

149   MILL CITY/UNIONVILLE: NO NEAR SERVICES!
CAMPGROUND: RV park to the South. No further information.
In 1862 Mill City was the latest silver bonanza and was buzzing with miners and plans for 40 stamp mills. And just down Buena Vista Canyon was Unionville, a town of 3,000. A ghost town today, but a few unghostly miners still live there.

SIDETRIP!

TO THE GHOSTTOWN OF UNIONVILLE: FOR THE ADVENTURESOME! Twenty miles South on a paved road, then a few miles to the Right on a gravel road. In the Spring of 1861 prospectors began arriving eager for gold and silver. Some of the first or poorer shelters were built within a week with adobe and poles with grass tied with rawhide to keep out the rain and snow. Young Mark Twain and his friends arrived in a driving snow storm and made a simple shelter near a spring, roofing it with canvas. A corner of it was left open for a chimney. Occasionally cattle would fall through their roof at night disturbing their sleep and smashing their belongings. Fuel was scarce so they shivered. Sometimes Paiutes came with brush to sell. Mark Twain found some sparkling ore and dreamed of millions until his partner pronounced it MICA. Read Mark Twain's "Roughing It" to see what life was like in those days.

But some men did find valuable mines that produced millions. Mills were built to process the ore. There were 50 businesses in town. The Chinese were at the bottom of the ladder, so they had the most dangerous jobs. Men died from cave-ins, explosions, consumption/silicosis. Today the town is a quiet haven of 22 souls. Roam around the old general store, the stage line building, the Odd Fellows, the brewery. Stay at the "OLD PIONEER GARDEN" B&B. Enjoy a quiet stay in a home of antiques in a real ghost town. $35-$55 includes breakfast. Call: 538-7585. Or camp at the "PERSHING CO. YOUTH CENTER" at the end of town. Free. Remnants of Mark Twain's camp is here. In the West, Mark Twain's "abodes" rank with "Washington slept here".

151   DUN GLEN/MILL CITY: ELEVATION: 4208 FEET.
Mill City is South of I-80. Dun Glen is North.
FUEL/FOOD/MOTEL: North to Burns Bros Truck Stop. Burns tried to call this "Puckerbrush, NV." with a population of 28. Don't know where they found the 28 souls, but Nevada would not let them use the name officially. From 1917 to 1958 the Springer Tungsten Mine operated to the Northwest. General Electric bought it in the 1970's, expanded and operated it until 1982 when the price of Tungsten dropped. At night you can see the lights of it North across the valley while it waits for the price to go up. You might see dust devils in the waste dumps of the mine. Tungsten has the mineral scheelite that formed in recrystallized limestone due to igneous (volcanic) action. It's used in making light bulbs and steel.

158   COSGRAVE/REST AREA: South of I-80. North to Thacker Ranch.

168   ROSE CREEK: NO NEAR SERVICES! Minimum security prison.

173   WEST WINNEMUCCA: NO NEAR SERVICES! ELEVATION: 4324 FEET.
Sonoma Peak Southeast of Winnemucca is 9,396 feet. To the North note the big "W" on Red Mountain/Winnemucca Mountain". Nevada towns have had these letter landmarks for so many years that no one seems to know how it all began. The letter is constructed with large stones that

are then painted white to make them visible. It used to be the tradition of the High Schools to have the Seniors repaint them each year. Then insurance liability costs made them discontinue this practice. Now someone else has to do it. The Irish in town paint it green when they are celebrating.

176 WINNEMUCCA BOULEVARD WEST/BUS 80: RADIO: 1400 AM. 92.7 FM.
EASTBOUND: Take Bus 80/Old US 40 into town to the Mall. Raleys Food/Deli-bar, Sprouse Ritz, etc. Rejoin I-80 East of town at Milepost 180. "Cruising Main Street" takes the boredom out of cross-country travel. Go through town and see how people live.
FUEL: Pump 'n Save, Flying J, Chevron.
FOOD: McDonalds, Winner's Lunch Buffet, A & W, Jerry's, Model T, The Breakfast House. Read Milepost 178.
MOTELS: Thunderbird, Star Dust, Model T, Park, Gold Country Inn, Town House, Motel 6*, Winners, Holiday, Neda, Nevada, Park, Ponderosa, Pyrenees, Red Lion, Val-U-Inn. More on East Winnemucca Boulevard, Milepost 178.
CAMPGROUND: "Parker's Model T Casino & RV Park": Private. On the North in Western Winnemucca. Scheduled to be built in 1993. Other campgrounds East end of town, Milepost 178.

WINNEMUCCA

Winnemucca provided the first route North to the Oregon Trail from the California Trail because it had the best crossing of the Humboldt with a good gravel base. It was the ONLY place where the river could be forded for miles in either direction. Fur trapper and explorer, Peter Ogden, first descended from Idaho and Oregon to Nevada and explored the Humboldt from this point. Winnemucca was first a fur-trappers' trading post in 1853 called "Frenchman's Ford". Later there was a ferry crossing; then a tollbridge. When the railroad reached here in 1868 and the railroad lots were sold, the settlement grew quickly into a town. It was named "Winnemucca" by an Army map-maker for the principal Paiute Chief of Northern Nevada. This became a busy trading center. By 1877 the stage was operating from Winnemucca to Boise, Idaho.

In 1865 sheep ranching began first by Scots, and then by Chinese, who were left stranded by the railroad. Finally Basque sheepherders were imported from the French/Spanish border. The Martin Hotel next to the railroad on Railroad Street, to the South, was a Basque Boarding house for wintering shepherds.

The next street East from Bridge Street. used to be "Chinatown". They had 400 Chinese here, mostly men, from 1900-1911. There were several wooden shops and an adobe Joss House. It was an important Chinese center visited by China's president, Dr. Sun Yat Sen in 1911.

Winnemucca ranchers have had good years when the price of beef was high and went bankrupt when the blizzards starved and froze their stock. Today, the town is supported by farming, ranching and mining including silver, gold, tungsten, mercury and barite. Opals and turquoise are also found locally.

If you're lucky enough to be passing thru here on Father's Day Weekend you will see the gathering of 14 Indian Nations for the "Red Mountain Pow Wow". You can experience an Indian rodeo, enjoy Indian dances, games, competitions. Labor Day weekend you'll encounter Nevada's oldest rodeo including many special features. Also you'll enjoy their Basque Festival in mid June.

CHIEF WINNEMUCCA: The high chief of the Paiutes, survived through first the invasion by the trappers and then the wagon trains. He led his men in a fight against the onslaught that ended at Pyramid Lake. He was wise enough to see that Major Ormsby would defeat him and stopped the war before his men were annihilated. He then led his tribes into the new era of living with the whites. He was very old when he went on horseback to Surprise Valley, California in 1882 to help settle an Indian problem. There he gave great speeches and then became ill and died at William Coppersmith's Road Station. The changes he lived through were staggering, yet he managed to lead his people and seek peace up to his dying day.

SARAH WINNEMUCCA HOPKINS: The daughter of Chief Winnemucca, also left a heritage of courage. She was born in 1840 and grew up during the "Great Migration" of the pioneers through her country. With only a few weeks formal education she taught herself to read and write in English and became the major spokesperson for the Paiutes. The Military used her to interpret their policies to the Indians. Promises were made to her that were rarely kept. Due to corruption in the Government's "Indian Agency". An appointed agent saw his chance to make money and confiscated supplies promised the Indians. Sarah saw the abuses and fought against them using the white man's own democratic procedures. She wrote letters to government officials and made several trips to San Francisco, Washington D.C. and Fort Vancouver to try to right things. She became a lecturer and wrote "Life Among the Paiutes" in 1882 and later "Solution of the Indian Problem". She founded a school for Indian children in Lovelock but was beaten by hostility, lack of funds and illness which forced her into a job as a domestic servant. She moved to Montana and died there in 1891. Her dedication and perseverance is an example to all women.

Driving through town on Bus 80 note the Redwood log on the North side by the Winnemucca Welcome sign. This tree was washed ashore in Crescent City, California in the 1964 flood. It is 1477 years old and the largest piece of driftwood ever collected.

WINNEMUCCA FINE ARTS GALLERY: In the "NIXON OPERA HOUSE". North at the Redwood log to the Melarkey Street entrance. Thurs-Sun 9-4pm.

VISITOR CENTER, BUCKAROO HALL OF FAME AND HERITAGE MUSEUM: Winnemucca Boulevard and Bridge Street in the East Hall of the Convention Center. Get information on Winnemucca here. The "Hall Of Fame" is a new idea with great potential!

HUMBOLDT COUNTY MUSEUM: Maple Avenue and Jungo Road. Go North at the Melarkey Street light by the Redwood log. Cross the river and take the first Left to the museum up on the hill. The museum has interesting historical and Indian artifacts. Mon-Fri 10-12 noon and 1:30-4pm. Donations. Legend has it that Butch Cassidy and the Sundance Kid robbed the First National Bank here in 1900, and that to celebrate the event, they sent the bank president a studio portrait of themselves. Well, it's a fun story and there are lots of interesting details, but they don't all jibe. There WAS a robbery and around $32,640 was stolen. They all got away and no one was ever positively identified. One tale has a robber reeking of skunk. Then there's the dropping of a bag of gold coins into the dust and a chase on a switch engine. It would make a great movie! Stop at the Humboldt County Museum and ask for copies of the stories.

Drive or walk along Bridge Street just East of Melarkey as this used to be the old town. At 1st & Bridge is the 1863 Winnemucca Hotel and Stage Stop where Basque lunch and dinners are still served family style. Check out the bar, a western heritage. From Winnemucca Boulevard and Bridge go South one block to the old blue building on the left corner of 4th Street. This was the old First National Bank Building where the famous robbery took place. One more block up the hill on your right is the Humboldt County Courthouse.

178   WINNEMUCCA BOULEVARD EAST, WINNEMUCCA/US 95 NORTH:
The North Fork of the Little Humboldt joins the Humboldt River here.
FUEL: Pump 'n Save, Maverick, Sinclair.
FOOD: This is Basque country so try out the Basque family-style dinners. AAA recommends Martin Hotel Dining Room to the South at Railroad & Melarkey Streets. Also there's Ormachea's Dinner House on US 95 North. Winnemucca Hotel at First and Bridge serves lunch at 12 noon for $5 and dinner at 6pm for $11.50. Read Milepost 176.
MOTELS: Bull Head, Frontier, Val U Inn, Cozy, Downtown, Stardust. Many more along West Winnemucca Blvd, Milepost 176.
DUDE RANCH: "Stone House Dude Ranch": Private. 30 miles North on US 95 to Paradise Valley. Cookouts, hay rides, horseback riding, etc. $35-$100 a day includes all. Call: 1-800-447-6411.
EASTBOUND CAMPGROUNDS: "KOA" and "High Desert RV Park": Left turns off East Winnemucca Blvd.

180   EAST WINNEMUCCA/BUS 80:
WESTBOUND: Bus 80 will take you past 3 campgrounds and onto the main street, Winnemucca Boulevard. You'll rejoin I-80 West of town at Milepost 176. Read Mileposts 176 and 178 for services in town.
CAMPGROUNDS: "Hi-Desert": Private. .5 mile. Pool. $23. Free Van to casinos.
"KOA": Private. 3/4 mi. Pool. $17-$20.
"Western Trailer Lodge" .5 mile further to 4th Street. East one block.

187   BUTTON POINT REST AREA:
As you go around this curve on the Northern end of the Sonoma Mountains, note the purplish rocks of volcanic origin. Just East of here you can see dikes/spines of intrusive rocks South on the Sonoma Mountains.
HUMBOLDT RIVER: Here the Humboldt is just to the North but you can't see it because it has washed out such a deep canyon through the alluvium. A California Trail pioneer said the Humboldt "was filled only with mineral and vegetable poisons". Alkali in the river made the

water taste like bile. They tried putting vinegar or citric acid in it. They nicknamed it, "The Humbug"! They buried their dead along it and abandoned their wagons, and goods by it. In one 42 mile stretch, 1,000 wagons were abandoned. Someone counted 1500 dead animals in 50 miles of trail. Due to the dry climate, long afterwards the skeletons of animals and wagons remained. Even today you can find items. Hunger was a such a big problem that they ate anything! Their bacon was rancid or gone by this time. The flour very low. They ate wild parsnips and sliced steaks from dead oxen and ate it raw even if it was old and putrefied.

The Paiutes harassed the wagon trains unmercifully. They didn't usually hurt the people but they wanted their stock. So they used rattlesnake venom to poison their arrows to shoot an ox, wounding it so that it would have to be left behind. Then they would carry it away to eat. Some historians say that the Paiutes considered their taking of animals as a toll for the passage of a wagon through their territory.

194 **GOLCONDA:** GAS AND POST OFFICE.
Golconda used to have a resort hotel and spa with several hot springs.
MILEPOST 200 GOLCONDA SUMMIT: ELEVATION: 5145 FEET. Parking area only.
WESTBOUND: See the view of Golconda six miles away and Winnemucca 20 miles in the distance. There is very old Cambrian metamorphosed sandstone here that is rather greenish brown.
MILEPOST 203 IRON POINT: A famous dispute took place here. There are several versions as there are to every fight, but let's try this one: The Donner-Reed Party was struggling up a hard grade with "double-teams". John Snyder's and the Reed's teams became entangled. Snyder became enraged and Virginia Reed said that her father tried to calm him. She said that Snyder hit him with his whip-stock. Mrs. Reed stepped into the frey and was hit. James Reed drew his knife and in the ensuing scuffle, Snyder was stabbed to death.
The law of the trail would have sentenced Reed to hanging and there was animosity toward him for choosing the Hastings Cut-off. However, Reed had already rescued them by bringing water to them on the Salt Flats, so they banished him from the train with no weapon and no provisions. During the night his 12 year old daughter, Virginia, and a hired man sneaked out to take him a horse, gun and provisions.
Reed knew how low their food supply was, so he hurried ahead into California to get help. He was pressed into the army for the Mexican War and sent to Monterey, but when he got there the war was over, and he hurried back to Sutter's Fort to get food supplies. When he brought a rescue party into the Donner Lake area he found the first relief party coming out with his wife and two of his children staggering through the snow. He went on to the camp and found little Patty sitting on a snow bank above a shelter, and his son Thomas inside. Patty's tiny four-inch doll was still in her pocket; perhaps it helped her to survive. Today it is at Sutter's Fort in Sacramento.

205 **PUMPERNICKEL VALLEY:** NO NEAR SERVICES! Great name though.
MILEPOST 209: Strip mining in distant North.
MILEPOST 211 LONE TREE MINE, SANTA FE PACIFIC GOLD CORPORATION.
South of I-80 is Nevada's newest gold producer. The red dumps on the nearby ridge were explored for copper. Gold was found just two feet down in faulted and fractured rock. The Ore vein here is 150-250 feet wide, 4500 feet long and 700 feet deep. Lone Tree moves 20 million tons of rock a year to obtain 120,000 ounces of gold at a cost of $295 an ounce. They use power from the Valmy Power Plant to the North. The ore is crushed and leached on a pad with a cyanide solution for 30 days. It is rested and then leached again. Recovery of the gold is by activated carbon, heat and pressure until the solution is a brown mud. Later the gold is melted in a furnace and poured into gold bars. Lone Tree is fortunate that they have both low grade ore AND high grade ore that leach well.

212 **STONEHOUSE:** NO NEAR SERVICES!
Paleozoic quartzite here. There is a hot sulphur spring in which the early settlers scalded their pork. This also became an early Stage Station. Can you see prospect pits from I-80? They called them "Coyote Holes". Sante Fe Pacific Gold has also purchased the Stonehouse Extension of the Lone Tree ore body.

216   **VALMY/REST AREA:** POST OFFICE.
      FUEL/FOOD/MOTEL: Shell, Golden Grill Cafe and motel.
         There were so many battles here over the springs that the town was named after the French Battle of "Valmy". Stretch your legs at the Rest Area and look for signs of life on this desert. You'll see small plants, lots of insects, lizards, maybe small rodents. The big black and white bird is the black-billed magpie. The larger black solitary bird with the beard is a raven. To the Northwest note the two tall chimneys of Sierra Pacific Company's "Valmy Power Plant" run by coal.
         MARIGOLD MINE: South of I-80. Closed in the 1930's, Marigold is a small mine gaining a new life with an ore body under 300 feet of gravel. The mine has 1.9 million tons of "mill ore" at 0.115 ounces gold per ton, and 18.5 million tons of "leach ore" at 0.032 ounces per ton. The leach ore is placed on 3 feet of compacted fill over the leach pads. The gold is extracted with the cyanide and activated carbon processes recovering 73% of the gold. The mill grade ore is crushed first by a "jaw crusher", then a "cone crusher" and then a "rod and a ball mill" that gets it down to fine silt. Chemicals, pressure and heat remove the gold and pump it through steel wool where the gold is precipitated by electricity. The gold plated wool is melted in a furnace and the gold poured into bars. This milling process recovers 91% of the gold. Their production cost is $237 an ounce.

222   **MOTE:** NO NEAR SERVICES!

229   **WEST BATTLE MOUNTAIN/NV 305 SOUTH TO AUSTIN:** ELEVATION: 4518 FEET.
      EASTBOUND: All services are in town on Bus 80/Old US 40.
      FUEL: Texaco Colt Truck Stop, Shell, Jackpot, Bonus, Conoco, Standard, Goodyear.
      FAST FOOD: Geno's Pizza, Kwik, Pack Out, Food Market.
      FOOD: Nevada and Owl Casinos, Colt Restaurant, Donna's Diner with home cooking.
      MOTELS: Vips, Colt, Best Western, Ho, Uptown, Owl, West Coast, Holiday, Bell Court.
      CAMPGROUND: "Colt Service Center": Texaco's on Bus 80. No further information.

BATTLE MOUNTAIN

The peaks to the South are North Peak nearer the highway at 8550 feet, and Antler Peak at 8236 feet with pit mining below it. You can see the scars on the hills. This town was named for a big bluff to the South where an Indian/Emigrant battle erupted in 1857. As an old Indian said in 1877, "Heap white men killed." Minerals were found 15 miles South in Copper canyon in 1870 and the original town of Battle Mountain was near there. When the railroad arrived, the present site became a trade center with a stage stop and a permanent settlement. Malachite, azurite and turquoise are also found here. However gold mining is more prevalent now.

In 1877 the Paiutes were described as having rabbit skin coats with the skins twisted in ropes and woven together with animal sinews or hemp. In the past the Paiutes hunted bison and antelope, but by this time the bison had fled North and the antelope were quickly following them. The Paiutes had rabbit hunts by making a trap of a "V" fence of saplings and stretched willowbark with a hemp net across it. Then they would chase the rabbits toward the trap with lots of noise, where they would catch their heads in the network and be clubbed. The skins were woven into cloaks and blankets.

As you drive through the dry Nevada basin remember that the California Trail and I-80 both took the easiest route through Nevada following the Humboldt, not the most scenic! Nevada conceals much of its beauty in its short North/South ranges that the highways skirt.

BATTLE MOUNTAIN GOLD COMPANY: Fifteen miles South. Duval Corporation was doing open-pit copper mining of low grade ore. They were owned by Pennzoil when they discovered gold ore in the "Fortitude" deposit and started mining that in 1984. The company was reorganized and renamed. The ore here is spectacular as "calc-silicate skarns". Molten rock intruded and combined with country rock to make the skarns. It is iron, copper, zinc and lead with sulfur. This high grade mill ore is milled at .157 ounces gold per ton where it is reduced to a flour-like consistency and leached in tanks. They achieve 96% recovery of the gold. Leach grade ore at 0.035 ounces of gold per ton is mined from four other sites and leached on a pad obtaining two parts silver to one part gold. The company produces 190,000 ounces of gold a year at a cost of $179 an ounce.

233   **EAST BATTLE MOUNTAIN/NV 305 SOUTH TO AUSTIN:** HOSPITAL
      WESTBOUND: Take Bus 80/Old US 40 for services in town. Continue through town to return to I-80 at Milepost 229. Read Milepost 229 for services.

244 ARGENTA: NO NEAR SERVICES!

I-80 and the Humboldt River are passing between the Sheep Creek Mountains and the Shoshone Mountains. There are often cattle grazing here in the Humboldt Valley. Herefords, first bred in England, predominate in dark red- brown with white markings. Often you'll see a French breed of white cattle, Charolais, in a mixed herd producing a leaner meat. As you look South to the Argenta Rim of the Shoshone Mountains, note two ridges of Cenozoic volcanic material. There is basalt in the top rim, an andesite ridge lower down, and an alluvial fan at the base.

254 DUNPHY: NO NEAR SERVICES! RADIO WEATHER INFORMATION: 1240 AM.

MILEPOST 257: You are crossing the Humboldt River and the railroad. From Carlin East of here to this point the river and the railroad go around the Tuscarora Mountains to the South, while I-80 goes over the mountains through volcanic rocks. The Humboldt River Valley Southeast of here is in a narrow fault block that dropped down. It's too narrow for a highway. Even the California Trail could not follow it but had to climb over the mountain.

259 REST AREAS: EASTBOUND: The next Rest Area is 167 miles.
WESTBOUND: The next Rest Area is 42 miles.

261 BEOWAWE/CRESCENT VALLEY/NV 306: NO NEAR SERVICES!

South two miles from Beowawe to "Beowawe Geysers". These are natural geysers that perform when surface water is heated by hot rocks underground. You used to be able to see them from the highway, but now the action has been destroyed by drilling for geothermal energy. Note the masses of yellow sunflowers with the brown puffy centers that you'll see from here through Nebraska.

MILEPOST 267 TWIN SUMMIT. ELEVATION: 5672 FEET. Climbing up over the head of two caterpillars this time.

268 EMIGRANT: NO NEAR SERVICES! How very green around the springs!

270 EMIGRANT SUMMIT: ELEVATION: 6114 FEET. PARKING ONLY.

These Tuscarora Mountains were a boundary for the Native Tribes. To the West were the Paiutes, to the East the Shoshones. The road cut here shows a black lava flow capped by a white tuff formed from volcanic dust.

EASTBOUND: Can you see the snow-capped Ruby Mountains to the East?

271 PALISADE: NO NEAR SERVICES!

The town is to the South. In 1877 there were tepees around the town. The canyon through which the train passed was called the "Twelve-mile Canyon" and the "Palisades of the Humboldt". There are sheer rock cliffs there. That's why the California Trail and I-80 had to detour over this mountain.

WESTBOUND: Steep up-grade now over two passes.

279 WEST CARLIN/NV 278/BUS 80:

FUEL: Sinclair.

EASTBOUND: We are now rejoining the route of the Humboldt River and the railroad.

WESTBOUND: Say "Good By" to the river and railroad while you cross over the Tuscarora Mountains.

280 CENTRAL CARLIN: FUEL: Sinclair.

Early gold miners said that this is "Where the train stops and the Gold Rush begins." Today the big "Newmont" gold mine is about ten miles North of here.

282 EAST CARLIN/NV 221/BUS 80:

EASTBOUND: The canyon ahead has always been one of the prettier spots along this route. Old US 40 wound down the mountain following the river past horses grazing in the green meadows. You can see its remains. Now we tunnel quickly past it and it is gone.

MILEPOST 286 CARLIN TUNNELS/CARLIN CANYON: The tunnels were completed in 1974 at a cost of $8 million. They are 1900 feet long and lined with white tile. There are two for the railroad and two for I-80. Just West of the tunnels there is a big curve of the river where the West hill contains fossils. Geologists might want to check out this ridge as it has several geological features. Watch for the angular unconformity with Mississippi Rocks vertical and Pennsylvania rocks on top. These are very old Paleozoic and carboniferous.

MILEPOST 288: Now note the pillars on the North wall. Soft materials on the hills have eroded away and left the hard rock towers.

292 **HUNTER:** NO NEAR SERVICES!

THE END OF HASTING'S CUTOFF!: Here the South Fork of the Humboldt comes tumbling out of the snow-capped Ruby Mountains to the South, and joins the Humboldt River about a half-mile from here. You can see the gap in the Rubies where the river has cut through. The Donner Party came straggling down onto the California trail after their arduous detour across the Wasatch Mountains, the Salt Flats, and three passes in Nevada. They had just made a long detour South to go through this Ruby pass. By the time they reached here they had been through so much, you can imagine their relief. Westbound travelers will remember Eddie Breen whose leg they wanted to amputate back at Ft. Bridger and his mother wouldn't allow it. He came riding his horse out of this canyon, the leg healed. He could walk again! Mother knew best! **EASTBOUND:** Read Wyoming Milepost 34, Fort Bridger History.

298 **ELKO WEST:** ELEVATION: 5000 FEET. RADIO: 1240 AM. 93.5 FM.

301 **DOWNTOWN ELKO/NV 225 NORTH/NV 227 SOUTH/BUS 80:**
EASTBOUND: Take Bus 80 through town to return to I-80 at Milepost 303.
MALLS: RALEYS FOOD and K MART North of I-80. South to IGA Food.
FUEL: Texaco Truck Stop, Shell, Sinclair, Exxon, Conoco.
FOOD: North to Arbys. South to Dairy Queen, Dinner Station, Toki Ona, The Coffee Mug (home-style dining), Golden Corral, Star Hotel (Silver Street at 3rd. Basque food in moderate price range.) Casinos also have food.
MOTELS: North to Shilo Inn. South to Westward, Key, Centre, Thunderbird, Esquire, National, Best Western, Starlite, Nelson, Roadway, Elko, Louis.
CAMPGROUNDS: "Cimarron West RV and Camper Park": Private. South just 2 blocks. Includes a beauty shop, car wash, cafe and miniature golf. $15.

SIDETRIPS FOR THE ADVENTURESOME!

JARBRIDGE WILDERNESS AND WILD HORSE RESERVOIR: North 50 miles on NV 225. This is beautiful country with several primitive campgrounds, fishing and deer hunting. Enquire at the Information Center by the Nevada Museum.

LAMOILLE CANYON: Southeast on NV 227 some 35 miles. Lamoille Canyon is "U" shaped with rock walls towering 2,000 feet above the valley. Waterfalls send ribbons down from small glacial lakes. Picnicking, primitive campgrounds except for one in Thomas Canyon with water and restrooms. NV 228 goes South off NV 227 to Jiggs and 50 miles to the Ruby Marsh. That is where the Donners came across the mountains meeting the South Fork of the Humboldt near Jiggs. Get local directions first.

ELKO

Elko was born when the Central Pacific Railroad pushed its tracks there in December 1868. On New Year's Day there were a few tents in the sagebrush. Two weeks later town plots were selling for $300 to $500. In March 1869 Elko was made county seat of Elko County which is 17,000 square miles and the 6th largest county in the U.S. That's as big as the five New England States plus the District of Columbia.

In 1869 after the Golden Spike was driven at Promontory Point, Utah, hundreds of Chinese laborers came West by foot and some settled around Elko. During the summer months they raised vegetables for the town in their gardens on the Northern banks of the Humboldt. They watered their crops by hand until they built the first water system in Elko.

In 1877 Shoshones camped here in their lodges. The men wore blankets and black hats tied with string. Women were in calico gowns. They were described as very dirty, begging around the train station for any scrap to eat. These must have been terrible years for the Natives with the game gone and no means of survival. Scottish herders brought sheep into Nevada from California and Oregon in the 1960's They grazed on the public lands which the cattlemen thought of as their own. Battles were fought, but the sheep stayed. Sheepherders from the Pyrenees Mountains in Spain were the preferred herders. In the fall the lambs were sold, the flocks combined and the herdsmen were no longer needed. Basque Hotels were built to house them over the winter. Today Basque dinners are served family style in these hotels. Try one!

HOT HOLE/CHICKEN SOUP SPRINGS: South on Mountain City Highway (the street leading off I-80) to a Right over the bridge. One block then Right onto Bullion Road. About .5 mile up the hill and turn right onto a wide gravel pad. A high cyclone fence will be on your right circling a deep hole. Get out and look! The springs are WAY down there! It's a blue pool bubbling up with a shelf of mineral deposit. This was a landmark on the California trail since 1940's. It was used in more recent years by the traveling hobos who camped there, and appreciated the hot water for washing. Today they call it Elko Hot Springs. Other hot pools nearby have been capped and used. Too bad that the town doesn't develop the area. It could be such a pretty spot!

THE GUNFIGHTERS: On Bus 80 at the Western end of town at the Commercial Hotel Casino. It used to be the finest casino in town but at this writing it is in need of a facelift. This is unimportant to the locals who like to congregate here. Maybe its the cook! Watch for the giant mounted Polar bear that towers over you as you walk from the coffee shop to the casino. Then search for the BACK casino room for the life-sized portraits of "The Gunfighters". In the 1950's the hotel asked Lea Franklin McCarty to paint the West's outlaws for their new Casino room. Being very conscientious, Lea searched out the descendants of these notorious persons. He was given family snapshots and descriptions to inspire his paintings. The dramatic results are the large oils that line the walls of this dark room. Their setting does not do them justice. They should be in a well-lighted art gallery. Lea wrote a biography that hangs by each portrait and brings each character to life. You may purchase a book at the Cash Register which includes prints of the oils and the stories. WESTERN HISTORY BUFFS DON'T MISS IT!. While you're there try the dining room. The back wall has all the cattle brands registered in Nevada burned into the wall.

NORTHEASTERN NEVADA MUSEUM
Photo credit: Northeastern Nevada Museum

PONY EXPRESS CABIN & NORTHEASTERN NEVADA MUSEUM: East end of Elko on the North side of the main street. The 1860 cabin was brought here from Ruby Valley. The museum is excellent with displays on the Native tribes, the flora/fauna of the area and Nevada history with a pioneer schoolroom and kitchen. Next door is the CHAMBER OF COMMERCE INFORMATION CENTER.

303   **EAST ELKO/BUS 80:** HOSPITAL.
     WESTBOUND BUS LOOP: Exit on Bus 80 to return to I-80 at Milepost 301 or 298.
     ELKO SHOPPING PLAZA: South to Penny's, Sproutz Reitz, Albertsons, Car Service, Western Auto, Payless Drug, Post Office.
     FUEL: Texaco, Chevron, Exxon.
     FOOD: Red Lion Casino Buffet (North side of Street), McDonalds, Taco Time, Pizza Hut, Wendys.
     MOTELS: Gold Rush Inn, Red Lion, Motel 6*, Holiday Inn, Econo Lodge, Super 8, National 9 Inn.

CAMPGROUNDS: "Red Lion Inn RV Park": Private. Small. Behind the Casino on the South side of the street, register inside. Small vehicles only.

"Valley View RV Park": Private. South of I-80, .5 mile East of the Mall. NEAR I-80. SEE ALSO MILEPOSTS 301 AND 314.

MILEPOST 307: "NEVADA CHUGARS UNLIMITED": An effort to save the native chicken-like bird called the "Chugar". Pens to the North of the highway.

310 **OSINO:** NO NEAR SERVICES!
MILEPOST 313: EASTBOUND: Great view of the Ruby Mountains in front of you. The Rubies, with more than two dozen alpine lakes hidden in their canyons are one of Nevada's favorite deer hunting areas.

314 **RYNDON-DEVIL'S GATE:**
CAMPGROUND: "KOA": Private. South of I-80 back from the road, near the Humboldt River. Stroll over to the river and you might see an egret. $15-$18.

317 **ELBERZ:** NO NEAR SERVICES!
EASTBOUND: Now you have the BIG PICTURE of both the North and the South Rubies in front of you. Can you guess where "Secret Pass" cuts through the Rubies?

321 **HALLECK-RUBY VALLEY/NV 229:** NO NEAR SERVICES!
Ruby Dome in the South Rubies is 11,299 feet. You'll see more ravens along this stretch. These solitary large black birds have heavier necks than crows. Crows are smaller and always hunt in flocks. More black and white magpies seen only in the West and North to Alaska.

EASTBOUND ALTERNATE ROUTE

SECRET PASS: FOR THE ADVENTURESOME! Take NV 229 South and up between the two ranges of the Ruby Mountains over the pass at 6457 feet. Return to I-80 at Wells via NV 229 and US 93. It's about a 60-mile scenic drive.

328 **RIVER RANCH:** NO NEAR SERVICES!
MILEPOST 330: Look Eastward toward the Ruby mountains. Find the highest jagged peak, "Hole-in-the-Mountain" at 11,276 feet. It's a pyramid-shaped peak that has a hole through which horseback riders can pass. You'll need strong binoculars.

333 **DEETH-STAR VALLEY:**
Deeth is at a junction of rivers. Boulder Creek, to the South of I-80, comes running down from "Hole-in-the-Mountain" where it is teased by the beaver. Mary's River, Tabor Creek and Bishop's Creek come in from the North all joining to make the Humboldt River. This is also where the California Trail came down from the Oregon Trail via Thousand Springs and Bishop's Creek to join the Humboldt in its Westward push.

EASTBOUND ALTERNATE ROUTE

THROUGH RANCHLAND: For a tiny taste of Nevada ranch country, take this exit South and follow Starr Valley Road/Old US 40 East for just 10 miles until it connects again with I-80 at Milepost 343. Lots of yellow headed blackbirds in the marshes here by the road. The Humboldt Valley has many large ranches often hidden in the canyons where they have a water source. The cattle are raised on range grass until they are yearlings. Then they are sold to mid-east farmers and feed lot owners who fatten them on corn-silage to produce more tender meat. The black cattle you see are "Black Angus".

There used to be a Dude Ranch up this road. It could be 100 degrees on US 40 while up this hill to the ranch, just 3-4 miles, you could sit by a cool mountain stream and watch a beaver. You could ride a horse up into the Ruby Mountains to high meadows where there were stone cabins built by early settlers. If you were a good rider you might even make it up and through "Hole-in-the-Mountain". In the 1960's when the host needed meat for a barbecue, the men flagged down the cars on old US 40 (there were just four) so that a small plane could land to deliver the meat flown in from Idaho.

343 **WELCOME-STARR VALLEY:** RADIO WEATHER STATIONS: 1240 AM, 93.5 FM, 95.3 FM.
CAMPGROUND: "Welcome Station RV Park": Private. North of I-80 in the trees. NEAR I-80.

WESTBOUND ALTERNATE ROUTE
THROUGH NEVADA RANCHLAND: Take Starr Valley Road just ten miles Southwest to I-80 and Milepost 333. Read Milepost 333.

348 **CRESTED ACRES:**
CAMPGROUND: Private. NEAR I-80. No further information. In August the green Rabbitbrush may be covered with yellow blossoms. The grey bushes that you see are sage with only puffs of grey blossoms. Stop and pick a piece and you'll smell the difference.

351 **WEST WELLS/BUS 80:** ELEVATION: 6245 FEET. Post Office.
EASTBOUND: Take Bus 80 through town for services. Back to I-80 at MP 352.
FUEL: Shell.
FOOD: Burger Bar. (This is also Well's information center.)
MOTELS: Mountain Shadow, China Town, Motel 6*, Sage, Crest, Sharon, Big Pillow, Ranch House, Snor Haven.
CAMPGROUNDS: "Mountain Shadows RV Park": Private. Pull-throughs. North two blocks on Bus 80.
"Snor-Haven Motel & RV Pk": Private. Three-fourths mile North on Bus 80. West two blocks.
Wells was named for the 30 very deep springs in this area. They had slightly brackish water often with minnows in it. Wells got its start in 1869 with a log shanty saloon, a railroad office in a boxcar, and a Wells Fargo Office. In 1877 it was a very primitive town with many "dugouts" in which white families lived. Today Wells enlivens things with Chariot races in February and Pony Express races in May.

352 MAJOR INTERCHANGE!
EAST WELLS/BUS 80/US 93:
US 93 NORTH TO TWIN FALLS, ID. SOUTH TO ELY, NV.
WESTBOUND: Take BUS 80 through Wells to MP 351 for services.
FUEL: Texaco Auto/Truck Stop, Phillips Truck Stop, Stinker Sinclair, Chevron.
FOOD: 4-Way Cafe, Frontier Foodtown, Burger Bar (Tourist information).
MOTELS: Motel 6*, Rest Inn.
CAMPGROUNDS: Crossroads RV Park: Private. NEAR I-80.
"Angel Creek" and "Angel Lake": Forest Service. South 8 miles on NV 231 to Angel Creek and 13 miles to Angel Lake. Enquire at the Burger Bar in Wells first. It's a very steep road up to the lake. For more services in Wells, read Milepost 351.

SIDETRIPS FOR THE ADVENTURESOME!
BEFORE STARTING ON ANY OF THESE SIDETRIPS, ENQUIRE AT THE "BURGER BAR" IN WELLS. THIS IS THEIR INFORMATION CENTER. YOU MUST KNOW IF YOUR RIG IS APROPRIATE FOR THE TRIP AND YOU'LL NEED MAPS AND KNOWLEDGE OF THE AREA.
ANGEL LAKE AND HOLE-IN-THE-MOUNTAIN: Thirteen miles up NV 231. Probably best for smaller vehicles, but ask first. Small peaceful lake in a glacial cirque. If you're a hiker, you'll want to hit the trail for "Hole-in-the Mountain" at 11,000 feet, or Winchell or Grey's Lake.
RUBY VALLEY AND RUBY MARSH: South 50-70 miles via US 93 and NV 229 to fish and hike. In the pioneer days, prospectors found garnets in this area and mistaking them for rubies named the mountain range.
CALIFORNIA TRAIL, BACKCOUNTRY BYWAY: North 23 miles on US 93 to the Thousand Springs turnoff onto gravel County Road 765. This parallels the original California Trail down from Idaho for 63 more

miles. You can continue on to Jackpot or to Oakley, ID. In the Back-country like this you must be prepared for all emergencies. Check at Burger Bar.

The Oregon Trail came through Wyoming about where US 30 is today at Little America, entered Idaho and went on up to the Snake River. The California Trail turned off the Oregon Trail at the Raft River in Idaho and followed it Southward upstream and along what is ID 77 from Malta to Elba, then Almo, past the City of Rocks. They crossed into Utah for just a corner at Granite Pass, and "Goose Creek Road" today, past Record Bluff and on down to follow Thousand Springs Valley in Nevada for 20 miles. A short trek took them to Bishop's Creek just above Wells which they followed down to the Humboldt.

Trail markers identify the old trail. Some of the old wagon ruts have eroded into deep depressions. This is a Wilderness area with springs and creeks, junipers, fishing, hiking, hunting and primitive camping. Pickups do best here. Get a Bureau of Land Management Map before going. Also a pioneer diary from a museum would be helpful. Elko Museum would be a good source.

SECRET PASS: US 93 South to NV 229 over Secret Pass to I-80 at Milepost 321. About 60 miles.

MILEPOST 354 EASTBOUND PARKING AREA:
MILEPOST 355 WESTBOUND: Look Westward toward the Ruby Mountains. They're often snowcapped. Just below the top of the mountain, note a sharp rock jutting up like a chimney on top of a pyramid. There is a small glacial lake nestled just behind it called, "Angel Lake".

360   **MOOR:** NO NEAR SERVICES! ELEVATION: 6,000 FEET.

South of I-80 are the Wood Hills where Paleozoic limestone and sandstone have pushed over dolomites and quartzites. Up into the hills now with the short pinon pines. A welcome relief from the deserts on either side. Pine nuts from these pinon pines are very good and sweet. When the Bidwell party was here, Bartleson decided he could travel faster than the rest of the train. He took seven others and left. They got lost but were rescued by the Indians who fed them pine nuts to bring them back from the brink of starvation. Note how some of these trees seem to be growing out of solid rock. Careful, the pitch on the trees and cones will stick to your hands.

365   **INDEPENDENCE VALLEY:** ELEVATION: 6000 FEET. NO NEAR SERVICES!
Nevada Prison. Not so independent for the inmates!

EASTBOUND: Steep climb up Pequop Mountain up 1,000 feet in six miles. The Devonian (very old Paleozoic) limestone walls here rise like castle battlements. There are many small caves in them from the limestone being dissolved. Good nesting sites for eagles, owls and swallows.

373   **PEQUOP SUMMIT:** ELEVATION: 6967 FEET. NO NEAR SERVICES! PARKING ONLY.
Note the black Mississippian shale that has eroded down to form this pass. Steep downhill now so take it easy!

376   **PEQUOP:** NO NEAR SERVICES!
This name will always be in the history books because this is where the first wagon train to attempt the California Trail left their wagons. In 1841 the Bartleson/Bidwell party of 31 men, one woman and infant and nine poor wagons followed the Oregon Trail to Idaho. They followed the Bear River South into Utah and then struggled along following whatever mountain-man trails they could find and going by stories passed by word-of-mouth. But when they got to the base of the Pequop Mountains they gave up on their wagons and left them here. They packed their mules and walked, using their oxen for food one by one. They crossed the Sierras at Sonora Pass, got lost in the Stanislaus canyons where they finished their last ox and ate mule meat. Finally on Oct. 30th they reached the San Joaquin valley and the young mother walked barefoot into Marsh's Ranch.

WESTBOUND: Very steep grade ahead for three miles. If it's a hot day and you're pulling a heavy load, you might turn your air-conditioner off.

378   **OASIS/MONTELLO/NV 233:**
FUEL/GARAGE/FOOD/MOTEL/CAMPGROUND/POST OFFICE: Clean restrooms, lawn, picnic table, home-style food (nothing artificial). Gift shop of Native American and Mexican crafts. This is the paved road turnoff for Pilot Valley which extends from Montello down to near

I-80's Milepost 298. There is good soil and water that supports cattle-raising and hay production. Nevada Ranchers put in a lot of miles. The children go to Montello to school. The High School students are bused into Wells. Parents go to jobs in Wendover or Wells.

So much sagebrush, but it has a purpose. The seeds feed rodents and grouse while the Bighorn sheep and deer eat the leaves. It won't grow in high alkalinity soil, so ranchers see its presence as designating favorable soil. It's a silvery-grey with tiny greyish toothed leaves that are aromatic. It blooms in the late summer with greyish puffs. Sage brush is free! Take home a trunkfull!

WESTBOUND: You'll climb the Pequop Range up 1,000 feet in the next six miles.

387 SHAFTER: NO NEAR SERVICES!

Travelers on old US 40 used to stop here at Johnson Springs for cool water. Now it is Wendover, NV's water supply. Before that, the Donner Party on Hastings Cutoff got their first water here since the Pilot Peak springs. Their next stop was Flower Spring and Flower Pass then over the hills to Ruby Valley. After crossing the Ruby Mountains, they joined the California Trail at the Humboldt River just Southeast of present day Carlin.

MILEPOST 390 SILVERZONE PASS: ELEVATION: 5940 FEET.

Although the Toana Range is mostly Paleozoic limestone, what you are seeing here on top is granite that has fractured and weathered. It looks like the Devil just tossed these rocks around.

Note that the Railroad crosses I-80 twice, once on each side of the summit. In order to climb this steep grade it makes a long loop North of I-80 at Milepost 390, and then back again at Milepost 393. At the Eastern crossing of the railroad, see if you can see the signs of the Western edge of ancient Lake Bonneville.

EASTBOUND: You have your first view of Pilot Peak, 10,716 feet, to the Northeast. This was an important milepost on the pioneer trail. It is part of the Pilot Range.

398 PILOT PEAK: NO NEAR SERVICES!

WESTBOUND: First view of Pilot Peak, the tall mountain to the North. Although it looks like a volcanic cone it is really granite.

PILOT PEAK SPRINGS

In 1845 when John C. Fremont was making his surveying expedition across the desert, he sent his scout, Kit Carson, ahead to find water. Kit found springs at the foot of Pilot Peak and sent smoke signals to guide the party there. Kit guided both Fremont and Stephen W. Kearny through the West.

When the Donner-Reed Party was struggling across the Salt Flats, James Reed and William Eddy went ahead to Pilot Peak for water to take back to them. While they were gone, Reed's 18 oxen panicked with thirst and ran off. The family walked until they were received by Jacob Donner's wagon. Graves and Breen each lent an ox to Reed, so that with his cow and one remaining ox his wagon could be pulled. In the morning the Pequop pass had snow on it. It was time to take stock. There were not enough provisions to get them into California. C.T. Stanton and William McCutchen were sent ahead to get relief supplies at Sutter's Fort.

Later emigrants struggling over the Salt Flats East of here were often rescued with water from Pilot Hill's springs. Pilot Valley farmers/traders with a water-wagon would drive 20 miles out onto the Salt Flats to rescue people. They would be repaid in trade goods. One farmer told of finding a woman delirious wandering in the desert. Usually the water wagon went only out to "Silver Island", a mountain near the edge of the Salt Flats just North of Wendover. It looked like an island from the Salt Flats because of its floating appearance through the heat waves. They spoke of a gap in the "Island" that the wagons went through. Actually it was the gap between Silver Island and Crater Island where the trail passed. There was never enough water for the animals. They died of thirst and mummified in the heat of the desert. Today Pilot Peak's springs provide water for Wendover, UT.

VIRGA: Often in the West and in this area particularly, you'll see storm clouds forming, the sky underneath becoming darker and darker. Then you'll see streaks coming down from the clouds. It looks like it is raining but it doesn't reach the ground. It evaporates first. This is called Virga. You may be surrounded by dark storm clouds but only get a few drops on your windshield.

LENTICULAR CLOUDS: Another Western phenomena! You'll see single clouds that are in smooth oval shapes. They have been described as "a pile of pancakes" or as if a giant bowl-scraper swept around beaten eggwhites.

MILEPOST 408: HORIZON VIEW: EASTBOUND: Slow down here and move onto the wide shoulder which becomes the Viewpoint Area. Look out across the Salt Flats. Although I-80's lanes to the distant left out on the Salt Flats appear to be curving, they're really straight and level. This indicates the curvature of the earth. The pools you see in the distance are evaporation pools for the production of potash. The rectangular pools at the foot of the hill are sewage treatment tank for Wendover.

410   WEST WENDOVER/ALT US 93 SOUTH TO ELY:

EASTBOUND: Exit here for the business loop through Wendover. You need a rest anyway and there will not be a single service station for 70 miles and no other service for 99 miles. You will get back on I-80 just inside Utah. There is a big new truck stop at Utah Milepost 4.

As you turn Left onto Wendover's main street, on your immediate Right is the **NEVADA WELCOME CENTER.** If you'd like any information on Nevada before leaving the state, stop here.

WESTBOUND: As you come West through town to Nevada, watch for the little park with the playground equipment and picnic area on the South side of the street in Nevada. It's the Nevada Welcome Center. And an excellent one! Nevada maps and brochures here.

MALL: In Nevada, far West of all the casinos. On the Utah side there's S & D Food.

FUEL: Chevron, Texaco Nevada Crossing Truck Stop, Conoco, Sinclair.

FOOD: Salt Flats Grill, Pizza Hut, Taco Burger, Great China, Burger Time, Hide- a-Way Casino. Silversmith has a coffee shop and a buffe; Nevada Crossing a restaurant and salad bar; Red Garter a restaurant; Peppermill a buffet with seafood on Friday night; State Line a coffee shop, a dining room and a Prime Rib Buffet.

MOTELS: State Line-Silver Smith, Peppermill, Nevada Crossing, Heritage, Motel 6*, Bonneville, Western, Super 8. Shuttle buses available between the motels and the casinos.

CAMPGROUNDS: "KOA": Private. From the West you'll make a Right at the stop sign. Go one block and turn Left/South behind "Nevada Crossing" for a block down the hill. Pool. $15-$19.

"Silversmith Casino Resort RV Park": Private. Just one block East of the Giant Cowboy waving his arms. One block South down the hill. Laundry and full hookups. No tents. Walkway to Silversmith Casino. $15.

Wendover was born when railroad workers piped water from Pilot Peak to the railroad and roundhouse here in 1907. The settlers were completely dependent on the railroad until the first road was built between Wendover and Knolls in 1917. But it was 1926 before the road reached Salt Lake City. To build the road across the Salt Flats, the 4-foot deep salt had to be removed. Then 15-foot deep trenches were dug to obtain mud for the embankment. The railroad brought in gravel for the roadbed. The town had to use kerosene lamps until 1947. Wendover is two towns in two states, two governments, both supported by tourism.

EASTBOUND: Wave "Goodby" to the giant cowboy and you are in Utah. Refresh yourselves before you start across the Salt Flats.

WESTBOUND: Say "Hi, Cowboy!" Cattle country! Watch out for a bum steer!

GIANT COWBOY WELCOMES YOU TO NEVADA
Photo credit: John A. Kost

NEVADA I 80 MILEPOSTS

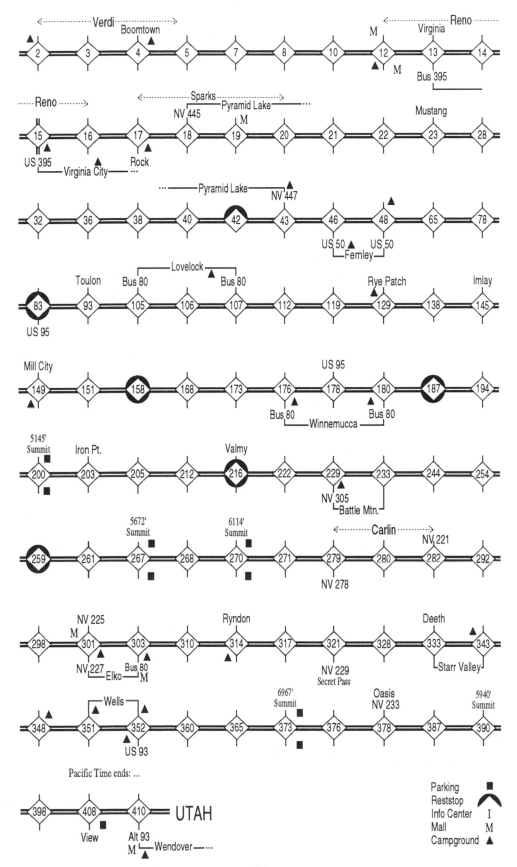

"SALT FLATS in SPRING RUNOFF, SILVER ISLAND in DISTANCE
Photo credit: John A. Kost

Utah

The Beehive State

The "Beehive" symbolizes "industry," hard work. Exactly what it took to settle this state! Utah is a very unique state in geology, geography, history and religion. It spans from the desolate desert of the "Salt Flats" in the West to the beautiful high peaks of the Wasatch and Uinta Ranges in the East. The Salt Lake Valley and the Salt Flats are NOT below sea level as expected, but are a giant basin on a 4000 foot plateau. Utah's lowest point is NOT on the Salt Flats but at Beaver Dam (2200 feet) in the North. Western Utah is the same Basin-Range area as Nevada where in ancient times large blocks of land tilted up and formed crests of mountains oriented North and South. Prehistoric Lake Bonneville has it's Western edge on the Eastern side of Silver Zone Pass in Nevada where I-80 crosses the railroad. It's remnant is the Great Salt Lake. I-80 stays in the basin and skirts around the North side of three ranges, the Cedar Mountains, Stansbury Mountains, and the Oquirrh Mountains.

Lake Bonneville was a Pleistocene fresh water lake that covered 20,000 square miles in Nevada, Utah and Idaho, with the site of Salt Lake City under 900 feet of water. If you watch carefully you will recognize benches/terraces along the edges of the ranges, that indicate ancient shores of receding Lake Bonneville. The remaining Salt Lake is 92 miles long and 48 miles wide. It is shallow with an average depth of 10 to 20 feet and a maximum depth of 42 feet. Utah's streams carry minerals from the mountains to the Salt Lake Basin. As there is no outlet to the sea, the water evaporates increasing the concentration of the minerals from 5 to 15 per cent. That's 6 times saltier than the ocean! Only the Dead Sea is saltier.

The Wasatch, dotted with popular ski resorts, is the range just East of Salt Lake City through which you will climb in your Eastbound journey. Skiers prize this area for its dry powdered snow. The Uintas in the Northeast are 150 miles long by 30 miles wide and contain 1400 glacial lakes. Twenty-four peaks in the Uintas are over 13,000 feet. When you are on Wyoming's I-80 you will see the snow-capped Uintas to the South.

But Utah has more that you won't see from I-80! In Southeastern Utah there are ranges from 3,000 to 13,000 feet where rivers, wind and rain have sculpted spectacular canyons, arches, and buttes. There are the magnificent "Arches National Monument" that dwarfs man, the piercing towers of "Monument Valley", and the brilliant red forms of "Bryce Canyon". Utah has fourteen National Parks, Monuments, and Recreation Areas! All are worth a visit! Maybe next trip?

Utah is our eleventh largest state with 84,990 square miles. It's population of 1,722,850 lives mostly along the Wasatch Front, the base of the mountains, where water is available for irrigation. Most Utah citizens are white-Anglo Saxon, descendants of the Latter-day Saints, the pioneers who came here seeking religious freedom. Gentiles came here to mine and in 1906 started the giant Bingham Canyon Mine, one of the world's largest copper mines. Agriculture, mining and now manufacturing keep the state stable.

Utah chose as its State flower the "Sego Lily", a lovely wild white lily. The root of this lily was the staple that kept some of the early settlers alive while waiting for their crops to mature. Utah's bird had to be the "California gull". Not a SEAGULL! The "California gull" migrates East/West, breeding in the basin and wintering along the Pacific Coast. Utah's tree is the "Blue Spruce", that perfectly formed cone-shaped tree. It's animal is the majestic "Rocky Mountain Elk". It's fish, that probably also helped the Mormons survive, the delicious "Rainbow trout".

Sego Lily

UTAH HISTORY

The first known inhabitants of Utah were the ancient "Anasazi". They lived on the sides of sandstone cliffs, climbed ladders to the top of the Mesas (table mountains) and tilled their corn, beans and squash. They disappeared in the 1300's for which scientists have a variety of explanations. Today, their fascinating homes and kivas (ceremonial rooms) remain all over Southern Utah, Arizona, Colorado and New Mexico. Nomatic Navahos roamed Southern Utah while the Shoshoni tribes inhabited Northern Utah, Nevada and Idaho. The Utes resided in the Northeastern and Central regions. Also a tribe of Shoshones, the Goshutes, the poorest of all the tribes, managed to survive in the dry basins.

Next came the Spanish, with Fathers Dominguez and Escalante exploring the Southern part of the state in 1776. They were told about the Great Salt Lake but they never saw it themselves. Then in the 1820's the demand for beaver felt hats brought the fur trappers from the North, among them Jim Bridger, Etienne Provost, Jed Smith and William Ashley. The first two DID see the Salt Lake in 1824-25. They penetrated the Uintas and the Wasatch Ranges where several fur-trading rendezvous were held. Jedediah Smith went Southward across Utah to California and almost died of thirst on his return trip across the unknown Salt Basin.

THE MORMONS

In far off New York state a young man searching for faith and truth unleashed a power that attracted thousands, marked the history of the nation, and gave birth to a new state. His name was Joseph Smith. He told of visits by an angel, "Moroni", who gave him some ancient records describing three migrations from the Middle East to America between 2,000 BC and 400 AD. Over several years he was able to transcribe these plates and to write "The Book Of Mormon". His brother and many others quickly joined him. Since they had been given these Christian teachings by the angel "in these latter days" and since St. Paul had called Christians "Saints", they called themselves "The Latter Day Saints" or "LDS". In 7 years Joseph Smith had many followers but also incurred the animosity of his neighbors. So the saga began! First they moved to Kirkland, Ohio, started their temple there, and spread out their missionaries. On to Missouri with more and more converts joining them. They dispersed missionaries to Europe. With their numbers increasing, fear of differences and too much power was a threat to others and they had to find somewhere else to go. Their anti-slavery views did not endear them to their fellow Southerners. They could not go West because that had been declared "Indian Territory" where Americans were forbidden to settle. The government was clearing all of the Indian tribes from East of the Mississippi to the West as the "permanent solution". At that time, West of the Mississippi was thought to be all desert wasteland, uninhabitable by whites, fit only for "savages".

In 1838 while Joseph Smith was being held in jail in Missouri, Brigham Young, a member of the Council of Twelve Apostles, led the Saints to Illinois. They were able to purchase some swampy land which they drained and reclaimed. They had to start all over again. They called their city "Nauvoo the Beautiful" and by 1841 they had built a new temple. Joseph Smith, escaped from his Missouri jail, had talked the state of Illinois into giving him a charter for his new city that left him in full political power. He even had his own newspaper, army and police force. His followers accepted this because an integral part of their dogma was obedience to the church and they wanted protection from the non-believers. But again all of this power frightened the "Gentiles" so that in 1844 Joseph Smith ended up in the county jail at Carthage, IL. A mob gathered, shots were fired, and both Joseph Smith and his brother, Hyrum, were killed.

The next year was very hard as persecution of the Saints continued. Mormon homes and crops were burned. Violence surrounded them! They had to leave, so careful plans were made to begin the trek West through Iowa and Nebraska. They were to leave as soon as the weather warmed and the Spring grass was high enough for cattle feed. However things became so violent that they began leaving in February 1846, crossing the Mississippi still in winter's grasp. Unable to sell their homes and goods, they had to leave most of their possessions. They endured terrible hardships, many dying along the way. They stopped along both sides of the Missouri River and Omaha became their "Winter Quarters".

The Mormons planned and prepared for the greatest (and certainly the best organized) migration in history. Their destination was the Salt Lake Valley, unsettled by anyone; even the Native Americans shunned it. It had been surveyed in 1843 by Fremont's Topographical Expedition, the accounts of which were carefully studied by the Elders of the church. In 1847 the first contingent of skilled, specially chosen male pioneers led the way preparing the trail for the thousands to follow. When they reached the Wasatch Mountains, Parley's Canyon was blocked (today's I-80), so they entered the valley through Emigration Canyon just to the North. Brigham Young became ill and was delayed in the mountains. But even before he had arrived the advance contingent had dug irrigation ditches and planted crops. By the end of the summer there were 2,000 Saints in the Salt Lake Valley and they continued to arrive the following years.

There was a great plague of locusts in 1848! The Saints had tried everything they knew to fight them. A cloud of these insects were destroying every living blade of grain in sight. This new settlement, 1,000 miles from anywhere, would perish without a harvest. When all their efforts to kill the locusts had failed, they gathered to pray for deliverance from this scourge. Suddenly a great flock of California gulls descended, devouring the locusts and saving the remainder of the crops. You can see the statue to the gull in Temple Square, Mileposts 117. The Mormons survived through backbreaking work and low rations! In 1850 this became the "Utah Territory", but because of difficulties with the U.S. Government, particularly concerning polygamy and church political control, statehood was delayed.

Converts from Europe were encouraged to come to the new land. Many were very poor and did not have the price of a wagon and oxen. In 1856 the first group of 1500 Europeans arrived at the end of the railroad in Iowa City, Iowa Milepost 240. This migration was as well-planned as the first. With the guidance of Saints from Salt Lake City, they built 6-foot hand-carts into which they loaded their most essential supplies and pulled them over the plains and mountains to the new Zion. Incredibly the first two contingents were quite successful, making the trip in comparable time to the wagon trains. The third band began too late and was caught in the Wyoming winter where many froze to death in the snows of South Pass. Their troubles were not over when they arrived in Utah. Many were sent to Southern Utah to establish new colonies where

SALT LAKE CITY
Photo credit: Utah Travel Council/Capitol Hill

they struggled to survive while they developed their fields, eating roots and grasses to sustain them. You will read more of the story of the Mormon migration as you travel Eastward on I-80.

The power struggle and mistrust that had plagued the Saints in the East followed them here. In 1857 President Buchanan sent the US army in to settle the conflict between the Mormons and the Gentiles. Known as the "Mormon War", it never really materialized. The Mormons "fought" them obliquely by cutting their supplies and making them think that in Echo Canyon, Milepost 168-185 they were surrounded by Mormon troops. At any rate compromises were made and the war was over before it began.

Salt Lake City was the site of the joining of the East and West telegraph lines. (Telegraph Office on Main Street.) In the 1860's the Central Pacific Railroad inched Eastward from California, while the Union Pacific feverishly pushed its tracks Westward from Omaha, NE. They met just North of Salt Lake City at Promontory Point in May 1869, Milepost 117. By that time there were already some 60,000 Mormons in Utah. The railroad brought an end to Utah's isolationism since it was so much easier for the dreamers and the opportunists to travel West. As more Gentiles arrived in the 1970's a new political party and a rival newspaper were born. Finally in 1889 the first Gentiles were elected to office. The church owned businesses, and some of the church leaders had plural marriages, so this more than anything else led to opposition. Finally the church ended the polygamy and sold its businesses and in January 1896 Utah became the 45th state to join the union. There are other churches in Utah today, but the Church of Latter Day Saints is still most predominant.

Salt Lake City is the capital of Utah. It's the only state capitol, and the only state, founded by a single religion and also organized, settled, and governed by it for many years. The Pilgrims, Puritans and the Quakers began such colonies but were quickly diluted by other religions. It was a disciplined and dedicated people who shared their talents and materials for the freedom to practice their religion. Individually they could never have survived in this terrain and climate. Together they could whip any odds. This was a social innovation that succeeded! Today, Salt Lake City, by far the largest city in the state, is the "Crossroads of the West."

UTAH MILEPOSTS

UTAH HIGHWAY PATROL: 801-965-4505
UTAH ROAD CONDITIONS: 801-964-6000 SALT LAKE AREA. ELSEWHERE: 1-800-752-7600
UTAH TRAVEL COUNCIL: 801-538-1030

TELEPHONE AREA CODE FOR ALL OF UTAH: 801.

MILEPOSTS:

2   **WENDOVER/BUS 80/NV 58: TIME CHANGE: PACIFIC TIME/MOUNTAIN TIME**
S & D SUPERMARKET on the East/Utah side of town.
See Nevada Milepost 410 for services in Wendover.

EASTBOUND: You're heading out across the Salt Flats! Milepost 4 will be your last Fuel, Food, Ice and Water for 66 miles, until Milepost 70, Delle. Little else until Salt Lake City at Milepost 115. Be prepared!

WESTBOUND: Exit here on Bus 80 for all services. You will find almost no services for 58 miles ahead until Wells, NV. As you drive up the hill see the giant cowboy waving you into the Stateline-Silversmith Casino that spans the road? That's the border of Nevada! Motels and restaurants are listed under Nevada Milepost 410. Be sure to go to the Nevada Welcome Center just over the hill on your Left across from the Peppermill. Get your Nevada maps there, picnic, let the kids exercise on the playground equipment.

MOTELS/HOTEL: Stateline-Silversmith Inn, Bonneville*, Heritage, Motel 6*, Western*.

CAMPGROUND: "Stateline RV": Private For RV's only: South one block East of Stateline Casino. Showers and laundry. Pool and spa in hotel.

BONNEVILLE SPEEDWAY MUSEUM: At the far Eastern edge of town at the bottom of the hill on the South. A small new museum exhibiting some of the cars that have broken world speed records on the Bonneville Racetrack. Beautifully restored cars and a film on "Golden Rod", a race car with an interesting history. Also a 1906 inlaid grand piano, a sleigh, early slot machines, record players, bathtub and doll collection. Fee.

SIDE TRIP OVER SILVER ISLAND LOOP

FOR THE ADVENTURESOME: If you're a history buff and have a pickup, you can take the two-hour Silver Island Loop. Go North along a rocky road through the historic "Silver Island Gap" traveled by the Donner Party and others. INQUIRE LOCALLY BEFORE ATTEMPTING!

4   **BONNEVILLE SPEEDWAY:**
FUEL AND FOOD: Phillips Truck Stop/Cafe/Mini Mart.

BONNEVILLE SPEEDWAY: Five miles to the Speedway where world speed records are made! This track is VERY smooth with none of the bumps in the salt that you see from I-80. If you're here in August you might get to see some of the action. First the cars submitted are "qualified" to determine into which class each vehicle is most suitable. Then the races for each class are conducted. Bring your own shade and refreshments. There are absolutely NO facilities of any kind there.

MILEPOST 10 REST AREAS: VIEWPOINT OF SALT FLATS AND BONNEVILLE. Do stop and experience the Salt and walk up the ramp for a great view. To the North here is the extensive "Newfoundland Evaporation Basin" where the Salt Flats are mined for Potash. To the South are Government test ranges. Also note the "Bonneville Limited Potash Plant", a sub-sidiary of Kaiser Aluminum.

THE SALT BEARS: Wendover tells the story passed on by a Pony Express rider, of savage Salt Bears that killed and ate the riders and their horses, but only when the moon was full. However the baby Salt Bears are gentle and love children and bring them good luck.

MILEPOST 27 METAPHOR, THE TREE OF UTAH: Sculpture by Karl Momen just North of the Westbound lanes. This is an 87-foot high cement sculpture slightly resembling a saguaro cactus, with massive cement balls, some "broken" and lying on the ground. It cost $1.5 million to construct. The six balls of the tree are tiled with Utah rock and minerals. The broken ones on the ground symbolize the tree changing with the seasons. No stopping, so look while you can.

In the 1950's to 1960's the highway through the salt flats used to be littered with tires, hoses and fan belts from cars that overheated and broke down. Now it seems to be bottle-throwing time! Along the salt flats notice the base of the fence posts and the telephone poles. The salt water permeates the wood. As the water evaporates, the salt expands and the wood fibers split, creating posts with splintered bases. If it's a hot summer day you'll see a shimmering of what appears to be water on the road ahead. This is a "mirage", an illusion due to the air close to the highway being less dense than the air above it. Hills such as "Silver Island" to the North appear to be floating in a lake. Some call it "Floating Island". As the Donner Party struggled over the Salt Flats on Hasting's Cutoff, they headed for Silver Island and the gap through it that led to Pilot Peak and WATER.

41 **KNOLLS:** NO NEAR SERVICES!

These gypsum sand dunes mark the Eastern end of the 40-mile salt flats. Now the road rises from the flats for forty more miles of desert to the East! As the Donner-Reed Party crossed the salt flats, the heat and the thirst were terrible. Oxen went insane and charged off into the desert. Thirty-six oxen died and wagons were abandoned. The lips and noses of men and animals were caked with salt. James Reed and William Eddy went ahead to the springs at Pilot Peak (found by Kit Carson and noted in Fremont's writings) and returned 20 to 40 miles with water. Near Silver Island they left Grandma Keye's fancy over-sized wagon. It was found there in 1927 and taken to Donner Lake State Park, but no one seems to know where it is today. When men and animals reached Silver Island they rested in its shade and some died there. Henry Bloom called it, "Rock of Misery" and noted it as "65 miles out".

49 **CLIVE:** NO NEAR SERVICES!

MILEPOST 55 REST AREAS: NO RESTROOMS! PARKING ONLY!

THE DONNER-REED TRAIL: Exit for a great view of the desert, the Knolls and Pilot Peak to the West. Also a good place to get some exercise. The Eastbound Rest Area has a trail up into the rocks for a Westward view. Pilot Peak with its springs is the highest mountain you see to the West. In front of it is "Silver Island", and to the Right of that, "Crater Island." Now pretend you are a member of the Donner Party and sight your trail through that lower dip on Silver Island to Pilot Peak. Now look to the Southeast to the Cedar Mountains composed of Late Paleozoic limestone, quartzite and dolomite. Hasting's Cutoff went over these mountains right where you might be able to see a dirt road going up to a mine. Now trace with your eyes the possible trail heading West from there and crossing I-80 going toward Pilot Peak. Visualize the Donners struggling with their heavy wagons and thirsty oxen. Want to try it walking? There used to be a cement monument near the wagon tracks about 50 feet North of Highway 40 before I-80 was completed.

56 **ARAGONITE:** NO NEAR SERVICES!

A dirt road South from here goes to an Aragonite mine and then East over "Hastings Pass" over the Cedar Mountains. It is not passable today. Now you are traveling up around the North end of the Cedar Mountains and just South of the Lakeside Mountains. Then across Skull Valley with more flat salty desert.

62 **MILITARY AREA/LAKESIDE:** NO NEAR SERVICES!

70 **DELLE:**

FUEL: Gas & Diesel. There used to be a sign telling you "Last chance for gas before the Salt Flats." The road was first built across these salt flats after World War I.

77 **ROWLEY:** ELEVATION: 4226 FEET. NO NEAR SERVICES!

The road to the North goes to "Timpie Springs Waterfowl Management Area". This is alive with ducks and geese during the migrations. In the summer, the area is closed to visitors to protect the nesting birds. To the North notice the piles of processed salt and the salt ponds. This is the Western edge of the Great Salt Lake. It's surprising to see the water this far West! In the 1950's to 1970's there was no water until 27 miles East of here, past the Tooele exit near Black Rock. Rainfall and snow melt have increased in the last few years and caused year-round flooding of new areas. The road going South is to the Government "Dugway Proving Grounds" and to "Skull Valley Indian Reservation". The latter is the home of the Goshute Indians, a Shoshone tribe. Like the Paiutes they learned to survive in the hostile basins by eating everything from insects to birds, rodents, plants and roots.

But there is another history down this road. The Donner-Reed Party struggled South around the marshes to "Kanaka Ranch"/"Iosepa". They found a note from Hastings who was perpetually and uselessly ahead of them. The note said that the desert/salt flats ahead would take two days and nights instead of one as he had said in his book. It took the Donner Party almost 6 days from the Kanaka Ranch, but first they had to climb 1,000 feet up "Hastings Pass" of the Cedar Mountains. Altogether it took them 9 days and several nights to cross 100 miles of this desert.

The Stansbury Mountains are to the South. Deseret Peak is 11,031 feet with a wilderness area and the Wasatch-Cache National Forest. Can you pick out the terraces of old Lake Bonneville? Stansbury is an anticline of Paleozoic rocks with light Cambrian on the crest.

84   GRANTSVILLE WEST/OLD US 40/UT 138: NO NEAR SERVICES!

I-80 had been only newly built here to bypass Grantsville when the rising waters of the Great Salt Lake reached out to inundate the land. So now you pass between pools of water, where it used to be farm land South of the road. Watch for waterfowl in all the ponds. On an overpass you'll have a good view of the American Salt Company pools. Water is let into blocks of land and is left to evaporate drawing up the salt from the desert leaving thick slabs on top of the ground. This is dozed up and refined. On the East side of the Stansbury Mountains you'll note that the strata has been tilted into a vertical position. There is a dolomite lime quarry and plant in these Paleozoic rocks.

88   GRANTSVILLE: ELEVATION: 4300 feet. NO NEAR SERVICES!

Explorers and pioneers camped at "20 Wells" ten miles South of I-80 for its springs. The Donner-Reed Party traveled from Tooele to "20 Wells" where poplars lined the road leading to the springs. A young man died of TB in Tamsen Donner's arms and was buried nearby. The Donners were relatively intact by the time they got here. This quiet farming town was settled in 1850 by the Mormons and named "Grantsville" after George D. Grant who saved them from the Indians. Many of the springs were capped to supply water for homes and irrigation.

DONNER-REED MEMORIAL MUSEUM: Ten miles South of I-80 on the Southwest corner of Cooley and Clark Streets. As you come into town you'll curve to the left to Clark Street. Go Right/West on Clark to Center Street. An old adobe building that served as school house and then city hall now houses Donner-Reed and Indian artifacts found on the salt flats. The problem is that it is not manned any certain hours and you have to search out someone to open it. One neighbor said that "It's only open between twelve and one on the day of a total eclipse of the sun." If you are determined to see it, call: Ruth Mathews 884-3348. Or ask at the City Building at Park and Main Streets (one block South and a couple blocks East) for someone to open it.

DESERET PEAK WILDERNESS AREA: FOR THE ADVENTURESOME! Try one of the 6 National Forest Campgrounds in South Willow Canyon 9 to 11 miles South of Grantsville. There are 15 and 20 foot RV Maximums here. Check locally for campgrounds and hiking trails.

99   TOOELE/STANSBURY/UT 36/UT 138: ELEVATION: 4400 FEET.
Named for Chief Tuilla, it is pronounced "Too-willa". All services are to the South of I-80.
FUEL: Texaco, '76 Truck Stop, Chevron.
FOOD: McDonalds, Texaco.
MOTEL/CAMPGROUND: Private. Oquirrh Motor Inn. Just South of exit. RV spaces from March to Oct. Also: S & W Trailer Park: No further information.
The Oquirrh Mountains, pronounced O-kwer, to the East are composed of a thick section of Late Paleozoic limestone, quartzite and dolomite like the Cedar Mountains. They have also been intruded (coming up from under the earth) with granite and folded and faulted (bent/split). Also note the terraces from ancient lake Bonneville and on these the Tufa formed by the lake as it receded. These are the same kind of formations that occur near Lovelock, NV. The "Stockton Bar" on the mountainside near Tooele is sand and gravel, left there by waves of the ancient sea.

MILEPOST 101 REST AREAS: VIEW OF GREAT SALT LAKE.

102   MAGNA/UT 202:

Eastbound in the 1950's to 1970's the first view of the Great Salt Lake was from this point. But the water was WAY out there. The big rock in front of you in the water is "Black Rock". Apparently it was well surrounded by water in 1849 when Captain Stansberry erected an observatory on it. He would lower beef from the rock into the salty water to make "Corned Beef". South of I-80 you'll see the Kennecott Copper Corp's Tailings Piles and against the hill the Copper Smelter. There used to be little cars dumping red hot tailings on the top of the pile, but Linde Gas Products are using the plant now.

EASTBOUND ALTERNATE ROUTE

TO BINGHAM COPPER MINE: The mine is 25 miles South of this exit. It is a sight you will never forget and may not have the chance to see again. Find your Salt Lake Area Map on the back of your Utah State Map. Exit here on UT 202 to Magna. South on UT 111 to UT 48 to "Bingham Canyon Mine". EASTBOUND: Return to I-80 via UT 48 to I-15 North. This is the world's largest open pit copper mine, "Kennicott Utah Copper". It is 2.5 miles wide and has a .5 mile deep terraced pit. There is a Visitor Center and a platform on which you can stand to view the drilling, blasting and loading. At one time, railroad cars carried the ore out. Now it is all trucked out. The electric shovels can scoop up 55 tons at a time yielding 12 pounds of copper per ton of ore. Gold and silver are found here along with the 200,000 tons of copper per year. April-Oct 8 AM to dusk. $2 per car. Copperton has a "Bingham Canyon Museum" at 301 East State Highway where you'll see cowboy relics and Indian and railroad exhibits.

MILEPOST 104 REST AREA: GREAT SALT LAKE STATE PARK/"SALTAIR RESORT":

Exit to the front of the domed Saltair building. Parking is limited. In 1992 the Park Visitor Center was located in a trailer to the West. The beach access is to the East. You can wade out and float on the lake. You are guaranteed not to sink!

The first Saltair Palace was built one mile out on pilings on the lake in 1893, accessible by open-air railroad car. Built by the Mormon Church it resembled a Moorish Palace, 1100 feet long with a restaurant, shops, funhouse and bathhouses and the world's largest ballroom on the second floor. It burned down in 1925 but was rebuilt in 1926 on the same foundation. Then times changed, the lake receded until it was some distance from the building, and the great domed edifice came into disuse and deteriorated. It was donated to the State of Utah in 1959, but remained neglected until it burned in 1970. Nostalgia took hold and the building was rebuilt on a new site closer to I-80 and opened in 1983.

In 1984 the lake rose 12 feet and flooded the new building. In the winter of 1986-87 there were very heavy snows in the Wasatch Range East of Salt Lake City and also in the other ranges. The lake filled to a record high of 4212.5 feet above sea level

SALTAIR
Photo credit: Utah Travel Council

and inundated 17 miles of I-80 from the Grantsville area past Saltair. In June the wind was high and the waves splashed 10 feet higher on the building. Water came within an inch of inundating the Salt Lake City Airport just East of here. A protective levee was built beside the lake and I-80 was elevated. With all this water the salinity level is now only 5.5%. In 1981 with the lake at a 4200 foot level, salinity was 23%. In the record low-level year of 1963, salinity was 27%. Prior to 1986 brine shrimp was the only life that could be sustained in the salty water of the lake. It was harvested as tropical fish food. Then with the high waters of 1986 and the resulting lower salinity, the "Rain Water Killey", a fresh water fish, washed in. Only time will tell how long it will survive here.

Three giant Aqua Pumps have now been installed 12 miles West of Lakeside to prevent future flooding.

The Salt Lake had its share of supernatural stories including a monster with a gigantic head that stuck its head up out of the lake and bellowed. Tales were also told of whirlpools and a subterranean outlet to the Pacific.

111 NOT OPEN IN 1992:

113 UT 172 SOUTH/5600 WEST: NO NEAR SERVICES!

115 AIRPORT/40TH WEST/NORTH TEMPLE/TEMPLE SQUARE:
Take 40th West to North Temple for services:
FUEL: Rainbow gas, Cash Saver Gas, Circle K.
FOOD: Apollo Burger, Burger King, Kentucky Fried Chicken (KFC), Dennys, and Pioneer Pies (5th or 6th West), Dee's Family, Honey's.
MOTELS: Days Inn, Comfort Inn, Raddison, Se Rancho*, Scotty's Travel*, Village Inn, Travelodge, Continental, Overnight*, Motel 6*, Chateau*.
EASTBOUND CAMPGROUNDS: "KOA": Private. 1400 West North Temple. Right on North Temple for 3.5 miles. Pool. $15-$22.
"Camp VIP": Private. 1350 North Temple. Right on North Temple for 3.5 miles. Pool. $14-$18.
PICNIC AREA: Hidden in the maze of freeways and streets is the famous Jordan River. The Donner Party camped here on September 3rd, over one month from Ft. Bridger, WY. You will cross over the Jordan on I-80 between I-215 & I-15 or on North Temple. 900 West will take you from North Temple, South to Jordan Park where you can picnic where history lies. The International Peace Park is also there. Or just drive North on North Redwood Road from North Temple to the Parkway which borders the Jordon River.

117 M A J O R   I N T E R C H A N G E !
REDWOOD ROAD/I-215: NORTH TO OGDEN. SOUTH TO PROVO.
REDWOOD ROAD, SALT LAKE CITY/TEMPLE SQUARE: ELEVATION: 4390 FEET.
EXIT ON REDWOOD ROAD FOR DOWNTOWN: North on Redwood to North Temple to either Left or Right for FUEL, FOOD, MOTELS. Right on North Temple for CAMPGROUNDS. Read Milepost 115. FOR TEMPLE SQUARE: Right on North Temple Street. Read "Salt Lake City" tours and sights below.

EAST BOUND ALTERNATE ROUTE

TO PROMONTORY POINT, LOGAN, BEAR LAKE: If you have already been East on I-80 through the Wasatch and Echo Canyon you might want to see new country. Go North on I-215/I-15 to just North of Brigham City. Take Exit 368 off I-15 and onto UT 83 to "Promontory Point", the site of the meeting of the Central and the Union Pacific Railroads, May 10, 1869. This is where the Golden Spike was driven. Visitor Center, 6-mile auto tour, and a 1.5 mile trail. $3 per car. Then back to Brigham City, South on I-15 to Exit 364 to get onto US 89. This highway goes through some beautiful country to Logan and up to Bear Lake. Although scenic it does get steep and twisty. You should find many RV parks and campgrounds between Logan and Bear Lake with swimming and fishing on the lake. From Bear Lake go East on UT 30 to East on US 30 to "Fossil Butte National Monument" joining I-80 at Wyoming Milepost 66 just before Little America. Read about Fossil Butte in Wyoming Milepost 18.

SALT LAKE CITY

The city streets are extra wide because the Mormons wanted plenty of room in which to turn their oxen teams around. The streets were carefully laid out with the Temple the very center of town. On the North side of the Temple is North Temple Street, to the South, South Temple, to the West, West Temple. To the East it became "Main Street" when the Gentiles came. Main and State Streets are the main North/South streets. All streets North of North Temple are "North" streets, all South are "South" streets, West are "West" streets, East are "East" streets. There are many gas stations, motels, hotels, and restaurants especially on both North and South Temple and on Main and State Streets with which you will soon become quite familiar.

Your first stop in Salt Lake City should be Temple Square via North Temple Street. Parking is provided in three large lots on the North side of North Temple (North of Temple Square) between West Temple and 200 East Street. If you have an RV you'll want to go to their special "RV Park Place". They have 60 foot long parking spaces for RVs for just $2. Going East on North Temple Street turn Right onto 300 West Street/UT 186 and go just one block. Then turn Left onto South Temple Street and you'll see the large lot and RV's to your Left.

SALT PALACE/VISITOR INFORMATION: Corner of South Temple/West Temple across the Street from the RV Park Place. Get your important MAP OF THE CITY, a current "Utah Guide" and other information here. They have walking and driving tours.

TEMPLE SQUARE: Entrance on South side. If you don't have your City Map and information, ask at the entrance. The free Tour of Temple Square is rather extensive. You might want to start with a tour and then just walk through parts yourself. Completed in 1867 the Tabernacle is especially impressive for its excellent acoustics. A pin drop can actually be heard in the back of the hall!

Organ recitals: Mon-Sat noon-12:30pm.
Youth Chorus Rehearsal: Tues 8-9:30pm.
Youth Symphony Rehearsal: Wed 8-9:30pm.
Choir Rehearsal: Thur 8-9:30pm.
Choir Broadcast: Sunday enter at 9am.

BEEHIVE HOUSE: Walk East on South Temple past Brigham Young's monument. A MUST! This is Brigham Young's original home. They conduct a great tour with many fascinating details. Mon-Sat 9:30-4:30pm. Sun 10-1pm. Free. Spanning State Street out front is the "Eagle Gate" which used to be the entrance to Brigham Young's farm. On top is a 4,000-pound Eagle with a 20-foot wingspread.

LION HOUSE: Just West of Beehive House. This is another Brigham Young house with a tour of the furnished upstairs rooms.

HANSEN'S PLANETARIUM AND MUSEUM: Diagonally across the street from Beehive House. Museum is free. Star Chamber shows are $3. Take a trip to the planets or enjoy some other star show. Adult $3. Senior $2.50. Child $2.

GENEALOGICAL LIBRARY: 50 North Temple. Want to research your ancestors? It's all here!

A DRIVING TOUR: Ready to sit now? Drive North up the hill on State Street.

BEEHIVE HOUSE/SALT LAKE CITY
Utah Travel Council Hall/Capitol Hill

OLD CITY HALL: West side of State Street. This is a Visitor Information Center and exhibits furniture and paintings from the 1860's.

STATE CAPITOL: The copper-domed building in front of you has exhibits and murals on the walls and ceilings.

PIONEER MEMORIAL MUSEUM: 300 North Main, just West of the Capitol. Doll collections, furniture and handmade textiles and other memorabilia from earliest times to 1869. The "Carriage House" has period vehicles and farm machinery including Brigham Young's covered wagon. Donations.

MARMALADE HISTORIC DISTRICT: A block to the North. Ask for self-guiding map at the Museum above. Many original pioneer homes that demonstrate the way the pioneers were able to use local materials.

ZIONS COOPERATIVE: South on Main between South Temple and First South. The first department store in the West was built and owned by the Mormons but sold later. Note its cast-iron facade.

EXCHANGE PLACE HISTORIC DISTRICT: Between 3rd and 4th South. This used to be a major financial district at the turn of the century and has nine neoclassic structures.

DRIVE PAST TURN OF CENTURY HOMES: Drive slowly East on South Temple Street.

GOVERNOR'S MANSION: 603 South Temple. Originally the "Thomas Kearns Mansion".

CATHEDRAL OF THE MADELEINE: 331 East South Temple Street. The land was donated by the Mormon Church to the Catholic Church and the Cathedral was built by the first Catholic Bishop of Salt Lake City. Spanish style with Venetian mosaics, Tennessee and Utah marble and oak. Daily 8-7:30pm.

UNIVERSITY OF UTAH: East on South Temple.

UTAH MUSEUM OF FINE ARTS: A Rubens, Louis XIV furniture and 17th Century tapestries.

NATURAL HISTORY MUSEUM: Dinosaurs, animals, birds and minerals.

ARBORETUM CENTER: Ask for a self-guiding tour.

SOUTH ON FOOTHILL DRIVE TO A LEFT ON SUNNYSIDE AVENUE.

PIONEER TRAIL STATE PARK and EMIGRATION CANYON: This is where the Mormons first entered the valley. There is a monument here and a large mural of the Mormon migration. Also "Old Deseret" is a recreated pioneer village of 1847-1869 with original homes from dugouts and adobe to Brigham Young's farm home.

PIONEER TRAIL STATE PARK
Photo credit: Utah Travel Council

HOGLE ZOOLOGICAL GARDENS: 2600 Sunnyside, near Pioneer Trail State Park. Great zoo with 1,000 animals and birds in natural habitat. Children's zoo. Summer 9-6pm. Spring & Fall 9-5pm. Winter 9-4:30pm.

If you're heading East from here, go South on Foothill to I-80.

MORE SIGHTS AROUND THE CITY: Try back down town again:

UTAH HISTORY MUSEUM: South on State Street to 2nd South Street. Turn West/Right about six blocks to a Left on Rio Grande. Collection of over 3,000 objects. Emphasis is on the various ethnic groups that settled Utah.

INTERNATIONAL PEACE GARDENS: 100 West/1000 South. From the museum go South about five blocks to a Right turn onto 9th South Street. Go West about four blocks to turn Left onto 900 West Street. A garden for each country. May-Sept daily 8-5pm. Free. Jordan Park is also here.

TROLLEY SQUARE: Go East to 6th East Street. It's between 5th South and 6th South. A unique shopping center originally an old trolley barn built in 1908 by E.H. Harriman (the Union Pacific Railroad Magnate). Some shops are in trolley cars. The stained-glass windows and antique lighting fixtures add to the Victorian atmosphere.

PIONEER CRAFT HOUSE: 3271 South 500 East Street. For lovely handmade quilts, needlework and other articles. Lovely things for gifts. Mon-Fri 9-3pm. Free.

LIBERTY PARK: 13th South Street/5th East Street. The park has picnicking and a swimming pool. "Tracy Aviary" is 11 acres with hundreds of birds. On summer weekends they have a "Free Flight" bird show.

120   M A J O R   I N T E R C H A N G E !

I-15: NORTH TO OGDEN. SOUTH TO PROVO.

EASTBOUND: To stay on I-80 watch the signs CAREFULLY and follow the I-80 signs South on I-15 to a maze of overpasses and the exit of I-80 Eastward.

WESTBOUND: To stay on I-80 watch signs CAREFULLY. Unusual traffic design here!

EXITS ON I-15/I-80:

MILEPOST 310 WESTBOUND: *CITY CENTER, TEMPLE SQUARE.* You'll exit onto 6th Street and go about three blocks to 300 West Street/US 89. Turn Left and go North to North Temple Street. For parking, walking and driving tours read "Salt Lake City" above. **MOTEL:** Motel 6*.

MILEPOST 309:

MILEPOST 308: FUEL: Flying J Travel Plaza.

WESTBOUND: Watch I-80 signs here! You'll be joining I-15 for three miles. Keep in the center lane until signs say otherwise.

WESTBOUND ALTERNATE ROUTE

TO KENNICOTT COPPER'S BINGHAM CANYON MINE: Go South on I-15 to UT 48. West on UT 48 to Bingham. North on UT 111 and UT 201 & 202 to I-80 at Milepost 102. Read Milepost 102. Check your Salt Lake City Area Map.

SIDETRIP TO TIMPANOGOS CAVE

FOR THE ADVENTURESOME: South on I-15 to East on UT 92 up the American Fork Canyon. About 30 miles total. Three joined limestone caverns with beautiful formations. The lime in solution has dripped for centuries forming frozen "falls", cascades and stalactites. National Forest Campgrounds nearby. Visitor Center at the trailhead. You must hike 1.5 miles up a 1,000-foot trail, so this is not for shirkers. Great views from the road and the trail.

121   M A J O R   I N T E R C H A N G E !
EASTBOUND: I-80 LEAVES I-15 SOUTH AND TURNS EASTWARD:
WESTBOUND: I-80 ENTERS I-15 NORTH:

122   300 WEST STREET:

124   STATE STREET:
    FUEL: Shell has diesel.
    CAMPGROUND: "Ideal Trailer Park". South to 2855 South State Street.

125   7TH EAST STREET/UT 71:
    FUEL: Shell, Texaco.
       PIONEER HOUSE AND ARBORETUM: South here several blocks to a Right on 3300 South Street.

126   13TH STREET EAST/SUGAR HOUSE/UT 181:   WESTMINSTER COLLEGE.
    FOOD: "Chuck-a-Rama", A favorite I-80 restaurant. South on 13th Street to the second light. Left on Highland Drive about three blocks to Chuck-a-rama on your Right with a covered-wagon out front. Different type of menu every day. Beautifully presented. Opens daily at 11-4pm for lunch, 4-9pm for dinner. Large rigs park carefully in rear or on sidestreet as the lot fills quickly.

127   UT 195 SOUTH:

128   M A J O R   I N T E R C H A N G E !
FOOTHILL DRIVE/UT 186 North into Salt Lake City.
I-215 BELT SOUTH/WASATCH BLVD:
WATCH SIGNS CAREFULLY TO STAY ON I-80.
      UNIVERSITY OF UTAH/UNIVERSITY MEDICAL CENTER
        North on UT-186, Foothill, Right on Wasatch, Right on Medical Drive.

WESTBOUND ALTERNATE ROUTE

    TOUR OF SALT LAKE CITY: You can begin your visit to the sights in Salt Lake City from this exit. (Read Milepost 117 above.) Go North on UT 186/Foothill Drive and begin with "Hoogle Zoo", "Pioneer Trail State Park" and "Emigration Canyon". Ask for a Salt Lake City map and brochures here. Then continue North to the "University of Utah". From there go West on South Temple into the downtown area. You will note that you are taking the "Driving Tour" in Milepost 117 in reverse.

130   WESTBOUND TO I-215 SOUTH: ELEVATION: 5,000 FEET.
    EASTBOUND: I-80 now goes up one of its steepest climbs and into the Wasatch Mountains. In 10 miles it rises 2,000 feet. Signs say 3% and 6% grade. Some cars pulling trailers vapor-lock on this grade. Turn off your air conditioner to keep your vehicle from overheating. This area is beautiful year round whether it's snow-covered in winter, alive with wildflowers in the spring or flaming with reds, oranges and yellows in the fall.

131   RANCH EXIT: NO NEAR SERVICES!

132   RANCH EXIT: NO NEAR SERVICES!

133   RANCH EXIT: NO NEAR SERVICES!

134 UT 65: MOUNTAIN DALE RECREATION AREA:

WESTBOUND ALTERNATE ROUTE
WESTBOUND ENTRANCE TO SALT LAKE CITY VIA EMIGRATION CANYON: If you have the time to spare you may want to experience the Mormons' first entrance into the valley. Take this UT 65 North to its intersection with Emigration Canyon and enter Salt Lake City from there. Begin your tour of Salt Lake City with "Pioneer Trail State Park." Read Milepost 117 and reverse the direction of the tour. When the Donner Party went down Emigration Canyon, large boulders blocked the way and they had to go over the hills. But when the advance Mormon party arrived here, they were experienced road builders. Their lead work party cleared the boulders and built a road. They arrived in the Salt Lake Valley just 111 days after leaving Omaha, NE. An erroneous concept is of Brigham Young not knowing where they were going until he sighted the valley and said "This is the Place!" They had studied maps and writings of the explorers carefully to find a place beyond "Indian Territory" where they would be isolated from those who had different religious beliefs.

137 LAMB'S CANYON: NO NEAR SERVICES!

140 PARLEY'S SUMMIT: Summit Park. ELEVATION: 7,000 FEET.
  WESTBOUND: Ahead is a 6% downgrade for ten miles. If you're pulling a trailer, be prepared. In ten miles you'll go from the Wasatch Mountains onto the desert valley of the Great Salt Lake.

143 SKI AREA/RANCH EXIT: NO NEAR SERVICES!
  WESTBOUND: This is a deceivingly hard climb up to Parley's Summit. If it's a hot day and you're pulling a heavy load, turn off your air conditioning until Milepost 140.

145 PARK CITY/PARK WEST/DEER VALLEY/UT 224: Visitor information here.
  FACTORY OUTLET STORES.
  FUEL: Chevron, Citco, Texaco.
  FOOD: McDonalds, Arbys, Dennys, Hardees.
  MOTEL: Best Western.
  CAMPGROUND: "Hidden Haven": Private. North of I-80. It appears too close to the road, but after you enter, you'll see that you can go behind this camp, down the hill and into a lovely green campground next to a gurgling creek. $9-$13.

SIDETRIP TO PARK CITY
  UT 224 goes South to Park City, a famous winter ski resort area. The town began in the last century with silver mining. There is a museum on main street in the old City Hall and you can walk through a mine tunnel, a jail and a dungeon. Free. There are many motels, hotels, cafes, shops. Since this is a resort area you might find them expensive. Summer prices are lower. Alpine Prospector Lodge and Budget Lodging are less. The "Imperial Hotel" is on the National Registry of Historical Places. Hot air balloon rides for $150.
  ALPINE SLIDE: Ride a gondola to the top and a special sled down. Riders control the speed. $3.50.

MILEPOST 147 REST AREAS:

148 MAJOR INTERCHANGE!
  US 40 EAST TO HEBER CITY/DENVER: WEATHER RADIO: 1320 AM.
    FUEL: Sinclair Truck Stop.

EASTBOUND ALTERNATE ROUTE
  TO DINOSAUR NATIONAL MONUMENT AND FLAMING GORGE: If you have been on I-80 before and would like a nice scenic alternate route, go East on US 40 to Heber City and Vernal, UT. Return to I-80 by going North on US 191 to Rock Springs and I-80 at Wyoming Milepost 99. Heber City was founded in 1859. The recreated Frontier town has wooden sidewalks, blacksmith shop, jail and Chinese laundry. Ride the "Heber Creeper Scenic Railroad" steam train ($10) to "Wasach Mountain State Park" and "Provo Canyon".

Many motels in Heber and Vernal and campgrounds along US 40. Now drive on to Vernal, Utah. Vernal has "Utah Pioneer Museum" and "National History Museum." Dinosaur National Monument is a fascinating place! Watch archeologists picking and carefully brushing the exposed dinosaur bones at the Visitor Center. Campground here also.

North then up over the Uintas to Flaming Gorge. Get a map on the gorge so that you'll know which exits to take to get the views, boat ramps and campgrounds. Read Wyoming Mileposts 91 and 99.

152 **RANCH EXIT:** Going through a nice canyon here! Notice the "conglomerate". This layer of jumbled rocks was subjected to heat and pressure over the centuries until they became cemented into solid rock. Also note the small towers on the North. They are of a harder rock, so the soft material around them eroded away and left these pillars standing.

EASTBOUND: You are seeing the first of the "snow-fences" used to keep the snow from drifting out over the highways and railroads. You'll be seeing them all across Wyoming.

156 **WANSHIP/KAMAS/ROCKPORT STATE PARK/US 189:** ELEVATION: 6100 FEET.
FUEL: Chevron.
FOOD: Spring Chicken Inn.
CAMPGROUND: "Juniper CG": Public. Rockport State. Park. Five miles South on US 189. Showers, fishing, boating. $8. Reservations: 800-284-CAMP. Also 8 primitive campgrounds with boating and swimming. $5.

EASTBOUND SCENIC ALTERNATE ROUTE

UP THE MIRROR LAKE HIGHWAY: FOR THE ADVENTURESOME! Almost 100 miles on US 189 and UT 150 to Evanston, Wyoming Milepost 5, and I-80. Utah considers this one of its most scenic highways! It's open from about Mid-June to Oct. The route is first through Kamas where you should check at the Ranger Station at 50 East Center. Phone: 783-4338. There might be a Maximum Vehicle Length. No motels in town but one B&B, "The Kamas Inn" (80 South Main, $25.) Cafes in town. From Kamas it's 65 miles of mountain meadows, cliffs and beautiful views to Mirror Lake and "Bald Mountain Pass" at 10,687 feet. Many campgrounds, hiking trails and major trailheads on this route. Campgrounds are limited to 20 and 25 foot RV lengths.

164 **COALVILLE:** ELEVATION: 5591 FEET.
FUEL: North to Flying W Travel Plaza. South to Chevron, Phillips, Texaco.
FOOD: Dean's Cafe.
MOTELS: Blonquist*, Moore Motel*.
CAMPGROUNDS: "Flying W RV Park": Private. West of road. A very pleasant place back from the highway in the trees. Opening under new management.

"Echo Park Resort": Private. On Echo Lake in grove of cottonwood trees. Into Coalville and Left in town to go around the East side of Echo Reservoir. Electricity, showers, water but no sewer hook-ups. Swimming, boating, fishing. Tents/RVs. Peaceful site with lots of birds. Office is in the front of the Restroom. Two camping loops and two sets of restrooms. Run by two retired educators. $6.75. Eastbound from the campground continue on North to I-80 North of Echo Lake at Milepost 169.

MILEPOSTS 166-168: VIEWPOINTS over privately owned Echo Reservoir.

168 **I-84 NORTH TO OGDEN:**
YOU ARE NOW AT THE BOTTOM OF ECHO CANYON: This is one of the oldest and most used trails: first by the Indians, then the trappers, the Donners, the Mormons, the Pony Express, the Overland Stage, the railroad, and old US 30 South. In the 1940's, cars had to drive very carefully down the narrow, twisty, potholed road. One man had four flats driving down this canyon. It required many years before I-80 had carved four lanes out of the steep canyon walls.

It took the Donner-Reed Party six days to traverse Echo Canyon to this point. The trail down Weber Canyon (I-84) was blocked by "Devil's Slide". The Harlan Young Party with Hastings had windlassed their wagons over the rocks, but the Donners were trapped. They found a message from Hastings (forever ahead of them) in the cleft of a stick by the trail. He warned them of the dangerous trail ahead, but advised no way out. They waited there five days while three men went ahead to catch up with Hastings to lead them out. They found him but he would not return to help. Actually Hastings was lost so much of the time himself that the route was disconnected, uncertain. The Donners went down East Canyon, UT 65, and had tried Emigration Canyon but big rocks blocked their way. Then on to try Mountain Dell Canyon and Parley's Canyon, now I-80. All were impassable so they crossed over Little Mountain into a lower part of Emigration Canyon and finally made it through. It had taken them a month from Fort Bridger down these Wasatch canyons.

169 **ECHO:** The Village of Echo has restored the "Echo Church House". Check it out to see if it is ready for viewing.

WESTBOUND: If you're looking for a campground you might want to exit here to go around the East side of Echo Lake and check out "Echo Resort". Read Milepost 164. You would rejoin I-80 at Milepost 164.

ECHO CANYON

EASTBOUND: You are entering the Western edge of Echo Canyon with its high pock-marked walls. Eagles nest up in the highest parts, but owls and swallows prefer a little lower down in those convenient holes. There was a Stage Station here in 1853 and the Pony Express had several Way Stations up the canyon. In Echo Canyon the Union Pacific Railroad achieved its Mile 1,000 from Omaha and celebrated. On a train trip down this canyon many years ago, an accommodating conductor pointed out and named the different formations. Perhaps he just made up those names. See if you can locate any of them, or label them yourself.

"Steamboat rocks", looks like the prow of a vessel.

"Sentinel Rock", a squared column.

"Bromley's Cathedral", a mile long with spires, pinnacles and domes.

"Pulpit Rock", a turret.

"Battlement Rocks", red sandstone. Maybe this was Castle Rock.

"Witches", thin belts of red, grey and yellow.

"Monument Rock", a hooded giant with a conical cap.

MILEPOST 170 REST AREA, ECHO JUNCTION WELCOME CENTER:

A MUST STOP! Get out and walk around and enjoy the grandeur of the canyon walls towering above you. You need to stretch your legs anyway! On the Eastbound side of I-80, walk up the trail to see the old 1857 Mormon War fortifications on the hill.

There are a lot of stories about Echo Canyon and "The Mormon War" in 1857. At the "Canyon Narrows" the Mormons piled rocks along the top edge of the canyon to roll down on General Johnson's Army. They tell their children that 50 Mormons marched around the top of the canyon walls to make it look like 1,000 men, and ladies entered the soldiers' camp bringing homecooked food to lighten their hearts.

WESTBOUND: Just stand out there and feel the magnitude and power of this canyon. You will want to stop here for a map of Utah and Salt Lake City and a "Utah Travel Guide". Make your decisions as to where you will stop tonight. If it is summer, it is cool and lovely in the Wasatch Mountains but very hot on the Salt Lake Desert. You might want to stop in the woods. Or you might want to spend the night in Salt Lake City and take in the many sights there. There's almost no place to stay from Salt Lake City to Wendover.

MILEPOST 173-179: Notice old US 30 South on the other side of the canyon. Some rocks from the canyon wall jutted out so far over the highway that trucks and trailers had to move out across the center line to get by them. Note the rock cliffs just above the railroad tracks. This is a conglomerate of stones cemented together over millions of years.

180 **EMORY:** NO NEAR SERVICES!

185 **RANCH EXIT:** NO NEAR SERVICES!

This is the East Gate to Echo Canyon that the trappers and pioneers noted. On the crest of a hill North of the railroad, is a red sandstone formation they called "Castle Rock" that crowns the summit. Look for the mouth of a cave 150 feet deep. When "Hastings Cut-off" left Bridger, it first came to "Cache Creek", then "Needles" and then Castle Rock.

WESTBOUND: Beginning of Echo Canyon. As you go down this canyon, try to visualize it as the narrow passage it was before the bulldozers cut I-80 through. The Donners were driving wagons down a pack trail traversed previously only by horses and mules. They hacked their way through, crossing and recrossing the creek between the rocks. The weary undisciplined Donners also rested another precious five days here. See Milepost 169 for the list of the rock-formations that you will see on your way down the canyon.

EASTBOUND: End of Echo Canyon and climbing again.

189 RANCH: NO NEAR SERVICES!

Lots of sheep grazing along these canyons. You'll often see the little "sheep-herders' wagons". As the Mormon advance party entered Echo Canyon in July 1847, they followed the narrow trail of the trappers and the errant Donner Party. More than just "get through" the canyon they blazed a trail for the thousands to follow. So a work party led the way, cutting down brush, moving boulders, laying down a passable roadbed. From 1846 to 1869, 60,000 Mormons came down this canyon. Pioneers got sick with "Mountain Fever". It might have been "Rocky Mountain Spotted Fever" or "Colorado Tick Fever". They had pains in the joints, headache, fever, sometimes delirium. It lasted several days. Brigham Young succumbed to it and was so weak that he had to be carried and was delayed from entering the valley.

193 WASATCH SUMMIT: ELEVATION: 6850 FEET. NO NEAR SERVICES!

198 UTAH BORDER: NO NEAR SERVICES!

EASTBOUND: Entering Wyoming and the High Plains!

WESTBOUND: Entering Utah, beautiful Echo Canyon and the Wasatch Mountains. Read Milepost 169 ahead of time so that you know about the rock formations of Echo Canyon.

UTAH I 80 MILEPOSTS

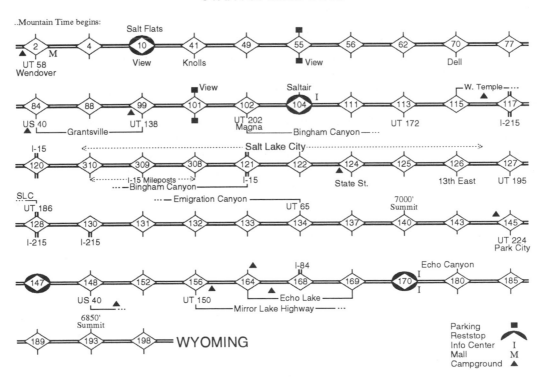

VEDAUWOO

"A magnificent placing of gargantuan sized Ice Age rocks awaits the traveler along I-80 between Cheyenne and Laramie. Known as Vedauwoo Glen, the large rocks were believed to have been "earth spirits" by the Arapaho Indians native to the area. The Indians thought that their god piled the rocks and make the trees and other flora specifically for them, as a place of worshop. The Arapaho people were noted for fighting other tribes over maintaining the sanctity of the area."

Photo credit and quote: Wyoming Division of Tourism

Wyoming

The Equality State

Wyoming calls itself the Equality State, but the other 49 states think of Wyoming as "The Cowboy State", the REAL WEST. Wyoming was the first state to give women the right to vote and the men of Wyoming would not accept statehood until the U.S. GUARANTEED that it would not interfere with women's voting rights.

Wyoming is too big and beautiful to describe in words. You have to experience it with the clean sweet air blowing in your face, the expanse of land and bright blue sky above you, the antelope running wild and free, the eagle high on a rock, the coyote trotting casually across the desert and the acres of wildflowers! You can't just DRIVE through Wyoming, you must walk, bike, hike, or ride horseback through it. I-80 finds the easiest route over the Rockies and that's across the Red Desert at the edge of the Great Divide Basin. The Red Desert is barren, but don't judge all of Wyoming by this! The rest of the state has some of the most beautiful mountain scenery in the United States. Everyone knows about Yellowstone and the Grand Tetons but if you lack time they may be too distant from I-80. This chapter will give you some easy Alternate and Side Routes just within your reach. Don't leave Wyoming without seeing some of its grandeur!

Wyoming is in the Rocky Mountains with several 13,000 foot peaks, four large basins and a lowest point at 3100 feet. It is the 9th largest state with 97,000 square miles and a population of just 453,588. The climate is semi-dry but precipitation varies from 5 to 45 inches a year. Summer days may be hot, to 100 degrees, but nights are cool. It's a dry heat here in the West so all you need is a little shade. Winters are cold and blustery but leave beautiful snow for winter sports.

The state flag has a buffalo in a blue field (the monarch of the plains and the blue skies of Wyoming). The red border represents the many Native American tribes that lived here. The state bird is the meadowlark which sings so clear a song and the state flower, the Indian paintbrush.

You'll probably see more wildlife in Wyoming than in any other state. Especially prolific are the pronghorn antelope. Just watch for a spot of white, his rump spot, out in the bunch grass and sage brush. You'll soon become quite adept at spotting them. They are North America's fastest animal! Although usually found in groups of 4 to 8, as many as 20 may be seen in a herd. Make a game and tally them. Bob gets all those on the North side of the road, and Karen all those on the South.

Watch for a coyote out for a stroll. On the plains there may be golden eagles, vultures and sage grouse. In the mountains you'll see deer, elk, marmots and bald eagles; in the marshes, beaver, muskrats, blue herons, and moose. Fishing and hunting are great sports in Wyoming. Enquire at an information center. Wyoming has our first National Monument, Devil's Tower, and the newest, Fossil Butte. Both well worth a visit!

"MINIMUM REQUIREMENTS FOR 'RANCHING?"

"At least two head of livestock, preferably cattle—one male, one female."
"A new air-conditioned pickup with automatic transmission, power steering and trailer hitch."
"Two dogs to ride in the bed of the pickup."
"A $40 horse and $300 saddle."
"A pair of silver spurs to wear to barbecues."
"A little place to keep the cows, on land too poor to grow crops."
"A spool of barbed wire, three cedar posts and a bale of prairie hay to haul around in the truck all day."

Indian Paintbrush

"Credit at the bank."
"Credit at the feed store."
"Credit from your father-in-law."
"A good wife who won't get upset when you walk across the living room carpet with manure on your boots."
"A good wife with a good full-time job at the courthouse." (Author Unknown)

WYOMING HISTORY

Wyoming was first seen by white men when the Verendrye brothers explored the Bighorn Mountains in 1743. John Colter came in 1807 and saw the geysers of Yellowstone, but no one believed him. "Colter's Hell" they called his description of the boiling lakes, just more tall tales passed around the campfire! Then came the fur trappers and traders seeking beaver to make those tall beaver felt hats that were so fashionable. In 1812 Robert Stuart led the American Fur Traders from Astoria, Oregon Eastward and found "South Pass" over the Rockies Northeast of Rock Springs. In 1822 William Ashley was followed by many others who traveled much the same route as I-80 from Laramie to Ft. Bridger. This later became known as the "Overland Trail". In 1824 William Ashley and Jed Smith rediscovered "South Pass". It was a good route by which wagons and stock could follow the North Platte River and cross the forbidding Rockies to Ft. Bridger so this became the "Oregon Trail". Fur traders' rendezvous were held near the routes of these trails. Then the Native Americans, fur traders and trappers would gather for a month, hawking their wares to their best advantage.

Most of the Oregon Trail in Wyoming is North of I-80. You will follow one part of it through Bridger Valley and cross it as it follows Blacks Fork River into Fort Bridger. Then you will loosely follow the Overland Trail from Bridger to Laramie, and see its remains at Rock Point, Milepost 130; Bitter Creek, Milepost 142 and Arlington, Milepost 272. The more rapid development of this part of Wyoming came after 1868 when the railroad chose much of the Overland Trail route, tying the country together and laying-out towns. I-80 follows somewhat the route of the railroads.

Wyoming became a Territory in 1869, the same year that it passed the first women's suffrage law in the U.S. The Territorial women of the state could vote thanks in a large part to Esther Hobart Morris who was instrumental in convincing the territorial legislators. In these early days the state encouraged women to settle here to stabilize the territory. Wyoming had the first woman judge, Esther Morris, in wild South Pass City. She was a rugged, six-foot tall, 200 pounds with a forceful personality. There was little that she could not handle!

In negotiations for statehood, Wyoming refused to become a state until Congress agreed not to interfere with women's right to vote. This delayed statehood until 1890 making it the 44th State. Women were also given control over their own property, guardianship of their children, and equal compensation with men for equal work. Wyoming had the first woman governor in the nation in 1924. Governor Nellie Ross made significant gains in education in Wyoming and reduced the state debt by $1 million. Her stance for prohibition and against prize fighting caused her defeat at the next election. She was appointed Director of the U.S. Mint in 1933 and held that post for 20 years.

The Utes, Cheyennes, Shoshones, Arapahoes and the Sioux had been defeated and confined to reservations in order to build the railroad. Then the great cattle drives began with vast herds of longhorns being driven North from Texas. The cattle multiplied until there were too many and the beef market collapsed. On top of that the vicious winter of 1886 killed a sixth of the herds. Then came the farming settlers, rustling increased, and sheep were brought in. Stockmen versus "Nesters" erupted into the "Johnson County. War" in 1892. After the army quelled that, the cattlemen and sheepmen still battled it out. This was a time of murder, arson, and slaughter of livestock, the "meat" of many Western movies.

Most of the towns along I-80 got their start as Union Pacific Railroad stops. They did not start as quiet villages as did other settlements, but with the noisy clang of railroad workers and their entourage. Today these towns flourish with intensified mining, oil drilling, agriculture, and sheep and cattle ranching. Wyoming raises a million head of cattle and a greater number of sheep, and leads all other states in coal reserves.

Lodging and services are often very far apart, so plan these stops carefully or you'll find yourself after dark in the middle of the plains or mountains with no where to rest or refuel. Most public campgrounds have pit toilets. They're usually well-monitored and clean. Wyoming has an excellent tourist guide, "Wyoming Vacation Guide," that lists all campgrounds, motels, and points of interest.

WYOMING MILEPOSTS

WYOMING HIGHWAY PATROL: 1-800-442-9090.
ROAD CONDITIONS OUTSIDE OF MAIN TOWNS IN WESTERN WYOMING: 1-800-442-7850.
ROAD CONDITIONS IN EASTERN WYOMING: 1-800-442-8321.
WYOMING DEPT OF TOURISM: 307-777-7777.
TELEPHONE AREA CODE FOR ALL OF WYOMING: 307.

MILEPOSTS:

3 **HARRISON DRIVE, WEST EVANSTON/BUS 80:**
EVANSTON RADIO STATIONS: 1240 AM. 106.3 FM.
FUEL: North to Flying J Travel Plaza Truck Stop, Chevron, Texaco, Standard, Sinclair. South to Phillips.
FOOD: North to J B's, Legal Tender, Burger King. South to Kentucky Fried.
MOTELS: North to Best Western, Weston Lamp Lighter, Western Plaza, Super Budget*.

EVANSTON

Evanston was originally known as "Bear River City" since the Bear River flows through here from Bear Lake. A famous riot erupted here in 1868 instigated by the rough elements that followed the railroad. Soldiers had to be called in from Ft. Bridger to restore order. As often happened in the West, Evanston got its name from its surveyor. Many of the early settlers were uneducated, often unable to read or write. A trained topographer drew a map of an area and topped it off with his name or with whatever suited his fancy.

Evanston like other towns along the railroad, became a commercial and shipping center. Both crude oil and natural gas are produced from what is known as "The Overthrust Belt". Evanston has WYOMING DOWNS RACE TRACK (8 miles North of town) with thoroughbred and quarter horse races May-Sept, Fri-Sun and holidays. At DEPOT SQUARE PARK they have square dances, melodramas, band concerts and barbecues. Real Western type entertainment! Labor Day Weekend heralds a big celebration in Evanston.

5 **EVANSTON/WY 89 NORTH/WY 150 SOUTH:** ROAD CONDITIONS CALL: 789-9966.
STATE HOSPITAL. WALMART.
FUEL: South to Conoco.
FOOD: North to McDonalds, Arbys, Shakeys Pizza, Main Street Deli.
MOTELS: North to Super 8, Western Super Budget*, New & Western*, Classic Lodge*.
UINTA COUNTY HISTORICAL MUSEUM: 36 10th Street. In County Library and Chamber of Commerce Building. History of Wyoming from the Shoshone and Arapahoe to the Chinese who worked the railroad and the mines. Also a pioneer parlor, ranching and bootlegging. Summers Mon-Fri 8-6pm. Sat-Sun 10-4pm.

WESTBOUND ALTERNATE ROUTE

MIRROR LAKE HIGHWAY TO KAMAS, UT: Take WY 150 South over 10,687 foot Bald Mountain Pass to Kamas, Rockport, and I-80 at UT Milepost 156 in the Wasatch Mountains. If you have a vehicle under 20 or 22 feet you will enjoy this beautiful side trip over the Uinta Mountains. Wyoming and Utah consider this one of their most scenic drives. It's about 120 miles of mountain scenery versus about 50 miles of open highway on I-80. Check your map and read Utah's Milepost 156. There are many campgrounds and trailheads along this route but there are length limits. Enquire locally to be sure! If you're only going to see high plains this trip, then this is your chance to see one segment of the high Rockies without going too much out of your way.

6 **BEAR RIVER DRIVE, EAST EVANSTON/BUS 80 LOOP:** ELEVATION: 6748 FEET.
BEAR RIVER INFORMATION CENTER: South of I-80 on hillside. **WYOMING'S ONLY INFORMATION CENTER ON I-80!** Your only chance to get a state map. Exit and follow the signs. (WESTBOUND: Exit and an immediate Left under the viaduct.) The new flagpole, donated by a man in honor of his brother, was recently installed at a cost of $120,000. Open Summers 7am-7pm. Winters 8-5pm. Next door is **BEAR RIVER STATE PARK** with picnicking only in 1992.
FUEL: North to Amoco, Texaco Truck Stop.
FOOD: North to Outpost Restaurant.
MOTELS: North to Prairie Inn, Budget Host, Evanston Inn, Prairie Inn, Super 8*, Friendship Inn.
CAMPGROUNDS: "Phillips RV": Private. Good Sam. West 6 miles on Bus 80 (Bear River Drive.). "Sunset RV": Private. Good Sam. One mile West on Bus 80 Loop. Next to City Park.

10 **PAINTER ROAD:** NO NEAR SERVICES!
MILEPOST 14: DIVIDE ROAD/ PARKING AREA: ELEVATION: 7800 FEET.

Can you believe you're this high? The Wyoming Rockies sit on a 3,000-foot plateau.

18   US 189 NORTH:

> **EASTBOUND:** If you're headed North to Kemmerer, Fossil Butte, Idaho, the Tetons or Yellowstone take US 189 from here. Note "Medicine Butte" to the North.

ALTERNATE EASTBOUND ROUTE

Take US 189 to Kemmerer and West on US 30 to Fossil Butte. To return to I-80 take US 30 East to Milepost 66. Kemmerer is the coal mining town where in 1902 J.C. Penny opened his first store, "The Golden Rule" with a $500 investment.

> **KEMMERER PIONEER MUSEUM:** In "Triangle Park". You'll see fossils and historical artifacts.

> **FOSSIL BUTTE NATIONAL MONUMENT:** Ten miles west of Kemmerer on US 30. Fossil Butte is a rainbow of red, purple, yellow and grey bands of the Wasatch Formation. Overlying these layers are the buff to white beds of the Green River Formation. An ancient sea once covered all this land and left its remains of sea animals. This is one of the world's largest deposits of fossilized fresh-water and salt-water fish that lived 50 million years ago. The museum has fossils of several varieties of perch, herring, paddlefish, garpike, stingray, snails, clams, birds and bats, palms and ferns. Fossil Butte, established in 1972, is one of our newer National Monuments. It has a Visitor Center and a self-guiding hiking trail for 2.5 miles to a fossil quarry. Ranger guided hikes and talks are held in the summer. Picnicking and Campfire programs in the park. Motels, food, fuel and private campgrounds are in Kemmerer.

> **ULRICH'S FOSSIL FISH GALLERY:** You'll pass it on your Left on the way to the Visitor Center. Mounted fish fossils are for sale in a wide range of prices. You can purchase your own fossil embedded in rock and learn how to "pick it out" yourself. Ask about a trip to a private quarry where you can help excavate a fossil.

> **MILEPOST 20: EASTBOUND:** See that ribbon of highway in front of you? How many miles would you estimate that it is to the next hill? Everyone pick a number. These rolling hills are beautiful in the spring. You may see your first pronghorn antelope here.

21   COAL ROAD: NO NEAR SERVICES!

> **WESTBOUND:** Say good-by to the pronghorns.

23   RANCH EXIT/BAR HAT ROAD: NO NEAR SERVICES!

> **WESTBOUND:** This is a hard climb for some vehicles.   Turn off air conditioning.

24   RANCH EXIT/LEROY ROAD: NO NEAR SERVICES!

> **PIEDMONT, A GHOST TOWN FOR THE ADVENTURESOME!** Check this out locally for type of vehicle and distance. You'll go South and West to a crossroads, then straight South for 5 miles to three 1868 Charcoal kilns built for the Utah iron industry. They are 30 feet high and 30 feet round. One-half mile more on the Right is the remains of the town of Piedmont, a logging town and then a tent town for the railroad with a roundhouse and water tank. In 1869, 300 unpaid railroad workers put ties on the track and stopped Thomas C. Durant's special train on his way to Promontory Point, Utah. He had to telegraph for funds to pay the men before they would let him pass. This delayed the Golden Spike Ceremony. The railroad built a tunnel changed the route and the town died. The last man there died in the blizzard of 1949.

> **MILEPOST 27:** Notice the "Central Pivot Irrigation". From the air it makes a circle of green. This irrigation system makes a round instead of a rectangular field! You will see this many times crossing the high plains.

28   FRENCH ROAD/PARKING AREAS: NO NEAR SERVICES!

> Another 7800-foot hill! You're on top of the world! Note the snow-clad Uinta Mountains to the South.

30   BIGELOW ROAD:

> **FUEL:** North to Bingo/Burns Truck Stop.

33   UNION ROAD, EASTBOUND PARKING: NO NEAR SERVICES!

34   BUS 80 TO FORT BRIDGER:

EASTBOUND ALTERNATE ROUTE

THROUGH BRIDGER VALLEY: Take Bus 80 South to Ft. Bridger and Lyman and back to I-80 at Milepost 48. A MUST STOP! It's only 3 miles further through this lovely valley with its farms and lilacs in the spring. Services on Bus 80 are listed below. The fertile valley of the Blacks Fork River was well-traveled by the pioneers. They always stopped at Ft. Bridger to replenish supplies, repair equipment at the blacksmith shop and get the news. And YOU must stop here too! Your whole family will enjoy Ft. Bridger as they stretch their legs and walk back into history. If you're interested in "Piedmont", the ghost town, ask here.

FORT BRIDGER HISTORY

In 1842 the fur trade was in recession. Beaver felt hats were going out of style. So Jim Bridger, a fur trapper and guide and his partner, Louis Vasquez, decided to build a fort here and settle down. Bridger was known for the "Tall Tales" that he told the "green" Easterners. The fort was opened as a trading post in 1843 just in time for the Great Westward Migration. It was second only to Ft. Laramie as an outfitting station for the pioneers.

The Donner-Reed Party spent four days at Ft. Bridger in 1846. While there, 13 year old Eddie Breen fell off his horse and broke his leg. The current treatment was to amputate it, but his mother would not allow it. So they splinted it expecting he'd never walk again. However, in spite of the trials of the Wasatch and the Salt Flats his leg did heal and he came off the Hastings Cut-off in Nevada riding his horse.

"The Emigrants' Guide to Oregon and California", written by an Ohio Lawyer, Lansford Hastings, gave a vision of health and wealth in California. He told of a Cut-off from the Oregon trail that would save 300-400 miles from the California Trail. He had explored it once, with only pack animals and horses like the trappers before him. He was just another one of hundreds of opportunists of the day trying to make a fast buck.

James Reed, afraid of early Sierra snows, was intrigued by the possibility of a "shorter" route. Jim Clyman, who had traveled the Cut-off with Hastings tried to discourage the Reeds and Donners with tales of the Wasatch canyons and the desert heat. Twelve-year-old Virginia Reed said years later that Bridger and Vasquez encouraged them to take the Hastings Cutoff. Hastings had just left a few days ahead of them with the Harlan-Young party. So undeterred by Clyman and sure that Hastings just ahead would help lead them, they started down the trail that began just behind where the Fort Bridger barracks are today.

The "Pioneer Mormon Train" met Bridger just North of here on the Little Sandy River. They were excited to hear Bridger talk about the Salt Lake Valley, their destination. Bridger always claimed that he was the first to discover it and references today seem to authenticate it.

In 1853 the Mormons built Ft. Supply just 12 miles to the South. They purchased Ft. Bridger from Vasquez in 1855 and used both forts to outfit the Mormon immigrants and other pioneers traveling West. The Mormons in Salt Lake Valley and President Buchanan were at odds in 1857, so he sent troops here to oust Governor Brigham Young and replace him with a non-Mormon governor. This was the "Mormon War". The Mormons burned

Ft. Bridger and Ft. Supply to slow the army and then retreated to Salt Lake City. Colonel Johnson arrived with his troops, to find nothing but charred remains. They set up a temporary camp for the winter. In the Spring the army started for Salt Lake City. Soldiers left behind began to rebuild the fort and transform it into an Army fort incorporating the stone wall built by the Mormons.

In the 1860's besides being an army fort it was also a Pony Express and an Overland Stage stop. During the Civil War the fort was garrisoned by the Fort Sutler, W. A. Carter and volunteer groups. In 1866 a company of "Galvanized Yankees" (Confederate Prisoners of War) were here. The fort was also the Shoshone Indian Agency where a treaty was signed that same year. Later troops stationed here were commissioned to keep the Indians from interfering with the building of the railroad. Up to 350 men were stationed here at one time. In the 1870's Ft. Bridger was the base of many mining, geological

Fort Bridger
Photo credit: Wyoming Travel Commision

and archeological expeditions. The fort was abandoned in 1878 but reactivated during the Ute Indian Uprising of 1880. New buildings and improvements were made. When things settled down, homesteaders began farming the Bridger Valley South through Urie and the Mountain View area. In 1890 the fort was again abandoned, but it remained a community center and the home of Judge Carter. Some of the buildings were sold, remodeled and are still in use in the area. The state acquired the site in 1920 and began restoration.

FORT BRIDGER STATE HISTORIC SITE: A great living history museum, a picnic area, the first school house in Wyoming, guardhouse, the original Pony Express Stable, and a commissary and officer's quarters. Staff is in period costume. Tours available. Bridger's original fort and store have been reconstructed. It includes a well-stocked store of desirable and reasonable gift and hand-made items. Summers daily 9-5:30pm. Living History 10-5pm. April-May & Sept-Oct 9-4:30pm. Winter weekends 9-4:30pm. Admission $2 per vehicle.

LYMAN TOWN COMPLEX TRONA INDUSTRY MUSEUM: On the South side of the road in Lyman you'll see a modern building housing the City Hall. They are planning a museum here on the Trona industry. Scheduled to be open in 1992 or '93. Trona mining is the major industry here. Trona is a combination of sodium carbonate and sodium bicarbonate. It is mined, crushed, dissolved, and recrystallized and dried to convert it to soda ash. This material is then used in the manufacture of glass bottles, jars, fiberglass, solar energy panels, baking soda, detergent, light bulbs, etc. The trona beds were laid down 30 to 50 million years ago when ancient Lake Gosiute covered these lands. There are five trona mines and plants between Lyman and Green River producing 90% of the soda ash used in the U.S.: FMC, Rhone-Poulenc, General Chemical, Texas Gulf and Tenneco. Church, Dwight and Rhone-Poulenc produce baking soda. Arm And Hammer Baking Soda made here is familiar to all cooks.

The largest Trona mine in the world, FMC, is at Milepost 72. There is a 10-foot thick seam of trona there. It is a "room and pillar" underground operation with over 2,000 miles of tunnels/streets covering a square mile 1500 feet below the surface of the earth. (This is more streets than the city of San Francisco.) The "Streets" are 14 feet wide and 8 feet high. The museum will depict the trona mining process, and have artifacts, ore samples, mining attire and the end-use products.

FUEL: Texaco, Chevron Maverick, 7-Eleven.

FOOD: Foodtime, Hidden Faces, Pizza Hut, Wagon Wheel Restaurant.

MOTELS: Wagon Wheel Motel* in Ft. Bridger. Valley West* in Lyman.

CAMPGROUNDS: "KOA": Private. At Lyman turn North for .5 mile on WY 413 at the intersection of the Valley West Motel and the Chevron Station. Pool, cabins, basketball and tennis courts, horseback riding, laundry. Lovely quiet spot.

Check out the free camping area across the road from Ft. Bridger.

39   URIE/MOUNTAIN VIEW/WY 412/WY 414 SOUTH: ELEVATION: 7000 FEET.

41   LYMAN/WY 413/SOUTH TO REST AREA: Solar-heated facility.

FUEL: North to "Gas-N-Go" Truck Stop.

CAMPGROUND: "KOA": Private. One mile South of I-80. Read above. Pool, camping cabins with beds. Peaceful and quiet here and the air is so clear! This is an Oregon Trail campsite. Wagons were parked all along this valley as the pioneers rested, washed clothes, and prepared for the long journey ahead. $15-$17.

WESTBOUND: Continue on this road into Lyman, and then West on Bus 80/Old US 30 to Ft. Bridger and West to connect with I-80 again.

MILEPOST 44: You are crossing Blacks Fork River, trailguide for the pioneers. Slow down and drink in history! Blacks Fork River tumbles North out of the Uinta Mountains in the South. The pioneers came down from the South Pass of the Rockies, Northeast of here, crossing the Green River to meet the Blacks Fork and then following it up to here. Can you visualize the almost continuous line of wagons crossing here from the 1840's to the 1860's heading for Ft. Bridger? Or the Mormons in 1856 pulling their handcarts? The Overland and Pony Express Trails also converged with the Oregon and Mormon Trails along this river.

48   EAST LYMAN/BUS 80:

WESTBOUND ALTERNATE ROUTE

TO LYMAN AND FORT BRIDGER: Exit on Bus 80. It's only three miles further than I-80. Follow the

trail of those sturdy pioneers and visit beautiful Bridger Valley. Ft. Bridger has been a MUST stop for all travelers since 1843. Read Milepost 34.
> **MILEPOST 49: WESTBOUND PARKING.**

53 **CHURCH BUTTE ROAD/WY 374:** NO NEAR SERVICES!
> **CHURCH BUTTE** was a landmark on the trail to Fort Bridger.
> **MILEPOST 59: PARKING AREAS:**

61 **CEDAR MOUNTAIN ROAD/GRANGER:** NO NEAR SERVICES!

66 **KEMMERER/US 30 WEST:**

WESTBOUND ALTERNATE ROUTES

TO FOSSIL BUTTE NATIONAL MONUMENT: Take US 30 West and visit Kemmerer and Fossil Butte (Read Milepost 18). From there you have two choices. Go South on US 189 to Milepost 18 on I-80. Or continue West to Bear Lake, US 89 South to Logan and possibly Promontory Point, and down I-15 to Salt Lake City to meet I-80 again. This last choice is possibly 185 miles versus 140 on I-80. Read UT Milepost 120 for more details.

THE FUR TRADERS

In 1825 William Ashley, a fur trader, decided to take his trade goods into the mountains instead of waiting for the trappers to bring the furs out. He set the place of the first **MOUNTAIN MAN RENDEZVOUS** at Henry's Fork and sent out word for all the trappers to be there. It was so successful (he made so much money) that it was held each year at a different site. Just North and West of here on Blacks Fork is the site of a "Mountain Men Rendezvous" in 1834. In 1835 Dr. Marcus Whitman joined the American Fur Company on its trek West to the Trappers' Rendevous 100 miles North of here near Daniel. He told how hundreds of Native Americans were there with some 200 white men including a Scottish sportsman. There was lots of "carousing". Kit Carson killed a braggart in a duel and Whitman preached to anyone who was sober. Whitman also practiced his medical arts and removed a three-inch iron arrowhead from Jim Bridger's back. Jim had had it for three years, yet it had not become infected. He said, "In the mountains meat don't spoil."

Whitman took his new wife to Oregon on his second trip West in 1836. In the winter of 1843 Whitman went East telling about his life in Oregon and the need for missionaries there. By May, 1,000 pioneers including Jessie Applegate were ready to go West with him. In 1846 Applegate founded the Applegate Road across the Black Rock Desert in Nevada (read Nevada Milepost 145. Whitman, his wife and 11 others were killed in 1847 in Oregon in an uprising by the Cayuse Indians.

The Fur Companies, John Jacob Astor's among them, made fortunes on the furs that were very popular especially for those tall felt "Beaver Hats". The trade goods they used to "buy" furs from the Natives and trappers were exorbitantly overpriced. Their most popular item, whiskey, purchased in St. Louis for three cents a gallon, was diluted and sold for $3 a pint. Coffee, tobacco and sugar purchased for under ten cents a pound, sold for $2 a pound. The cheap beads and calicos they sold to the Native Americans were marked up 2000 percent. Trappers and Natives sold their year's work for barely enough rations to last them another year. Some drank away all their profits and were left destitute. The last rendezvous, held in 1840, was poorly attended. Beaver hats were out and silk hats were IN!

68 **LITTLE AMERICA/WY 374:** ELEVATION: 6500 FEET.
> **FUEL, TRUCK STOP, FOOD, MOTEL, GIFT SHOP, POST OFFICE ALL IN ONE:**
> You need to stretch your legs, check out the gift shop, get one of their famous cones and mail your post cards. Ask a clerk in the giftshop for the postcard of "The Legend of Little America". "A Promise Kept, A Dream Come True!" the signs used to say. The card tells the story of the founder who as a teenager was herding sheep on this high plain and was lost in a blizzard. He had to camp out all night. He thought of the need for a shelter and promised to build one here someday. Many years later he constructed "Little America" to fulfill his youthful dream.
> **MILEPOST 71: PARKING ONLY.**

72 **WEST VACO ROAD:** NO NEAR SERVICES!
> To the North there are usually busy trucks serving the FMC Trona mines.

MILEPOST 77: Blacks Fork River flowed North from Bridger Valley. But now it has curved South heading for the Green River and we cross it again.

83   LEBARGE ROAD/WY 372/FONTENELLE DAM:

Exxon Natural Gas Company, Shutte Creek Project here.

BRONZE BELT: Rock formations North on WY 372. No further information.

SEEDSKADEE NATIONAL WILDLIFE REFUGE: 26 miles North via WY 372. Refuge on the Green River with 200 species of birds including five nesting colonies of Blue Herons. Also 14 historic sites there.

EASTBOUND EXTENSIVE ALTERNATE ROUTE

TO TRAVEL THE OREGON TRAIL: FOR THE ADVENTURESOME! If you have been on I-80 before, you're a history buff and want to follow the Oregon Trail Eastward, this is your chance! Get a brochure on the Oregon Trail at your first stop so that you won't miss any of the sights. Take Wy 372 for 27 miles North. Then Northeast on WY 28 (Big Sandy Recreation Area there). Over the famous South Pass through which thousands of pioneers crossed. Then take US 287 South and East. And Wy 220 East past famous Devil's Gate and Independence Rock (climb to the top). Beautiful country there in the spring! At Caspar you'll take I-25 East and South to US 26. You'll see Ft. Laramie and Scott's Bluff. Great Stops! Don't miss the museum at Scott's Bluff! or the hike downhill through a tunnel. Continue on East past Chimney Rock and Ash Hollow into Ogallala, NE and I-80. Hike up the hill at Ash Hollow. Wonderful trip! You'll need an extra day or even two to see and experience all of this! Read NEBRASKA MILEPOST 107 on Ash Hollow.

85   COVERED WAGON ROAD, GREEN RIVER: ROAD CONDITIONS: CALL 875-9966.

Adams RV Parts and Service.

EASTBOUND CAMPGROUND: "Tex's Travel Camp": Private. Good Sam. South .25 mile on WY 374. East one mile. Green River swimming, fishing.

THE GREEN RIVER: Meet the river of history flowing majestically Southward to the Colorado River. But look South and you see the Uintas! To DRIVE South you have to go up over an 8600 foot pass in the Uintas. Long ago in geologic time the Green River rushed Southward through the sedimentary layers cutting such a precipitous canyon that it can only be explored by boat. The canyon walls of red and yellow sandstone are the "Flaming Gorge". The first white men

"TOLLGATE GUARDS the PALISADES"
Photo credit: Sweetwater County Historical Museum

to see them were floating South by boat on John Wesley Powell's Expedition in May of 1869. Today this is still the best way to see this canyon. From the road there are just a few vantage points from which to view the gorge. The river flows out of this deep canyon near Dinosaur National Monument in Colorado.

As you enter the town of Green River from the West, towering over the river are **THE PALISADES,** a colonnade of rocks with lovely colors as the sun and shadows dance on them. The artist, Thomas Moran, made them famous with his painting of a fur-trading scene. The rock tower standing alone on the South side of I-80 is **TOLLGATE ROCK.** The old "Tollgate Trail" went through here and pioneers had to pay a fee to pass. In the late 1860's, W. H. Jackson brought more attention to the area with his photograph of **CASTLE ROCK** which guards the city on the North.

89   GREEN RIVER/BUS 80 EAST: RADIO STATIONS: 11.40 AM. 100.3 FM.

RV PARTS & SUPPLIES: West of Green River on WY 374.

FUEL: South to Conoco, Standard, Texaco.

FOOD: South to Golden Corral, Pizza Hut. Cowboy Restaurant.

MOTELS: South to Prairie Dog Inn, Wesern, Coachman Inn, Super 8, Mustang.

CAMPGROUND: WESTBOUND: "Tex's Travel Camp": Private. Good Sam. West three miles on Frontage Road/ Wy 374.

SWEETWATER COUNTY HISTORICAL MUSEUM: 80 West Flaming Gorge Way. In the Courthouse. South on Bus 80 which becomes Flaming Gorge Way. The story of the mines from 1867, including the story of the Chinese miners. Weekdays 9-5pm. Free.

MILEPOST 90: Tunnels through Castle Rock. Just think! You are traveling UNDER layers of rock that are the remains of an ancient sea bottom!

91   GREEN RIVER/WY 530/BUS 80 WEST: ELEVATION: 6100 FEET.
RV PARTS AND SERVICE.
FUEL: South to Mini Mart, Shell.
FOOD: South to McDonalds, Cafe, Pizza Hut, Dairy Queen, Trudel's Restaurant on East Flaming Gorge Way.
MOTEL: South to Super 8, Western, Mustang*, Flaming Gorge*, Coachman Inn.

GREEN RIVER

The first town of "Green River" was 30 miles upriver where the Oregon/Mormon trail crossed the Green River. Today's Green River is one of the few towns along I-80 in Wyoming that was not given a violent birthing by the railroad. This town had already been established with a population of 2,000, and was on the Overland Stage route when the railroad came through. Men cut down trees in the mountains to the South and floated them down the river to town. Here they made the railroad ties and then carted them off to the construction site.

Green River was made famous in the courts for the "Green River Ordinance". The railroad nightshift found that their sleep was disturbed by door-to-door depression salesmen knocking. So in 1931 they passed an ordinance prohibiting such selling. Merchandising organizations fought the law as unconstitutional but it held and thousands of towns passed "Green River Ordinances". Today they call Green River the "Trona capital of the World". The Trona industry has increased the population of Green River from 4,000 in 1970 to over 15,000 in 1992. Trona mining and use is described in Milepost 34.

FOREST SERVICE INFORMATION CENTER/CHAMBER OF COMMERCE: 1415 Uinta Drive, Green River. South on WY 530, on the Right as you go up the hill. Information, books and maps on Green River and Flaming Gorge.

EXPEDITION ISLAND PARK: South on WY 530, across the railroad tracks to a Right on East 4th Street. Left on South 2nd to cross a bridge to the island that is dedicated to one of our great explorers, Major John Wesley Powell. From this point on May 24, 1869 the one-armed Major Powell commenced the first Expedition down the Green River to the Colorado, through the Grand Canyon to where Lake Mead is today. Entering the unknown, they traversed wild waters and knew hunger. Ten men started out, one left in six weeks, and three men deserted and were killed by Natives just two days before journey's end. On Aug 30th the six men went ashore at the Virgin River, Nevada. Major Powell mapped and recorded all, naming this area "Flaming Gorge". He made a 2nd trip in 1871 again leaving from this same island.

FUR-TRADERS' RENDEZVOUS: Forty miles South of here off WY 530 is McKinnon. In 1825 William Ashley of the Rocky Mountain Fur Company called all the fur trappers to come for the month of July to "where Birch Creek runs into Henry's Fork". This then became the first fur-trading rendezvous in the Rocky Mountains between traders and trappers. Future meetings were always designated by rivers and creeks whose names were established long before towns and states were even a dream.

FLAMING GORGE NATIONAL RECREATION AREA: A dam was built across the Green River which formed a lake 90 miles long. It has 375 miles of shoreline bordering flatland to 1500 foot cliffs visible only by boat. The National Recreation Area was established in 1968 and encompasses 201,000 acres surrounding the lake. The terrain was laid down some 40 million years ago in early Tertiary time, by the sediments on the bottom of a great fresh water sea that covered most of Wyoming. Highpoints of this area are the colored rock formations, chimneys and pinnacles carved by wind and water.

You can take a boat down the river from various launching ramps and see the cliffs from a fish-eye view. Fishing is reported to be excellent here so hope you brought your gear! From here it is 26 miles to the nearest campground and boat rental at **BUCKBOARD CROSSING**. Actually I-80's closest **OVERLOOK**, campground and boat rental is **FIREHOLE CANYON** off US 191 on the East side of the lake 24 miles from Rock Springs and Milepost 99.

If you are Adventuresome you can make a 150-mile round trip by taking Wy 530 South up to UT 44 and UT 260 returning to I-80 on Wy 191. However, the lake and cliffs are NOT visible from the highway! Spur roads lead up to them and have campgrounds, boat launching, etc. Be sure to get an area map first so that you will know which spur roads to take.

99 **EAST GREEN RIVER/FLAMING GORGE/US 191 SOUTH:**
FUEL/FOOD: Conoco Car/Truck Plaza.
EASTBOUND CAMPGROUND: "KOA": Private. North on Service Road. Turn Left/North. One mile East to KOA. NEAR I-80.
FLAMING GORGE NATIONAL RECREATION AREA: Read Milepost 91.
FIREHOLE CANYON: South on US 191 24 miles. Views of colored chimneys and pinnacles, plus picnicking, camping, showers and boating. Ask for a map of the area at a store, service station or at Firehole Canyon. Rental boats are available to explore this colorful Green River canyon.

WESTBOUND EXTENSIVE ALTERNATE ROUTE

TO DINOSAUR NATIONAL MONUMENT: If you have been on I-80 before and you'd like an Alternate Route take US 191 up over the Uintas via Flaming Gorge and down the other side to Vernal, Utah to see "Dinosaur National Monument". Then West on US 40 to join I-80 at Milepost 148 in the Wasatch Mountains. A beautiful route! Read UTAH Milepost 148. If you take this loop you can also see the marvelous view from 1360-foot high "RED CANYON" at the Southern end of Flaming Gorge. Be sure to get an area map so you won't miss it.

102 **DEWAR DRIVE, ROCK SPRINGS/BUS 80 EAST/US 191 NORTH:**
ROCK SPRINGS RADIO STATIONS: 1360 AM. 95.1, 96.5, 104.5 FM.
VISITOR INFORMATION CENTER: South on Dewar to Info Center on right.
MALLS: North to Penney's, Walmart, K-Mart. South TO PLAZA MALL.
FUEL: South to Texaco, Chevron. North to Amoco, Chevron, Exxon.
FOOD: South to McDonalds, Hardees, Burger King, Arbys, Pizza Hut, Wendys, Sizzler, Hong Kong House, Golden Corral. North to Dennys.
MOTELS: South to Motel 6*, Village Inn, Lamplighter, Holiday Inn, Comfort Inn. North to The Inn, La Quinta, Motel 8*,
WESTBOUND CAMPGROUND: "KOA": Private. North on Service Rd. Turn Right to traffic light by K-Mart, Left two miles to KOA. NEAR I-80!

103 **COLLEGE DRIVE, ROCK SPRINGS:** NO NEAR SERVICES!
ROAD CONDITIONS: 382- 9966. HOSPITAL. WESTERN WYOMING COLLEGE.
FUEL: South to Mini Mart.

104 **ELK STREET, ROCK SPRINGS/US 191 NORTH/ WY 430 SOUTH:**
FUEL: North to Flying J Travel Plaza Truck Stop, Phillips Truck Stop, Conoco, Sinclair, Exxon. Texaco, Amoco.
FOOD: Frosty Freeze, Daylight Donuts, Santa Fe Trail Restaurant.
MOTELS: North to American Family, Outlaw Inn, Best Western. South to Nomad, Cody's*. Elk Street*, Irwin*.

ROCK SPRINGS

Rock Springs began as an Overland Stage stop in 1862. The discovery of coal here helped determine the route of the Union Pacific in 1868 as coal was needed for their engines. Millions of tons of coal from this area fueled the Union Pacific steam engines that passed through. The town was named for its springs that were disrupted by the coal mining, so Railroad tank cars brought water from Green River until a pipeline was finally built from there. This area only receives 8 to 9 inches of rain a year, so water is precious. In more recent years buildings have been subsiding into the coal mines so some tunnels had to be filled and houses moved.

Miners of so many nationalities arrived here that they called it the "Melting Pot of Wyoming". Chinese contract laborers were imported in 1875 for cheap labor. The local jobless rebelled resulting in the "Chinese Massacre of 1885". The white miners burned Chinatown and chased the tenants away. The U.S. army was sent here to restore order and build a fort. In the 1950's when the railroad converted to oil, mining and sheep raising also declined and Rock Springs was reduced to a quiet village. But as the natural gas and oil industries expanded, and Trona was discovered, the area boomed again. It was easy to convert coal miners into trona miners, and with others arriving, the town population quadrupled to 22,914. They still continue to produce coal with the new "Jim Bridger Plant", the largest such plant in Wyoming, generating electricity from the coal.

    ROCK SPRINGS HISTORICAL MUSEUM: Broadway & B Streets. South on WY 430/Elk Street to Left on Broadway. In old city hall with a tower. Signs might say "Old City Museum". On National Register.

    FINE ARTS CENTER: 400 C Street. One block South. Upstairs of Library. Noon-5.

    WILD HORSE HOLDING FACILITY: North 3 to 4 miles on Elk Street. The RED DESERT to the Northeast is host to one of the largest herds of wild horses anywhere. The Bureau of Land Management tries to control their numbers by rounding them up and bringing them to Rock Springs where they have an "Adopt a Horse" program. Buyers must pay fees for inoculations, etc. Want a horse?

    RELIANCE TIPPLE: North ten miles on US 191. Historic site. A monument to the coal industry.

106   **PILOT BUTTE STREET, ROCK SPRINGS/BUS 80 WEST:** HOSPITAL.
    FUEL: Chevron Truck Stop, Amoco, Gas for less, Phillips, Texaco.
    MOTELS: South to Thunderbird, Springs, El Rancho.
    PILOT BUTTE: A famous landmark of the early settlers is to the North here.

111   **BAXTER ROAD:** NO NEAR SERVICES!

122   **SUPERIOR/WY 371 NORTH:** NO NEAR SERVICES!

130   **POINT OF ROCKS/JIM BRIDGER POWER PLANT:** ELEVATION: 6509 FEET.
    FUEL & FOOD: North to Conoco and a cafe.
    ROCK POINT STAGE STATION. Just the remains here. This was a relay point on the "Ben Holladay Overland Trail Stages" in 1862. The Overland Trail had first been traveled by William Ashley in 1822 and became a route for trappers. Fremont followed this route in 1843. It was 200 miles shorter than the Oregon Trail. In 1849 a large party of Cherokees obtained permission from the government to leave their reservation in Kansas for the goldfields. Led by Captain Evans of Arkansas, they came up through Colorado following the trappers' trail and giving it the name "Cherokee Trail". Until the Sioux uprisings during the Civil War, the mail and stage went over the Oregon Trail and South Pass. When Ben Holladay bought the Overland Mail in 1862 and used this route to avoid the Sioux, the name of the trail was changed to "The Overland". Sioux and Cheyenne raids spread onto the Overland in 1865 with several attacks between Fort Collins, Colorado and Rock Creek Station/Arlington. Therefore 200 miles of the Overland were abandoned for awhile. "Bitter Creek" is to the South of the road near the railroad. Eastbound I-80 follows the Overland Stage Route up Echo Canyon, through Bridger Valley and Rock Springs following Bitter Creek to Point of Rocks. From here the Overland followed Bitter Creek South about 20 miles to parallel I-80 until it again joined it from Elk Mountain to Laramie. From there the trail went South to Colorado and the South Platte River.

136   **BLACK BUTTE:** NO NEAR SERVICE!

139   **RED HILL ROAD:** NO NEAR SERVICES!

142   **BITTER CREEK ROAD:** NO NEAR SERVICES!
    To the South along Bitter Creek was another stop on the Overland Trail, the "Bitter Creek Station".
    MILEPOST 143: PARKING AREAS.
    MILEPOST 144: BITTER CREEK REST AREA: This is an innovative solar-heated facility. Wyoming has built 18 of them.

GREAT DIVIDE BASIN:

To the North of I-80 is the Great Divide Basin. In the far distant North are "Antelope Hills" and the "Green Mountains" that cradle the "Oregon Trail" and form the Northern boundary of the Great Divide Basin. Mule deer and elk roam in the mountains. The Table Mountains to the South are the Southern boundary of the Basin. All waters flow down into the center of the Basin. There is very little rain or this basin would be a mammoth lake.

There are great moving sand dunes in the Northwestern side of the basin that rival the Sahara desert. Petroglyphs and pictographs tell a story of ancient people in this basin. This is a rock hounder's paradise with many gemstones found here. Other precious commodities of the Great Divide Basin are the "black gold" of oil plus natural gas. This is the longest stretch of desert on I-80, 108 miles from Rock Springs to Rawlins. It's one of the most important Pronghorn antelope ranges in the state. Also watch for hawks, eagles and grouse. You might see a coyote, a bobcat or even a mountain lion. This basin was the home of the last herd of wild bison in Wyoming. Wild horses, mustangs, can sometimes be seen from I-80. They look no different than domesticated horses, in fact they are rounded up, trained, and used as cow ponies.

146   **PATRICK DRAW ROAD:** NO NEAR SERVICES!

150   **TABLE ROCK ROAD: FUEL:** Major gas & diesel.
THE GREAT DIAMOND HOAX
Table Rock, a big sandstone formation to the South, held a secret. In 1872 two humble-looking miners walked cautiously into the Bank of California in San Francisco. They asked for use of a safe-deposit box for their diamonds, rubies and emeralds. When questioned they said that the source was secret, but it was somewhere in the Utah Territory. Bank President, William Ralston convinced them to let him send some of the gems to Tiffany's in New York where they were appraised at $150,000. Now Ralston wanted IN on this wonderful find but the miners were reluctant to tell him where the mine was located. So Ralston talked the men into letting two blindfolded engineers go with them to their Utah Territory claim. They were brought here to Table Mountain. The engineers reported finding gems just below the surface. So Ralston formed a company of 25 of his San Francisco friends plus famous people like Louis Tiffany, the Rothschilds, and Horace Greeley. Just to be sure, Ralston sent in one more engineer who agreed with the others and was rewarded with 1,000 shares of stock. Now as Ralston's company made plans to develop the mine, the miners told him that they didn't want to be involved in the mining business and sold their interests for $300,000 each and left. The last engineer sold his shares for $40,000. Then a young geologist back in the "states" heard the story and was skeptical. Diamonds and rubies are never found together! He went to the site and not only found diamonds with rubies but found one diamond that was already "cut". The miners had "salted" the area with $25,000 worth of reject gems from a German source. Ralston had to pay off the investors.

152   **BAR X ROAD:** NO NEAR SERVICES!

154   **BLM ROAD:** NO NEAR SERVICES!
SAGEBRUSH: Sagebrush is a major food source for antelope and sage grouse. It has a deep taproot that allows it to survive with only six inches of rain a year. There are 13 species of sage in Wyoming. All those low bushes out there on the desert are NOT sagebrush, just the grey almost dead-looking ones. If they're a little green, they could be **RABBIT BRUSH** or **GREASEWOOD**, with tiny shiny leaves. In some parts you'll see **MORMON TEA** a taller bush with jointed stems. It was used as a tea by the Native Americans and is still used today, especially for arthritic symptoms.

156   **GL ROAD:** NO NEAR SERVICES!

158   **THE CONTINENTAL DIVIDE:** ELEVATION: 6930 FEET. NO NEAR SERVICES!
You will cross the Continental Divide twice today as it encloses the Great Divide Basin. Look at your Wyoming map. Use your highlighter to trace the Continental Divide. Now the basin is more prominent. On the other side of the hills to the South of I-80 all waters flow toward the Green and the Colorado Rivers, the Gulf of California and the Pacific Ocean. North of the Great Divide Basin, waters flow into the Missouri, the Mississippi and the Gulf of Mexico. To the West of the Great Divide, the waters flow toward the Pacific via the Snake and the Columbia Rivers. You will be traveling through the Great Divide Basin for 52 miles. Enjoy!

165   **RED DESERT: FUEL:** Emergency services to the South only.

166 BOOSTER ROAD: NO NEAR SERVICES!

168 FREWEN ROAD: NO NEAR SERVICES!

170 RASMUSSAN ROAD: NO NEAR SERVICES!

173 WAMSUTTER: ELEVATION: 6709 FEET.
  FUEL: North to Texaco. South to Conoco Truck Service, Sinclair, J.T. Truck Amoco Service.
  FOOD: South to Broadway Cafe on Broadway Street.
  MOTEL: South to Conoco Motel.

184 CRESTON JUNCTION/WY 789: ELEVATION: 7500 FEET.
  The Continental Divide ROAD crosses the divide and goes down into Colorado. An Old Continental Divide Marker is South of the road up on that rise. Check your map and you'll see that it was not accurate. The Highway Department is planning a Rest Stop here.

187 BAGGS ROAD, CRESTON/WY 789 SOUTH: South to Sinclair gas only.
  MILEPOST 190: PARKING AREAS: Tables and "Summer Rooms". (Some are for men and some are for women.)

196 RINER ROAD: NO NEAR SERVICES!
  Did you ever wonder how the Interstate Highway System got started? It was all because of Dwight D. Eisenhower who during his younger army days had to take an army unit across the country. It took him 63 days! Later, as a General, he felt the need to move traffic and materials more efficiently. He had probably also appreciated the wonderful Autobauns that Hitler had built in Germany. As President he pushed for legislation to build our own super highways. In June 1956 he signed legislation creating the "Interstate Highway System" to build the roads and the "Federal Highway Trust Fund" to finance and maintain them. Because of Eisenhower's pursuit of the Interstate System, in 1973 Congress designated this section of I-80 as the "Dwight D. Eisenhower Highway".

201 DALEY ROAD: NO NEAR SERVICES!

204 KNOBS ROAD: NO NEAR SERVICES!

206 CONTINENTAL DIVIDE/HADSELL ROAD: ELEVATION: 7000 FEET.
  This marks the East side of the Great Divide Basin. From here all streams flow toward the Platte and the Missouri. **WESTBOUND:** Check your map and mark the extent of the Basin.

209 JOHNSON ROAD, WEST RAWLINS: ELEVATION: 6755 FEET. RADIO: 92.7 FM.
  FUEL: North to Gay Johnson's Texaco Truck Stop, Laundramat & Store.

211 SPRUCE STREET, RAWLINS/US 287 NORTH/BUS 80 EAST: HOSPITAL.
  ROAD CONDITIONS: 324-9966 RAWLINS RADIO STATIONS: 1240 AM. 92.7 FM.
  FUEL: North to Conoco, Sinclair, Texaco. Amoco, Mini Mart, Gas for Less, Auto parts.
  FOOD: North to J.B.'s, Cappy's, Bel Air Inn, Golden Spike, Taco John's, Ideal Foods.
  MOTELS: Bel Air Inn, Best Western, Super 8, Buckaroo*, Bucking Horse*, Cliff*, Golden Spike*, Hi Top*, Jade, Rawlins Ideal*, Rawlins, Sunset, Holiday Lodge, La Bella, Rifleman*.
  CAMPGROUNDS: "Western Hills CG": Private. Good Sam. North two blocks on 23rd Street to Wagon Circle Road. West two blocks. NEAR I-80. $9-$15.
  "RV World CG": Private. .5 mile West on Wagon Circle Road. Pool, wading pool, whirlpool, miniature golf. NEAR I-80. $12-$15.
  "Golden Eagle RV Park": 2346 West Spruce Street. No further information.

RAWLINS

Rawlins is another town that grew up around a spring with the mines and the railroad heightening the life. It was a wild lawless town in the 1870's until the citizens took over and lynched one of the worst outlaws, "Big Nose" George Parrott. Notices were given to 24 other outlaws who took the hint and left town. At this time prospectors were arriving by train to go North to the gold fields of South Pass City. Mines here produced the "Rawlings Red" pigment which was used to paint the Brooklyn Bridge in 1874. Today Rawlins produces coal, uranium, oil and natural gas as well as sheep and cattle.

CARBON COUNTY MUSEUM: 9th and Walnut. Historical items including stained glass windows, an old sheep wagon and a 1919 fire truck. Summer afternoons. Free.

WYOMING FRONTIER PRISON: 5th and Walnut. Take Spruce East to 5th St. 1898 prison. A tour takes you from the "Search" room to the Death House. On the National Registry. Summers: Mon-Sat 8:30-4pm. Sun 10:30-4:30pm. Adult $3. Senior & Child $2.

FERRIS MANSION": 607 West Maple. A beautiful red & white Victorian that is Carbon County's Visitor Council Building.

214 HIGLEY BLVD, RAWLINS: STATE PENITENTIARY.
    FUEL/FOOD: South to Rip Griffin Texaco Truck Stop.
    MOTELS: South to Best Western, Sleep Inn.

215 CEDAR STREET, EAST RAWLINS/BUS 80 WEST/US 287:
    FUEL: Chevron, Phillips.
    FOOD: McDonalds, Daylight Donuts, Pizza Hut, Country Kitchen, City Market.
    MOTELS: Budget Inn, Super 8, Ramada, Days Inn, Bridger, Rawlins Inn, Key Motel, Quality Inn.

219 WEST SINCLAIR: Sinclair Refinery.
    FUEL: Phillips Truck Stop.
    FOOD: Country Kitchen.
        FRONTIER PRISON: National Historic site.

221 EAST SINCLAIR: ELEVATION: 6592 FEET.
    FUEL & FOOD: Burns Bros Truck Stop/Cafe.

228 FORT STEELE STATE HISTORICAL SITE REST AREA:
    FUEL: South to Sinclair.
        A relaxing Rest Area with solar-heated facilities, shade trees and lawn. The Calvary Base (a mile down the road) was established in 1868 to protect the railroad that was being constructed. Not much to see at the site, just one building left and a few plaques. The road has a BIG unexpected bump and there is a small turn-a-round at the end. Eastbound, this is your first view of the North Platt River, you won't see it again until Ogallala, Nebraska. The North Platt river is born in the high Rockies 70 to 100 miles South of I-80, and flows Northward through the Saratoga Valley and Casper before it turns East to Nebraska.

235 WALCOTT/US 30 NORTH/WY 130 SOUTH:
US 30 NORTH TO HANNA & MEDICINE BOW:
WY 130 SOUTH TO SARATOGA & COLORADO:
    FUEL/FOOD/MOTEL: Major gas.

EASTBOUND ALTERNATE ROUTE

TO SARATOGA HOT SPRINGS AND OVER THE SNOWY RANGE SCENIC BYWAY: Take WY 130 South 20 miles through the resort town of Saratoga and eight miles past to turn East over "Snowy Range Pass" 10,847 feet. Then to Centennial & Laramie to rejoin I-80 at Milepost 311. It's about 100 miles of Wyoming at its best. This was designated as the second "National Forest Scenic Byway" in 1988. It's open from Memorial Day to September. Elevations range from 8100 feet to 10,847 feet. Beautiful scenic drive, glacial lakes beneath the peaks, gurgling creeks, and tall trees. You'll pass through three Life Zones from the Treeless Prairie through the Conifer Forest to the Treeless Alpine Zone. And from lodgepole pine, to spruce-fir, to alpine tundra with its little lakes and perpetual snowbanks. Watch for mule deer and at the higher elevations for elk. Late evening and early morning are good viewing times. Many birds! The Pine Siskin and Pine Grosbeak thrive here. In the rocks and talus slopes watch for marmots (like groundhogs) and pika (like tiny rabbits). Fish for trout at Lake Marie. Park and hike to Medicine Bow Peak, 12,013 feet. Watch for interpretive signs at the parking areas. Walk the "Libby Flat Wildflower Trail", 13 miles West of Centennial.

SERVICES IN SARATOGA:

FOOD: Family Diner, Mom's Kitchen, Stumpy's Eatery, Wally's Pizza, Wolf Hotel.

MOTELS: Silver Moon*, Wolf Hotel*, Saratoga Inn, Riviera Lodge*, Hacienda, Cary's Sage & Sand.

GUEST RANCHES: "Medicine Bow Guest Ranch": Stay in a log cabin, fish, ride, hunt. Call: 307-326-5439. "Sierra Madre Guest Ranch": Lodge, cabins, RV parking, hiking, fishing. Call: 307-326-8407. "Bolten Ranch Adventures": Working cattle ranch. Wagon trains, floats, fish, ride. Call: 307-3266-5332. "Brush Creek Ranch": Working cattle ranch. Lodge, cabins, fish, hike ride, etc. Call: 800-726-2499.

CAMPGROUNDS: "Saratoga Lake": 1.5 miles North of Saratoga. Fish, swim. $5 to $8. "Saratoga Inn and RV": Private. Good Sam. East four blocks on Bridge Street. Hot mineral water pool. Tennis courts, golf course, other sports. Fish, float, ride horses, hunt. $19 to $26. "Saratoga Camper Trailer Court.": 116 West Farm. $7 to $10.

WILDLIFE VIEWING AREA: North of Saratoga. Bird sanctuary. Check in town.

SARATOGA NATIONAL FISH HATCHERY: North of Saratoga, two miles West of WY 130. Visitor Display Room depicts management of big game and waterfowl. View small fish and eggs in incubators. Open daily 8-4pm. Free.

SARATOGA HOBO POOL: From Wy 130 turn Left on East Walnut Avenue. The pool is open 24 hours a day all year. Temperature ranges from 117-129 degrees. Free.

SARATOGA MUSEUM: From WY 130 turn Left on Constitution. In the old Union Pacific RR Depot. Exhibits the heritage of the Platte Valley people, their homes, stores and the railroad. Free.

OVER THE SNOWY RANGE PASS

Forestry campgrounds: "Libby Creek-Willow", "Silver Lake" and "Ryan Park" have 32 foot RV limits. The rest have 22 foot limits and are one to two miles off on Forestry roads. Picnicking, hiking and fishing in this area. Ryan Park has a self-guiding trail to a World War II Prisoner-of-War Camp.

CENTENNIAL: On the Eastern side of the pass. This town experienced the discovery of gold in 1876, the U.S. Centennial, therefore, it's name. Four gold mines were here at one time but they all played out. Today it's a gold mine of recreational activities with fuel, groceries, restaurants, motels, and resorts. **NICI SELF MUSEUM:** In the old railroad station on the East side of Centennial. See an old kitchen with a round ice box, the making of railroad ties, an old newspaper, etc. Open weekends July to September, 1-4pm.

SIDETRIP TO ENCAMPMENT:

About 18 miles South of Saratoga. Encampment is an historical Native American meeting place where they gathered to hunt bison and other animals. It also became a fur-traders encampment, then ranchland and a copper boomtown. It's

MIRROR LAKE - SNOWY RANGE
High in southwest Wyoming's Snowy Range, Mirror Lake sits at the base of 12,000 foot Medicine Bow Peak
Photo credit: Wyoming Division of Tourism

snuggled in the Rockies between the Medicine Bow Range to the East and the Sierra Madre Mountains to the West. In 1897 copper was found and men rushed in to get rich quick. Many relics of the old mines around.

GRAND ENCAMPMENT MUSEUM: 817 Barnett Street. Turn Left on 8th Street. There are several buildings in the Museum Complex including a 2-story outhouse, a school house, a tiehack cabin & stage station. Displays include minerals, photos, Indian artifacts, a folding oak bathtub and a square grand piano. It's open summers and weekends in the Fall. If you're there on the third weekend in June you might make the "Woodchoppers Jamboree and Rodeo."

FOOD: Beartrap Cafe in Riverside. Pine Lodge and The Oasis in Encampment.
MOTEL/LODGING: "Lorraine's Bed & Breakfast Homestay": $30 to $40. Elk Horn Motel*: $21 to $32. Lazy Acres Motel*: $20 to $35.
CAMPGROUND: "Lazy Acres RV Court": 110 Fields Avenue, Riverside. $5 to $13.
"Encampment Town CG": 300 Rankin. Turn Right on 3rd Street.

238   PETERSON ROAD: NO NEAR SERVICES!
> **MILEPOST 242-244:** Note the different type of fence here, tall and short posts alternating with horse-fence on it. Government rangers try to discourage elk, deer and antelope from using ancestral crossings. Tunnels were built under I-80 in certain places, with hay as bait, to encourage the animals to cross under I-80 instead of over. WESTBOUND: Big view of Saratoga Valley.
> **MILEPOST 246:** Summit elevation 7400 feet.
> **MILEPOST 247-250:** View to South of Sheephead Mountain, Elevation 8,997 feet.

255   HANNA/ELK MOUNTAIN/WY 72 NORTH:
"ELK MOUNTAIN HOTEL AND VILLAGE": Accommodations FOR THE ADVENTURE-SOME. Go 3.5 miles South to the village of Elk Mountain. Left across a narrow bridge onto a County Road. (No large rigs!) This was the site of a Stage Station on the Overland Trail. Now on the National Registry with rooms & food. Across the road from the Hotel is the **GARDEN SPOT PAVILION.** This old dance hall was built in 1895 and in the 1940's was still alive with bands and entertainers. The floor was especially built with flexible lodgepole pine logs to have "spring". **Elk Mountain** village is like a secret hideaway, a wonderful surprise! It is secluded in the willows with Medicine Bow Creek splashing through, a haven for 128 souls. (But the mosquitoes like it there too.) Many deer feed in the meadows in the evenings. Old Fort Halleck was built just West of here in the 1860's to protect the Overland Trail. Apparently not constructed as a permanent fort, it had dugouts, huts and log cabins. In 1864 the surgeon there recorded the numbers that passed the fort: "Waggons 4264; Stock, 50,000, Men etc. 17,584." The notorious Jack Slade went into the Fort Commissary and shot up the canned goods. Abandoned in 1866, the original blacksmith shop still stands. It is on the Palm Livestock Company Home Ranch.
> **EASTBOUND:** In the Spring the next 40 miles are gorgeous! The swampy meadows are a riot of color with wild flowers, the most dramatic being the wild purple iris, called the "Western Blue Flag". Who will be the first to spot them? In August yellow sweet clover lines the highway.

259   EAST FORK OF MEDICINE BOW RIVER:
FUEL: North to Gas. South to Texaco & towing.

260   COUNTY ROAD 402: NO NEAR SERVICES!
> **MILEPOST 262:** PARKING AREAS. ELEVATION: 7800 FEET.
> **MILEPOST 265 WESTBOUND:** Great view to the South of Elk Mountain 11,162 feet, Pennock Mountain 10,043 feet, and Kennedy Peak 10,805 feet.

267   WAGONHOUND ROAD/REST AREA: ELEVATION: 8,000 FEET.
> South of I-80 on hill. Trailer Dump station. There are Tipi Rings here from early Native American encampments. These are rings of rocks that the natives used to surround their tipis. The Overland Trail went through here.
> **FISH & GAME'S ELK CORRAL:** Wagonhound Creek area is a wintering ground for elk, deer and pronghorn antelope. In the winter the winds blow as hard as 70 miles per hour through these hills, blowing the snow off this particular area exposing the grass as forage for the animals. Game naturally gathers here to feed. Elk are corralled and fitted with radio tracking collars.
> **MILEPOST 268 WESTBOUND:** First view of Elk Mountain ahead.

272   ARLINGTON:
FUEL/CAMPGROUND: The gas station is open all year, but the campground is open only from May to October. "KOA": Private. Close to Road but very pretty area with Rock Creek flowing through and antelope grazing nearby. Expect mosquitoes. Antelope came right up to the

campground. It's the only Campground between Rawlins and Laramie. NEAR I-80. $14.00.

OVERLAND STAGE WAY STATION: On the South side of I-80. Park and walk around. For the history of the Overland Trail read Milepost 130. Joe Bush built the first buildings here in 1860 and in 1862 this was Rock Creek Station on the Overland. In 1868 the Williams family bought it and operated a Way Station. Then a U.S. Post Office was built called "Rock Dale". An Inn, a blacksmith shop, a dance hall and of course a saloon, (in the 2-story building) were built. This building had other lives as a bunkhouse and a school. The army also used Rock Creek with three army barracks still here in 1883. The original homestead, hidden in the trees is one of the oldest standing log cabins in Wyoming.

MILEPOSTS 276-279: Wild Irises all through here in the spring! Acres of them!

279   COOPER COVE ROAD: NO NEAR SERVICES!

MILEPOST 282 BENGOUGH MONUMENT/GRAVE: On the hill North of the road.

Clement Bengough, son of the High Sheriff of Gloucestershire, arrived in Laramie in 1887 from his ancestral mansion in England. He was painfully shy, sometimes violent, but loved books and flowers. He lived as a recluse in a barren, cobwebby log cabin (South of I-80) cluttered with the London Times, books and magazines. He took his daily bath summer and winter in a big barrel outside his door. He raised steers as pets until they were 5 years old; the largest neighbors had ever seen. He also raised eleven vicious Siberian wolf hounds, had terrible fits of temper, and answered his door with a shotgun in hand. He jumped fences with his fine horses fitted with his English saddle. When he died in 1934, he requested that he be buried "on the hillside east of my cabin where I have resided." So there lies Bengough under the monument, this recluse who cherished solitude for eternity, with hundreds of cars and trucks rumbling past daily. What a rage he would have had he known!

290   QUEALY & DOME ROAD: FUEL: Phillips Truck Stop.

297   HERRICK LANE/WY 12: NO NEAR SERVICES!

WESTBOUND: In May-June watch for wild irises, the Blue Flag, for the next 40 miles!

MILEPOST 307 PARKING AREAS.

310   LARAMIE/BUS 80 EAST/CURTIS STREET: ROAD CONDITIONS CALL: 742-8981.

RADIO: 1210 & 1290 AM. 91.9, 95.1, 102.9, & 105.5 FM.

EASTBOUND: Drive through town on Bus 80 for K Mart and many services.

FUEL: Pilot, Vickers Truck Stop.

FOOD: Shoney's, Pizza.

MOTELS: Super 8*.

CAMPGROUNDS: "KOA": Pri. .25 mile East on Curtis Street. Right/South on McCue Street past the truck stop. Tents OK. NEAR I-80. $10-$18.

"N-H Trailer Ranch": Private. 1.3 miles on Curtis. South 2 blocks on 3rd Street. No tents. $11.

"Riverside CG": Private. East on Curtis. Right/South on McCue Street. South 100'. Fishing in Laramie River.

311   SNOWY RANGE ROAD, LARAMIE/WY 130: ELEVATION: 7000 FEET.

FUEL: Phillips, Conoco, Sinclair Truck Stop, Michelin Tires.

FOOD: North to Hardees, Foster's Country Corner.

MOTELS: Best Western, Camelot. Rodeway Inn, Ranger, Downtown, Travel Inn all on 3rd Street.

CAMPGROUND: "Ankeny's RV": Private. West two blocks on Snowy Range Road and Left. Just a big gravel parking lot, but quiet enough and clean restrooms. $12.

GUEST RANCHES: "Two Lazy 3 Y Ranch": 12 miles Southeast of Laramie near Vedauwoo. Rates are competitive with motels. Pets OK. Fishing & guide trips. Call: 307-745-7051.

"Vee Bar Ranch": 21 miles West on WY 130. Lodge & cottages. Horseback ride, fish, hike, raft, camp. The Excursion Train stops here. Call 307-745-7036.

LARAMIE

Native Americans have been in this area since 8000 BC. Jacques LaRamie was the first of a long line of trappers and explorers, who came this way. This was an ideal location for a camp or a town since it had two springs and the Laramie River. In 1868 it was a tent city. Then in May the Railroad reached it and six months later it had a population of 5,000. The boom busted shortly thereafter and brought the count down to 1500 people. Today it is Wyoming's third largest town. Just South of town is "Fort Sanders" where the calvary was stationed to protect the building of the railroad. As with Rawlins, it took a local vigilante group to get rid of the lawless who followed the railroad. Laramie's grasslands make it a prime livestock center but like the rest of Wyoming it also has mineral deposits and oil. If you're here the week before July 10th you can enjoy "Laramie Jubilee Days".

The first newspaper was published by Bill Nye, a famous writer. He named it after his favorite mule, "The Laramie Boomerang", and it is still on the newsstands today. He was a colorful character like Mark Twain. He arrived here with just 35 cents, became Editor of the newspaper, Justice of the Peace, and Postmaster. He left in 1883 after penning a letter to the President of the U.S. resigning his position as Postmaster. The safe was a mystery to him: "The safe combination is set on the numbers 33, 66 and 99, though I do not remember...which comes first or how many times you revolve the knob, or which direction you turn it at first in order to make it operate..."

Women made the biggest strides here as well as in the rest of Wyoming with the first women jurors in the U.S. in 1870. The next year Grandma Louisa Swain cast her ballot as the first woman to vote.

BIRD of PARADISE SALOON SHOW
Photo credit: Wyoming Territorial Park

WYOMING TERRITORIAL PARK: East of I-80 on WY 130. Site of the restored "Wyoming Territorial Prison" built in 1872. It's the only original Territorial Prison left in the country. This Living History Museum includes an "End-of-Tracks" town with shops and a "rip-roaring" show at the saloon. Also a "Dinner Theater" serving Western food and offering dancing and comedy. An outdoor barbecue pit serves everything from buffalo burgers to pioneer potato candy. There is a broom and brick factory where prisoners worked. One prisoner got out of jail and went into the lumber business supplying fence for the prison. Costumed guides lead the tours and Stagecoach and trail rides are available. Summers daily 11-8pm. Weekends through October. Adult $5.95. Senior & Child $4.95. Dinner Theatre $16.80.

Elnora L. Frye researched the lives of former prisoners and has written a fascinating book about them. Jehm Mountain Publications. 209 Park Street, Laramie, 82070. $17.95.

LARAMIE PLAINS MUSEUM: From the prison or from I-80 go East over the railroad tracks to 3rd Street/US 30. Right/South 3 blocks to Ivinson Street. Left to 6th Street & large towered Victorian Mansion. Purchase your tour ticket at the Carriage House. The museum is in the fabulous Ivinson mansion built in 1892. On the National Registry. The delicate hand-carved furniture was made at the Territorial Prison. There is also a log schoolhouse. It's a great museum, well worth the stop! Edward Ivinson, 26 years old with his wife, 18 years, arrived in one of the first trains in 1868 when this was known as "Laramie City, Dakota Territory". They brought with them the stock for a grocery and mercantile business. He became the chief supplier of ties and timber for the Union Pacific and made a fortune. The museum contains only objects actually used in the Laramie area. Summer Mon-Sat 9-8pm. Sun 1-5pm. Winter 1-4pm. Adult $4. Senior $3. Child $2.

OLD TOWN: Laramie suggests you walk the streets of their old town between Ivinson & University and 1st & 2nd Streets.

WYOMING/COLORADO EXCURSION TRAIN: Day Train rides Southwestward over the Snowy Range. Photostops are made. May 18-Dec 23rd. Lv 10:30am. Return 4:30pm. Call: 307-742-9162. Adult $24. Child $20. Includes lunch.

WESTBOUND ALTERNATE ROUTE
OVER THE SNOWY RANGE MOUNTAINS TO SARATOGA HOT SPRINGS: Take WY 130 West

over the mountains to Saratoga and North to Walcott and I-80 at Milepost 235. Beautiful scenic drive. Read Milepost 235.

MILEPOST 312: Crossing the Laramie River.

313 **3RD STREET, LARAMIE/WY 230 SOUTHWEST/ WY 287 SOUTH:** ELEVATION: 7165 FEET.
EASTBOUND: To get to the services on Grand Avenue that are listed in Milepost 316, exit here on 3rd Street to a Right on Grand.
FUEL: North to Texaco, Conoco.
FOOD: North to Hardees, The Laramie Stage Stop (with 2 restaurants). South 1.5 mile on Wy 287 to Calvaryman. (Locals recommend.)
MOTELS: North to Circle S, Comfort, Downtown, Gas Lite, Boswell, Park Inn, Ranger*, Sunset*, Thunderbird*, Motel 8, Laramie Inn. South to Motel 6*, Holiday Inn.
UNIVERSITY OF WYOMING: Ivinson & 9th. Founded in 1886 just four years before Wyoming became a state. **OLD MAIN** was the first building on the campus.
     ANTHROPOLOGY MUSEUM: Presents the cultural history of Northwest Plains Indians.
     ART MUSEUM & GEOLOGICAL MUSEUM: North on 3rd Street. Right on Lewis. With Tyrannosaurus Rex greeting you outside, and a skeleton of a brontosaurus reaching to the 2nd floor in the inside. And have you ever seen a primitive elk with 9.5-foot antlers? Also camels, bison, mammoth and rhino.
     ROCKY MOUNTAIN HERBARIUM: Check locally.
     WYOMING CHILDREN'S MUSEUM AND NATURE CENTER: 710 Garfield. 2nd floor of Laramie Plains Civic Center. Children may experience the qualities of light, sound, touch, or try out an animal home. Tues 8:30-12:30pm. Thurs 1-5pm. Sat 10-4pm. Adult $1.50. Child $.75.

316 **GRAND AVENUE, EAST LARAMIE BUS I-80 WEST:**
WESTBOUND: WEST ON GRAND AVENUE TO ALL SERVICES, MARKET & WALMART.
FUEL: Conoco, Texaco, Coastal.
FOOD: Mc Donalds, J.B.'s, Wendys, Burger King, Arbys, Taco Bell, Kentucky Fried, Sizzler.
MOTELS: Circle S, Wyo Motel.
     EASTBOUND: You are ascending Pole Mountain to the highest pass on I-80, 8640 feet, your last pass through the Rockies. In 10 miles you'll go up 1640 feet. The first four miles are easy. Then the last six miles are very steep. Turn off your air conditioner. Photographic red cliffs here with a mixed conifer forest of Englemann Spruce, Limber Pines, Lodgepoles and Ponderosas. Lodgepoles are usually tall and thin. But here, because of the winds and stressful conditions, they remain short and stubby.
     WESTBOUND: You just came over your first pass in the Rockies on I-80. Ahead of you is Laramie and the "Snowy Range" which usually boasts some snow all year.

323 **HAPPY JACK ROAD/WY210:** ELEVATION: 8640 FEET
SUMMIT REST AREA INFORMATION CENTER: Exit to the Rest Area to the North of I-80. Larger rigs park in the lower Truck Parking area as it is level. Take time to walk around, stretch your legs, breathe that stimulating air and get a delicious drink of mountain water. At the Visitor Center you can get maps and information on the nearby campgrounds. Ask about rig length restrictions. Walk to the back of the Visitor Center to the large window. Look toward the Vedauwoo rocks to the East and the Colorado Rockies to the South. Chipmunks and prairie dogs are busy on the ground below. A 42.5 foot tall statue of Abraham Lincoln looks out over I-80. Formerly US 30, the highway was designated as the "Lincoln Highway" in 1912 on the centennial of Lincoln's birth. Lincoln had pressed hard for transcontinental transportation. He would be pleased with the success of his dream.

     CAMPGROUNDS ON HAPPY JACK ROAD/WY 210: All are beautiful woods settings. "Tie City, Upper & Lower": National Forest. One mile on Happy Jack Road. On right. Pit toilets. "LOWER" has "No Trailers."
     "Yellow Pine" & "Pole Creek": National Forest. Three miles. Pit toilets.

ALTERNATE EASTBOUND ROUTE

ON HAPPY JACK ROAD: For a lovely ride into Cheyenne through rose-granite formations. From the Summit take WY 210 East entering Cheyenne on 19th Street. There are views of massive rock formations weathered into odd shapes. Watch for elk, deer, antelope, coyote.

CURT GOWDY STATE PARK: 15 miles. Fish, hike, boat, picnic, camp. Steep downgrade into it. No problem going down but a hard pull coming back UP. Two lakes, "Granite" with water sports and "Crystal Lake" for fishing and hiking. Beautiful area! Pit toilets at both.

VEDAUWOO
Children love exploring the rocks of Vedauwoo.
Photo credit: John A. Kost

329 VEDAUWOO: A MUST stop!

There is NO PLACE like this anywhere! North one mile to the National Forest Picnic Ground. Turn Left at the Picnic Area sign. The first Right takes you to a small campground that is usually full. But check it out, you may be lucky. (32 foot RV limit.) Now drive on down to the picnic area. Cars and pickups can explore the roads, but larger rigs and all hikers/climbers park at the turn-around at the National Forest Bulletin Board. This is an incredible picnic ground nestled under towering Pre-Cambrian pink granite. Vedauwoo is an Arapaho word meaning "Earthborn spirits"; "Home of the Gods" to the early tribes. They always knew the most beautiful places and reserved them for their retreats. So too this spot today is a retreat for people to experience God's beauty at its finest. The rose-colored granite outcroppings have weathered with wind and rain into chaotic shapes: pancakes on top of pillars, balancing rocks, mushrooms. You need to experience this on foot. Take your camera! Walk in to the farthest loop to the Left. From the end of this cul-de-sac follow the switchback trail up to the top of the rocks. Ramps are provided here and there to make walking easier. From on top you have a superb view West towards the Summit, and down to the beaver ponds below you. If it's summer you'll find the rocks alive with climbers. Your children will love it and remember it forever!

AMES MONUMENT: South at this exit and Left over a gravel road. You'll pass the old "Sherman" townsite where train-brakes were checked before proceeding downhill to Laramie or Cheyenne. This was a busy train inspection station before the tracks were moved. The 1882 monument is a 60 foot pyramid to the promoters/financiers of the Union Pacific RR, Oliver and Oakes Ames.

MILEPOST 333 LONE TREE PARKING AREA: Between the lanes is a tree growing out of a stone. The tracks used to go right past it. Thinking it to be endangered, the early railroaders tended it by splashing it with buckets of water as they passed. They need not have worried. Water in the crack of the rock freezes and expands splitting the rock more forming a larger reservoir for yet more water to keep trees like this growing out of solid rock. Note the gingerbread rocks of Vedauwoo on the North; to the South are the Colorado Rockies.

335 BUFORD: RADIO: 1240, 1370, 1480, & 650 AM. 97.9, 100.7, 101.9 & 106.3 FM.
FUEL & FOOD: Conoco, Diesel.

339 **REMOUNT RANCH:**
Soldiers "remounted" here. This is the ranch where Mary O'Hara Alsop wrote "My Friend Flika" and "Green Grass of Wyoming". Parts of the movie were filmed here. Riding horseback off across these rolling hills deer, coyote, killdeer and many other animals can be seen. Why not stop at a Dude Ranch for a few days and LIVE Wyoming style? Visitor Centers and museums have information on Dude Ranches and B&Bs.
MILEPOST 341 PARKING AREAS. Eastbound: Goodby Rockies!

342 **HARRIMAN ROAD:** NO NEAR SERVICES! ELEVATION: 7500 FEET.
MILEPOST 343 EASTBOUND PARKING AREA. View the Great Plains.

345 **WARREN ROAD:** NO NEAR SERVICES!

348 **OTTO ROAD:** NO NEAR SERVICES! ELEVATION: 7000 FEET.

358 **WEST LINCOLNWAY, CHEYENNE:**
EASTBOUND THROUGH ON I-80: Signs are confusing here. Do NOT take the I-25 or West Lincolnway exits.
EASTBOUND SERVICES: Follow the Lincolnway signs for one mile to services.
FUEL: Phillips, Conoco Truck Stop, Sinclair.
FOOD: Country Kitchen, Crossroads.
MOTELS: Motel 6* (next to tracks), Hitching Post, Little America, La Quinta, Stagecoach, Super 8, Atlas, Days Inn, Frontier*, Guest Ranch, Luxury 8*, Pioneer*, Ranger, The Sands.

359 **M A J O R   I N T E R C H A N G E !**
I-25 NORTH TO CHUGWATER, SOUTH TO DENVER:
WESTBOUND SERVICES: To get to West Lincolnway motels/stations, exit on I-25 North and take the West Lincolnway Exit #9. Go North or South. Read Milepost 358 for Services.
WYOMING INFORMATION CENTER: South on I-25 to College Drive/Exit 12. Get map & brochures on Cheyenne.
CAMPGROUNDS: "Hyland Park/MHP": Private. Good Sam. North on I-25. 1.6 miles to Missile Drive/Exit 10 D. East .3 mile. Adult park, no tents, no pets.
"AB Campground": 1503 West College. Cabins, play ground.. South on I-25 to College Drive/Exit 7. East 1.5 miles.

WESTBOUND ALTERNATE ROUTE
ON HAPPY JACK ROAD: Through marvelous rose granite rock formations. North on I-25 to Exit 10. West on WY 210/HAPPY JACK ROAD for 38 miles. You'll climb from rolling grassy hills into rocky mountains of tall pines past campgrounds to end up at Summit Rest Area and I-80. Read Milepost 323.

362 **CENTRAL AVENUE, CHEYENNE/I-180/US 85:** ELEVATION: 6000 FEET.
Radio: 650, 1240, 1370 & 1480 AM. 97.9, 100.7, 106.3, 101.9 FM.
MALL: To South. HOSPITAL.
FUEL: Bingo-Burns, Vickers Truck Stop, Conoco.
FOOD: South to Burger King, Taco John's, Arby's, Los Amigos. North to Owl's Inn & Whipple House (block North of US 30). Golden Corral Buffet on Lincolnway.
MOTELS: Holiday Inn, Lariat*, Plains, Roundup.
CAMPGROUND: "Hide a Way": 218 South Greeley Highway. South on US 85.

CHEYENNE
The town of Cheyenne was named for the Cheyenne Nation of Native Americans by General Grenville M. Dodge, chief engineer for the building of the Union Pacific Railroad. The armys main function at this time was to protect and aid the railroad. Dodge set up camp on Crow Creek (that snakes through Cheyenne) in 1865 at the junction of roads leading to army camps. In 1867 he put a terminal there and the area was soon swamped by opportunists such as developers, gamblers, and salesmen even when the track work was 100 miles East. This

ever-moving front of the railroad was called "Hell on Wheels" because of the riff-raff that moved with it. Cheyenne became a trade center for railroad supplies for the expanding construction. The town was incorporated in 1867 with a unique justice system that included a log cabin that housed the tramps & drunks.

Telegraph crews had their own problems with the bison who used the poles to scratch themselves, for there were few trees on the prairies. They could destroy a pole in a few hours. Spikes were put on the poles but these did not detract the bison. Cowboys told stories of bison lining up to use a spiked pole.

Fort Russell, just Northwest of town, had orders to protect the railroad from attack and maintain order so that construction could proceed. The fort was later named for Wyoming's first governor Francis E. Warren, who held office for 37 years. It is now Warren Air Force Base where a museum traces its early history.

Cheyenne is in the center of rich grasslands for cattle. With the railroad here to ship them to the Eastern markets, the cattle industry was quickly established. Longhorns were herded up from Mexico and Texas. They were just $3 a head, were nimble and hardy and needed little water, but their meat was tough and stringy. Ranchers learned to interbreed them with Eastern English-bred cattle like the Hereford, producing better meat and higher profits. Wyoming became a land of cattle barons and cowboys.

If you're in Cheyenne the LAST FULL WEEK OF JULY you'll find crowded facilities (reserve ahead) but a whopping good time western style. Cheyenne's Frontier Days is one of the world's largest rodeo spectaculars with exciting quarterhorse and chuckwagon races. Additional festivities include a parade of horse-drawn vehicles, nightly shows, pancake breakfasts, Comanche dancers, square dances, old fashioned melodramas, and even an air show by the Thunderbirds from WARREN AIR FORCE BASE. Call 1-800-227-6336.

NORTH ON CENTRAL AVENUE TO TOUR CHEYENNE:

ATLAS THEATRE & MELODRAMA: 211 West 16th Street. Call 638-6543.

CHEYENNE STREET TROLLEY: Historic summer 2-hour city tour. Call: 800-426-5009.

WYOMING STATE CAPITOL: The highest capitol in the U.S. at 6062 feet, built in 1877, is a beautiful white classic building with a gold-leafed dome. Out front is a spectacular bronze bucking bronco. In the rotunda are mounted bison and elk, murals, and marble floors. Guided tours weekdays, 8:30-4:30pm. Free.

GOVERNOR'S MANSION: 300 East 21st Street. This Georgian mansion was built in 1905 and housed, among others, the United State's FIRST woman governor, Nellie Taylor Ross. Lovely mansion visited by Bill Cody, Teddy Roosevelt, & Harry Truman. Tues-Sat 9-5pm. Free.

SPIRIT of WYOMING
This statue, the "Spirit of Wyoming", stands outside the Wyoming Capitol Building in Cheyenne.
Photo credit: Wyoming Division of Tourism

WYOMING STATE MUSEUM: Central Avenue & 24th Street. An excellent museum telling the story of the sheepherder, the cowboy, and the men and women of Wyoming. Mon-Fri 8:30-5pm. Sat 9-5pm. Also contains the "Wyoming State Art Gallery". Free.

NATIONAL FIRST DAY COVER MUSEUM: 702 Randall Blvd. This is a $750,000 collection of first edition postage stamps with original artwork. An oldtime post office and a general store are open. Mon-Fri 9-12 noon & 12:30-5pm. Free.

HOLLIDAY PARK: East of the capitol at 17th & Morrie. The World's largest steam locomotive, called "Big Boy". It used to run from Cheyenne to Ogden, Utah carrying 28 tons of fuel and 25,000 gallons of water. This is twice the capacity of normal steam engines.

LIONS' PARK: Carey & 8th. West on 8th Street. Relax here and picnic. Give the kids a chance to see the bison and elk at the zoo, or swim or check out the amusement park, miniature golf and solar-heated Botanic Gardens.

CHEYENNE FRONTIER DAYS OLD WEST MUSEUM: West on 8th to Carey Avenue. Turn North. Western collection of horse-drawn vehicles, rodeo history and Ogallala Sioux artifacts. Summer Mon-Sat 8-7pm. Sun 10-6pm. Winter Mon-Fri 9-5pm. Sat-Sun 11:30-4:30pm. Adult $2. Senior $1. Child free.

WYOMING GAME AND FISH DEPARTMENT VISITOR CENTER: Central & I-25. Information on wildlife and the wetlands. Mon-Fri 8-5pm. Summers Sat-Sun 8-5pm. Free.

364 COLLEGE DRIVE, CHEYENNE/WY 212/NORTH TO EAST LINCOLNWAY/US 30:
MALLS: CHEYENNE PLAZA: North one mile to Left at 2nd light. FRONTIER MALL: North to Prairie Dell Range and Left to K MART and WALMART.
FUEL: South to Vickers, Conoco.
FOOD: North one mile to McDonalds, Country Kitchen, Wyatt's Cafeteria in Frontier Mall. Taco, Burger King, Hardees, Shari's at Lincolnway Mall.
MOTELS: North to Fleetwood, Firebird, Home Ranch, Rodeway, Big Horn*, Cheyenne, Twin Chimneys*. South to Roundup.
CAMPGROUNDS: "Karl's KOA": Private. 364 East Lincolnway. North 1.5 mile on College Drive/WY 212. East on Charles Street for .25 mile.
"Greenway Travel Park": Private. North on College Drive 1.5 miles.
"Restway Travel Park": Private. Good Sam. North on College Drive to East Lincolnway. Right and Northeast 1.7 miles to Whitney Road. North one block. Pool, playground, miniature golf.

367 CAMPSTOOL ROAD:
WYOMING HEREFORD RANCH: Operating ranch with tours available. Call 634-1905.
MILEPOST 368: WESTBOUND: First view of the Rockies!

370 ARCHER: ELEVATION: 6000 FEET.
FUEL & MOTEL: Texaco/Sapp Brothers Truck Stop. Motel*.
MILEPOST 376: EASTBOUND PARKING AREA.

377 HILLSDALE/WY 217 NORTH:
FUEL & FOOD: Bingo-Burns Truck Stop and Motel.
CAMPGROUND: "WYO Camp": Private. North of I-80. Pool, playground. NEAR I-80.
MILEPOST 379: Note the wheatfields here in alternate ribbons. This is a good example of dry farming (no irrigation in a low-rainfall area). It takes two years of moisture to grow a crop. So Wyoming wheat farmers plow up the land and plant alternate ribbons, leaving the other ribbons to "lie fallow" (grow nothing) for a year to store the moisture. They even plow up the weeds as they sprout so that they won't use up the moisture. The next year they plant the alternate field.

386 ANTELOPE/WY 213/WY 214/BURNS/CARPENTER:
FUEL: Cenex Truck Stop.
WESTBOUND: Watch for antelope from here to the Fort Bridger area. You'll see their white rumps and undersides that stand out against the darker grass.
EASTBOUND: Say goodby to the antelope.
MILEPOST 389: ELEVATION: 5000 FEET.

391 EGBERT: NO NEAR SERVICES!

401 PINE BLUFFS/BUS 80 NORTH:
REST AREA TO SOUTH: A MUST STOP! Visit the University of Wyoming Archeological Digs and learn about Tipis. Information, maps, brochures, playground, RV dump, nature loop trail through the bluffs. The "digs" are around the bluff to the West. It's a pleasant 15 minute trail past yucca and prickly pear plants that may be blooming May to July. The Sioux used this area to pass from the hunting grounds in the valley to their tipis on the Bluffs. The Sioux words "Tipi" and "Tiyata" mean "home". Indian Tipis have been reconstructed, carefully painted with authentic Indian designs. A brochure in the Information Center will tell you all about them. Walk up the hill at the back of the Rest Area. Tipis were placed in a circle open to the East to remind them to give thanks for the new day. Walk further up to see remnants of "Tipi rings". These are piles of rocks used to surround the tipis and anchor them. There are remnants of authentic Tipi

rings at Wagonhound Road, Milepost 267.

PINE BLUFFS

FUEL: North to Ampride Truck Stop, Phillips Truck Stop.

MOTELS: North to Sunset*, Travelyn.

CAMPGROUND: "Pine Bluff RV CG": 10 Paint Brush. Private. Good Sam. Exit North on Bus 80 and follow it to the East of town. Right turn into the campground. NEAR I-80.

TEXAS TRAIL MUSEUM: 3rd & Market Street. North into town and follow the road until after it turns Right. The Museum includes Indian lore, pioneer and ranching displays, and a collection of Western "Fur" coats. Other buildings include a furnished Union Pacific boarding house, a railroad caboose, an 1879 one-room school house, and a log home. Summers 9-5pm. Pine Bluffs marks the area of the greatest cattle drives in history. As a Union Pacific shipping center, cattle were herded here from Brownsville, Texas and Abilene, Kansas up the "Texas Trail". In just one of those years, 1871, 600,000 cattle arrived here from Texas. In 1884 Pine Bluffs shipped more cattle on the Union Pacific from here than any other station. Some were herded North to Wyoming, Montana and the Dakotas to be raised. Others were sold to brokers who shipped them to Eastern markets.

REHER PARK: A block East of the museum. Picnic, playground, shelter, miniature golf. Free pool.

ARCHEOLOGICAL ARTIFACT CENTER: 2nd & Elm Street. Two blocks East of the Museum. Artifacts from the University Digs are displayed here.

EASTBOUND: Say "Goodby" to the Equality State and "Hello, Nebraska!"

WESTBOUND: Now you'll climb up into and over the Rockies. Take at least one sidetrip off I-80 to experience these wonderful mountains. Read Wyoming History and prepare to enjoy Wyoming.

WYOMING'S FIRST SCHOOLHOUSE
Restored at Fort Bridger.
Photo credit: John A. Kost

LONE TREE GROWS OUT OF SOLID ROCK
Photo credit: Wyoming Travel Commission

106

WYOMING I 80 MILEPOSTS

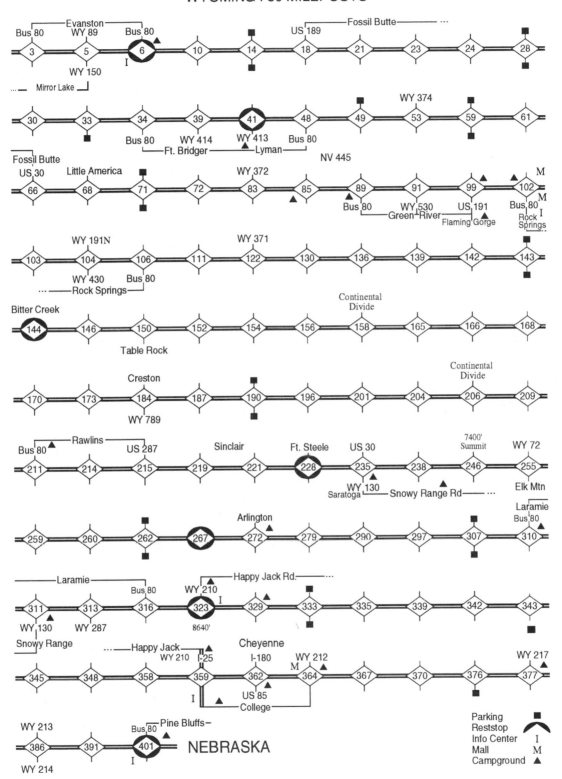

Evanston
Bus 80   WY 89   Bus 80   Fossil Butte ──── ...
                            US 189
3   5   6   10   14   18   21   23   24   28
                    I
WY 150
... ── Mirror Lake ──┘

                                    WY 374
30   33   34   39   41   48   49   53   59   61
      Bus 80   WY 414   WY 413   Bus 80
      └── Ft. Bridger ──┘ Lyman   NV 445

Fossil Butte
US 30   Little America   WY 372   M
66   68   71   72   83   85   89   91   99   102
                                                                        M
                        Bus 80   WY 530   US 191   Bus 80   I
                        └── Green River ──┘ Flaming Gorge   Rock
                                                            Springs

WY 191N   WY 371
103   104   106   111   122   130   136   139   142   143
WY 430   Bus 80
... ── Rock Springs ──┘

Bitter Creek   Continental
                                        Divide
144   146   150   152   154   156   158   165   166   168
      Table Rock

                                        Continental
      Creston   Divide
170   173   184   187   190   196   201   204   206   209
      WY 789

      ── Rawlins ──
Bus 80   US 287   Sinclair   Ft. Steele   US 30   7400'   WY 72
                                                              Summit
211   214   215   219   221   228   235   238   246   255
                                          WY 130   Snowy Range Rd ── ...   Elk Mtn
                                        Saratoga
                                                                          Laramie
                                Arlington   Bus 80
259   260   262   267   272   279   290   297   307   310

── Laramie ──   ── Happy Jack Rd ── ...
              Bus 80   WY 210
311   313   316   323   329   333   335   339   342   343
WY 130   WY 287   8640'
Snowy Range

... ── Happy Jack ──   Cheyenne
              WY 210   I-25   I-180   WY 212   WY 217
                                      M
345   348   358   359   362   364   367   370   376   377
                I   US 85
                └── College ──┘

WY 213   Pine Bluffs ──
              Bus 80
386   391   401   **NEBRASKA**
WY 214   I

Parking   ■
Reststop   ⌒
Info Center   I
Mall   M
Campground   ▲

PRONGHORN ANTELOPE ROAM the HIGH PLAINS
Photo credit: Wyoming Division of Tourism

Nebraska

The Cornhusker State

Corn was a staple to the early settlers and they husked tons of it by hand. "Cornhusker" is a fine name for a football team, but it doesn't do Nebraska justice. It's so much more! Nebraska is a giant bridge spanning lands, cultures and climates. It begins in the East at the Missouri River at around 900 feet and climbs very slowly but steadily to its highest point in Western Nebraska at 5426 feet. It's a vast flat prairie rolling into hills toward the West until the final climb up the foothills toward the Rockies. Nebraska climbs also from Eastern farm country and industrial cities to Western ranches. From cornfields to cattle country; from cottontails to jackrabbits, antelope and bison. And man's innovation, from Central Time to Mountain Time just East of Ogallala. Even Nebraska's first native settlers had two different cultures East to West. In the East the Omahas, Otoes, Pawnees and Poncas, were farmers who lived in permanent earth lodges and grew their major food supply. They had cooperative drives to kill bison and deer. But in the West the Cheyenne, Sioux and Arapaho, were excellent horsemen and nomads with easily collapsible tipis to follow the bison herds.

As a country we are becoming more homogenized now from TV, McDonalds and K Mart. But the East used to have cinnamon rolls while the West had "snails". The East had the baseball cap and the West the cowboy hat. The headgear of the road crews changed as you crossed the state.

Eastern Nebraska averages 24" of rain a year for its rich brown soil and long-grass. The Western Panhandle is lucky to get 12" of rain for its light-colored soil and short grass . For Westerners returning home from the East Coast, spanning Nebraska is traveling from the humid East to the dry West. Going West the skies clear, the clouds roll away, and the air is light and free.

The "Ogallala Aquafir", an extensive subterranean reserve of water, stretches from Nebraska to Texas, The Platte River may be wide and shallow but it has this tremendous reserve of water under it. Since the water table is so high there are many lakes in the sand hills to the North where seabirds nest in the marshes. When digging post holes along the Platte River, the settlers could not dig too deeply or they hit water and sand. Windmills were most important to the early settlers to pump water for their livestock and crops. Watch for the windmills along I-80 especially at "Windmill State Recreation Area", Milepost 285.

Nebraska has 77,355 square miles with a population of 1,578,385. Its flower is the goldenrod with waving spears of blossoms seen near the roads along with the brown and yellow sunflowers. The state received its name from the Otoe and Omaha Indians who called it "Nibthaska" meaning "flat water". This referred to Nebraska's main nourishing river, the Platte. The first writings describe the Platte as so wide that it resembled an ocean lined with sand dunes. It was the guide for the first trails Westward for some 340,000 pioneers, the route of the railroad, and now it leads I-80 on its way. The Missouri River at its Eastern boundary carried Lewis and Clark on the first exploration West.

Nebraska like Kansas is storm and tornado country. The warm wet humid air comes up from the gulf while the cold air comes down from the North and West. When these two meet, it's trouble with a capital T. One minute it's a sunny day with just a dark cloud in the distance. Suddenly it hits! You reach for the windows or dash for shelter but you're drenched immediately. The drivers

Goldenrod

on I-80 are facing a curtain of water as they hang on to their steering wheels and slow down. And then it is gone! It's over as quickly as it started and man is left weak with awe at the power of a prairie storm.

Nebraska has a unique legislature of one house of 49 non-partisan representatives at their capital in Lincoln. Today the state is still largely agricultural, but has large food processing and machinery manufacturing industries. As you pass from East to West, first you'll see fields of corn and soybeans like Iowa, then towards the West the field crops of oats, rye and barley. The irrigated valleys of the West will have alfalfa, potatoes and sugar beets. Nebraska also has oil and natural gas. All of these riches the early pioneers bypassed as they wound their way through "Indian Country" to the Far West.

NEBRASKA HISTORY

Various Native tribes had occupied this territory for centuries, when in 1739 Pierre and Paul Mallet explored the Platte and called it "La Riviere Plate". Americans had not ventured this far West until the United States had acquired the Louisiana Purchase from France. Now Lewis and Clark were sent out in 1804 to find a way West to the Pacific. They held their First Council with the Indians on the Missouri at "Council Bluffs" just North of Omaha, Nebraska. At this time there were a half million Natives and 25 million bison West of the Missouri.

The trappers moving West found the Missouri route too hazardous, the Black Feet too deadly, until they found the "Great Platte River Road." In the 1830's it was the missionaries who initiated the Westward Movement with trappers as their guides. The first wagon train, the Bidwell-Bartleson Party with 20 wagons and 69 members, went through in 1841 and Marcus Whitman guided 1,000 people and wagons through in 1843. Numbers increased from 3,000 in 1845 to over 44,500 in 1850 until 350,000 people had crossed Nebraska via covered wagons from 1840-1866.

There are more trails through Nebraska than any other state. The most-used "Oregon Trail" entered Nebraska from Kansas near Rock Creek, met the Platte at Ft. Kearny and followed its Southern bank West. The stage coaches and the Pony-Express followed most of the same route through Nebraska. The wide sandy Platte River was impossible for wagons to cross so they stayed on the South bank until near Big Springs where they crossed the South Fork and traveled up to the North Platte. The "Mormon Trail" actually began at Nauvoo, IL. It entered Nebraska above Omaha and joined the Platte to follow it along on its Northern bank. The freight companies used both the Oregon Trail and the "Nebraska City Cutoff" (Nebraska City to the Platte River).

The pioneers had many descriptions of the Platte, but they usually centered around its configuration, "A mile wide and a foot deep", or its water "Too thick to drink, too thin to plow". Or they called it "The Upside-down River", sand on top, water underneath! The river's grasslands spread out one to 12 miles each side of the river. This was no narrow trail as each wagon could fan out and seek its own road through the tall grass to avoid the dust of the wagons in front.

Bison trails wound down from each ravine of the rolling hills on both sides of the river, where they came to drink and to "wallow" in the sand. A wagon train would be held up for hours waiting for the massive herds to pass. (A single herd on the Arkansas River was reported to be four million strong, 25 miles wide and 50 miles long.) In the early years game was quite plentiful and tame. Early travelers reported antelope grazing near the campsites and a young antelope becoming as tame as a pet. Of course this all changed as hunting increased and more emigrants came.

The first emigrants along the Platte were from the Southern and Middle states. The government had made Kansas and Oklahoma "Indian Territory" so new land for Southern settlers could only be sought South to Texas or North to the Platte. The Northeasterners could still find new land in Iowa, Michigan, Wisconsin and Minnesota. The last pioneers West were immigrants from Germany, Ireland and Scandinavia from 1856 to 1890. By 1870 most of them were using the train instead of the trails. But some farm families from the Central and Midwestern states migrated West in wagons long after the trains came.

Watching the never-ending line of wagons in utter dismay and desperation were the Sioux and the Cheyenne. Their hunting grounds were trampled, their bison slaughtered and left rotting, sometimes just for tongues or hides! The Natives were aghast at the waste! How could these whites destroy the gifts of the Great Spirit? Before each hunt, they asked the blessings of the Great Spirit who gave them their game as a sacred trust. They killed only what they needed for food and used EVERY part of it.

The death of the bison coincided with the death of so many Natives. When white men first came they estimated there were some 13-25 million bison. The settlers saw an endless supply, and the railroad needed food for the crews, so many were killed. However it was 1871 when the bison hides were found to be good for leather that the animals were doomed. Between that year and 1874, three million were killed for just the hides, $1 each. By 1878 the Southern herds were exterminated and by 1883 the North saw no more. Some ranchers in these

Western States have been trying to increase the number of bison by breeding them.

In the 1840's-50's the pioneers passed up Nebraska land for the Far West because Nebraska was designated as "Indian Territory" and the government would not allow whites to settle there. Since 1845 the idea of "Manifest Destiny" had been growing; a United States all the way to the Pacific! If this was to be, before Nebraska could be settled, the government had to reverse itself and find somewhere else to put all these Native Americans. Oklahoma Territory had been designated as "Indian Territory" and the government had forcibly moved the Eastern tribes there by 1838. What could they do with the Nebraska tribes? The government came up with a unique plan. They instigated charges of Civil War treason against the Eastern tribes in Oklahoma, took their land, gave them smaller plots for a price and thus made room for the Plains Tribes on the same land. In 1854 the Omaha and Oto Indians of Nebraska ceded their lands. The Pawnees surrendered in July 1859 in Northeast Nebraska. The Poncas were next and were herded to Oklahoma some dying along the way. (The Western nomadic tribes endured on into the 1870's and 1880's). Now the "Indian Territory" label was removed from Nebraska and emigrants could settle in the Eastern part of the state.

Statehood plans for the West had to be designed by Congress before any new states could be admitted. Would states be admitted as slave or free? A hot and not just a moral issue! It had to do with the balance of the votes in Congress to retain the status quo. Finally in 1854 the "Kansas-Nebraska Act" was passed by which states could CHOOSE slave or free for themselves. This was a device of Stephen A. Douglas that he called "Popular Sovereignty" debating Lincoln on this issue.

The year 1862 was a dramatic year for Nebraska. The Civil War began in 1860, field crops were needed, and immigrant farmers were arriving from Europe. So the "Homestead Act" of 1862 was passed to encourage farming. Any citizen over 21, (or man who intended to become a citizen), who was head of a family, could claim 160 acres of public land. He just had to live on it for 5 years and pay a registration fee. Or a man could buy the land after 6 months at $1.25 an acre. This same year Lincoln signed the "Pacific Railroad Act" to begin the Transcontinental Railroad. These events brought hundreds of settlers to Nebraska.

After 1867 the railroads were also in the land business selling off the alternate one square mile of land for 10 miles each side of the railroad that they acquired as a bonus for building the railroad. They spent $1 million advertising in Europe for the sale of their land and sometimes offered free passage to those immigrants who bought it. This encouraged settlers to make their homes on the prairies and gave Nebraska her rich ethnic and cultural heritage. Former fortune seekers who had failed to find their dreams in the Far West, now remembered the prairies and came Eastward again to settle down.

NEBRASKA INDIAN WARS

It's a common misconception from movies that pioneers along the Oregon and the Mormon Trails in the 1840's-1850's were constantly in peril of attack. Not true, as most of the Tribes were too busy in their own boundary struggles. Black Hawk's Sauk tribe, pushed to Nebraska from Iowa, was struggling with the Pawnee for a place in their territory, keeping both tribes on edge. On the other side were the Sioux perpetually harassing the Pawnee. Emigrants felt threatened by the Pawnees who pestered them by begging, and demanding fees for passage through their territory. But in spite of the settlers fear and hatred of the Natives, less than 400 of 10,000 emigrant deaths were caused by Native Americans.

But now "Manifest Destiny" was demanding ALL of Nebraska. The idea of a United States all the way to the Pacific had been festering for years, especially since Alta California had been won from Mexico. The U.S. decided to divide and conquer the Indians as they had in the East. First they needed set boundaries for each tribe so that they could deal with weak individual tribes instead of a strong confederation. Thus in 1851 Thomas Fitzpatrick met with the Plains tribes at Ft. Laramie and lands were allotted. Cheyenne and Arapaho had the land South of the Platte to half of Colorado "for all time". The Sioux were guaranteed all the land North of the Platte. Peace reigned for 8 years. Then came the Colorado gold rush of 1859 with 100,000 miners crossing Nebraska and invading Cheyenne territory in Colorado. As their land was overrun, conflict erupted. In response, in 1861 Federal agents called a meeting of the Cheyenne and Arapaho. ALL their lands were taken except for a small plot between the Arkansas River and Sand Creek. The warriors rebelled, rejected their chiefs, and went on the warpath raiding the stagecoaches and the miners. In June 1864 the Colorado Territorial Governor demanded that all chiefs come to another meeting or be exterminated. This goaded the Natives into full war extending from the Platte to the Arkansas Rivers.

By the fall of 1864 Chief Black Kettle tried to make peace first with the Army Commander and then with the Governor. But he got only threats that when the Civil War was over in the South the Army would destroy him and all his people. Then he approached a new Commander who vacillated. Black Kettle thought that his pleas for peace were accepted so he led his tribe of 700 to a camp at nearby Sand Creek. On Nov 28, 1864 Colonel Chivington with 1,000 men surrounded the camp in early morning and attacked. The Chief's white flag and his

American flag were ignored. Men, women and children were not only slaughtered, but 450 were viciously mutilated. The few who survived told the story to the other tribes to the North. The Sioux were already on edge because of the installation of "The Singing Wires" (the telegraph lines), and the surveying of the railroad along the Platte. Fired up by the Sand Creek Massacre they attacked the surveying crews, wagon trains, and settlements, and cut down the telegraph wires. Read Mileposts 237, 272, 305, and 312. In Oct 1865 the Cheyenne surrendered! But now miners had spread up to Montana. A new road to the mines was being surveyed through Sioux Territory from Ft. Laramie to Boseman, Montana. In 1865 when the Sioux learned that this road was to go through their sacred hunting grounds at Little Big Horn (awarded them by treaty in 1851) Sioux attacks multiplied. The government finally decided to let the Sioux keep the Little Big Horn, until they needed it. In 1868 the Sioux settled for a reservation in Northern Nebraska and South Dakota. This brought some peace to the Platte River Road. But up North the Sioux still struggled for their freedom on through the battles of the Little Big Horn and Wounded Knee.

NEBRASKA REST AREAS

For the Bicentennial, Nebraska had a competition with 100 artists designing sculptures for the Rest Areas. The theme was to dramatize the past and visualize the future. Use your imagination to understand and appreciate these nine large diverse sculptures along I-80. They're made of stone and metal and are meant to be climbed on and touched by children of all ages.

Nebraska provides its travelers with some of the finest Rest Areas on I-80. They are well-designed and spaced, and have friendly attendants. Each Rest Area has a large plaque describing an historical event or something locally significant, along with other displays and photos. Stop, read and be informed! Stretch your legs and jog along the walkways. From March 1st to November 1st, 9-5 pm the following rest areas will be staffed: 124 Eastbound and 132, 430, and 454 Westbound. From Memorial Day to Labor Day, 9-5 pm. Rest Areas will be staffed at least every 100 miles. (Before cutbacks they were staffed every 45 miles.)

Information Centers have audio tapes that you can check out, "Nebraska: Highway to a Heritage". These are hour-long tapes by folklorist Roger Welsch with a lighthearted look at the history, culture, museums, folklore, food and people of Nebraska. Leave a $12 check for a deposit with the hostess. Return the tape and booklet in the postage paid envelope within 10 days and they'll return your check. Get them at the EASTBOUND Visitor Centers at Mileposts 9, 51 and 124, and at the WESTBOUND Centers at Mileposts 404, 430, and 454.

Nebraska has old US 30 paralleling I-80 to the North and connecting all the towns for 2/3rds of the way across the state. To go into the towns for more services, you drive 1-4 miles North and you are on US 30, no Bus 80's here. If you get tired of I-80 and want to see the ranches and towns, just travel US 30 for awhile. In the summer you'll see and smell where the alfalfa is cut, dehydrated and formed into pellets.

NEBRASKA MILEPOSTS

EMERGENCY HIGHWAY HELP LINE: 1-800-525-5555.
STATEWIDE CRIME STOPPERS: 1-800-422-1494.
TOURIST INFORMATION: 1-800-742-7595.
TELEPHONE AREA CODES FOR NEBRASKA: WESTERN: 308. EASTERN: 402.
NEBRASKA STATE PARKS AND RECREATION AREAS REQUIRE A $2 DAILY ENTRY FEE OR A $10 ANNUAL FEE.

MILEPOSTS:

1 **EAST PINE BLUFFS:** ELEVATION: 5,000 FEET.
WESTBOUND: Exit North into Pine Bluffs for services, Campground, Texas Trail Museum, and Archeology Artifact Center. Read the descriptions in Wyoming Milepost 401. Then say goodby to the great bridge of Nebraska and get ready to climb onto the high plains and mountains of Wyoming.
EASTBOUND OLIVER LAKE STATE REC AREA: North to US 30 and East to the lake. Take time off from driving to relax, picnic and swim off a sandy beach. Or stay and fish, boat, and use the primitive camp.

8 **BUSHNELL:** NO NEAR SERVICES!
MILEPOST 9 EASTBOUND RESTSTOP AND VISITOR CENTER: Get your

Nebraska map here and your one-hour cassette of "Highway to a Heritage". Playground. Walk up the hill for a Big View of the Plains.

20   **KIMBALL/NE 71:** ELEVATION: 4695 FEET.
WESTERN ENTRANCE: On the Southwest corner of I-80 is an oil derrick that commemorates Kimball as the oil capital of Nebraska.
FUEL: North to Phillips Truck Stop. South to Sinclair Truck Stop.
FOOD: North to Pizza Hut.
MOTELS: North to Super 8*, Best Western, I-80 Inn, Slumber J Lodge.
CAMPGROUND: "I-80 Camp & Mart". Private. Good Sam. North .25 mile on NE 71. Playground. $7-$11.
  WESTBOUND OLIVER LAKE STATE REC AREA: 8 miles West of Kimball off US 30. Read Milepost 1.
  GOTTE PARK: North 1 mile on NE 71 to US 30. East for 9 blocks. A 100 foot Titan-1 ICBM Missile represents the 200 Intercontinental Ballistic Missiles that are in silos in the Tri-State Area. Overnight trailer parking, playground, tennis court, pool.
  PLAINS HISTORICAL MUSEUM: North one mile to US 30. Antique furniture, clothing & tools, Indian artifacts, and dolls. Summers 1-5 pm.

22   **KIMBALL/EASTERN ENTRANCE:** Services are all 2 miles North on US 30.
 FOOD: 5 Restaurants and Safeway groceries.
 MOTELS: 8 including Best Western and Western* Motels.
 CAMPGROUNDS: "Daz End KOA": Private. North one mile on 53 E Link. Pool and Playground. $12-$18. City Park is also a Tourist Park.
  MILEPOST 25 WESTBOUND RESTSTOP: (on the hill) Displays on trappers and explorers. Playground.

29   **DIX:** NO NEAR SERVICES!
  MILEPOST 33: Note the Central Pivot Irrigation.

38   **POTTER:** ELEVATION: 4,000 FEET. All services one mile North.
"FAR-MOR CO-OP": Hitches, tires, car repairs.
FUEL: Texaco, Cenex.
FOOD: Buffalo Bend Restaurant, Sandy's Cafe, Potter Sundry (an old fashioned soda fountain).
MOTEL/CAMPGROUND: "Buffalo Bend Camp-Motel": Private. North to US 30. East three miles. $10. Hiking, fishing, small zoo with bison & deer, cafe, museum, summer stage show. There was an especially big curve on the railroad here as it went around "Point of Rocks".

48   **COMMUNITY COLLEGE:** ELEVATION: 4085 FEET. RADIO: 98.7 FM.
  The college was previously an Army Ordnance Depot and also a Prisoner of War Camp during World War II. (From swords to plowshares!)
  MILEPOST 51 EASTBOUND RESTSTOP AND VISITOR CENTER: Note that you're in the Bluffs now. Get your "Highway to a Heritage" tapes here. A few trees and a playground. Get some exercise by taking the path up the hill for a Big View. Displays on the Sidney-Deadwood Trail. A plaque tells you about the Golden Link. Nebraska was the first state to complete its section of I-80 and in 1974 Nebraska connected its final section of I-80 here. A Golden Link is embedded in I-80 just North of the Rest Area where the last two sections of NE I-80 joined. You'll need your binoculars to see it.
  LODGEPOLE CREEK: To the North is Lodgepole Creek, the longest creek in the world, and the site of battles between the Sioux and the railroad.

55   **SIDNEY/NE 19:**
  Sidney was layed-out by the railroad when it arrived in 1867.
Eastbound into Sidney for services:
FUEL: Amoco.

FOOD: Kentucky Fried and 14 cafes.
MOTELS: Econo Lodge*, Super 8*, and 9 others in town.

59 **SIDNEY/US 385 NORTH:** HOSPITAL.
FUEL: Sapp Bros, Texaco Truck Stop, Amoco.
FOOD: McDonalds, Pizza Hut.
MOTELS: On US 30: Right to Conestoga Motel, Roundup Motel. Left to Generic Motel, El Palomino Motel, Ft. Sidney Motor Hotel, Sidney Motor Lodge.
CAMPGROUND: "Conestoga RV Park": Private. North 2.2 miles on US 385 to US 30. West .5 mile. No tents. Pool. $10.
CABELA'S: Northwest of I-80. North to Left at McDonalds. Undoubtedly the largest and most spectacular store for outdoor wear. You must see it to believe it! Two sides of the 2-story high building have large bronzes of two elk with locked horns. Inside are dioramas of North American wildlife with one on the back wall two stories high! The walls are lined with mounted animals and fish. Mounted geese fly overhead and glass cases display mounted ducks and geese. A pond outside is for practicing fly-casting. A cafe inside features smoked buffalo meat.
CHEYENNE COUNTY MUSEUM/FORT SIDNEY: 544 Jackson Street. North to US 30 and into town. One block South on 6th Street. Museum is in the former Ft. Sidney Officers' Quarters. In the 1860's this fort served to protect the pioneers on the Oregon Trail, the Overland Stage and the Pony Express. As the railroad built Westward the army protected the construction workers. Later when gold was discovered in the Black Hills, it struggled to keep peace on the Sidney to Deadwood Trail. Daily 1-5pm. Free. The Post Commander's Home is on 6th Avenue, 1.5 blocks away. Go East to 5th Avenue and drive by the 8-sided Powder House of the old fort.
LEGION PARK AND MEMORIAL GARDENS: On 10th Avenue, eleven blocks South of US 30. Recreation, swim, tennis, kid-fishing pond, playground, a steam engine, box car, caboose and a rose garden.

The Oregon and Pony Express Trails closely parallel I-80 on the North from Chappell to Sidney. Then the trails crossed the Lodgepole just West of Sidney at Milepost 59 and turned North traveling just West of US 385 toward Bridgeport, Courthouse Rock and the North Platte. This route was used in the 1860's to avoid the difficult descent into Ash Hollow from Brule East of here. Using this trail the Pony Express riders reached Ft. Laramie on their 3rd day from St. Joseph, Missouri. Later, the stage connecting Deadwood South Dakota's goldfields and Sidney crossed here also. Just visualize those young wiry Pony riders heading up the hills to the North. Or that Deadwood Stage bounding up the hill toward that golden El Dorado, the pot of gold.

MILEPOST 60 WESTBOUND REST AREA: On the hill. The Sculpture is "Roadway Confluence" by Hans Von DeBovenkamp. Displays on Pine Ridge and Sidney-Deadwood Trail. Notice that the Railroad parallels you across Nebraska. First the trails, then the railroads, then US 30 and now I-80.

69 **SUNOL:** NO NEAR SERVICES!

76 **LODGEPOLE:** ELEVATION: 3831 FEET. Three miles North to services.
MILEPOST 82 EASTBOUND REST AREA: Overlooking Lodgepole Creek that I-80 follows for 100 miles. There is a plaque on Lodgepole Creek and displays on the Ogallala Aquafir and the Transcontinental Railroad.

85 **CHAPPELL:** ELEVATION: 3696 FEET. WEATHER RADIO: 99.7 FM.
FUEL: South to Texaco.
FOOD: North to Big Red Cafe.
CAMPGROUND: "El Rancho CG": Private. North to town and East on US 30. No further information.
"Husky Streamsite Kampark": Private. .5 mile North of I-80. No further information.
The Oregon Trail and Pony Express Trail had followed the South Platte River Southwest dipping down to the Julesburg, Colorado Station, then crossing the South Platte and following Lodgepole Creek North. Now I-80 is crossing those trails that are going to the North.

MILEPOST 88 WESTBOUND REST AREA: Displays on the Transcontinental Railroad.

95 **SOUTH TO JULESBURG/NE 27:** NO NEAR SERVICES!

Julesburg was named for one of the most brutal and most notorious Overland Stage Division Agents who manned that station. Horses disappeared and stages were delayed by this accomplice of rustlers. He was supplanted by Slade who got the stages running again by killing several men. Jules and Slade were mortal enemies. Slade finally captured Jules, tied him up and shot him piece by piece. Slade was the most feared man West of Ft. Kearny as he carried Jules' ear in his pocket while he added more killings to his name. He was finally hanged in Montana. Stage and Pony Express Station personnel were not acquainted with social graces.

MILEPOST 99 EASTBOUND: Great view of the SOUTH Platte Valley to the South!
WESTBOUND: Viewpoint Turnout.

101 **US 138:** NO NEAR SERVICES!

WESTBOUND: Cattle Country: The largest number of cattle you see along I-80 are the red and white "Herefords". You'll also see some all black herds, "Black Angus". Watch for the grey humpbacked Brahma bulls that are often bred into a herd for stamina. If you see all-white cattle, they may be the French Charolais, preferred for their leaner meat.

102 **MAJOR INTERCHANGE!**

I-76 TO DENVER: NO NEAR SERVICES! Crossing the South Fork of the Platte.

107 **BIG SPRINGS:**
FUEL: North to Phillips, Amoco Truck Plaza.
FOOD: North to Grandma Max, Budget 8 Restaurant.
MOTEL: North to Budget 8.
CAMPGROUND: "McGreer Camper Park": Private. North on Big Springs Road to Frontage Road. East 500 feet. NEAR I-80.

The "Big Springs" are on the hill North of town and the old Railroad Depot has been moved there to be a museum. The town swimming pool nearby was given in memory of Riley Lintz who died in the explosion of US Navy ship "Leyte" in Boston harbor. Go have a swim, cool down and check out the historical markers. There's a buffalo sculpture of chains and the site of a giant cottonwood tree that was a landmark for the pioneers. Sam Bass's Gang held up a train here in 1877 and got $60,000. This must have encouraged him for he held up 4 banks in Texas until the Texas Rangers got him on his 27th birthday.

SIDETRIP TO ASH HOLLOW

WESTBOUND: North about 12 miles to US 26 and West to "Ash Hollow". Return to I-80 the same way.

OR EASTBOUND ALTERNATE ROUTE: North to Left/West on US 26 a few miles to Windlass Hill and Ash Hollow State Historical Park and then East on US 26 to Ogallala.

The pioneers on the Old Oregon Trail in the 1840's had been traveling on fairly level land on the South side of the Platte River. The South Platte River branched off at the present town of "North Platte". The Oregon Trail continued on the South side of SOUTH Platte until they came to Milepost 115 where they crossed it and headed North. Now came their most dangerous navigational trial East of the Rockies. Between the North and South Branches of the Platte is a ridge of hills extending from here to North Platte, which the Oregon Trail had to surmount. Then suddenly the trail went sharply down a steep grade to Ash Hollow. One pioneer said that the "road hangs a little past the perpendicular". This is "Windlass Hill" where the Pioneers had to winch their wagons down, the wheels locked with chains, and men pulling back on the ropes. Park at either turnout and hike the trail up the hill to get a Pioneer's eye view from the top. Take your camera! The original tracks were deepened first by wheels and then by erosion so that part of the downward trail today is a deep gully. Go Northwest two miles more on US 26 and follow the signs to "Ash Hollow State Historical Park", a fine Visitor Center, a trading post, restored schoolhouse, and a picnic area near the spring at the bottom of the hill. Just a short distance over the hill from the Center you can walk into Ash Hollow Cave with a glassed-in viewing area of the digs and a taped story. Visitor Center open summers 9-6pm. Adult $2.

Ash Hollow is an unusual Geological formation, like the landscape of the Great Plains before the Ice Age. Prehistoric man lived here 6,000 years ago where bones of prehistoric rhinoceros, mammoths, and mastodons have been found. When the pioneers finally got to Ash Creek it was an oasis for them. Now they had fresh water, Ash trees, forage, wood and trading posts. There would be hundreds of wagons here at one time, resting, repairing equipment. The first major battle between the Calvary and the Sioux took place at Blue Creek North of Lewellen.

CAMPGROUNDS: On Lake McConoughy 11-13 miles East.

MILEPOST 115: I-80 crosses the Oregon Trail of the 1840's. The trail then crossed the SOUTH Platte (which is to the North) at **CALIFORNIA CROSSING**, and headed almost due North. At Milepost 116 look Northwest to follow the trail up **CALIFORNIA HILL** where the power line is today. Over the hill is Ash Hollow and the NORTH Platte River. The original trail was made by the buffalo and the Natives followed by the Mountain Men who trod it for 20 years before the settlers came.

117 **BRULE:** NO NEAR SERVICES! TOURIST INFORMATION RADIO: 530 AM.
CAMPGROUND: "Riverside CG": Private. North to CG on Left between South Platte River and Service station. Shielded by trees. NEAR I-80.
WESTBOUND: If you go North here to US 30 and West you'll see several Historical markers about a Pony Express Station and the Oregon Trail.

MILEPOST 120: "Ogallala's Prosperity"! You smell it before you see it! Cattle raised on the open range have tough meat. Therefore they are rounded up and brought to "feed lots" like this one where they are fed on fattening grains before being slaughtered.

MILEPOST 124 EASTBOUND REST AREA AND VISITOR CENTER: Pick up your maps and "Highway to a Heritage" tapes here. Plaque on Nebraska's "Chain O' Lakes"/borrow pits. There are 100 of these lakes along 215 miles of I-80 along the Platte River. The water table is just 10 feet down, so as soon as they dig out the sand and gravel to build the overpasses, the excavation fills with water. The lakes are 5 feet deep and vary in size from 3 to 5 acres.

126 **OGALLALA/US 26/NE 61:** ELEVATION: 3216 FEET. ANTIQUE MALL to South.
RV PARTS & SERVICE: North to Right on 4th Street.
GROCERY STORE: North to West a few blocks on US 30.
FUEL: North to Sapp Bros Texaco Truck Stop, Standard, Phillips. South to Conoco, '76 Truck Stop & Restaurant.
FOOD: South to Kentucky Fried, Wendys, Family Restaurant. North to Arbys, Mc Donalds, Amigo, Valentino, Taco John's. Pioneer Trails North to West on River Road behind Arbys.
MOTELS: North to Best Western, Holiday Inn, Stagecoach Inn, Plaza Inn, Lazy K Motel, Elms Motel. South to Super 8*, Western Paradise, Interstate Inn, Motel 8*. North in town to Oregon Trail, Western Paradise, Plaza Inn.
CAMPGROUNDS: "Meyer's Campground": Private. Good Sam. South .75 mile on NE 61 to Park Road. East .2 mile. Heated pool, playground, big trees, lawn, quiet. A favorite. $15.
"Open Corral Camp": SE corner of I-80. East of '76 Truck Stop. Heated pool. NEAR I-80. $9-$11.
"Gold Dust RV Park": Private. North of I-80. NEAR I-80. $9-$13.
LAKE OGALLALA/ LAKE MCCONAUGHY: 10 State Park Campgrounds. The nearest is: North East on NE 61 for 9 miles. Showers, playground and lake fish, boat. $6-$9. Check locally for locations of other Campgrounds.

OGALLALA

Ogallala was named after the "Oglala" tribe of the "Sioux". It was a railroad and cattle town, where Texas ranchers herded their cattle North on the Texas-Ogallala Trail to sell and ship them East on the railroad. This was such a wild town with many fights and shootings that they dubbed it "Gomorrah of the Plains". Now it's "The Cowboy Capital of Nebraska". If you're passing through in August you might see the "OGALLALA ROUND-UP-RODEO" and the "KEITH COUNTY FAIR".

FRONT STREET: North to East on US 30 .2 mile. Ogallala's oldest buildings are rebuilt here to represent the wild frontier town that it once was. The action is in the evenings. See a shoot-out & have a "Sarsaparilla" or a "Red-eye". Summers 8am-10pm. Nightly show "Crystal Palace Revue", a melodrama of Texas Trail Days is in the saloon. Show: Sun-Thurs, 8pm. Fri-Sat, 7:15 & 8:30pm. Adult $4. Museum next door has exhibits from the Texas Trail to the dustbowl days.

OGALLALA'S MANSION ON THE HILL: Spruce & 10th St. 2.5 miles North on US 26. Built for the bride who married another, this 1887 mansion now houses Ogallala's history. Summers Thurs-Tues 1-7pm. Free.

BOOT HILL CEMETERY: 10th & West C Street. 4 blocks West of the Mansion. Read the epitaphs on the tombstones. Here lie the losers of the gun battles who died with their boots on!

WORLD OF ANTIQUES: North to West .2 mile on US 30. Many antique dealers under the same roof. 9am-5:30pm.

PETRIFIED WOOD GALLERY: On NE 61. 1 mile West of water tower near I-80 interchange. Art and music boxes made of petrified wood.

WESTBOUND ALTERNATE ROUTE

TO ASH HOLLOW: Follow US 26 North about 21 miles to **WINDLASS HILL** and **ASH HOLLOW** where thousands of pioneers wound their way. Read Milepost 107. You can return to I-80 at Big Springs. Or go a little further North on US 26 to "Bennetts Thunder Valley Ranch" near Oshkosh. This is a working ranch with horsedrawn carriage rides & outdoor steak feed. Reservations: 308-284-8411. From there you can return to I-80 via NE 27. Or on to **CHIMNEY ROCK** and to "Oregon Trail Wagon Train" at Bayard, (308-586-1850) where you can have a wagon ride to Chimney Rock. Time to go further? At **SCOTTSBLUFF** you can walk in the old eroded wagon tracks, and hike down the mountain through a tunnel in the bluff. Choose your own route South again to I-80.

MILEPOST 132 WESTBOUND REST AREA: Sculpture "Up and Over" by Linda Howard. Displays about Ogallala.

133 **ROSCOE:** ELEVATION: 3,000 FEET. NO NEAR SERVICES!

To the North see some of the sand hills of Nebraska. They extend North for more than 100 miles. Did you ever wonder how the pioneers baked things? They had big iron pots called "Dutch Ovens" with close-fitting lids and a strong wire handle. The food, e.g. biscuits or potatoes, were put into the Dutch Oven which was then buried in heaps of coals raked from the campfire.

145 **PAXTON:** TOURIST INFORMATION RADIO: 530 AM.

FUEL: North to Phillips.

FOOD: "Ole's Big Game Lounge and Grill": One mile North. One block North of railroad. Eat midst 200 big game trophies from every continent. Includes an 11 foot polar bear. 10am to 10pm.

B & B: "Gingerbread Inn". On your left on your way into town. Lovely restored home.

Guess what's running under I-80? Water. Water from the North Platte River is tunneled under town, I-80 and the South Platte River to the Sutherland Reservoir. It's all part of Nebraska's extensive irrigation system that makes this formerly dry land green.

Pioneer wagon trains moved 15-20 miles a day, 65 miles or more a week. They needed to know their mileage. Sometimes they tied a rag to a wagon wheel and then had a child walk beside it counting the turns. Multiplied times the circumference of the wheel gave them their mileage.

MILEPOST 149 CHANGE TIME ZONES: MOUNTAIN TIME/CENTRAL TIME. RADIO: 970 & 1240 AM. 85 FM.

158 **SUTHERLAND/NE 25:**

FUEL: South to Sinclair, Parr's.

MOTEL: Park Motel.

CAMPGROUND: "Sutherland State Recreation Area": 1 mile South on NE 25. Lake swim, boat, fish. $6. Golf course near the campground. Historical markers on the trails.

Here in the sandhill country, wagon wheels sank in the sand and the oxen struggled. They called one hill, "The Ox Killer" because it was so difficult to negotiate. The emigrants had many problems on the trail. People and animals drowned at crossings and animals and wagons broke down. Children, numb with heat and fatigue, fell off the wagons to be run over by the iron-rimmed wheels. Rattlesnakes bit animals that sickened and died. Dysentery made people sick for days or weeks.

MILEPOST 158 HISTORIC O'FALLON'S BLUFFS.
MILEPOST 160 REST AREAS: WESTBOUND: Displays about the trails.
EASTBOUND OREGON TRAIL WAGON RUTS:. Take the path at the far East end of the park and go out to where you see the wagon wheels. Stand in the eroded trail. O'FALLON'S BLUFFS hug the South bank of the Platte so that there was only a narrow trail available. Sometimes it was flooded. In 1856 the new Secretary of the Utah Territory and his companions were ambushed by Indians on this trail. This made other wary pioneers avoid it by climbing up around the Bluffs through this Rest Area. Just think, these ruts are 140 years old!

164 **HERSHEY:** ELEVATION: 2500 FEET.
FUEL: North to Sinclair, Hershey Truck Stop.
FOOD: North one mile to Jack & Jill Market.
CAMPGROUND: "Ron's I-80 Sinclair": Private. North East corner. Small. NEAR I-80.

177 **NORTH PLATTE/US 83:** ELEVATION: 2805 FEET.
WINTER ROAD CONDITIONS: 532-0623. RADIO: 1410 AM.
TOURIST INFORMATION: South on US 83. Left at first light. In a Union Pacific Caboose.
SMALL MALL: North on US 83 across South Platte River to Philip Avenue.
MICHELIN TIRES & K-MART to South. WALMART to North.
FUEL: South to Texaco, Conoco, '76, Phillips. North to Standard, Tomahawk Truck Stop, Texaco (has towing).
FOOD: North to Burger King, Perkins, Arbys, Bonanza, A & W, McDonalds, Long John Silver, Hardees, Chinese Restaurant, Mr Donut, Runza hamburgers (North to B Street, Left one block), Maxwell's (prime rib), Merrick's (North to East on US 30 just past the park. Family food and pies). South to Country Kitchen, Holiday Inn (breakfast and luncheon buffets).
MOTELS: South to Nebraskan, Luxury Inn, Sands, Super 8*. North to Far West, Stockman, Holiday Inn, Motel 6*, Blue Spruce, Travelers Inn, Pioneer, Dunes, Best Western, Watson Manor Inn B&B, Rambler Motel.
CAMPGROUNDS: "Holiday Trav-l-Park": Private. Good Sam. North one block on US 83 to Right .5 mile on Frontage Road. Pool, miniature golf, playground, waterslide. NEAR I-80. $12-$15.
   "Lake Maloney State Recreation Area": 4 miles South on US 83. West .6 mile. Lake swim, fish, boat. Dump station, grills, playground. Vault toilets. $4.
   "Cody Park": City. North on US 83. .5 mile North of Rodeo Road to City Park on the river. No showers. Swim, tennis, small zoo, depot, engine, and rides. Primitive Campsites.
   "Buffalo Bill Ranch" is planning a campground. It will be a nice quiet place when it is ready.

BUFFALO BILL CODY'S SCOUT'S REST RANCH
Photo credit: Nebraska Department Economic Development

NORTH PLATTE

At North Platte, the North Fork of the river from Wyoming joins the South Fork from Colorado. The Oregon Trail remained South of the South Platte until "California Crossing" near Brule, Milepost 115. The Mormon Trail continued on the North Bank of the North Platte. As you drive North into town you'll cross the South Platte first. North of Cody Park you would cross the North Platte.

Grenville Dodge laid out North Platte in 1866. The town had an instantaneous founding in 1867 as 2,000 people, the railroad construction crews, moved in and headquarters were set up here. This traveling mass of brawling humanity was dubbed "Hell on Wheels". They were largely Irish who at the time were at the bottom of the work force in Eastern U.S. With them came the footloose, thieves and speculators looking for easy money. North Platte lacked law and order until Vigilantes took over. In later years when homes were built, the danger from dry prairie grass and lack of rain,created fearful prairie fires. In 1893 a fire started by sparks from a Union Pacific locomotive 9 miles West, swept through the area destroying ranches and 35 houses in town.

BUFFALO BILL'S RANCH: State Historical Park. A MUST STOP! North three miles on US 83. West 1.6 miles on US 30. North 1.2 miles on Buffalo Bill Avenue. Buffalo Bill began as a Pony Express Rider, shot buffalo for the Kansas Pacific Railroad, was an Army Scout during Indian Wars, and a guide for hunting parties. He joined with an author who elaborated on Bill's stories and put him in his "dime novels" and on stage. At his home in North Platte he organized the "Congress of Rough Riders of the World" and for 30 years put on "Wild West" shows all over the world.

Stroll through Cody's 1886 mansion, barn (that held 180 horses) and grounds. View 15 minutes of rare film of Cody's "Wild West Show" taken by Thomas Edison in 1898. Sing-a-Longs are held some evenings. Summers 10-8pm. Spring & Fall 9-5pm weekdays, 1-5pm weekends. Family Admission: $2. Summer 45 minute trail rides Wed-Sun at 10:30am, noon, 1:30pm, 3 & 4:30pm. $6. Buggy rides Wed-Sun 1-4pm.

LINCOLN COUNTY MUSEUM: 2403 North Buffalo. On your Right just before you turn Left to Cody's Parking Lot. Includes a Western Prairie Village: 2-story log home, 1900 middle class home, church, school, library, store, train depot, and Pony Express station. Main museum building has a wide variety of items. The glasswear, china and gowns are fabulous. Summers daily 9-8pm. Donation.

WORLD WAR II CANTEEN: Part of the County museum, but it deserves special note. During the war there was never enough food on the trains. The dining cars serving only breakfast and dinner, were overcrowded, too expensive for most service people, and often ran out of food. The passengers, 99 percent service people, were always hungry. It was December 1941 and the local National Guard unit was rumored to be coming through North Platte. The residents collected goodies for them and waited but their train was rerouted. Then a train-load of Kansas boys arrived so the citizens served them instead. Thus began one of the most amazing feeding and morale programs of the war. Spearheaded by Rae Wilson, people gathered food from merchants and citizens and began passing it out to 3,000 to 5,000 service people a day. The former Lunch Room of the Railroad Station was lined with tables of food and smiling attendants. Troop trains made special 10-minute stops when servicemen could eat all they wanted, or could carry. And it wasn't just the food that they appreciated. Many were young, homesick and often frightened and the expression of love was a Godsend to them. Townspeople as far as 200 miles away spent a monthly 10-hour day working the Canteen (after having spent a week or two before preparing the food). Their efforts did not go unnoticed. The museum has received thousands of letters from service people all over the nation expressing gratitude. Be sure to stop and thank these beautiful people for their expression of love.

FORT CODY TRADING POST: Northeast Corner of I-80. A large souvenir shop with a small "Buffalo Bill Wild West Show" every half hour.

NORTH PLATTE RECREATION COMPLEX: North on US 83 to West 9 blocks on Philip Avenue. South three blocks on McDonald Street. If you're staying overnight how about a workout here? They have a heated swimming pool, weight room, gym, racquetball courts, etc. Visitors: Adult $1.75. Family $3.50.

BAILEY YARD VISITOR CENTER: North on US 83 across South Platte River, to Front Street. West three miles. Past the Yard Office take the Right/North turn into the yard. North Platte was founded by the railroad in 1867 and it is still a railroad town. Bailey Yard is 7 miles long, one of the largest Railroad Classification Yards in the U.S. The diesel repair shop with 11 tracks, is as big as 3 football fields. There is a covered observation platform near the "Hump" where trains are formed continually. A speaker tells visitors about the lighted yard while they watch trains form. This yard is also unusual because it uses the constant Westerly Wind to sort ALL the cars, both East and Westbound. Open 24 hours a day. Free.

SIOUX LOOKOUT: South 1 mile on US 83. East at State Farm Road. Follow paved road that curves through. About 10 miles in all. A marker on the Left will direct you. Statue of a Sioux Indian is on a rise to the Southwest. The Sioux used this rise to watch for approaching soldiers. The statue was built in 1931. Take an hour to climb the hill a quarter mile, get some exercise and a Sioux Warrior's view.

D.A.R. LOG CABIN MUSEUM: 1100 E 4th Street. North to 4th Street/US 30 and East 10 blocks. On your right in Memorial Park in an 1867 log cabin. Artifacts from Civil War to World War II, guns, dolls, music boxes, and spinning wheel. Summers 1-4pm. Closed Mon. Free. Rest awhile in the park, picnic, tennis, playground.

UNION PACIFIC RAILROAD MUSEUM/CODY PARK: North on US 83 to North edge of town. Two blocks North of where US 30 turns Westward. World's Largest Steam Locomotive, "Mighty Challenger Engine #3977"! Also one of the largest diesel-electric locomotives, a mail car and an old depot. Guided tours. Summers Thur-Mon 10-2pm & 3-7pm. Carnival rides for children in the summer. Picnic and playground along tree-shaded lands of the North Platte River.

North Platte has a nightly rodeo in the summer. South on US 83 and West/Right two miles on Walker Road past the golf course. Right/North .5 mile on a gravel road. If you're in town in July, you might join their Buffalo Stew Cookout held each Wed, Thurs, and Fri for 6 weeks at Buffalo Bill Ranch. Must reserve ahead. Adult $5. Child $4.

179   NORTH PLATTE, EAST ENTRANCE/56 G LINK: NO NEAR SERVICES!

190   MAXWELL:

FUEL/FOOD: North to Texaco Truck Stop.

MOTEL/LODGING: "Valley View Guest Ranch": Ride through the cedar studded hills. Call: 308-582-4320.

CAMPGROUND: "Ft. McPherson CG Valley View Stables": Private. Two miles South to Ft. McPherson National Cemetery. West .5 mile. South .5 mile. Working ranch on Oregon and Pony Express Trails. Horseback riding up the hills for a great view of the North Platte. Mini frontier town, playground, fishing, hiking, pool, shady, grassy. $8-$11.

FORT MCPHERSON NATIONAL CEMETERY: Two miles South. Here beside soldiers who died in the battles with the natives are buried those who died in Korea and South Vietnam. This area was first called COTTONWOOD SPRINGS. Bill Cody was a scout at the old fort that operated here from 1863 to 1880. No sign of it remains. The headquarters cabin from the old fort is in the Lincoln County Historical Museum in North Platte. An historical Marker at the exit tells the importance of the old Indian Wars fort.

Life along the trail, even along this flat flood plain was not easy. Trees were found only on the islands in the Platte, not on the shores. One emigrant said that there were scarcely two trees from Grand Island to Ash Hollow. Women collected "buffalo chips" to use as firewood to cook the evening meal. Water was a problem. there were so many hundreds of wagons passing that the Platte River was muddy. Pioneers might put a handful of cornmeal in a bucket of water overnight to clear it. They drank from lagoons, their stock also, leaving the water muddied for other pioneers. They dug 8-10 foot wells but they also became polluted. Cholera was rampant. One could contract cholera and die within 24 hours.

Tributaries of the Platte had to be crossed. Shifting sand (they called it "Quick Sand") often took the livestock not by suction but by panic and entanglement in their harness. Men cut down willow broughs to form a "road" through soft/sandy terrain. Sometimes after their company wagons had crossed over, men would stay awhile and charge subsequent wagon companies to pass over. When the white men left, Pawnees took over the sites and charged a steer, or such, per wagon to cross.

The Platte valley looks very different today than it did 150 years ago. Settlers have planted trees, dams have been built to contain the Platte and reduce its flow, fields are irrigated and green. The OLD Platte was viewed a mile wide with no obstruction over the prairie grass, and lined with sand dunes. The wind, as today, blew constantly with lightening starting fires in the dry Western grass and burning everything, one reason why there were no trees on the prairies for the pioneers.

MILEPOST 194 REST AREAS: EASTBOUND: Learn about the Pony Express, water sports in Nebraska and the **ROAD RANCHES**. Some of the first people who settled in Nebraska started a little "Road Ranche" or "Inn" where you could buy food or stay the night. Some were built like forts with very primitive accommodations in little sod houses. "Guests" just threw their own blankets on the dirt floor.

WESTBOUND: Lots of shade trees and a sculpture, "Nebraska Gateway" by Anthony Padovano. Also displays about Fort McPherson, Buffalo Bill and North Platte.

199   BRADY:

FUEL/FOOD: North to Sinclair, Stuckey's, Dairy Queen.

CAMPGROUND: "Ault Fur & Tackle Company Trading Post & Campground". North .1 mile on 56-d Link. showers/playground.

MILEPOST 201: I-80 crosses the Platte river to the North Side, the Mormon Trail side, and Eastbound remains there until Grand Island.

211   GOTHENBURG/NE 47: HOSPITAL:

FUEL: North to Phillips, Texaco Truck Stop.
FOOD: Pizza Hut. Jack & Jill Market at 10th & F Streets.
MOTEL: Western Motor Inn.
CAMPGROUNDS: "Lafayette" Public Park: City. Norht 1.5 miles on NE 47. showers, playground. Lake Helen fish, swim, canoe, paddle boats. $9. THE STATE'S ONLY COVERED BRIDGE IS HERE.

"Pony Express RV": Private. North one block. Behind the Phillips Station in the trees. river fishing, playground. NEAR I-80. $7-$9.

"Stage Stop Inn KOA": South a block. Pool, river swim, fish, playground. NEAR I-80. In thick trees so is shielded from I-80. $13-$19.

GOTHENBURG

SOD HOUSE MUSEUM: City. North on Left behind Phillips Station by the giant plow. A farmstead setting of a Sod House, a barn and a wooden windmill with life-size sculpture of buffalo, horse and rider made from 5 miles of barbed wire. Daily 9-6. Free.

ORIGINAL 1860 PONY EXPRESS STATION: City. In "Ehmen Park". Two miles North on NE 47. shady park in which to relax picnic, take a carriage ride. this station was about 18 miles West of here and 4 miles East of Ft. McPherson on the "Upper 96 Ranch". (There is another station, "Midway", 4 miles south of gothenburg at the "Lower 96 Ranch".) Built in 1854 as a fur-trading post it was later used as a bunk house. the owner gave it to Gothenburg in 1931 and the American Legion moved it to the park. Historical souvenirs for sale. Summers daily 8-9pm. May & Sept 9-6pm. Free. A sign here says that mail took 9 days to get to Sacramento from Gothenburg via Pony Express. Compare today's mail service by mailing a card from here which the clerk will stamp with "Pony Express".

THE PONY EXPRESS

On April 3, 1860, the fifth rider from St. Joseph, Missouri completed the first 230 miles of the Pony Express Trail. He dashed into Ft. Kearny early the second day with the first mail. The trail had come up from Kansas following the Oregon Trail to the Platte River. They guided their ponies on the turf between the wagon ruts. From here their trail was South of the Platte River and I-80 all the way to Chappell.

The riders were young men, under 135 pounds, between 15 and 20 years old. Buffalo Bill Cody was a rider when he was just 14 years. They carried 10 pounds of mail, no gun, changed horses every 10-12 miles and riders every 75 miles. Thus the mail was carried from St. Joseph, MO. to Sacramento in 10 days. At the occasion of Lincoln's inaugural address, they made it in 7 days, 17 hours. The charge for the mail was $5 for .5 ounce plus postage, later lowered to $1. In the 1966 miles 308 runs were made in each direction between the 200 stations. Only one rider was killed by Indians, and one man, Richard Erastus, rode 330 miles without rest. The Pony Express operated from April 1860-Oct 1861 when the Transcontinental Telegraph was completed. In 1864 the Indians wiped out all the Pony Express Stations East of Ft. Kearny.

If you're in Gothenburg in September you might enjoy their "Harvest Festival" or the "An-

GOTHENBURG PONY EXPRESS STATION
Photo credit: Gothenburg Chamber of Commerce

tique Airplane Fly-in" at the Quinn Airport East of town. Precision flying, spot landing, and flour bombing contests.

MILEPOST 221: Note the GRAIN ELEVATORS: They have been called the "Skyscrapers of the West", or "Cathedrals of Plenty". A million bushels of wheat can be stored in each elevator.

222 COZAD/NE 21: ELEVATION: 2486 FEET.
FOOD: Dairy Queen, PIzza Hut.

MOTEL: North to Best Western, Cozad Motel.
CAMPGROUND: "Muny Park": City. 14th & O Streets. Small. No further information.

C O Z A D

You are now on the 100th Meridian of Longitude! Look at a globe and note the vertical lines that connect the North and South Poles. Find the 100th Meridian. This is a very important line especially to Westerners. For this is where the humid East meets the dry West, or visa versa. The 100th Meridian is in line with the West shore of the Gulf of Mexico. The humid air and the storms come up from the Gulf of Mexico and swing Eastward increasing the humidity from this point Eastward. On the other hand, the air West of here is dry because the storms, come from the Pacific and the Rockies have already removed most of the moisture. However, the two systems coming together for 100 miles East or West of here, breed the potential for violent storms. Go North on NE 21/E Street over the railroad tracks. Turn Left at the first street. A second Left takes you to the Railroad Station where the 100th Meridian marker and sign stand. At the next street, turn Right onto Meridian Street and you are driving on the 100th Meridian. **WESTBOUND:** Stay on US 30 to Gothenburg to the Pony Express Station. Pioneers traveling West of Cozad noted that their lips cracked and their nostrils were dry. The wind blew constantly. They also noted the difference in the land. Dry grass, dust 4"-6" deep, and the danger of prairie fires that the wind whipped across the land. Men wore bandanas over their noses and mouths. The women pinched their bonnets together in front. They could rarely wash themselves or their clothes. Maybe only once in a month. They got boils on their unwashed necks. Pioneers also noted that the grass changed from the "Turf grass" of the East to the "bunch grass" of the West. The animals were different now too. Bison, antelope, jackrabbits, prairie dogs and horned toads were new experiences for them.

Congress required that the Union Pacific be in Cozad by Jan 1868. When they reached this point ahead of schedule in October 1866 they had a big party. Grenville Dodge and Durant invited Congressmen and Senators to the celebration and 169 arrived.

In 1872 John J. Cozad in coat and tails, gold cane and diamond stick pin walked along the lonely railroad tracks here where there was no station, and dreamed of a town along this 100th Meridian. He built his town and his hotel. Ten years later he fled, suspected of murder, and changed his name. Researchers finally found his son, Robert Henri, who had become a leading artist in the early 1900's. The Cozad Depot building was designed by Gilbert Underwood.

ROBERT HENRI MUSEUM AND WALKWAY: 218 East 8th Street. North on NE 21/E Street to 8th Street. On your Left. The works of this artist are displayed in the home and hotel built by his father. A Brick walkway next to the hotel takes you to the Pony Express Station in the park. This building had a previous life as a trading post and a stage station. Next up the street are a pioneer school ready for its pupils and a church with Bible verses on the walls. Summers Mon-Sat 9-5pm. Sun 1-3pm. Rest of year 1-5pm. Adult $2. Child $.50.

MILEPOST 227 REST AREAS: Displays on towns on the prairies. A plaque on the Central Platte Valley, the trails and **PLUM CREEK**.

231   **DARR:** NO NEAR SERVICES!

237   **LEXINGTON/US 283 SOUTH/NE 21 NORTH:** TRAVEL INFORMATION RADIO: 1580 AM. WAL MART AND FOOD STORE. HOSPITAL.
FUEL: South to Conoco. North to Phillips, Sinclair Truck Center & Goodyear Tires.
FOOD: North to McDonalds, A&W, Kentucky Fried, Amigos, Wendys, Arbys, The Don, Pizza.
MOTELS: South to Super 8*. North to Econo*, Best Western, Budget Host, Ranch, Toddle Inn.
CAMPGROUNDS: JOHNSON LAKE STATE PARK: Two Campgrounds: "Inlet": Seven miles South on US 283, then Southeast .6 mile. Fish, swim, boat, showers, playground, graveled pads. Hookups $9. Tents $6. Golf course nearby. "Main": A bit further South, includes showers.
"Masten's Camper Haven": Private. South 200 feet to Frontage Road. West one mile. Fish, boat, playground. NEAR I-80. $8-$11.

L E X I N G T O N

PLUM CREEK MASSACRE: Lexington began as "Plum Creek" in the 1860's with a Pony Express Station and a trading post on the Oregon Trail South of the Platte. On August 7th, 1864 a small wagon train had stopped near a post where there were a few soldiers of the 7th Iowa Cavalry. The wagon train pulled out heading West and were still in view of the post when 100 Indians attacked the train killing 11 men and taking a boy and a woman hostage. The men at the post wired for help but were too few to do anything themselves. The boy was released a month later but died of his injuries. The woman gained her freedom six months later.

THE TURKEY LEG RAID: The Plum Creek settlement moved North of the Platte River near the Railroad Depot in 1867. On Aug 7th, Sioux Chief Turkey Leg led his warriors to cut the telegraph lines and sabotage the new railroad track. This was off the South side of US 30 just 3.5 miles West of US 30/US 283.

The first thing down that track was a handcar with two men. Both were shot and scalped. Then a Westbound train came and was derailed. The engineer and fireman were killed but the train crew in the caboose were able to escape back to Plum Creek under the cover of darkness. The Indians ripped open the freight and found liquor among other merchandise. They must have caroused around all night as they were still there when a rescue train came out from Plum Creek in the morning and chased them off. The historical marker says that the Indians were tying yards of calico to their horses tails! It may have appeared that way as they rode off with a bolt under an arm and the calico streaming behind them. One man on the handcar survived his scalping, retrieved his lock and tried to have it sewed back on. He was taken to Omaha for the surgery but it was not successful. Today his scalp is in the Union Pacific Museum in Omaha.

Major Frank North and 44 of his Pawnee Scouts from Fort Kearny pursued the Cheyennes and though outnumbered 2 to 1 they were successful and captured a woman and also a boy who was Turkey Leg's nephew. These two were later exchanged for the Campbell girls. Read Milepost 312, Grand Island. Plum Creek, with much of Nebraska, survived a drought and a plague of grasshoppers. In 1889 it changed its street names to those of presidents and its town to "Lexington". Today some want to change it back to "Plum Creek".

DAWSON COUNTY HISTORICAL MUSEUM: 805 North Taft Street. A MUST STOP! US 293 North three miles to East on 7th Street. North on Taft Street. Excellent Museum on the history of the Platte Valley from prehistoric times to the 1920's. Includes period rooms, barber shop, optometry office, restored buildings, depot, schoolhouse, log cabin. Also shows the history of agriculture in the valley. See the unusual McCabe experimental airplane of 1919, hard to believe it could fly! March-Nov Mon-Sat 9-5pm. Sun 1-5pm. Adult $1. Shady park next door with great playground equipment.

If you're interested in architectural styles get a local map and "cruise downtown" to see the courthouse in Classical Revival style, the bank in Richardsonian Romanesque and three Queen Ann houses. Ask at the museum.

248   **OVERTON:** ELEVATION: 2,000 FEET. RADIO: 1340, 1460 AM. 97.7 FM.
FUEL: North to Burns Bros Truck Stop and restaurant. South to Phillips.
CAMPGROUND: "Phillips CG": South of I-80. No further information.

The Oregon Trail was crowded. Emigrants all planned their travel between the fresh green grass of spring and the mountain snows in Western passes. So they were all traveling at the same time across Nebraska, often 12 teams abreast over the level prairie. Campgrounds were crowded, unsanitary, soon bereft of fuel and clean water and grass for the stock. Each campsite had its graveyard.

257   **ELM CREEK/US 183:**
FUEL/FOOD: North to Texaco Truck Stop and Pump & Pantry.

CHEVYLAND USA AUTO MUSEUM: North of I-80 to one mile East on gravel road. Over 100 Chevys here from 1914 to 1975. Daily, 8-5pm. Admission.

FIRST BRIDGE ACROSS THE PLATTE: The Platte was shallow but it was so sandy that wagon wheels would just sink into it claiming many wagons that tried to cross. The first bridge across the Platte in Central Nebraska was one mile long, one lane, with turnouts for vehicles to pass. It is US 183 today.

263   **ODESSA:**
FUEL: South to Citco. North to Sapp Bros Phillips Truck Stop.
MOTEL/CAMPGROUND: "Betty's I-80 Budget Motel & RV Park": Private. North .3 mile on Odessa Road. Small.

UNION PACIFIC WAYSIDE: Public. North of I-80. A borrow pit lake/campground. Restrooms, no swimming and scant shade. NEAR I-80.

MILEPOST 268 EASTBOUND REST AREA: Lots of trees here. Displays on the Frontier Forts and a Plaque on Fort Kearny.

MILEPOST 271 WESTBOUND REST AREA: Stretch your legs and see the 7200 pound "Nebraska Wind Sculpture" by artist George Baker in the lagoon behind the building. It resembles a space ship but it has wide propellers that turn. Displays about prairie towns and water sports. The Plaque tells you that you are leaving the Eastern Prairies and entering the "Great Plains". They used to call this semi-arid area from Canada to Mexico, "The Great American Desert", since with little rain it was dry and dusty.

272 **2ND AVENUE, KEARNEY/NE 44 SOUTH/NE 40 NORTH/NE 10 NORTH:**
ELEVATION: 2146 FEET. RADIO STATION: 1340 AM. WEATHER STATION: 100.3 FM. KEARNEY STATE COLLEGE. HILLTOP MALL: North of town at 48th Street.
FUEL: South to Amoco, Gas 'n Shop. North to Texaco. RV Onan Auxillary Generator Service.
FOOD: South to Grandpa's Steak House, Ft. Kearny Inn, Burger King. North to McDonalds, Bonanza, Perkins, Wendys, Hinan Chinese, Golden Dragon (320 3rd Street. North to Left to get on 3rd), Dairy Queen, Golden Corral, U Save Bakery/Deli.
MOTELS: North to Western, Budget, Ramada (Wed-Sun buffets), Best Western, Super 8*, Budget 8, Luxury Inn 8*, Kearney Inn*, Holiday Inn.
CAMPGROUNDS: "Clyde and Vi's": Private. Good Sam. North .5 on NE 44 to 4th Street. West 200 feet. Heated pool, playground. $9-$14.
"Budget 8 Motel & RV": Private. North two miles to US 30. West one mile. Pool. $10.
COTTONMILL LAKE RECREATION AREA: City. 3 miles West of Kearney on US 30. Flush toilets. RV/Tents. Swim, playground, "Nature Barn", picnic, trails.
FORT KEARNY STATE RECREATION AREA: State. Two miles South on NE 44. Three miles East past the Fort. One mile North to campground. Showers, swim, playground, shelters, grills. Enjoy a hike/bike trail across two branches of the Platte and along the former segment of the Burlington/Missouri Railroad bordering the Platte River. There are 8 sand-pit lakes for fishing and swimming. Year-round recreation area. Modern rest rooms are available from May-Oct. Primitive camping rest of year. Pets on leash only. $6-$9.

KEARNEY

First you must pronounce it right, it's "Car Knee". It was named after Colonel Stephen Kearny who in 1845 led the first military up the Platte to meet with the Sioux at a trading post that became Fort Laramie. General Kearny was also the commander of the army that came upon the Donner Party Death Camp in California and buried the remaining bodies and parts of bodies. Kearney, the town, somehow got an extra "e" that is not in the name of the man nor Fort Kearny. The town was established after the Burlington Railroad line was built to connect with the Union Pacific Railroad. In 1872, 750,000 trees were planted as snowfences from Kearney to Lincoln along the Burlington Railroad. These tracks were torn out but the trees are still there making a pleasant hiking/biking trail!

FORT KEARNEY MUSEUM: North on NE 10 to the first street, Talmadge. Right to Central Avenue and the museum.

MUSEUM OF NEBRASKA ART: North to US 30. East two blocks to Central Avenue and South one block. In the former Post Office Building. Art by Nebraskans, the official art collection of the State of Nebraska. Tues-Sun 9-5pm. Donation.

TRAILS AND RAILS MUSEUM: 710 West 11th Street. North on NE 44 to Left at light on 11th Street for three blocks. Old Union Pacific depot, wagons, trains, cars, Freighters Hotel, school & church. American farmers didn't lose time producing an excess to sell. They were shipping prairie hay and sugar beets by 1870. The school was built by Mormons in 1871. Summers: Mon-Sat 10-12 noon and 1-5pm. Donations.

FRANK HOUSE: Four miles North on NE 44. Left on US 30. Right on College Drive. Built in 1889 by George Washington Frank from New York, it included electricity and steam heat before its time. The building itself is spectacular with a tiled roof and pillared veranda. It's even unusual inside today with its Corinthian columns, Tiffany windows and carved woodwork. Summers Tues-Sun. Adult $2.

SANDHILL CRANE MIGRATION

The gigantic Annual spring migration of the sandhill cranes is between Grand Island and Lewellen (West of Ogallala). Fort Kearny State Recreation Area is an excellent center for viewing the cranes. From March to April thousands of the majestic cranes reign supreme. North America's largest bird flies with an 8-foot wing-spread with neck and legs stretched out. To land, he billows down as if parachuting. Sandhills are regal-looking grey fowl with curving tail-feathers and a red cap. People come from all over the country to view these majestic birds as they fly between the river and their feeding places. The Platte River has been their spring resting grounds for centuries between their winters in Texas, New Mexico, Arizona and Southern California, and their summers in North Dakota, Michigan, Wisconsin and Canada. The waters of the Platte receive 75% of the world's cranes.

Plans are being discussed of yet one more dam on the Platte which it is feared will destroy this valuable Crane Resting Area.

SOD HOUSE BLACKSMITH SHOP, FORT KEARNY
Photo credit: Nebraska Department of Economic Development

EASTBOUND ALTERNATE ROUTE

TO FORT KEARNY STATE HISTORICAL PARK: A MUST STOP! South on NE 44 to Left on Link 50 A, East to Fort Kearny. To return to I-80, continue East to NE 10 and North to I-80. At the junction of NE 10/ Link 50 A, watch for an unusual tile barn.

In 1848 Fort Kearny was built as the first of a chain of forts to house the calvary protecting the growing number of pioneers going West on the Oregon and Mormon trails. As the only official representative of the United States, it became the headquarters of both military and civil government. Ft. Kearny is where the Oregon Trail Pioneers including the Donner-Reed party met the Platte on their way up from their starting point in Kansas or St. Joseph, Missouri. They had already lost some members to disease before they arrived here. James Reed's mother-in-law was one of them. They had built her a special wagon that her granddaughter, Virginia, referred to as a "two-story palace parlour car". They kept the wagon and hauled it all the way to the Salt Flats of Utah before they abandoned it.

Emigrants bought supplies, especially staples like beans, flour, bacon and cornmeal at the fort. The commanding officer was authorized to sell them at cost and needy emigrants might get some free. In 1850 the stage coach began operating from Independence, so the pioneers could mail letters. Some emigrants noted that this is where they saw their first bison.

One emigrant described 6-8 buildings, some with windows and some with just grates. The roofs were sod or soil. One had a garden of vegetables on it. A cultivated field had a mud fence around it and a ditch. The sod houses were warm in the winter and cool in the summer but impossible when it rained. They just leaked!

Ft. Kearny was a haven and a very busy place logging 22,500 pioneers in 15 days in 1849 and 45,000 in 1850. One '49er said that he counted 90 wagons in just one "train" and there were many, more trains as far as the eye could see in both directions.

The fort was built in 1848 and the first years gave no hint of an uprising. In the 1860's Cheyenne and Sioux joined to fight off the miners and trains of settlers invading their territory by attacking the wagon trains killing, scalping, taking goods and burning wagons. Soldiers cared for survivors of massacred trains and rode out in escort for the wagons. The Fort then became an outfitting station for war campaigns and was the base for the famous Pawnee Scouts led by Major Frank North. The Pawnees were a former Eastern Nebraska tribe, which had been forceably moved to Oklahoma in 1859. Major North, with the Pawnee Agency, had organized several companies of Pawnees to help fight the Cheyenne and Sioux, their historical enemies, from 1864 to 1876.

Two miles West of Ft. Kearny was Dobytown. A wide-open town with gambling, "Tanglefoot" whiskey, and prostitutes it took care of the "needs" of the soldiers and wagon drivers and was an outfitting point. The town had been bypassed by the railroad so when the fort closed in 1871 the town died.

In the 1860's a new trail, the "Nebraska City Cut-off", was widely used. It was shorter than the Kansas route to Fort Kearny. Russell, Majors and Waddell had a large freight depot in Nebraska City. So now Fort Kearny was a stage and freight station at the intersection of these trails. It also became a Pony Express Station and later a Telegraph Office. When the railroad was being built in 1867, the Fort's job was to protect the crews and the new construction.

Today there is a Museum/Visitor Center and a walking tour of the fort that includes a stockade and a sod blacksmith shop. They show an interesting 20 minute film. The fort was abandoned in 1871 but has been excellently restored. Adult $2. 9am-5pm.

279   NE 10: FUEL: North to Texaco Trading Post Truck Stop.

WESTBOUND ALTERNATE ROUTE
TO FORT KEARNY: South three miles on NE 10 to Link 50 A. Right about four miles to Fort Kearny National Recreation Area Campground. Continue on West to restored Fort Kearny State Historic Park. Then on West to NE 44 and North to I-80. Read Milepost 272. Fort Kearny is A MUST STOP for Easterners especially!

SIDETRIP TO PIONEER VILLAGE
HAROLD WARP PIONEER VILLAGE: 12 miles South on NE 10 to US 6/US 34. East 1 block. One of your trips across I-80 you MUST stop here. This is one of the largest museums in the nation with 26 buildings filled with Americana at its best! It is the story of how American life and technology changed since 1830, arranged in the order of its development. Fascinating! If you're over 50 it will really take you back down memory lane. Plan on a day or even two. Daily 8am to Sundown. Adult $4. Child $2.

Large private campground with budget rates nearby. Restaurant.

285   **NORTH TO GIBBON:**
EASTBOUND REST AREA: Displays about Lewis and Clark and people and goods on the Overland Trail. Plaque on the town of Gibbon.

FUEL/FOOD/MOTEL: South to all in one.

CAMPGROUND & PICNIC AREA: WINDMILL STATE RECREATION AREA: North .25 mile on 10C Link. Turn Right near the unique Windmill that was used by the Union Pacific Railroad to provide water for the steam engines. A choice park with ample shade under tall trees, showers, swimming beach, playground, laundromat. Westerners listen for the Eastern birds here, perhaps your first cardinal, bob white or wren. $6-$9.

GIBBON: The town of Gibbon was settled in 1871 by 129 Civil War Veterans as a "Soldiers' Free Homestead Temperance Colony". They named it after General John Gibbon. They came by train and lived in railroad boxcars until sod and frame houses were built. A prairie fire had just passed through when they arrived, and it was followed by a vicious blizzard. You had to be tough to homestead!

291   **SHELTON:** NO NEAR SERVICES!
CAMPGROUND: "War Axe State Wayside": North of I-80 by Borrow Pit. Shelter, flush toilet, no showers. Free. NEAR I-80. No swimming. However there is a swimming pool in the city park four miles North in Shelton at 4th and Cody.

300   **WOOD RIVER/NE 11:** RADIO: 1340 AM.
FUEL/FOOD: South to Texaco Truck Stop, Pump & Pantry.
CAMPGROUND: "Cheyenne State Wayside": North of I-80 by Borrow Pit. Shelter, flush toilet but no showers or swimming. NEAR I-80. Free.

305   **ALDA:**
FUEL/FOOD: North to '76 Truck Stop, Apco, Gas-N-Shop.
MONUMENT TO THE MARTIN BROTHERS: Three miles South on NE 40C at Platte River Road. The Sioux were on the warpath from 1862-1867 while protection by the army was limited until the Civil War was over in 1865. In 1864 Sioux attacked George Martin and his two sons while they were out in their fields. George leaped into his wagon, grabbed his gun and held off the Indians from the back while the two boys galloped the saddle horse back to the house. George was pierced through his neck by an arrow and fell into the wagon. The Sioux then pursued the boys shooting an arrow through both boys pinning them together. The boys were each hit again

before they fell off the horse and into a draw. The Indians saw that one boy was still moving so they hit him on the head, took the horse and rode off. The well-trained draft horse just walked on home with George. Wife and daughter got George into the house, removed the arrow and pinned his wound together to try to stop the bleeding. Thinking the boys dead they got George back into the wagon and headed for Ft. Kearny for medical aid and protection. With the army in pursuit of the Indians the Martin women brought critical George back to their cabin. They asked some wagoneers to help them bury the boys. Imagine their surprise when they found the boys were still alive. Amazingly all three survived!

> **MILEPOST 307 WESTBOUND REST AREA:** Displays concerning Nebraska forts, lakes and the Martin Brothers.

> **MILEPOST 311:** I-80 crosses the Platte River that is flowing Northward in a big curve. I-80 makes a sharp turn Eastward away from the river and follows the Nebraska City Cutoff. At this point the Platte River Valley is 10 miles wide. The Pioneer wagons could REALLY spread out! Now we have a mystery! You just crossed the Platte River and will cross it again at Milepost 312 and 315. Each time the river is flowing Northward. How?

312 **GRAND ISLAND/US 34/US 281/MORMON ISLAND:** ELEVATION: 1864 FEET. HOSPITAL. ROAD CONDITIONS PHONE: 384-3555.

TOURIST INFORMATION: North to the first Right. It's in a Union Pacific Caboose by the entrance to Mormon Island State Recreation Area.

ANTIQUE MALL: 215 East 3rd Street. North to US 30. East to downtown. North to 3rd Street.

MALLS: North on US 281. One mile North of US 30.

FUEL: North to Conoco, Amoco Truck Plaza. South to Conoco.

FOOD: North to Amoco Pump & Pantry, Grandma Max's. South to Holiday Inn Restaurant (Buffet 11-2pm & 5:30-9:30pm, some localites travel 20 miles to eat here). In Grand Island: Bonanza. Dreisbach's Steaks (North to US 30. East to Locust.)

MOTELS: North to USA Inn. South to Holiday Inn.

CAMPGROUNDS: MORMON ISLAND STATE RECREATION AREA: North .25 mile on US 281. Showers, playground, lake fishing/swimming. $6-$11. Part of Nebraska's Chain-of-Lakes developed into a campground with lots of shade from big trees.

"George H. Clayton Hall County Park": Three miles North on US 281. Just South of Stuhr Museum. Paved camping pads plus tenting, playground and nature trail.

GRAND ISLAND

The town of Grand Island is 8 miles North of here. It is not ON the island, but North of it by the railroad. The "Island" is 40 miles long and 2 miles wide and lies between Grand Island and Shelton, Milepost 291. The Pioneers especially noted its many trees while most of this countryside had none.

West of Brady, I-80 is on the South side of the Platte along the Oregon Trail. From Brady/Milepost 199 to Grand Island, I-80 follows the Mormon Trail along the NORTH side of the Platte River. Here at Milepost 312, I-80 crosses the Platte back to the South side. Note that the river is running Northward again. Solve it yet?

The Mormons remained North of the Platte all the way across Nebraska as they had no reason to cross to the South side to the Oregon Trail. From Omaha they followed the Platte to Columbus, then the Loup River to Palmer before they crossed it and went South to Grand Island and the Platte again. ("Loup" means "wolf" in French, named after the Wolf Pawnee Tribe who held much of this Eastern Nebraska land.)

Germans settled Grand Island in the late 1850's and prospered selling farm products to the migrating pioneers. Later it became a trading center for selling Nebraska mules to Southern buyers. An early leader was William Stolley who claimed some of the first land in Hall County in 1857. An early conservationist, he planted over 50 varieties of trees in groves. Many still live in "Stolley Recreation Area". Henry Fonda was born here and his home is exhibited at the Stuhr Museum "Town".

Bird lovers and ecologists flock here to "Mormon Island Crane Meadows" for 6 weeks in March and April when thousands of Sandhill Cranes rest here on their flight North. Read Milepost 272 on the "Sandhill Crane Migration".

STUHR MUSEUM: North 4 miles on US 281 and .25 mile East on US 34. A MUST STOP! It's a large Prairie museum, comparable to a metropolitan museum, attractively displaying pioneer history and art. You Senior Citizens will recognize the flour-sack clothing made by the depression women. Outside is a Railroad town with 60 authentically restored buildings brought here to form this pioneer town. Stroll the boardwalks, visit Henry

STUHR MUSEUM
Photo credit: Stuhr Museum

Fonda's birthhome, and ride the steam train. Summer weekends you might see craftsmen of the old school. Open May - October 9-5pm. Adult $6. Students $3.50. October 16 - April 20, Mon-Sat 9-5pm. with reduced prices. Sun 1-5pm.

L.E. RAY PARK: .75 mile East of Stuhr Museum. River beach, swimming.

GRAND ISLE HERITAGE ZOO: Eight miles North on US 281, East on Stolley Park Road. Delightful grounds where you can mingle with the animals. A miniature town, a railroad, and pony rides. Mon-Sat 10-6pm. Adult $2.50. Senior & Child $1.50.

CAMPBELL MONUMENT: 3 miles South of I-80 on US 281. Right on Platte River Road to monument nearby. In July 1867 the Sioux and the Cheyenne were raiding ranches in this area. They captured twin 4-year old boys and two teenage girls. Later, at Plum Creek/Lexington, Milepost 237: Pawnee Scouts took an Indian woman and boy hostage who were later tradedfor the girls.

SIDETRIP TO HASTINGS MUSEUM

US 34 South 17 miles to 3 miles North of Hastings. Pioneer and natural history including an exceptional exhibit of adult and infant animals. Includes birds, minerals, a planetarium, and their special "People on the Plains" exhibit. Includes a Discovery Center where you test your senses and have new experiences. Mon-Fri 9-5pm. Sun 1-5pm. Adult $4. Senior $3.50. Child $2.

FISHER RAINBOW FOUNTAIN: 2 blocks South of Museum at 12th Street entrance to Highland Park. Nightly show of colored lights on the fountain. Summers.

CROSIER MONASTERY: 14th and Pine. Collection of woodcarvings and artifacts of the Asmat people of New Guinea.

CAMPGROUND: "LAKE HASTINGS": Municipal. North of Hastings and the Union Pacific Railroad. One mile West of US 281 & US 34.

MILEPOST 315 EASTBOUND REST AREA: Tourist Information. Crossing the Platte River flowing Northward again. More than one island here! Ask about it at the information desk. Sculpture "Erma's Desire" by John Raimondi in the back by the lagoon. Displays on Lewis and Clark and a plaque on Grand Island.

EASTBOUND: I-80 is now leaving the Platte River and following the "Nebraska City Cutoff" Eastward. This trail was used by freighters and later pioneers coming from Nebraska City, which is directly East of here. You won't see the Platte River again until Milepost 426.

MILEPOST 316 WESTBOUND REST AREA: Tourist Information. Historical marker about Grand Island. Displays about the Mormon trail and the Sandhills to the north.

318 **GRAND ISLAND/NE 2:** ELEVATION: 1500 FEET. RADIO: 106 FM. 1430 AM.
CAMPGROUND: "West Hamilton RV Park": Private. Good Sam. South .2 mile on NE 2. Pool, playground.

324 **GILTNER:** NO NEAR SERVICES!

332 **AURORA/NE 14:** HOSPITAL.
FUEL: North to Phillips, Texaco, Casey's. South to Fast Fuel Truck Stop.
FOOD: Pizza. North to cafe.
MOTELS: North to Hamilton Motor Inn, Ken's Motel, Modern Motel.
CAMPGROUNDS: "Streeter Park": Municipal. North 3 miles on NE 14. West on US 34 for .25 mile. Heated pool and playground.
"Bader Memorial Park": Public. South 3 miles. Tenting. No further information.
The Nebraska Cutoff is now paralleling you to the South. I-80 will cross it at Milepost 335.

Pioneers on this trail stopped at the Relay Station Well which is about 2 miles South of I-80 on NE 14.

PLAINSMAN MUSEUM: 210 16th Street. 2.5 miles North on NE 14. An admirable museum with a large rotunda with 8 huge murals showing the history of Nebraska. Displays including an original log cabin, a sodhouse, a prairie chapel, a homestead, antique cars, firearms, and dolls. Also an exhibit of Harold E. Edgerton's work, the inventor of strobe photography. You'll note that the courthouse tower has a strobe light in honor of Edgerton. Summers Mon-Sat 9am-5pm. Sun 1-5pm. Adult $3. Senior $2. Child $1.

338   HAMPTON: ELEVATION: 1500 FEET.
       FUEL/FOOD: South to Conoco Truck Stop & Pump 'n Pantry, Kelly's Corner Truck Stop.

342   HENDERSON: RADIO: 104 FM. ANTIQUES: Mon-Sat 9-5pm.
       FUEL: South to Phillips Country Store Truck Stop, Fuel Mart Truck Stop.
       FOOD: Dell's Restaurant.
       MOTELS: South to Western. North to Wayfarer II Motor Inn.
       CAMPGROUNDS: "Henderson KOA": Private. North .2 mile on NE S 93 A. Playground,. beach, tents, RVs. In trees. $13-$19.
       "Western CG": Private. South 200 feet on NE S 93 A. Pool, playground. NEAR I-80.
       Henderson is one of the most Western Mennonite villages. The ancestors of these people courageously kept moving West seeking religious freedom and exemption from army service. They went from Holland to Prussia, the Crimea in 1790, and then to the U.S. and Henderson in 1874 where they purchased land from the railroad. They are credited with bringing "Turkey Red" hard winter wheat with them from the Crimea that was eventually grown all over the west. Only hard wheat could survive the great changes in temperatures on the prairies. But it required a special milling process which they called "New Process". This was Hungary's method of using rollers instead of millstones. Prairie wheat became famous!

348   BRADSHAW: NO NEAR SERVICES!
       Look fast at the North East corner under the overpass. This is the last remnant of the village of Charleston. The old school building left there had its bell tower removed.
       MILEPOST 350 EASTBOUND REST AREA: Tourist Information. Photos and displays on the Nebraska Tribes and the pioneers. Plaque on the Nebraska Cutoff.

353   YORK/US 81: RADIO WEATHER: 96.9 FM. YORK COLLEGE. HOSPITAL.
       SUPER MARKET: 1.5 mile North.
       FUEL: North to Sapp Bros, Amoco, Texaco. South to Conoco. Phillips.
       FOOD: North to Black Bart, Amigo, Wendy, Arbys, Country Kitchen, Pizza Hut, Bonanza, "Chances R Restaurant" (In town at 124 West 5th Street. Said to be unusual.) South to Hardee's, Hi Mark, Kentucky Fried.
       MOTELS: South to Comfort Inn, USA Motel. North to Best West, Super 8. Yorkshire, Motel 8, Luxury.

YORK

Named after York, Pennsylvania by English and German settlers. It was founded in 1869 by a Land Company and was a stop off for pioneers on the Nebraska City Cutoff. The town has a swimming pool, pool room and exercise machines. Stop and check it out.

       ANNA BEMIS PALMER MUSEUM: 211 East 7th Street. Right on 7th to Grant. In York's Community Center. It traces the history of York County through the years. Replica of a vintage bank and period rooms. Mon-Fri 8-4pm. Free.

       MILEPOST 355 WESTBOUND REST AREA: Tourist Information. The sculpture is called "Crossing the Plains" by Bradford Graves. The Historical Markers tell about the Overland Trail and the "Nebraska City Cutoff". There were many Trading Posts along the Missouri River and as more settlers and freighters came West they began to compete against each other to gain the growing Westward trade. Nebraska City wanted its share! The "OxBow Trail" began there and curved Northward to Columbus before it angled down to Ft. Kearny. But this trail was too long to gain attention and wider use. So the people of Nebraska City provided the money to send out an engineer to choose a more direct route to Ft. Kearny. Then a farmer with mules and a plow followed and turned a furrow to mark the 180-mile trail. It was successful especially from 1858-1865, but used more by freighters than by settlers. Russell, Majors and Waddell operated their freight service along this route. About Milepost 359, I-80 crosses the Nebraska City Cutoff which then runs South of I-80 Eastward to Nebraska City. In 1862 Joseph Brown brought his "Steam Wagon" here. Bridges and other facilities were built for it but it was unsuccessful.

360 **WACO/NE 93 B LINK:**
FUEL/FOOD: North to Burns Bros Truck Stop.
CAMPGROUND: "Double Nickel CG": Private. Good Sam. 300 feet on NE 93 B. Pool, playground, miniature golf, 9-hole golf nearby. Tennis court available. NEAR I-80. $8-$12.

366 **UTICA:** NO NEAR SERVICES!

369 **BEAVER CROSSING:**
CAMPGROUND: Sign to the South but no further information.

373 **GOEHNER:** NO NEAR SERVICES!
    MILEPOST 375 WESTBOUND REST AREA: Tourist Information. Displays about the Native tribes and the trails.

379 **SEWARD/NE 15:** RADIO: 1240, 1400 AM.
FUEL: South to Phillips. Tire Service.
FOOD: Valentina's, Hardees, McDonalds.
MOTEL: Dandy Lion Inn.
CAMPGROUND: "Seward Glue Valley CG": Municipal. 5.5 miles North on NE 15. Primitive.
    MILEPOST 380 EASTBOUND REST AREA: Tourist Information. The sculpture at this rest area is called "Arrival" by Paul Ringelheim. You must cross-over a bridge in the rear of the area to get to it. Who will find it first? Displays tell about farming in Nebraska. This area was settled after 1861 when the Nebraska City Cutoff brought more trade through. A plaque tells what is left of the historical Big Blue River after a water project. West of Lincoln you might see some red granite rocks left here by an ancient glacier.

382 **MILFORD:**
FUEL: North to Phillips, Conoco.
MOTEL: North to Milford Inn.
CAMPGROUNDS: "Motel N Camp" North. Near I-80
    "Westward Ho! CG": Private. North of I-80 turn Right. Sleep in tipi. NEAR I-80.

388 **PLEASANT DALE/NE 103:** RADIO WEATHER: 1370 AM.
CAMPGROUND: North on NE 103. Northwest corner. NEAR I-80.

395 **48TH STREET, LINCOLN:** ELEVATION: 1169 FEET. RADIO: 1610 AM.
FUEL: South to Gas-N-Shop, Shoemaker Texaco Truck Stop.
FOOD: South to Merle's, Popeye's, "Bonanza" at 8315 O St.
MOTELS: South to Congress Inn, Cobbler Inn, Super 8.
CAMPGROUNDS: "Pawnee Lake State Recreation Area": South then West 4 miles on US 6. Showers, playground. Lake fish, swim, boat. Few trees. $6-$9.
    "Sky View Mobile Home Park": Private. 1030 North 48th Street. To North. Trailers only.

396 **EASTBOUND ONLY EXIT:** LINCOLN/US 6/NE 2.
FUEL: South to Gas-N-Shop.
MOTEL: Super 8*.

397 **LINCOLN/US 6/SALT VALLEY ROADWAY:** ROAD CONDITIONS: 477-9202.

EASTBOUND EXIT TO DOWNTOWN LINCOLN. Check your city map.
FUEL: Shoemakers' Truck Plaza.
MOTEL: South to Super 8*, Senate Inn.

LINCOLN

Lincoln was first called "Lancaster" and was settled in 1863 by a Methodist colony. The first capital of the Nebraska Territory was Omaha. But most of the population was South of the Platte River and the river could only be crossed to Omaha in the winter when it was frozen. This was a big issue during the Territorial days. A commission was set up to solve the problem but by 1867 Omaha had the railroad and was a viable choice for the capital. There were charges of bribery. Proponents of Omaha as the site, backed the name change from Lancaster to "Lincoln" to discourage the choice of that town. (Nebraskans were angry with Lincoln for taking the army East for the Civil War and leaving them unprotected from the Sioux and Cheyenne.) But the Southern citizens were adamant and with a population of only 60 the new town of Lincoln won its bid as capital. To be sure their position was secure, one night citizens secretly moved State Archives and property from Omaha to Lincoln.

A grasshopper invasion in early 1870's discouraged many residents who packed up and went East. By the mid 1870's Lincoln had a new Capitol building, a railroad and a university, but still retained its western character. Wild animals such as deer and coyotes came into town. Pioneer wagons passed through and "Market Square" in the city center was an emigrant camp scene of wagons, horses, and cattle. Of course there was also the opportunist element such as gamblers, horse traders and land sharks. William Jennings Bryan, one of our nations finest men and a great orator, emerged here in the late 1880's. He was Nebraska's Congressman, who made such an eloquent speech at the Democratic Convention in 1896 that it will be remembered for generations. Another national hero was John J Pershing, commander of Allied forces in World War I and professor of military science at University of Nebraska. The University set the pace for Lincoln and made it a cultural center.

UNIVERSITY OF NEBRASKA: East on US 6 to downtown. You'll be on O Street.

STATE MUSEUM/MORRILL HALL: 14th and U St. Excellent collection of fossils, natural history, anthropological, and geological artifacts. Mon-Sat 9:30-4:30pm. Sun 1:30-4:30pm. Adult $1.

LENZ CENTER FOR ASIAN CULTURE: 14th and U Street. Asian philosophies through art and objects. Mon-Sat 10-4pm.

HALL OF NEBRASKA WILDLIFE: Mounted native animals in dioramas. Mon-Sat 9:30 to 4:30pm. Adult $1. Child $.50.

CHRISTLIEB COLLECTION OF WESTERN ART: 13th and R. Love Library. Second floor of South Wing. Collection of Charles Russell's and Frederick Remington's paintings and bronzes.

THE ENCOUNTER CENTER: A hands-on learning center. Great for kids! Mon-Fri 10:30-4:30pm (except lunch hour). Free.

RALPH MUELLER PLANETARIUM: Shows Tues-Sun at 2pm. Adult $2.50. Child $1.50.

SHELDON MEMORIAL ART GALLERY: 12th and R Streets. 20th Century American Art, paintings and sculpture. Tues-Sat 10-5pm. Sun 2-9pm. Free.

OTHER PLACES OF INTEREST:

STATE MUSEUM OF HISTORY: 15th and P Streets. North of the Capitol. Three floors of exhibits tell the history of Nebraska and of the Plains Indians, "The First Nebraskans". Mon-Sat 9-5pm. Sun 1:30-5pm. Free.

FOLSOM CHILDREN'S ZOO AND BOTANICAL GARDENS: 28th and A Streets. A child-sized Pioneer town and 200 animals, a train, botanical garden, and art gallery. Mon-Sat 10-5pm. Sun 10-6pm. Adult $2.75. Child $1.

STATE CAPITOL: K and 15th Streets. A bronze statue of "The Sower" is on top the central tower. The sculpture of Abraham Lincoln on the West side is by Daniel Chester French who sculpted the Lincoln Memorial in Washington, D.C. There is a mosiac dome in the rotunda, a walnut ceiling in the Supreme Court Chamber, and one of the world's largest chandeliers. Tours weekdays 8-4pm. Noon-4pm Sat. Tours every .5-1 hour. Free.

GOVERNOR'S MANSION: 14th and H Streets. Brick mansion South of Capitol. Thurs 1-4pm. Free.

LINCOLN CHILDREN'S MUSEUM": 12th and N Streets. Hands-on learning center of science, time, cultures, art. Sun-Mon and Fri 1-5pm. Tues, Thurs, Sat 10-5pm. $2.50 per person.

FAIRVIEW: HOME OF WILLIAM JENNINGS BRYAN: 4900 Sumner Street. From O Street/NE 34 go South on 48th Street about .5 mile to East on Sumner Street. Bryan moved to Lincoln in 1887, became their member of Congress, editor of Omaha World-Herald, ran for President three times, and became Secretary of State under Wilson. At the Democratic Convention of 1896 at 36 years of age he spoke eloquently against the Gold Standard: "You shall not press down upon the brow of labor this crown of thorns. You shall not crucify mankind upon a cross of gold". He also was the prosecutor of the Evolution theory in the famous "Monkey Trial" in Tennessee in 1925. Weekends 1:30-5pm. Adult $1.

NATIONAL MUSEUM OF ROLLER SKATING: 7700 A Street. Go East of Lincoln on US 34/O Street. South on 79th Street to A Street. East to Museum. Shows the development of the roller skate and the history of its use. Mon-Fri 9-5pm. Adult $2.75.

DOWNTOWN PARKING: 11th and N Streets. 1318 M Street. 1220 L Street.

FOOD: Many restaurants in town including, "Old Country Buffet": 23rd and O Street, Park Center Plaza.

MILEPOST 398: Capitol Beach Lake used to be a salt flat. Look for a white crust on the sides near I-80. The Natives dusted the salt up with feathers and put it into leather bags. Early settlers also obtained their salt here. Lincoln's underground water is too salty to drink so fresh water has to be piped in from wells along the Platte River. Look across the lake to the tower of the State Capitol in downtown Lincoln. It is 400 feet tall with a 32 foot bronze statue of "The Sower".

399 NORTHWEST 12TH STREET, LINCOLN/AIRPORT:
FUEL: South to Amoco, Phillips, KM Quik, Gas-N-Shop.
FOOD: North to Perkins, Dennys, McDonalds, Happy Chef, Bonanza.
MOTELS: South to Ramada, Econo*. North to Holiday, Best Western, Comfort Inn, Days Inn, Travel Lodge, Hampton, Motel 6*, Dillon Inn.

401 9TH STREET, LINCOLN/I-180 SOUTH/US 34: UNIVERSITY OF NEBRASKA: South to Vine.
WESTBOUND TO DOWNTOWN LINCOLN: South on I-180/US 77 and East between alphabet streets. Check your city map. Read Milepost 397 for the sights of Lincoln.
FUEL: South to Sinclair.
MOTELS: South to Super 8*, Sharon Motel & Oak Park Motel all East on Cornhusker.
CAMPGROUNDS: "Camp-a-Way": Private. South on I-180 to Superior Street. West .5 mile to Ogden Road. North to campground. Playground.
   "State Fair Park CG": Private. 14th and Cornhusker. South on I-180 to East on Cornhusker.
   MILEPOST 403: NEW INTERCHANGE UNDER CONSTRUCTION.
   MILEPOST 404 WESTBOUND REST AREA: (Solar Heated): Get your tape "Highway to a Heritage" here. Read "Nebraska History". Prairie grass and wildflower area with plaque on ecology of prairie.

405 56th STREET, LINCOLN/US 77: HOSPITAL.
All services are .5-1 mile South:
FUEL: Phillips, Conoco.
FOOD: Misty's, Holiday Inn.
MOTELS: Super 8, Econo Lodge*, Holiday Inn. South 2 miles to Imperial Inn.

409 EAST LINCOLN/WAVERLY/US 6: HOSPITAL.
FUEL: North to Gas-N-Shop.
MOTEL: North to Sleepy Hollow.
   MILEPOST 418 WESTBOUND REST AREA: Do you know the grasses and flowers along I-80? The tall feathery yellow flowers are sweet clover. The low ground cover with pink to orchid flowers is crown vetch.

420 GREENWOOD/NE 63:
FUEL: North to Phillips, Amoco Truck Plaza, Fuel Mart Truck Stop. South to Fine.
FOOD: Happy Chef.
MOTEL: South to Rath Inn.
CAMPGROUND: "Pine Grove Holiday Travel Park": Private. Good Sam. North 200 feet on NE 63. West .2 mile on County Road. Pool, playground. NEAR I-80.
   MILEPOST 422 EASTBOUND REST AREA: Tourist Information. Go to the Quiet park back behind the main building with the sculpture, "Memorial to American Bandshell", by Richard Field. The plaque is on the Platte River. Saline Salt Creek enters the Platte just North of here. Agrarian people lived here 1,000 AD, Oto Indians in 1718 and settlers in 1854.
   MILEPOST 424 WESTBOUND REST AREA:

426 **ASHLAND:** WEATHER RADIO: 590 AM, 660 AM, 1420 AM. 99.9 FM 100.7 FM.
MOTEL/LODGING: MAHONEY STATE PARK: North 2 miles off I-80. Follow signs. Cabins, Lodge rooms, restaurant. Call: 402-944-2523.
CAMPGROUNDS: MAHONEY STATE PARK: About 2 miles North. 500 acres of recreation along the Platte River. Two RV areas near the Owen Marina with pads, showers, hookups, dump station. Tent camping Southeast of Little Creek Campground. Swimming pool, water slide, horseback rides, hiking, picnicking, miniature golf, tennis, volleyball, camp store, paddleboats. Hookups $13. Tent $5.
MILEPOST 425: Look Southeast to the Platte River Valley where a stone canyon wall narrows the Platte Valley to .5 mile wide. Downstream further South it narrows even more to .25 mile across. So the mighty Platte with its wide valley as much as 12 miles wide to the West, is finally confined by stone before its final push into the Missouri River.
MILEPOST 427 CROSSING THE PLATTE RIVER.
MILEPOST 430 WESTBOUND REST AREA: TOURIST INFORMATION. GET YOUR "HIGHWAY TO HERITAGE" TAPE HERE. This is your first view of the Platte River Valley.

432 **GRETNA/US 6/NE 31:**
FUEL: South to Flying J Conoco Travel Center.
CAMPGROUNDS: "West Omaha KOA": Private. North .5 mile. In trees. Pool. $14-$21.
PLATTE RIVER STATE PARK: South about 5 miles on NE 31. Follow signs. Tipis $10, camper-cabins $20, housekeeping cabins $35. Call: 402-234-2217. Swim and hike, paddleboats, tennis, archery, horseback rides, buffalo stew cookout. Scott Lodge Restaurant. Climb 130 steps up "Lincoln Journal Tower" and you can see way up & down the Platte River.
LOUISVILLE STATE RECREATION AREA: South on NE 31 and East to Louisville. About 7 miles. On South bank of Platte River on North side of Louisville. Camping pads, showers, RV dump. Near Platte River State Park. $6-$9.
SCHRAMM PARK STATE RECREATION AREA: 6 miles South on NE 31. A 300-acre park of trails and nature walks, fish hatchery, museum, geology, water fowl, and wildflower exhibits. There are spectacular views of the Platte Valley from here. No camping.
AK-SAR-BEN AQUARIUM: Native and introduced fish in tanks and a large terrarium for amphibians and reptiles. Also outside ponds. Mon-Fri 10-4:30pm. Summers: Sat-Sun 10-6pm. Adult $1. Child $.50.

439 **156TH STREET, OMAHA/NE 370:** HOSPITAL.
FUEL/FOOD/MOTEL: North to '76, Happy Chef and Motel.

EASTBOUND ALTERNATE ROUTE

TO THE SAC BASE AND BELLEVUE, NE: East about 12 miles on NE 370 to Bellevue. To return to I-80 go East across Missouri River to I-29. North to I-80 at Iowa Milepost 4.
STRATEGIC AIR COMMAND MUSEUM: 2510 Clay Street, Bellevue. East on NE 370. Follow signs South on Galvin Road for .5 mile to 24th Avenue. East one block. Large building of artifacts plus 30 aircraft and 7 missiles. 8am to 5pm. Adult $3.
SARPY CO HISTORICAL MUSEUM: 2402 Clay Street, just a block from the SAC base. Displays of early Indians, fur traders and pioneer life. Ask directions to the historic old buildings of Bellevue.
FOOD: "Old Country Buffet": 701 Galvin Road South. Ask at the Museum or SAC base for directions.
CAMPGROUND: "Haworth Park": Municipal. NE 370 and Payne Drive. Tents and trailers. Showers.
BELLEVUE: This was Nebraska's first settlement. Just South of here Lewis and Clark raised the American flag for the first time in Nebraska. In 1820's-30's Bellevue was growing fast with trading and shipping. Peter Sarpy arrived in 1824, married an Indian woman, and took over the American Fur Company Post. He began a ferry service carrying pioneers across the Missouri. In the 1830's government agents checked upriver ships for liquor as it was outlawed for Natives. But this was traders' best trade item, most desired by both Natives and Trappers. So the traders used various means to smuggle the liquor through. They tried encasing it in flour barrels but it wasn't long before this was no longer successful. One ruse was to label it for the fur-trading agent at Bellevue and unload it there before the inspector came. Then when he had gone, they just loaded it back onto the ship.

In 1832 an Indian agency was established here for the Omaha, Pawnee, Oto and Missouri tribes.

John C. Fremont got his boats and supplies here on his return trip in 1842. Scout Kit Carson, and artists Karl Bodmer (1833) and J.J. Audubon (1843) visited here. Peter Sarpy bought a steam ferry in 1853, "The Nebraska", for $13,000. It carried 25-30 teams and wagons at a time. In 1854 Nebraska's first newspaper, "Nebraska Palladium" was published and the first Territorial Governor was inaugurated.

THE BELLE: Off NE 370 in Haworth Park near the bridge. Riverboat ride on the Missouri River. Tues-Sun 1pm. 1.5 hour ride. Adult $5.50.

440 **SPRINGFIELD/NE 50:** ELEVATION: 1,000 FEET. HOSPITAL.
FUEL: North to Sapp Bros Texaco Truck Stop, Amoco, Phillips Truck Stop, Ford truck dealer.
FOOD: North to Happy Chef, McDonalds, Catfish Charlie's Restaurant, Hardees.
MOTELS: North to Huntington Inn, Park Inn, Ben Franklin, American 9 Inn.
WESTBOUND CAMPGROUNDS: PLATTE RIVER STATE PARK & LOUISVILLE STATE REC AREA: South on NE 50 about 10 miles to Louisville. Read Milepost 426. You will return to I-80 at that milepost.

444 **HARRISON STREET, OMAHA:** NO NEAR SERVICES! New Interchange UNDER CONSTRUCTION IN 1992!

445 **L STREET, OMAHA/US 275/NE 92:**
FUEL: Exit and then Right to Amoco, Sinclair.
FOOD: Left at light to Shoney's. Right at light to The Choice Smorgasbord, Wendys, Hardees, Bonanza, Long John's, Arbys, Burger King, Shelldon's, Village Inn.
MOTELS: East to Village Inn, Hampton Inn, Omaha Inn, Carlisle Hotel, Bugetel Inn, Super 8*, Motel 6* (East on L Street to 108th St. Right 1 block. Left on "M" Street.) West to Sheridan Inn.

446 **MAJOR INTERCHANGE!**
I-80 THROUGH DOWNTOWN OMAHA TO COUNCIL BLUFFS, IOWA.
I-680 NORTH AROUND THE CITY AND CONNECTING WITH I-80 IN IOWA.

EASTBOUND ALTERNATE ROUTE ON I-680

I-680 skirts North around Omaha, joins I-29 North in Iowa for two Exits, then turns East to rejoin I-80 in Iowa at Iowa's Milepost 27. It's mostly in the country, avoids the business area of Omaha, and is usually less congested. You will also want to take this route if you want to visit **BOYS' TOWN, FORT ATKINSON**, and/or the **MORMON PIONEER CEMETERY** at Florence. (Outside of rush hours you may sail through on I-80.)

I-680 EXITS:

MILEPOST 1 FOOD: "Old Country Buffet", 144 and West Center Road. West on Center Road.
MILEPOST 1 B: Rockbrook Mall.
MILEPOST 3: MALL: Westwoods Shopping Center. On US 6. 160 stores, Penny's, Wards.
FOOD: "Old Country Buffet", 74th Street and Dodge Place. East on US 6.
BOYS' TOWN VISITOR CENTER: West 2.5 miles on US 6. Famous home for abused, homeless or neglected children. Recorded tape guides you on your tour. 8am-4:30pm. Free.
MILEPOST 12 FORT CALHOUN/FORT ATKINSON STATE HISTORICAL PARK: US 75 North 9 miles. .5 mile East. Lewis & Clark's first council with the Indians in 1804 was held here, not in Council Bluffs, Iowa. The Missouri has changed course over the years and those same bluffs are now 3 miles from the river. Lewis and Clark recommended that a fort be built here on the Missouri, but the government was slow and didn't build Fort Atkinson until 1819. It became the first military post West of the Missouri. With the only governmental authority in the territory, they regulated the fur trade, river traffic and "Indian Affairs" until the fort was abandoned in 1827. Much of the Old Fort has been reconstructed and living history demonstrations are held there. Summers: 9-5pm. May, Sept, and Oct weekends 1-5pm.
MILEPOST 13 FLORENCE:
CAMPGROUND: "N.P. DODGE PARK": Municipal. On the Missouri River. South to first light at McKinley. As you make a Left turn onto McKinley, note the **OLD MORMON MILL** on your Left. East 2 blocks to John Pershing Drive, under I-80 and North one mile. Showers, playground. $6.
VISITOR CENTER AND MORMON PIONEER CEMETERY: South to the first light. On your Left note

the old mill built by the Mormons. The 1856 restored Bank of Florence, Omaha's oldest building, is on your Right as you continue South. At State Street turn Right up over the hill to a Left at the sign. Park in the lot on the Left where the free tours begin. There is a restored cabin, a handcart and a covered wagon outside and a 20-minute film on the Mormon Migration inside. The tour continues across the street in the Mormon Pioneer Cemetery. Tours are from 8am to dusk. This is the site of historic "Missouri Bottoms" where for two years the population ranged from 3,000-5,000 Mormon pioneers at a time. They built a town of a thousand buildings including a meetinghouse, a school, and a water-powered gristmill. They produced supplies and built wagons preparing for the trek to the Salt Lake Valley. The cemetery tells the sad story of those who didn't make the trip, especially the infants and the elderly who died from fevers, starvation and exposure in the winters of 1846 and 1847. FOR OTHER SIGHTS IN DOWNTOWN OMAHA READ MILEPOST 452.

THE MORMONS AND MISSOURI BOTTOMS

The Mormons had fled Nauvoo, Illinois when their leader, Joseph Smith and his brother Hyrum were shot by a rioting mob in June 1844. Read Iowa History. Brigham Young was elected the new Church President. He called all his missionaries back to Nauvoo to help prepare for the Exodus. Converts on the Eastern Seaboard were told not to go to Nauvoo but to find passage by water to the West Coast as it would be an easier trip. Sam Brannan, a printer found a vessel, "The Brooklyn", and equipped it with supplies and 238 converts and sailed West February 4, 1846 to go around Cape Horn. They sailed through the Golden Gate on July 31st, 1846. On the same date that The Brooklyn set sail, Brigham Young led his flock Westward across the frozen Mississippi River and on across Iowa. They arrived at the Missouri River in companies. The government was reluctant to allow them to cross into "Indian Country". They had to get permission from both the government and the Natives to do so. Some stayed on the Iowa side for awhile. Others crossed on three different crude ferries at Bellevue, South Omaha and Florence. Their first camp on the Nebraska side was "Cold Spring Camp" at present Ak-sar-ben. They also camped at "Curler's Park" three miles West of Florence. Then they negotiated with the Indians for a campsite. They settled on "Winter Quarters"/Florence, Oto territory, and "Summer Quarters" just North of old Fort Atkinnson, Omaha Territory. They leased the land for just two years, and for payment, promised to leave all of their fields and buildings to the Indians when they had finished their move to Salt Lake City. This Missouri Bottoms/Winter Quarters site was dubbed "Misery Bottoms" that first winter when 3500 people huddled in 600-700 sod and log houses and dugouts. With their homemade 3-pounder cannon they felt they could defend themselves from the Gentiles at this site. Those unable to make the Westward Trek moved back across the river to Kanesville/Council Bluffs to keep their treaty with the Indians. By the spring of 1847 there were 10,000 Mormons on both sides of the Missouri River or scattered along the Iowa trail.

Brigham Young needed money to move his Saints West. He wrote President Polk with an idea to have his men build Forts along the Westward Trail for the government in order to earn money for supplies. Instead, the Mexican War had begun so Polk proposed that the Mormons form a battalion to help. This appealed to Young as he not only could obtain money from the soldiers' pay to buy supplies for the migration but the Mormons could prove their loyalty to the U.S. and he would then receive permission from the government to cross "Indian Territory". So in July 1846, the 536-man Mormon Battalion left Winter Quarters for Fort Leavenworth and for Los Angeles.

In April 1847 the Advance Group, the "Pioneer Mormon Band", headed west to blaze a trail for "The Saints" to follow. There were 154 men, 3 women and 2 children. (Brigham Young's wife included.) They had tools, farm equipment, grain, food for one year, 93 horses, 52 mules, 66 oxen, 19 cows, 17 dogs and unnumbered chickens.

The Mormons were strictly organized and disciplined with 14 captains, one for every 10 men. They traveled two abreast, guns ready. A bugle blew at 5am to rise and pray, at 7am to travel, and at 7pm to prayers and bed. Each man had his job, skills were assigned. Some kept logs. A scientist, Orson Pratt, kept a record of all measurements. He used his barometer and compass and invented a wheel of 60 cogs, a "roadometer" to measure distance. The company arched North along the North bank of the Platte, where US 30 is today. They stayed to the North when the Loup River entered the Platte and followed it past today's Fullerton and on South to the Platte just East of Grand Island. They remained on the North bank all the way across Nebraska. There was so much game that the men shot too many and Brigham Young reprimanded them for wasting food. In July 1847 the next group of 1553 people and 560 wagons started the trek West. In Sept 1848, 2500 left Winter Quarters. Thus continued the trek of thousands.

448 84TH STREET, OMAHA/PAPILLION:
   FUEL: South to gas.

FOOD: McDonalds, Dennys.
MOTELS: Motel 6 (South on 84th. Right on L Street. Left on 108th Street. Left on M Street.)
CAMPGROUND: "Omaha New City CG": Private. South one block to F Street. East 150 feet. In town. NEAR I-80.

449 **72ND STREET, OMAHA:**
FUEL: North and South.
FOOD: Restaurants to North.
MOTELS: Super 8, Best Western, Days Inn.
    AK SAR BEN RACE TRACK: 63rd and Center Street. North .5 mile then East on West Center Road. Watch signs. Thoroughbred horse racing May-Aug. Wed-Fri 4pm. Sat-Sun 2pm. Spell the name backwards. Nebraska humor!

450 **60TH STREET, OMAHA:** UNIVERSITY OF NEBRASKA. **FUEL:** To North.

451 **42ND STREET, OMAHA:** UNIVERSITY OF NEBRASKA MEDICAL CENTER
FUEL: '76, Texaco.

452 **M A J O R   I N T E R C H A N G E !**
I-480 NORTH & US 75/DOWNTOWN OMAHA: NO NEAR SERVICES!
ROAD CONDITIONS: 553-5000.
    Downtown is centered at US 6/Dodge Street and I-480/US 75. You might want to Exit on Milepost 454 at the Information Center first.

DOWNTOWN OMAHA

    The name of the city of Omaha came from the Omaha tribe meaning "above all others on a stream". In 1853 Chief Iron Eye of the Omaha sold 4,000,000 acres of land to the U.S. for 20 cents an acre and a 300 square-mile reservation, 80 miles North of here. The Otos made a similar settlement. Now settlers came across the Missouri and this time instead of just passing through, stayed and settled there. Omaha became an outfitting center, a wild town of lawlessness as were most of the frontier towns.

    President Lincoln chose Council Bluffs and Omaha as the beginning of the Transcontinental Railroad. Ground was broken in December 1863 but it was some time before construction was actually underway. Fort Omaha was built in 1868 and was in use through World War II when it became "Metropolitan Technical Community College".

    General Dodge, a Civil War army officer, was assigned to protect the railroad surveyors. Then after the war he was made "Chief Engineer for the Union Pacific Railroad". The second man chosen by Lincoln was Oakes Ames, a Congressman and financier, a wealthy man well-respected for his integrity. His brother became president of the railroad. The third man was the died-in-the-wool crook, Dr. Durant, a surgeon, who made deals to get things done.

    The famous trial in the 1870's of "Standing Bear", chief of the Poncas gave status to the Natives as a "person" for the first time. General Crook was credited with making sure the trial was just. All of the Tribes were being sent forcibly to Oklahoma to clear the way for the settlement of the Nebraska Territory. Many died along the way of disease, starvation and hopelessness. Standing Bear's oldest son died in Oklahoma with a final request to be buried in his homeland in Nebraska and the chief was honor-bound to fulfill his son's wish. So he brought the body to Nebraska and was arrested for being off the reservation. With the help of the media and General Crook he was not extradited but brought to trial. The defense attorney took the stand that a Native could leave his tribe and live under U.S. law and he won the suit. So in 1879 Standing Bear was allowed to stay and settle in Nebraska. However when other Indians tried to do the same thing, it was not allowed. In fact Standing Bear's brother was killed when he threatened to "take it to court".

    MUTUAL OF OMAHA: 33rd & Dodge. The dome of the building is a contemporary design and is energy efficient. Inside are exhibits from the TV show, "Wild Kingdom". Tours at 9am and 2pm.

    ST. CECILIA'S CATHEDRAL: 701 North 40th Street. Just South of Cuming Street/NE 64. This is a Spanish Renaissance-style building. It has a white Carrara marble altar from Italy, a chapel with stained-glass windows from a 16th Century cathedral in Pampeluna, Spain, and a hand-carved mahogany pulpit. 7-6:30pm.

    JOSLYN ART MUSEUM: 2200 Dodge Street/US 6. An unusual pink marble building. Emphasis on Western art with Carl Bodmer oils, but includes collections from ancient Greece, Italy and Egypt, the

Renaissance, and Middle Ages. Tues-Sat 10-5pm. Sun 1-5pm. Adult $2. Child $1.

UNION PACIFIC MUSEUM: 1416 Dodge/US 6. In lobby of UP Headquarters Build. Shows the development of the railroad. Has the furnishings from President Lincoln's funeral railroad car. Mon-Fri 9-5pm. Free.

OLD MARKET AREA: Off US 75 on Harney Street, then East. In a 4-block area including 11th and Howard. Browse in the shops. **OLLIE THE TROLLEY** runs along this street to the Market.

WESTERN HERITAGE MUSEUM: 801 South 10th Street. South 3 blocks of Old Market. Parking on North of the old Union Pacific Station Building. The history of Omaha with artifacts and old photos downstairs. Also an old fashioned soda fountain. Tues-Sat 10-5pm. Sun 1-5pm. Adult $2. Child $.50.

GREAT PLAINS BLACK MUSEUM: 2213 Lake Street. From US 75 North of downtown, turn East on Lake Street. Designed by the prominent architect, Thomas R. Kimball. Stories of black settlers, soldiers, trappers. Weekdays 8-5pm.

USS HAZARD AND USS MARLIN FREEDOM PARK: Minesweeper and submarine. 1600 Abbott Drive. Just East of US 75 and North of US 6. Abbott Drive goes across Carter Lake. The Minesweeper was used in the invasion of Okinawa. April-Oct Tues-Sat 1-sunset. Adult $3. Child $1.

HISTORIC FORT OMAHA/GENERAL CROOK HOUSE: North of town on 30th Street to Fort Street. West 200 feet to South Road. West .2 mile to West Road. North two blocks. Active post from 1868 to 1975 and presently "Metropolitan Technical Community College". General Crook was commander during the Sioux Wars of the 1870's. Read Milepost 445. Restored Italianate residence and gardens. Mon-Fri 10-4pm. Adult $3.

You can continue North to the **MORMON PIONEER CEMETERY AND VISITOR CENTER**. Read Milepost 13 of the I-680 Alternate Route above.

WESTBOUND ALTERNATE ROUTE

SOUTH TO THE SAC BASE AND BELLEVIEW SIGHTS: Read Milepost 439 for descriptions. Then go West on NE 370 to rejoin I-80 at Milepost 439.

453 **24TH STREET, OMAHA:** NO NEAR SERVICES!

454 **13TH STREET, OMAHA/VISITOR INFORMATION CENTER:**
> **WESTBOUND:** Stop here and get your Nebraska map and brochures! Also your tapes: "Highway to a Heritage". Read Nebraska History and Mileposts 452, 446 and 439 for Omaha sights.
> **EASTBOUND:** Stop here for information on downtown Omaha. Ask about the best route and parking if you have a large motor home or trailer. Also read the descriptions of downtown attractions on Milepost 452 and I-680's Milepost 13 above.
> **FUEL:** Both North & South.
>
> **HENRY DOORLY ZOO:** South on 13th Street a few blocks. Then East to 10th Street. Some rare species including a white tiger. Petting Zoo, aviary, aquarium. A 2.5 mile train ride takes you around the zoo. April-Oct 9:30-5pm. Adult $5.25. Child $2.50.
>
> **OMAHA CHILDREN'S MUSEUM:** 551 South 18th Street. South of Dodge Street. "Hands on" science for children. June-Aug Tues-Sat 10-5pm. Sun 1-5pm. Adult $3.
>
> **EASTBOUND:** Across the Mighty Missouri to Iowa!
>
> **WESTBOUND:** You are now off across the Great Bridge of Nebraska following the old trails of the pioneers. Stop at some of the historical sites along the way to gain an understanding of the pioneers as they set out on this "Great Platte Valley Road".

NEBRASKA I 80 MILEPOSTS

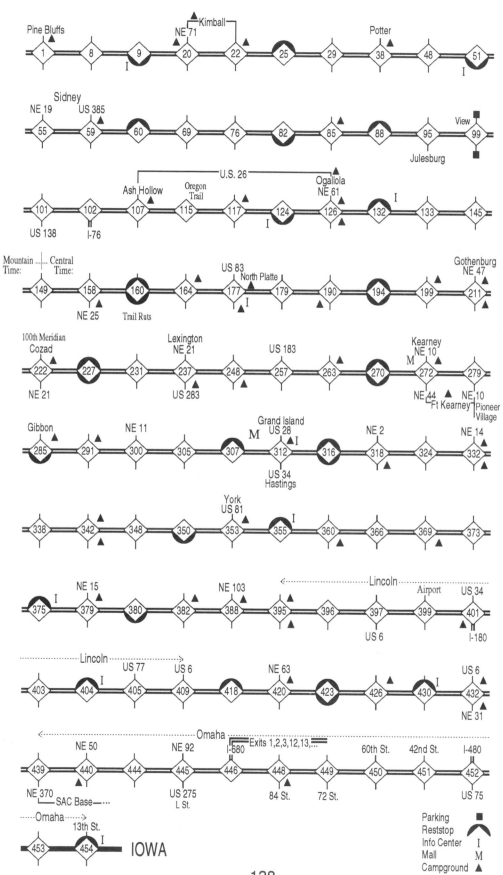

Pine Bluffs
Kimball
NE 71
Potter
1 · 8 · 9 · 20 · 22 · 25 · 29 · 38 · 48 · 51
I · I

Sidney
NE 19 · US 385
View
55 · 59 · 60 · 69 · 76 · 82 · 85 · 88 · 95 · 99
Julesburg

U.S. 26
Ash Hollow · Oregon Trail · Ogallola · NE 61
101 · 102 · 107 · 115 · 117 · 124 · 126 · 132 · 133 · 145
US 138 · I-76 · I · I

Mountain Time: · Central Time: · US 83 · North Platte · Gothenburg · NE 47
149 · 158 · 160 · 164 · 177 · 179 · 190 · 194 · 199 · 211
NE 25 · Trail Ruts · I

100th Meridian · Lexington · Kearney
Cozad · NE 21 · US 183 · NE 10
M · NE 10
222 · 227 · 231 · 237 · 248 · 257 · 263 · 270 · 272 · 279
NE 21 · US 283 · NE 44 · Ft Kearney · NE 10 · Pioneer Village

Grand Island
Gibbon · NE 11 · US 28 · NE 2 · NE 14
M · I
285 · 291 · 300 · 305 · 307 · 312 · 316 · 318 · 324 · 332
US 34 · Hastings

York
US 81
338 · 342 · 348 · 350 · 353 · 355 · 360 · 366 · 369 · 373
I

Lincoln
NE 15 · NE 103 · Airport · US 34
I
375 · 379 · 380 · 382 · 388 · 395 · 396 · 397 · 399 · 401
US 6 · I-180

Lincoln
US 77 · US 6 · NE 63 · US 6
I · I
403 · 404 · 405 · 409 · 418 · 420 · 423 · 426 · 430 · 432
NE 31

Omaha
Exits 1,2,3,12,13,...
NE 50 · NE 92 · I-680 · 60th St. · 42nd St. · I-480
439 · 440 · 444 · 445 · 446 · 448 · 449 · 450 · 451 · 452
NE 370 · SAC Base · US 275 · L St. · 84 St. · 72 St. · US 75

Omaha
13th St.
I
453 · 454 · **IOWA**

Parking · ■
Reststop · ⌒
Info Center · I
Mall · M
Campground · ▲

138

Iowa

The Hawkeye State

The proud Hawkeyes of Iowa date back to 1837 and David Rorer, an Iowa Attorney. He helped draft a petition to Congress to create the Territory of Iowa from the Territory of Wisconsin. He didn't want a derogatory designation that was common at the time like "The Suckers of Illinois" or "The Pukes of Missouri". He wanted a classic name for a proud new state. The Hawkeyes! His newspaper friend, James Edwards, agreed and published the proposals for both the Territory and the Name along with stories of Old Chief Black Hawk. Deliberate "anonymous" letters to other newspapers promoted the name further. Edwards even named his newspaper, "The Hawkeye". The name could also have been inspired by James Fenimore Cooper's hero in "The Last of the Mohicans" published in 1826. That stalwart frontiersman was Iowa's hero too. In 1838 when the Rorer-Edward plan succeeded and Iowa became a Territory, Governor Lucas was appointed. Lucas, who had previously been a governor of Ohio Territory, objected to the common practice of carrying pistols. Then another attorney got in an argument with Rorer and beat him with a cane. Rorer shot the man but was never prosecuted for his deed. Lucas later retired to Iowa City and built his home, "Plum Grove", Milepost 240.

Iowa is cradled between the country's two major rivers, the Missouri and the Mississippi, that brought the earliest explorers. It is "prairie" country, the French word for "meadow". The early explorers noted the tall waving shoulder high grasses, blue stem, switch grass, Indian grass, and others. Iowa's prairie is not in flat land like Indiana and Illinois, but in beautiful rolling hills! The rows of corn, soy and oats sweep over the hills with placid farm buildings cloistered between the fields. The perfect pastoral scene! Although you don't see it from I-80, Iowa has 1.5 million acres of forest on its Eastern side. The State Flower is the Wild Rose, the bird, the Goldfinch, and the tree, the mighty Oak.

We're in a smaller state now, 56,275 square miles, just 2/3rds the size of Nebraska. But the population explodes to twice as much, 2,776,755. The cities are larger with more industry, 276 manufacturers, who generate three times the income as does agriculture. But after traveling I-80 across Iowa you'll always think of this state as agricultural. All that corn you see is largely for feed grain for their hogs and that tender grain-fed beef that began as Wyoming range cattle. The oats is for the Quaker Oats Company in Cedar Rapids. Biochemical research with corn and soy has developed new food products for animals and for people. "Malto dextrin" is an innovative ingredient developed by Iowan, Dr. Al Morehouse, that provides viscosity to many prepared packaged foods.

You'll pass a lot of colleges here. Iowa has the highest literary rate in the nation with 60% of its High School graduates going into college. The violent crime rate is less than 38 percent of the national average. The Iowan composer, Meredith Wilson wrote "The Music Man", J. V. Atanasoff invented the first digital computer, and James Van Allen discovered the protective band of radiation encircling our planet.

IOWA HISTORY

The major 18th Century inhabitants of this area were the Sauk and Fox/Mesquaki tribes along both sides of the Missitheepi/Mississippi River. There they farmed corn and squash and had their permanent homes. But in the early spring they migrated to Minnesota to tap the maple

Wild Rose

sugar trees. They also roamed large territories hunting and fishing. The Ioway tribes lived along the Des Moines River, and the Otoe, Missouri and Omaha tribes along the Missouri River.

The French had hunted, trapped and traded around the Great Lakes when in 1673 Louis Joliet and Fr. Marquette found their way from Green Bay, Wisconsin down the Wisconsin River to the Mississippi, the Great Mother of Rivers described to them by the Natives. They walked on Iowa soil where the Iowa River enters the Mississippi. They only went as far South as Arkansas as they were looking for a way to the Pacific, and were not interested in the Gulf route. Fr. Louis Hennepin explored the upper Mississippi in 1680. In 1788 the first settlement allowed by the tribes was made by Julien Dubuque who had a farming community and mined lead in a place later named Dubuque, Iowa. But when he died in 1810 all was abandoned. No new settlers were allowed in since the government designated the Mississippi as the Eastern boundary of "Indian Territory". The government needed Iowa land in order to have somewhere into which to move the Eastern Indians to clear THOSE states for settlement. In 1803 the United States purchased the "Louisiana Territory" from France (who had obtained it from Spain) and President Jefferson sent Lewis and Clark up the Missouri to explore their new bargain. So now Iowa's Western shores were explored. In 1805 Zebalon Pike explored the upper Mississippi and then went into Colorado and New Mexico in 1807-8. In 1810 a book was published about his travels glorifying his expeditions and making extravagant claims. It is said his wife really wrote it from his notes in order to raise the Pikes' expectations in society and politics. Pike described barren wastelands with miles of sand dunes. Farmers were advised to "be constrained to limit their extent in the west to the borders of the Missouri and Mississippi, while they leave the prairies incapable of cultivation to the wandering and uncivilized aborigines of the country." By 1825 most literary people had read Pike's book and accepted the premise that the West was an arid waste.

Since 1801 President Jefferson had driven ahead his policy of teaching the Natives to become completely stationary farmers or moving them Westward across the Mississippi. The Potawatomes you'll read about in Indiana had been pushed West to Iowa. An 1804 Treaty sent many Sauk and Fox tribes here from Illinois. After the war of 1812, the U.S. policy was to coerce the Natives to move West. First the Indian lands were divided between the tribes. Then government agents negotiated with each tribe individually demanding that they sign-over their lands and go West of the Mississippi. President Monroe carried on Jefferson's concept and put a proposal before Congress that ALL Natives be forcefully moved yet further West and South, this time West of the 95th Meridian, the Missouri River, the new "Permanent Indian Frontier". Check your U.S. map.

THE BLACK HAWK WAR

In the face of government policy, the effort of a Rock Island chief to regain his Illinois land ironically led to the opening of Iowa to settlement. Old Chief Black Hawk's Sauk and Fox tribe were farming the rich riverbottom lands of the Mississippi and the Rock Rivers in Illinois. Indian farms were small; they had no plows like the settlers. They grew enough corn and squash to feed themselves, but had no need of a surplus. They also believed in disturbing the land the Great Spirit had given them as little as possible. They felt that it was the rape of the land when the settlers came in and plowed large fields. The white men were hungry for these rich lands and felt that the lands were not being used to their capacity.

You will read in "Illinois" how in 1804 Governor Harrison had forced the Sauk and Fox to cede these lands to the government by a treaty signed by bribed lesser chiefs. (Who then had to flee the wrath of the real chiefs and the rest of the tribes.) According to the treaty the tribes could still farm and hunt there until settlers moved in. In 1829 greedy settlers formed a mob and drove the Natives from their homes and cornfields. Wise Chief Keokuk knew the situation was hopeless and led his people across into Iowa. Black Hawk refused and stayed in Illinois until 1831 when 1500 militia felt that the peaceful tribe's presence was a threat and joined to drive them across the Mississippi. Black Hawk's tribe got to Iowa too late to plant their crops or prepare protection from the elements so they shivered and starved through the winter.

By spring, 63 year old Black Hawk just wanted to go HOME. He convinced himself that he could reassure the settlers of his good intentions and they would let him return. So his whole tribe with 600 women and children and 400 warriors crossed the Mississippi in full view of soldiers from Ft. Armstrong/Rock River. But panic swept the frontier and rumors of "Indian attack" multiplied so that 1300 settlers gathered at the Fort and chased the tribe up the Rock River. Black Hawk tried to surrender and sent three men under a white flag, but they were killed. The tribe moved North where the women and children could be protected while the warriors roamed the country searching for food, and killing some settlers.

As the army pushed Northward, Black Hawk led his starving tribe back to Iowa at the Bad Axe River. The warriors held off the troops as long as they could to allow the women and children to cross the river. Then the warriors staggered toward the river exhausted and weak from starvation. A gunboat was on the river in front of them, and the militia behind them. Once more Black Hawk tried to surrender but the boat fired on his white flag. A terrible 3-hour battle ensued while they were forced into the river at bayonet point and shot. Only 150 Sauk survived and Black Hawk was taken prisoner. As punishment, at the Treaty of Fort Crawford, the U.S. took not only the Illinois lands of this tribe of Sauk and Fox, but also ALL of Eastern Iowa that belonged to the other tribes. They called it the "Black Hawk Purchase". Chief Black Hawk was paraded before all the other tribes to show them how useless it was to resist the whites. He was not even present when the "Treaty" was signed. Ironically for them, the Winnebagoes who assisted the government in the capture of Black Hawk, also lost THEIR lands that same year. The Black Hawk War was the last resistance of the Eastern Tribes as they relinquished their homelands for land West of the 95th Meridian. Abraham Lincoln was a captain during this war, but he was forever ashamed of his participation in it.

In June 1833 the Iowa "Black Hawk Purchase" was opened to settlers who came in droves. One settler said that "The roads were literally lined with the long blue waggons of the emigrants wending their way over the broad prairies". In 1836 there were 10,000 settlers in Iowa; by 1838 it became the Territory of Iowa and in 1840 it had a population of 43,000. Iowa needed a capital and all the towns wanted theirs to be chosen. The problem was settled by establishing a new town, Iowa City, and hiring a farmer to plow a straight furrow 100 miles from there to the Mississippi to guide the emigrants there. Iowa's first I-80 was but a furrow! In 1840 when construction began on the new capitol building, there were only 20 families in town.

In 1842 all the "Black Hawk" land was settled so the government went to work on another "Treaty" taking Central and Southern Iowa from the Sauk, Fox, and Ioway Indians and sending them further West and South. This was just 13 years after the Sauk had been driven across the Mississippi to "Indian Lands"! Iowa was the site of the first "Land Rush"! Thousands of settlers lined up and when the starting shot was fired, they raced to be first to their chosen spots. Towns sprang up overnight along the Des Moines River. Just four years later the rest of Iowa was taken from the Otoe, Omaha, and Missouri Tribes. Some years later a few Fox/Mesquaki were allowed to PURCHASE some land North of Grinnell where they live today.

Des Moine became the capital in 1857 and the state of Iowa prospered. In 1869 Iowa published "Iowa, the Home for Immigrants" in 5 languages. Many Europeans responded and made Iowa rich in cultures. About 95 percent of the state is cultivated now but Iowa retains some of its original "prairie land" in protected areas. The closest to I-80 is at Milepost 70, the First Train Robbery site and then at "Sheeder Prairie" near Guthrie Center on IA 25 and IA 44, Milepost 86.

When Eisenhower herded his Interstate Highway system through Congress in 1954, Iowa responded with the first section in 1957. It used to take 8 hours or more to cross Iowa with her NARROW pre I-80 roads. Coast to Coast travelers were very happy when Iowa completed I-80 in 1966 and travelers could safely cross the state in 5.5 hours.

THE MORMON MIGRATION, IOWA'S TRAIL OF TEARS!

EASTBOUND: Iowa holds the beginning of the story of the Mormon trek which you have been following in reverse the last 3-4 days.

WESTBOUND: You will be able to follow the Mormon Migration on their Westward move to the Salt Lake Valley. It all began here when they crossed Iowa.

Mormons in Far West, Missouri had fled Northeastward in 1838-39 because the "Permanent Indian Frontier" prevented them from going Westward. They settled in a swampy area of Illinois on the Mississippi just off the Southern tip of Iowa. They gained an autonomous charter from the state to establish their town of Nauvoo, Illinois with their own laws, courts and militia. Mormon missionaries spread over the U.S. and Europe and more converts came. By 1844 Nauvoo had a population of 15,000, a thriving metropolis for that day.

Joseph Smith was President of the Church, Commander of the 4,000 strong Nauvoo Militia, and Mayor of the town. Dissention arose because of local laws, abolitionism and fear of power. The sanctioning of polygamy for some church leaders raised additional fears. When the Mormon town Marshall smashed the press of a dissenting newspaper, it was the last straw. The Gentiles in town rose up against them and Mormon leaders were put in protective custody upstairs in the Carthage Jail. On June 27, 1844 a street mob with blackened faces pushed through the protecting Illinois Militia. Joseph Smith went to the window to see what was happening, shots were fired, and he and his brother were killed. "The whole state of Illinois is a mob!" said Governor Ford. Tension ran high.

By September, Brigham Young had been chosen as the new leader of the Mormons. But mobs ruled the streets so the Mormons had to move on. They studied John C. Fremont's writings and maps carefully. They could not move West of the 95th Meridian because it was "Permanent Indian Frontier". But they could try to get permission to cross it to the Great Salt Lake Valley which was as yet unsettled by whites. Young held his enemies in check by promising to leave "as soon as the grass grows and the water runs." So preparations began. They tried to sell their Nauvoo homes and land and most of their possessions, but their buyers were angry and hardhearted so they got a pittance of the worth of their properties and abandoned the rest.

The Mormons were well-organized, divided into companies of 100 families each with a variety of skilled craftsmen in each company. The situation in Nauvoo was so inflammable that the first Pioneer contingent with Brigham Young leading, left Nauvoo on Feb 9, 1845 crossing the Mississippi over the frozen ice, (a very unusual condition for the river). As they traveled across Iowa there was so little grass that the stock ate limbs and bark of trees. March brought heavy rains and thick mud that made travel a quagmire. At night the wagon wheels would freeze in the mud. The winds blew their tents down and heavy rains put out their fires. They slept in caves, or any shelter they could find.

At Locust Creek near Sewel, Iowa, William Clayton wrote the stirring Mormon hymn "Come, Come Ye Saints, All is Well". At Garden Grove, just South of Des Moines, they built their first "Way Station" for the Mormon parties to follow. They cleared 715 acres in 3 weeks, cut 10,000 rails for fences, built shelters and planted crops. All along the trail they cut down river banks, made ferries, put up signs, and stored supplies for their brothers coming after them. At Mt. Pisgah 150 died of black scurvy, TB, cholera, typhoid and childbirth. Other parties followed them along the trail. (By 1852 800 had died at Mt. Pisgah.)

This large contingent of Mormons arrived at the Missouri in 1846. Some crossed the river to Missouri Bottoms/Florence for the winter, and then went on to Salt Lake the next year. Those who could not go to Salt Lake settled on the East side of the river and built a thriving town called "Kanesville". Many of those who followed, stopped here also until the population was 8,000. In 1852 Mormons left here en masse to follow Brigham Young to the Salt Lake Valley, depleting the town's population to 1,000. In 1853 the town was renamed "Council Bluffs". In 1856 when Iowa City was the Western terminus of the railroad, it became the staging ground for the European Mormon immigrants to build their hand carts and start west. Visit "Handcart Park" at Milepost 240. In 1862 when President Lincoln selected Council Bluffs as the Eastern terminus of the Transcontinental Railroad, it grew into a major rail center.

IOWA MILEPOSTS

EMERGENCY NUMBER FOR HIGHWAY PATROL: 1-800-525-5555.
ROAD CONDITIONS: 515-288-1047.
RADIO FOR WEATHER AND NEWS: 1040 AM.
DIVISION OF TOURISM: 515-242-4705.

MILEPOSTS:

1A   MAJOR INTERCHANGE!
COUNCIL BLUFFS/I-29 NORTH: ELEVATION: 984 FEET. NO NEAR SERVICES!
I-29 NORTH TO SIOUX CITY.
 WESTBOUND: LAST EXIT FOR COUNCIL BLUFFS, IOWA. Exit I-29 at Milepost 53A to see the sights of Council Bluffs.
 CAMPGROUND: "Friendship Park": Public. North on I-29 to exit 53A at 9th Avenue. West .5 mile. Max 30 foot RV. Showers, electricity, playground. On the Missouri River.

1   SOUTH 24TH STREET, COUNCIL BLUFFS:
 FUEL: Amoco, Texaco, Phillips Truck Stop.
 FOOD: Happy Chef, Bonanza at 16 South 17th Street.
 MOTELS: Finish Line, Best Western, Comfort Inn, Regal Inn, Super 8.
 BLUFFS RUN DOG TRACK: 2701 23rd Street. Follow signs. Greyhound racing. Jan 8 to Dec 19th. Tues-Sun 8pm. Sat-Sun 1:30pm. 4pm Wed. Dining available.

3   COUNCIL BLUFFS/IA 192:
 FUEL: '76 Truck Plaza.
 North on IA 192 into town. South to Lake Manawa.
 MOTEL: Motel 6*: 1846 North 16th Street.
 CAMPGROUNDS: "Lake Manawa State Park": 1 mile South on South   Expressway. Electricity, showers, campfires. Lake fish, swim, boat. $5-$8.
 "Long's Landing County Park": South through Lake Manawa State Park and 1 mile further

to the river. Showers, hookups, boating. $5-$8. Lewis and Clark stopped here on their return trip from the Pacific in July 1805.

COUNCIL BLUFFS

The original "COUNCIL" between Lewis and Clark and the Otoe and Missouri Tribes took place in August 1804 North of Omaha on the Nebraska side of the river near the present site of Ft. Atkinson State Historical Park, Nebraska. Read Nebraska's I-680 Milepost 12.

A LEWIS & CLARK MONUMENT, erected in 1935, stands atop a bluff North of Council Bluffs and has a great view. However, to get to it you have a mile of gravel road and **TWO LOW 9-FOOT RAILROAD UNDERPASSES.**

GENERAL DODGE HOUSE: 605 3rd Street. Right off IA 192 onto South 5th Avenue to 3rd Street. Start at the Bereshaim House next door where you'll see a film about the house and the General. General Grenville M. Dodge was a Civil War General and the Chief Construction Engineer of the Union Pacific Railroad as it clawed its way west. This elegant Victorian house was built in 1869, the year that the railroad was completed. It has fine woodwork, crystal chandeliers, marble and lace. Dodge's high class entertainment of Presidents even boasts a 3rd floor ballroom with a rosewood piano. Tues-Sat 10-5pm. Sun 1-5pm. Adult $2.50. Child $1.

POTTAWATAMIE COUNTY JAIL: 226 Pearl Street next to the Courthouse, three blocks West and one block North of the Dodge House. Called "The Squirrel Cage", it is a 3-story revolving drum divided into 10 pie-shaped cells on each level. The cage rotated to get to each cell. It was used until 1969, but no longer rotated. The jailer's family lived on the top floor while the wife cooked the inmates food in the downstairs kitchen. Wed-Sat 11-5pm. Sun 1-5pm. Adult $2. Child $1.

BAYLISS PARK: 1st & Pearl. One block North of jail. Plaque on the Mormon Trail and a fountain with a dramatic water show that is computer controlled. It may be for the summer season only.

STEMPEL BIRD COLLECTION: 227 South 6th Avenue. Two blocks South of the jail and in the Courthouse. Mounted birds are displayed.

THE BLACK ANGEL: Further North at Fairview Cemetery, North 2nd & Lafayette. The Angel of Death is a sculpture by Daniel Chester French who did the Lincoln Memorial in Washington, D.C. It is a memorial to Ruth Ann Dodge, the wife of Gen. Dodge. Watch for the black squirrels that are all around Council Bluffs.

TRANSPORTATION MUSEUM: 4041 Broadway. West on Broadway to Dodge Park on the River. Has two steam engines, a club car and a caboose. Golf course also.

GOLDEN SPIKE MONUMENT: 21st & 9th Avenue. At the Eastern beginning of the Union Pacific RR. 30 foot high replica of the Golden Spike.

LINCOLN PARK & MONUMENT: Lafayette & Oakland Avenues. Lincoln visited here in 1859 before he became President. The story is that he came on a quick trip up the River and didn't intend to stay, but the boat ran aground and was stuck for 3 days. They say that Gen. Dodge took him in hand and used the time to convince him that the much-debated Transcontinental Railroad should begin in Council Bluffs instead of further South at St. Joseph, Missouri.

4   MAJOR INTERCHANGE!
I-29 SOUTH TO KANSAS CITY: NO NEAR SERVICES!

WESTBOUND ALTERNATE ROUTE

TO THE SAC BASE AND BELLEVUE, NE: South on I-29. West across the Missouri River to NE 370 to the SAC Base and points of interest in Bellevue, Nebraska. Continue West to rejoin I-80 at Nebraska Milepost 439. Read NE Milepost 439 for descriptions.

5   MADISON AVENUE, COUNCIL BLUFFS: ELEVATION: 984 FEET.
MALL OF THE BLUFFS: North of I-80. Includes: "Hy Vee" Grocery store (Deli & Salad Bar), Pharmacy, Target, J.C. Penney's. If you need more shopping than is here, ask directions to Midlands Mall on Broadway.
FUEL: North to Amoco and Texaco. South to Standard and Phillips.
FOOD: North to Subway, Kentucky Fried, Garden Cafe, fine food, moderate price, Pizza Hut, Burger King and "Royal Fork Buffet Restaurant". The interior of the Mall has several fast food counters. South to Shoneys, Dairy Queen, McDonalds, Blue Ox Restaurant (tenderloins).
MOTELS: South to Western Inn, Heartland Inn.

FAIRMONT PARK: North. Get local directions. Flowers and a great view of the Missouri. For other Council Bluffs sights, read Milepost 3.

8 **COUNCIL BLUFFS/OAKLAND/US 6:** HOSPITAL.
POST HEADQUARTERS OF IOWA STATE PATROL
FUEL: West to Fina.
MOTEL: West to Iowana Budget Motel*.

17 **UNDERWOOD:**
FUEL: Phillips Truck Stop.
FOOD: West to I-80 Inn Restaurant.
MOTEL: West to I-80 Inn, Underwood Motel.
MILEPOST 19 REST AREAS: Historical markers.
EASTBOUND IOWA INFORMATION WELCOME CENTER: Get your Iowa maps.

23 **NEOTA/IA 244:**
FUEL: Phillips.
CAMPGROUND: "Arrowhead County Park": One mile North. In trees, pit toilets, no showers.

27 **MAJOR INTERCHANGE!**
JUNCTION I-680: NO NEAR SERVICES!
CONTINUING EASTBOUND STAY ON I-80.
WESTBOUND: TWO LEFT LANES REMAIN ON I-80.

WESTBOUND ALTERNATE ROUTE
I-680 BYPASS GOING NORTH OF OMAHA: This is a fast easy route around Omaha, especially during rush hours. Read Nebraska I-680 exits for Ft. Atkinson and Mormon Winter Quarters; Milepost 439 for SAC BASE and Bellevue; and Milepost 452 for downtown Omaha "sights" to decide which route you'd like to take through or around Omaha.

29 **MINDEN:**
FUEL: North to Burns Bros. South to Conoco & Phillips.
FOOD: South to Copper Kettle. North to Burns Bros Restaurant.
MOTEL: Midtown.
MILEPOST 32 PARKING-ONLY REST AREAS!

34 **SHELBY/COUNTY ROAD M 16:**
FUEL: North to Phillips, Texaco. South to Goodyear Tires.
FOOD: North to Cornstalk, Dairy Queen.
If you watch here North of the road you'll see a steel construction of a cornstalk.
CARSTEN'S MEMORIAL FARMSTEAD: South 1.5 miles on County Road M 16. West .5 mile. North .5 mile. This farm is run by the Historic Society of Pottawatamie County. Just wander around and experience a REAL Iowa farm.

40 **AVOCA/HARLAN/US 59:**
FUEL: North to Phillips. South to Texaco.
FOOD: South to The Embers.
MOTEL: South to Capri.
CAMPGROUND: "Parkway CG". South through Avoka. New, no shade trees yet. Quiet farm village.
NISHNA HERITAGE MUSEUM: South 15 miles to Oakland, IA. Southwest Iowa history with art & music.
AVOKA TOWN PARK AND POOL: South to Avoka then 1 mile East on IA 83. Stop and have a swim.

EASTBOUND ALTERNATE ROUTE

TO PRAIRIE ROSE STATE PARK: 5 miles North on US 59. 3 miles East on CR F 58. Return to I-80 by continuing East on CR F 58 and South on IA 173. This is a 422 acre park overlooking a winding lake. Hills are of wind-blown silt from glacial deposits. Paved roads, showers, hike, picnic, lake fish/boat. Quiet. $7-$11.

46   **WALNUT:**
    FUEL: South to Phillips, Standard. Apco.
    FOOD: The Villager.
    MOTEL: North to Antique Inn. South to Budget Inn.
        ANTIQUE CITY DRIVE: South 1 mile to Walnut. 1900 brick streets and storefronts with several antique shops & 1890 Opera House. There is a storefront Historical Museum across the street from the Post Office.

51   **MARNE:** NO NEAR SERVICES!

54   **ATLANTIC/ELK HORN/IA 173:**
    FUEL: North to Amoco.

WESTBOUND ALTERNATE ROUTE

TO PRAIRIE ROSE STATE. PARK: North 5 miles on IA 173 to Left turn by Elkhorn bank to 7 miles West on CR F 58. Return to I-80 by continuing West on CR F 58 to US 59 and South to I-80. Read Milepost 40.

SIDETRIP TO ELKHORN

DANISH MILL, WELCOME CENTER AND GIFT SHOP: 7 miles North on IA 173. In 1976 Danish descendants brought a 60 foot 1848 windmill from Norre Snede, Denmark and rebuilt it here at Elkhorn. Today the mill grinds wheat, rye and corn which may be purchased. They have a 12 minute Video and one hour tour through the mill. Adult $1.50.
    BEDSTEMOR'S HOUSE: College & Union Streets. Grandmother's house is restored and furnished as a Danish immigrant home.
    ELK GROVE also has a Danish restaurant, antique shops, quilt shop, deli, grocery, ice cream, crafts, bakery and 2 B&Bs.
    LITTLE MERMAID: 3 miles North of Elk Grove at Kimballton. This is another Danish town with a replica of Copenhagen Harbor's Little Mermaid in the city park North of town. There is also a small Danish house and a miniature windmill. On Main Street are ethnic and antique shops and the **GENERAL STORE MUSEUM:** June-Sept Daily 1-5pm.

57   **ATLANTIC:** HOSPITAL.
    FUEL: North to Amoco, Texaco.
    FOOD: North to food.

60   **BRAYTON/ATLANTIC/US 6/US 71:**
    FUEL: South to Phillips Truck Stop, Union, Conoco.
    FOOD: 1 mile South to Country Kitchen.
    MOTEL: North to Econo Lodge*.
        PURPLE MARTIN TRAIN: On Southwest corner of intersection. Tour 30 railroad cars, plus shops & food. Parking and admission are free, but a fee is charged for a guided tour of one train from engine to caboose. Also a fee to visit two cars with an extensive wildlife collection including 400 birds, nests and eggs.
        MORMON TRAIL MARKER: 20 miles South off US 6 in the town park of "Lewis". Just the marker here, but this is where the Hand Cart Trail of 1856 from Iowa City met the 1846 Mormon Trail from Nauvoo.

64   **WIOTA:** NO NEAR SERVICES!

70   ANITA/IA 148/CR 58:
ANTIQUE SHOPS IN ANITA.
CAMPGROUNDS: LAKE ANITA STATE PARK: South 4.5 miles on IA 148. West ollowing signs. Showers, electricity. Lake fish, swim, boat. $7- $11. A lovely park. Quiet country. Well worth the 4 miles.
LITTLEFIELD RECREATION AREA: 6.5 miles North on CR 58. Camp, picnic, swim on 60-acre lake. A park of open areas with only small trees.
LITTLEFIELD PARK: Just North of recreation area. Older park in woods by a stream. Picnic and camp.

75   COUNTY ROAD G 30:

FIRST TRAIN ROBBERY IN THE WEST:

Take CR G 30, .5 mile Southwest. (There is no room for a large trailer or RV to turn around.) In a 7 acre park of restored prairie planting, a steam engine wheel marks the spot where at 8 pm on July 21, 1873 Jessie James robbed the Chicago, Rock Island & Pacific Train. This train was just a year old at the time. Verdi, Nv. would dispute that it was the "FIRST" train robbery because THEY had one in 1870. However, this Iowa incident boasts one of the West's most colorful bandits.

Jessie had heard that $75,000 in gold bullion was arriving from the Cheyenne region. He sent his brother, Frank, and Cole Younger to Omaha to learn when the gold shipment was to arrive. (The five others in the gang camped out near Adair.) They reported when it was due, so Jessie set his trap. The gang broke into a handcar house and stole a spike bar and hammer. At a sharp curve on the railroad, they removed a rail splice connecting two rails and pulled out the spikes. They tied a rope around the disconnected rail and led the rope into a hole they had dug in the bank in which to hide.

When the engine came too near to stop at its uphill 20 mph, they pulled the rope to disconnect the rail. And they shot the engineer! The engine went into the ditch and turned over with the tender on top and a baggage car on top of that. As people started to emerge from the cars, bullets flew going through one man's coat and just missing two heads. When the four agents in one of the express cars opened the door to see what had happened, the robbers, masked like the Klu Klux Klan, jumped in and held a gun to the Express agent's head. Searching for the bullion and money they cut open the mail bags, but found just $1700. No gold bullion! A lot of bullets flew about but the engineer was the only fatality.

Of the 200 passengers on the train (four coaches and a sleeper) were included 30 young Chinese youths of the aristocracy on their way to 10 years of school in New England. They flattened themselves on the floor during the melee and called this "Hell Country". They had been 32 days crossing the Pacific and five days from San Francisco to Iowa. They rode in a "splendid Palace Car" called the "City of Leavenworth" and one baggage car was heavy with their belongings.

Since there was only a section house in Adair at that time, a trainman walked the 8 miles to Casey, Iowa to telegraph news of the robbery. By 1am the day of the robbery, work began on building a new track around the engine, and by 1:30 pm all the cars were back on the track except the engine and one baggage car. The railroad brought armed men and dropped off small detachments along the route where saddled horses were waiting to take them in pursuit of the robbers. Papers reported that the posse had the robbers surrounded and would capture them soon, but they were overly optimistic and never did. On April 3, 1883 in St. Joseph, Missouri, Jessie was shot by a gang member for the "$10,000 Dead or Alive". The rest of the gang, except for Frank James, were captured or killed in a bank robbery in Northfield, Minnesota in 1876. The town of Adair puts out a free paper with the old newspaper accounts of the robbery. This makes great reading for all ages and good for the kids to "Share and Tell" back at school.

76   ADAIR/IA 925: AAA SERVICE.
FUEL: North to Texaco, Amoco, Phillips, Casey 1/2 mile North in town.
FOOD: North to "Acres Back 40" breakfast and lunch. Right on Audubon Street, restaurant on left.
MOTELS: North to Best Western, Budget Inn*.
CAMPGROUND: "Adair City Park": Municipal. North .5 mile. Right turn into Park. Trees, shade, showers, playground, shelter, electricity, tennis court. Town cop plays host. $6.
WATERSHED DIVIDE: That tall yellow water tower in Adair with the big smile sits on top of the divide between the Missouri and the Mississippi River watersheds. You will cross over it on your way to town to the park. If you stop in the City Park you may suddenly hear a train

whistle very near, but can't see it because the tracks are in a deep cut next to the park. This cut was made to ease the grade of the railroad over the divide. Jessie James' robbery was possible because he took advantage of the train's slow speed up this grade from the West.

JESSIE JAMES MUSEUM: North just past Casey's and 3 blocks East on Audubon Street, the small house just past the Rock Island caboose on the North side of the street. This was the Section House built by Rock Island RR in 1858. In 1870, the railroad sent section foreman, Robert Grant and his wife (the first woman in these parts) and their children to live here. On the afternoon of the robbery, the gang stopped here to obtain some pies and other food from Mrs. Grant. The crude construction of the house is interesting. A spike and a rail-splicing section recovered from the robbery site are here. Also a spike bar used to remove rail spikes, and old photos of the James Gang. Gerald Wilson in the mobile home next door will show you around and tell you about each item. Fee.

EASTBOUND ALTERNATE ROUTE

TO SHEEDER PRAIRIE: North 11 miles on CR N 54 to East 3 miles on IA 44. Continue East to Guthrie Center and IA 25. South to I-80 at Milepost 86.

MILEPOST 80 REST AREAS: Trailer Dump.

83 CASEY:
FUEL: North in town, Apco.
CAMPGROUNDS: "Casey City Park": North .5 mile. Electricity, showers, playground. $5.
KOA: Private. North on CR N 72 just West of Casey.

86 GUTHRIE CENTER/GREENFIELD/IA 25:
FUEL/FOOD: South to Conoco, Kopper Kettle.

WESTBOUND ALTERNATE ROUTE

SHEEDER PRAIRIE: North 15 miles on IA 25 to IA 44 and West to see the original grasses of Iowa. South on CR N 54 to I-80 at Milepost 76.

88 MENLO:
CAMPGROUND: Swimming/no showers. No further information.

93 STUART:
FUEL: North to Conoco, Amoco. South to Phillips Truck Stop.
FOOD: North to Cyclone Drive Inn, South to Golden Griddle, Harris House.
MOTEL: South to Motel. North to "Summit Grove Inn" in Dexter. An affordable B&B.
CAMPGROUND: No further information.

97 DEXTER:
This town was named after the famous race horse of the 1860's that won 48 of 50 races. He's now on a Currier and Ives Print pulling a carriage carrying President Grant.
FUEL: North to Caseys.
FOOD: North to Dexter & "Our Place" (Home cooking?)
CAMPGROUND: North. No further information.

100 REDFIELD/US 6: NO NEAR SERVICES!

104 EARLHAM: NO NEAR SERVICES! This town was founded by Quakers.

106 DES MOINES:
CAMPGROUND: "KOA": 1 mile North. Pool, LP gas. $12-$20.

110 DESOTO/ADEL/US 169: ELEVATION: 600 FEET.

FUEL: South to Texaco Truck Stop, Amoco, Casey's.
MOTEL: to South.

JOHN WAYNE BIRTHPLACE: 14 miles South on US 169 to 224 South 2nd Street, Winterset. The town's other "birth" is that of the "Delicious Apple". The town park has a large boulder commemorating the apple, a covered bridge, playground, a tower, a settler's cabin and a campground.

MILEPOST 112: Crossing the Raccoon River where several branches of this river come together. They flow into the Des Moines River and thence into the Mississippi.

113 **VAN METER:** NO NEAR SERVICES!
TRINDLE COUNTY PARK: Picnicking. 1.5 mile South on hill overlooking Raccoon River Valley. Playground.

117 **WEST DES MOINES/WAUKEE/BOONEVILLE/CR R 22:**
FOOD: South to Steak House.
MOTEL: South to Hi Ho.
CAMPGROUND: "Waukee Timberline CG": Private. Good Sam. North one mile to CR F64. East .5 mile. Pool, playground. RV's and Tents.

MILEPOST 118 REST AREAS INFORMATION WELCOME CENTER: Get Iowa maps here. Trailer Dump.

121 **EASTBOUND ASHWORTH ROAD. WESTBOUND 74TH STREET:** NO REENTRY!
FUEL: South to Amoco.
FOOD: North to Zackary, West End Diner.
MOTEL: South to Super 8*.

123 MAJOR INTERCHANGE!
I-235/I-35/DES MOINES: ELEVATION: 817 FEET.
EASTBOUND I-80 NORTH OF THE CITY OF DES MOINES.
EASTBOUND I-235 THROUGH DOWNTOWN.
I-35 SOUTH TO KANSAS CITY.

EASTBOUND ALTERNATE ROUTE

THROUGH DOWNTOWN DES MOINES ON I-235: Find your Des Moines map your state map. Remember the perils of downtown traffic during rush hours. That's why they built I-80 to the North. (If someone needs emergency care, there are three HOSPITALS near I-235. Try the 2nd Ave exit.) After seeing the sights below, return to I-80 Eastbound via I-235 North to Milepost 138.

CAMPGROUND: WALNUT WOODS STATE PARK: Accessible from I-35 South. Exit 68 for one mile on IA 5 & 2 miles North on County Road. Or from I-235 and IA 28 go South to Southwest 48th Avenue and West about 3 miles. On the Raccoon River. Flush toilets.

DES MOINES

Des Moines began in 1843 as "Ft. Raccoon" after the Raccoon River that flows in from the West. French explorers had named the river from the North, "La Riviere des Moines" so eventually the town took on that name. The town's prominence was recognized in 1857 when the state capital was moved here from Iowa City. The city is a center for Iowa's grain industry, food products and manufactured goods. Downtown has 2.5 miles of "skywalks" linking 30 buildings. You can walk between restaurants and shops in weather-proof comfort with a high city view.

EASTBOUND SIGHTSEEING ROUTE OFF I-235: Grand Avenue parallels I-235 to the South:

DES MOINES ART CENTER: 4700 Grand Avenue. Take 63rd Street exit from I-235 and go South to Grand. Outstanding building! Modern sculpture, American and European oils. Tues-Sat 11-5pm. Sun noon-5pm. Free.

SCIENCE CENTER OF IOWA: 4500 Grand Avenue. Just East on Grand. This is a hands-on learning center. Great for families! Natural history, technology, physical and biological sciences exhibits. Foucault pendulum, computer equipment, anatomy display, and live native animals. Mon-Sat 10-5pm. Sun noon-5pm. Adult $3.50 includes planetarium.

SALISBURY HOUSE: 4025 Tonawanda Drive. Two blocks South of Grand off 42nd Street. A 42-room replica of a Royal manor house in Salisbury, England. Art objects and furnishings of the Tudor Age. Imported stained-glass windows, fireplaces, etc. Mon-Thurs guided tour at 2pm. Fri at 10:30am. Adult $2.

TERRACE HILL: 2300 Grand Avenue. Stay on Grand from the Art Center. This 1869 Victorian mansion is now the Governor's Mansion. Furnished with polished woodwork, statuary, paintings, crystal chandeliers, stained-glass windows. Mon-Thurs 10-1:30pm. Sun 1-4:30pm. Free.

HOYT SHERMAN PLACE: 15th & Woodland. From Grand, go North on 10th Street, West on Woodland to 15th. Victorian mansion of 1877. Carved woodwork, marble fireplaces, brass chandeliers, art gallery, and 19th Century art. Daily 8-4pm. Adult $2.

STATE CAPITOL: Grand Avenue. Between East 9th & 12th. Built in 1886 it has a main dome covered with 22K gold leaf plus 4 smaller domes. Designed after "Les Invalides" in Paris. Has paintings, statues, dolls dressed as the first ladies, a collection of war flags, a scale model of Battleship Iowa, and intricate carvings on doors and window frames. Drive all around the building to see it well. Daily 8-4pm. Free.

STATE OF IOWA HISTORICAL BUILDING: 600 East Locust Street. One block West of the Capitol. Displays Iowa's Indian, civic and military history, geological and natural development. Has one of few remaining Conestoga Wagons. Tues-Sat 9-4:30pm. Sun noon-4:30pm. Free.

DES MOINES BOTANICAL CENTER: 909 East River Drive. West of the Capitol take East First Street North to the North side of I-235. On the bank of the Des Moines River. Under a 150 foot dome 1500 species of plants, flowers, and the Ladany Bonsai collection flourish. Mon-Fri 10-6pm. Sat-Sun 10-5pm. Adult $1.

HERITAGE VILLAGE: At the State Fair Grounds at the East end of Grand Avenue. 10 acres of heritage buildings with a church, sod house, blockhouse from Ft. Madison, pharmacy, etc. April-Oct.

AQUARIUM CENTER: At State Fair Grounds. 60 aquariums of all sizes with 300 species of fish, tropical, marine, and freshwater. 10-5pm daily.

124   **UNIVERSITY AVE, CLIVE:** EASTBOUND RE-ENTRANCE ONLY.

125   **HICKMAN ROAD, URBANDALE/US 6:** HOSPITAL.
   FUEL: West to Flying J Travel Plaza Truck Stop.
   FOOD: West to Harveys and Flying J. East & then Left at First light to "Iowa Machine Shed". They pride themselves in their fresh farm products, home-made baked goods, and prize pork dishes. "Bonanza" is East 1.5 mile.
   MOTEL: Sheraton.

LIVING HISTORY FARMS
Photo credit: Iowa Department of Economic Development

LIVING HISTORY FARMS: 2600 Northwest 111th Street. .25 mile East. Contains: Ioway Indian Village of 1700, Pioneer Farm of 1850, Horse-powered Farm of 1900, and a "Farm of Today and Tomorrow". Mon-Sat 9-5pm (last tour at 3pm). Sun 11-6pm. Adult $6. Child $4. Senior $5.

126 **DOUGLAS AVENUE, URBANDALE:**
> **FUEL:** Bar B Travel Plaza Truck Stop, Phillips Truck Stop.
> **FOOD:** West to Bar-B Crossroads Restaurant.
> **MOTEL:** East to Interstate Inn.

127 **SAYLORSVILLE LAKE/IA 141/GRIMES:**
> **FUEL:** North to Fina Truck Stop.
> **CAMPGROUND:** "Cuddy's": North of I-80. Nestled in hills back from road. Pool, playground, miniature golf, paddle boats.

131 **MERLE HAY ROAD, URBANDALE/IA 401:** V. A. HOSPITAL. MALL: South 3 miles.
> **FUEL:** Texaco, Sinclair, Standard, C Mart, Amoco, QT.
> **FOOD:** North to Embers, Country Kitchen, Shoney's. South to Dennys, Burger King, Wendys, Howard Johnson. Hardees, McDonalds.
> **MOTELS:** South to Days Inn, Roadway, Howard Johnson. North to Best Inns.
> **CAMPGROUND:** "Saylorsville": US Corp Engineers. About 5 miles North. Fishing, hiking, boating, swimming, bike trail and nature walks.
>> **SAYLORVILLE LAKE & VISITOR CENTER:** North 5 miles on IA 401. Across the dam. US Corp of Engineers. Daily 10-4pm.
>> **CAMP DODGE:** 3.5 miles North on IA 401. They say that this is the World's LARGEST swimming pool open to the public in the summer. No Campground here!
>> **MILEPOST 133:** CROSSING THE DES MOINES RIVER. This river gathers its waters from the top to the bottom of Iowa, right down the middle and then flows into the Mississippi river.

135 **SECOND AVE, DES MOINES/POLK CITY/IA 415:** HOSPITAL.
> IOWA STATE PATROL HEADQUARTERS.
> **FUEL:** Phillips, C-Mart, Marathon. North to General Tires. South to Firestone Tires.
> **FOOD:** Golden Harvest.
> **CAMPGROUND:** "Prairie Flower": Public. North 5 miles on IA 415 to signs. Showers, playground. Lake fish, swim, boat. $8.

136 **EAST 14TH STREET, DES MOINES/ US 65/US 69:** North to K MART.
> **FUEL:** North to Sinclair, Amoco.
> **FOOD:** North to "Bonanza", Country Kitchen. South to Bontel's Restaurant.
> **MOTELS:** North to Motel 6*, Best Western.

137 **MAJOR INTERCHANGE!**
I-35 NORTH TO MINNESOTA: NO NEAR SERVICES!
WESTBOUND: I-235/I-35 SOUTH AND WEST THROUGH DOWNTOWN DES MOINES.
> **JOHN DEERE PLANT:** North 6 miles to Ankeny. Farmers might want to tour the John Deere plant that makes grain drills and cotton picks. You must reserve your tour beforehand.

WESTBOUND ALTERNATE ROUTE

THROUGH DOWNTOWN DES MOINES: Take I-235/I-35 South into Des Moines. Exit I-235 at IA 160 and go East to South on IA 48 to the fair grounds (If that is where you want to start your tour of Des Moines.) From here follow Milepost 123's sights in reverse order up Grand Ave. Rejoin I-235 and continue West to I-80 at Milepost 123.

142 **US 6/US 65:** HOSPITAL.
> **FUEL:** South to Amoco Truck Stop, Git-Go.
> **FOOD:** South to Burger King, Mc Donalds.
> **MOTELS:** South to Roadway, Archer, Country Inn.
>> **PRAIRIE MEADOWS RACETRACK:** Off US 65. Follow signs. Pari-mutuel track featuring quarter horse and thoroughbred racing, restaurants. Wed-Sun.

ADVENTURELAND: South. Follow signs. This theme park recreates Iowa of the 's: Main Street, River City, Last Frontier, and an Iowa farm. There's a wooden roller coaster and white-water raft. June-Aug Daily 10-10pm. May and Sept weekends. $14.95 all inclusive admission.
CAMPGROUND: "Adventureland CG": Private. South to Adventureland Theme Park. Pool, playground. $7-$14.

143 BONDURANT/ALTOONA:
FUEL: North to '76 Truck Stop, Texaco, Amoco.
FOOD: '76 Restaurant.
EASTBOUND CAMPGROUND: "Thomas Mitchell Park": Public. South 1 mile to US 6, East 4 miles. Showers, playground. To leave, continue East to Milepost 149. $6.
MILEPOST 146 REST AREAS: Trailer Dump.

149 MITCHELLVILLE:
FUEL: Union '76.
WESTBOUND CAMPGROUND: "Thomas Mitchell Park": Public. 4 miles. South to US 6 and West. Leave by continuing West to Milepost 143. Read Milepost 143.
MILEPOST 153: SOUTH SKUNK RIVER.

155 COLFAX/MINGO/IA 117:
FUEL: South to Phillips, Sunoco Truck Stop. North to Conoco.
FOOD: North to Kopper Kettle.
TRAINLAND USA: North 2.5 miles. Very large toy train museum of 3 eras, frontier, steam, diesel, depicting the development of the railroads across the U.S. Handpainted scenery, 4,000 feet of track, 120 automatic switches, 200 buildings and 35,000 hand-cut ties. The trains run through and by Mt. Rushmore, Devil's Tower, Boot Hill, Trolley cars in San Francisco, and the White House. A Rock Island passenger car has a snack bar. April-Nov Daily 9-7pm. Sept weekends. Adult $3.50. Child $1.50. Senior $3.
Colfax used to be a mineral springs resort with 9 hotels. You can see the 150 room yellow Hotel Colfax to the South. Look high on the hill East of the Colfax water tower.

159 BAXTER:
FUEL: North to Citco and Country Service Auto Repair.

164 NEWTON/MONROE/IA 14: ELEVATION: 768 FEET. HOSPITAL. CENTRAL COLLEGE.
FUEL: North to Sunoco, Conoco, Amoco.
FOOD: Country Kitchen, Kentucky Fried, Perkins, Sizzling Sam's. North to Village Inn.
MOTELS: South to Newton Inn. North to Econo Lodge*, Oak Tree Inn, Best Western, Days Inn, Terrace Inn.
If you're able to splurge you will enjoy La Corsette restaurant and Maison Inn Bed & Breakfast in an elegant old mansion at 629 First Avenue East, Newton. Must call 515-792-6833 for reservations.

NEWTON

Newton was built with Maytag Washing Machines. F.L. Maytag began with the hand-powered washer in 1907. He added an electric motor in 1911, and became the "Washing Machine King". Howard Snyder added the cabinet style of cylinder washer and the town grew. The county court house has some interesting murals. The town park at West 3rd Street & 11th Avenue has a pool, playground and picnic facilities.
JASPER COUNTY MUSEUM: 1700 South 15th Avenue West. Go North and then Right onto Frontage Road. A fine well-housed museum of Maytag Washing Machine History, rooms of a Victorian Iowa home, a one-room school, replica of the first area church, 19th Century barn-raising equipment, and clock collection. Also a 40 foot bas-relief sculpture of 4 historical periods. May-Oct daily 1-5pm. Adult $2. Child $.50.
FRED MAYTAG PARK: North on IA 14. Right on US 6. Right on West 4th. Left on 5th Avenue. Right on 3rd Street. Picnicking, tennis, playground, pool with 170 foot water slide. Fee for pool.
MAYTAG DAIRY FARM: 19th Avenue near East 8th Street. 3 miles North on IA 14. One mile East.

Produces blue cheese. Mon-Fri 8-5pm. Sat 9-1pm.

SIDETRIP TO PELLA

About 23 miles South. Founded in 1847 by 800 Dutch seeking religious freedom and led by Henry Peter Scholte. Tourists love this place! But never on Sundays as too much is closed.

PELLA HISTORICAL VILLAGE: 505 Franklin Street. 20 historic buildings including mill, store, cabins, bakery, Wyatt Earp's home. Summer 9-5pm. Winter 9-4pm. Adult $3.50. Child $1.

KLOKKENSPEL: East of town square. 147-bell carillon plays 4 times a day while figurines perform. The courtyard has lovely Delft tiles.

SCHOLTE HOUSE: Oldest house in town with old-world furnishings. Daily 1-4pm. Adult $2.50.

168 COUNTY ROAD, NEWTON:
> **MOTEL:** North to Mid Iowa.
> **CAMPGROUNDS:** "Rolling Acres": Private. North .5 mile to Camp Road. Left and South back toward I-80. Pool, playground, recreation room, pull-through sites. NEAR I-80. $13.

173 KELLOGG/IA 224:
> **FUEL:** North to '76. Camping by station. NEAR I-80.
> **CAMPGROUNDS:** "Lake Pla-Mor CG": Private. .5 mile South. Left/East 3 .5 miles on gravel road.
> **ROCK CREEK STATE PARK:** North 6 miles to East 3 miles on CR F27. Electricity, showers, campfires, lake, beach, fish, swim, boat, picnic & hike. $7-$10.

179 OAKLAND ACRES/LYNNVILLE: NO NEAR SERVICES!
> **MILEPOST 180 REST AREAS:** Great playground equipment for kids.

182 GRINNELL/IA 146: ELEVATION: 1011 FEET. HOSPITAL. GRINNELL COLLEGE.
> **FUEL:** North to Phillips, Casey's, C Mart.
> **FOOD:** North to Hardees, Country Kitchen, Dairy Queen.
> **MOTELS:** North to Super 8, Best Western.
> **GRINNELL:** The town was founded in 1854 by Josiah Bushnell Grinnell, a Congregational minister. He lost his pastorate of a Washington, D.C. church when he preached for abolition. This is one of the towns that John Brown visited in his push for abolition. Congregational missionaries from New England established Grinnell College on land that Grinnell donated.
> **BRENTON NATIONAL BANK:** Broad & 4th Street. Two blocks East of IA 146. Built in 1914, this bank was designed by Louis Henri Sullivan. Really beautiful with an ornate front and a lovely round stained glass window they call "The Jewel Box".
> **GRINNELL HISTORICAL MUSEUM:** 1125 Broad Street. History of Grinnell, old buggies, Civil and World War artifacts. May-Oct Tues-Sun 2-4pm. Donation.

191 MALCOM/MONTEZUMA/US 63:
> **FUEL:** South to Conoco Truck Stop, Fuel Mart Truck Stop.
> **FOOD:** South to Nicki's Salad Bar.

197 BROOKLYN:
> **FUEL/FOOD/CAMPGROUND:** North to Amoco Truck Stop, Brooklyn 80 Restaurant and Campground ($6) next door.

201 GUERNSEY/WHAT CHEER/BELLE PLAIN/IA 21:
> **FUEL:** South to Phillips Truck Stop. North to Sunoco, C Mart Derby Truck Stop.
> **FOOD:** North to C Mart Fountain & Deli. South to Star Inn.
> **MOTEL:** South to Star Inn.
> **CAMPGROUND:** "Belle Plain I-80 CG": Private. North 500 feet. Playground. NEAR I-80. $8.

205 VICTOR: NO NEAR SERVICES!
> **MILEPOST 207 REST AREAS: EASTBOUND INFORMATION WELCOME CENTER.**

211 LADORA/MILLERSBURG/CR V 52:
> CAMPGROUND: IOWA LAKE STATE PARK: South 1 mile. West 1 mile. South 3 miles. Peaceful lake and sites. Electricity, showers. Lake swim, boat, fish. $7-$10.

216 MARENGO/ENGLISH/CR V 66: HOSPITAL.
> FUEL: North to Conoco Truck Stop.
> CAMPGROUND: "Oak Park": Private. 7 miles North to US 6. West 500 feet. Playground. RVs and tents. Restaurant near CG has smoked ribs, chicken and Sunday Breakfast Bar.
> PIONEER MUSEUM: 6 miles North to Marengo. Two blocks East at South & Wallace. Inside a Quanset. Also an 1856 Log Cabin and 1861 house. Summers Sat-Sun afternoons.

220 WILLIAMSBURG/IA 149: LARGE OUTLET CENTER North of I-80.
> FUEL: South to Texaco. North to Phillips Truck Stop.
> FOOD: North to Landmark Restaurant, Mc Donalds, Subway. Or go North to the Amana Colonies.
> MOTEL: North to Crest or to the Amana Colonies.

225 AMANA COLONIES/US 151:
> FUEL: South to Phillips, Amoco.
> FOOD: South to Colony Haus, Little Amana. Or go North to the Amana Colonies to Colony Market Place and many other restaurants. (Dinners are over $10 in most of this area.)
> MOTELS: Colony House Motor Inn. South to Colony Budget Inn, Holiday Inn, Super 8. North 10 miles to Guest House Motor Inn.

EASTBOUND ALTERNATE ROUTE OR SIDE TRIP
THROUGH AMANA COLONIES: Go North and tour the Amanas and then return to I-80 by going SE on US 6 to I-380 and I-80 at Milepost 239. Check your map.

THE AMANA COLONIES

The Amanas are a religious sect that came out of Lutheranism, mainly from Germany and purchased this land in 1854. They established farms and industries as a communal group with high quality control. You're probably familiar with "Amana" refrigeration and air conditioning that is in Middle Amana. In 1932 they voted to change to private and corporation ownership. Don't confuse them with the Amish! The Amanas prospered by utilizing new technology, yet retaining their old crafts.

Ask for a local map/brochure to the 7 attractive Villages, available at Iowa Information Centers and at the shops at this intersection. They specialize in antiques, crafts, bakery goods, wine, furniture, wool, cheese and sausage. You can visit the **MUSEUM OF AMANA HISTORY** the **WELCOME CENTER** and the **WOOLEN MILL** in Amana. Or the **COMMUNITY KITCHEN MUSEUM** and **COOPERSHOP** in Middle Amana. Visit the **BARN MUSEUM** (extensive collection of miniature buildings) in South Amana. Or an Amana home and **BLACKSMITH SHOP MUSEUM** in Homestead. See an **OLD FASHIONED STORE**, 100 years old, in

AMANA COLONIES
Photo credit: Iowa Department of Economic Development

High Amana. And/or your choice of wineries, bakeries, and furniture shops. Most things are open 9-5pm weekdays and 12:30-5pm on Sundays. North 9 miles on US 151 is Amana and "Ox Yoke Inn" Family Style Dinners that you may have seen advertized. It is said to be very good, but you must reserve ahead especially on weekends when the area is crowded with visitors. There are at least 6 large restaurants in this one small village. "Ronneburg

Restaurant" and "Colony Inn" were recommended. The latter has an RV Park. Locals also liked "Bill Zuber's Restaurant" in Homestead. Customers come from miles around. Talk to some of the repeat tourists in the colonies to find their favorite stops.

230 OXFORD:
FOOD: North to Dairy Queen, Mini Mart.
CAMPGROUND: "Sleepy Hollow": Private. North 1.5 blocks. Right into CG. Pool, fish, playground. Park-like site nestled in hills. Just back off I-80.
EASTBOUND CAMPGROUND: "FW Kent Park": North 2 miles to US 6. East 4 miles. Quiet, rural area. Return to I-80 via Milepost 237 or 239.
MILEPOST 236 REST AREAS: WESTBOUND IOWA INFORMATION CENTER. Plaques about Hoover and the Mormon Hand Carts. Trailer Dump.

237 TIFFIN: NO NEAR SERVICES!
WESTBOUND CAMPGROUND: "FW Kent County Park": North one mile to US 6. West 3 miles. Return to I-80 via Milepost 230. Lake, beach, picnic. See Milepost 230.

239 MAJOR INTERCHANGE!
US 218 SOUTH TO UNIVERSITY OF IOWA, MT. PLEASANT.
I-380 NORTH TO CEDAR RAPIDS.

WESTBOUND ALTERNATE ROUTE

TO THE AMANA COLONIES: Go North here on I-380 to US 6 West to the Colonies. Return to I-80 on US 151 at Milepost 220. Check your map. Read Milepost 225.

240 CORALVILLE/NORTH LIBERTY/IA 965/US 6:
HOSPITAL. UNIVERSITY OF IOWA, OAKDALE CAMPUS.
FUEL: North to Texaco.
FOOD: North to Best Western.
MOTELS: North to Best Western, Inns USA.
CAMPGROUNDS: "Colony Country": Private. North 2 miles on IA 965, to Forevergreen Road. West .5 mile. New. Playground, RVs, tents. $8-$14.
"Jolly Roger Recreation & Marina": Private. North 4 miles on IA 965, to Scales Bend Road. East 3.8 miles. Campfire, playground. Lake swim, fish, boat. $7-$13.
"Sugar Bottom": Public. North 4 miles on IA 965. East 4 miles on CR F28. Showers, campfires, playground. Lake fish, swim, boat.

EASTBOUND ALTERNATE ROUTE

THROUGH IOWA CITY: Find your Iowa City Map on the back of your state map. Iowa City was founded in 1839. It was the capital first of the Territory of Iowa and then of the state of Iowa from 1841-1857.

JOHNSON COUNTY MUSEUM: 310 5th Street. Go South & Southeast on US 6 to Left on 5th Street. In the old schoolhouse in Coralville. Includes history of the area. March-Nov Wed-Sat 1-5pm. Sun 1-4pm. Donation.

"Iowa River Power Co": First Avenue & 5th Street. Locals like this restaurant in a former power plant near the river.

MORMON HANDCART PARK: South again & East on US 6 to Mormon Trek Blvd. Under the railroad overpass and 2 Right turns to the park. After the Mormons had settled in the Salt Lake Valley, converts came from Europe. In 1856 1,500 Europeans arrived via train to the end of the railroad here in Iowa City. They constructed 6 foot handcarts on this site and began their trek West. The first 2 groups made the journey amazingly well, as fast as the wagon trains. The third company started out too late in the year, was short of supplies but were told to "gird their loins" and go forward. Rations were cut and cut again. They sold everything they could to buy food at the forts. In October as they struggled up South Pass in Wyoming, they counted the daily toll of the dead frozen in their blankets. Over 200 had died before supply wagons from Salt Lake reached them. It was November 30th before they arrived at Salt Lake City. Between 1856 and 1859 3,000 European converts made the trip in ten companies. Read the story of the Mormons in the Utah Chapter.

MUSEUM OF ART: North Riverside Blvd. Back on US 6. Left on Riverside. African art, antique silver, paintings, sculpture and jade. Tues-Sat 10-5pm. Free.

OLD CAPITOL: Clinton & Iowa Avenue. Back on US 6 and East across the river. Built in 1846 in Greek Revival architecture. It was first a Territorial Capitol and then the State Capitol. It is now in the center of the University of Iowa. Mon-Sat 10-3pm. Sun 12:30-3pm. Free.

MUSEUM OF NATURAL HISTORY: Jefferson & Capitol. To the North of the Capitol. Exhibits birds, mammals, marine animals, plants and anthropological artifacts, a Marquette-Joliet diorama, and a giant ground sloth. Mon-Sat 9:30-4:30pm. Sun 12:30-4:30pm. Free.

PLUM GROVE: 1030 Carroll Street. Go East to Dodge Street. South to Kirkwood. Built by Governor Lucas, the first governor of Iowa, in 1844. Period furnishings, beautifully restored. April-Oct Wed-Sun 1-4:30pm. Free. Now back up North on Dodge to I-80 & Milepost 246.

242 **FIRST AVE, CORALVILLE:** HOSPITAL. SHOPPING MALL.
    FUEL: Amoco, KM, C Mart. South to Texaco Truck Stop, QT.
    FOOD: Country Kitchen, Perkins, Days Inn, McDonalds.
    MOTELS: North to Days Inn. South to Best Western, Super 8*, Comfort Inn, Motel 6*, Kings Inn & Mar-Kee Motel. 1.5 mile South into town to Blue Top, Capri Motor Lodge.
    CAMPGROUNDS: "Edgewater Park" Public. South .25 mile on First Avenue to 9th Street. East .5 mile to Quarry. North .5 mile. Electricity, showers, campfires, playground. River fish, boat.
        MILEPOST 243: Crossing the Iowa River.

244 **DUBUQUE STREET, IOWA CITY/CORALVILLE LAKE:** ELEVATION: 670 FEET.
    LAND'S END OUTLET. UNIVERSITY OF IOWA.
    NORTH TO CAMPGROUNDS NEAR CORALVILLE LAKE: Corps of Engineer Campgrounds, $6-$8.: "Cottonwood": North 2 miles to County Road. East 2 miles. Showers, campfires.
    "Linder Point": North 2 miles to County Road. East one mile. Showers, playground, campfires.
    "Tailwater East": North 4 miles to County Road. East .25 mile. Showers, campfires. Lake fish, boat.
    "West Overlook": North 2 miles to County Road. East one mile. Showers, campfires, playground. Lake fish, swim, boat.

246 **DODGE STREET, IOWA CITY/IA 1/LAKE MAC BRIDE:**
    FUEL: South to Sinclair. North to Phillips.
    FOOD: South to Country Kitchen, Johnsons. North to Highlander.
    MOTEL: Highlander Inn.

WESTBOUND ALTERNATE ROUTE

THROUGH IOWA CITY: Find your Iowa City Map on your state map. Take this exit into town to Kirkwood Street to "Plum Grove". Come back up North and turn West on Iowa Street to the "Old Capitol". North of that is the "Museum of Natural History" in Mac Bride Hall. West across the river and right up Riverside Drive to the "Museum of Art". Then back down to head West on US 6. Left on Mormon Trek Blvd. and 2 quick Rights to "Handcart Park". Back West on US 6. Turn Right on 5th Street to the "Johnson Museum". Back on US 6 to a Right/North on IA 965 to I-80 and Milepost 240. Read Milepost 240. You will follow it in reverse order.

249 **HOOVER HIGHWAY:** NO NEAR SERVICES!

254 **WEST BRANCH:** ELEVATION: 718 FEET.
    FUEL: South to Conoco Truck Stop. North to Amoco, Casey's.
    FOOD: West Branch Restaurant. North to Casey's General Store.
    MOTEL: Presidential Motor Inn.
        HERBERT HOOVER NATIONAL HISTORICAL SITE: .5 mile North. Cottage of Hoover's birth, his father's blacksmith shop, Quaker Meeting house, and Westbranch's First school. Daily 8-5pm. Free.
        HERBERT HOOVER PRESIDENTIAL LIBRARY AND MUSEUM: Documents, memen-

tos, photos of Hoover's life from mining engineer to political career and presidency. Daily 9-5pm. Adult $1.

259 SPRINGDALE/WEST LIBERTY:
FUEL: South to Sunoco Truck Stop, DX.
FOOD: South to Yesterday's Restaurant, buffet.
MOTEL: South to Budget Host.
CAMPGROUNDS: "West Liberty KOA": Private. South 500 feet. NEAR I-80. Pool, playground. $9-$14.

"Cedar Valley County Park": 4 miles North on County Road. Camp, picnic, fish, boat, hike. No information on the facilities.

JOHN BROWN

Just 3 miles North of here John Brown spent the winter of 1857-58 planning his attack on Harpers Ferry, Virginia. Now this might sound like a long way from Virginia, but there was a reason for it. The Southern representatives in Congress would only vote for the admission of new states if they could be "slave". The "Missouri Compromise" of 1820 admitting Missouri as a slave state and balancing Maine as a free state, designated the states West of the Missouri River as free states. In 1850 California was admitted as a "Free" state only with a "rider" that the old "Fugitive Slave Law" would be enforced and runaway slaves returned to their owners. (Northerners had long ignored it.) Instead of calming the slavery issue, this fired up the abolitionists and increased their numbers tremendously. More people than ever became active in protecting run-a-way slaves.

Stephen Douglas back in Illinois debating the slavery issue with Abraham Lincoln, argued for "Popular Sovereignty". That is, new states admitted to the Union could each vote as to whether to have slaves or not. (Douglas was trying to hurry the settlement of the North to get the Transcontinental RR through there.) Now in 1854 Douglas succeeded in passing the "Kansas-Nebraska Act" on his terms which let the new states choose. Pro Slavery advocates and the abolitionists rushed into those two states to sway the vote. Violence broke out as they clashed trying to gain control of the area. Of course, John Brown was in the midst of it. In fact he led the famous Pottawatamie Creek Massacre on May 24th, 1856. Brown wanted to arm the slaves to rebel. Thus from Kansas he stopped in Iowa to plan his strategy to get arms from the Arsenal to give to the southern slaves. Then on to the Arsenal at Harper's Ferry, Virginia and his destiny with death.

265 ATALISSA:
FUEL: South to Phillips Truck Stop.
Crossing the Cedar River that steamboats traveled as far as Cedar Rapids.

267 MOSCOW/IA 38:
FUEL: North to Sinclair.
FOOD: South to The Cove.
CAMPGROUNDS: "Cedar River": Private. North NEAR I-80. RV, tents, cabins, playground. Lake swim, fish, boat.
"Koch's Meadowlake": Private. 6.5 miles North on IA 38 to East to CG. Follow signs.
"Minifarm Acres": No further information.
MILEPOST 269 REST AREAS: INFORMATION WELCOME CENTER. Historical markers, nature trail, trailer dump station.

271 WILTON/US 6: NO NEAR SERVICES! MUSCATINE COMMUNITY COLLEGE.
CAMPGROUND: "Koch's Meadow Lake": No further information.
"CANDY KITCHEN": 3 miles South on US 6 to Wilton. East to Candy Kitchen and some good homemade ice cream!
EASTBOUND: Note how the terrain is leveling off here. Not rolling as high as Western Iowa.

277 DURANT/SUNBURY: NO NEAR SERVICES!

280 STOCKTON/NEW LIBERTY:

FUEL/FOOD: Bingo/Burns Truck Stop.
CAMPGROUND: "Davenport KOA": Private. South 500 feet. Pool, playground, cabins. NEAR I-80.

284 WALCOTT:

FUEL: South to Amoco Truck Stops of America, Pilot Truck Stop, Union. North to Standard, Phillips Truck Stop.
FOOD: North to TA Restaurant.

290 MAJOR INTERCHANGE!

DAVENPORT/US 280: ELEVATION: 571 FEET. NO NEAR SERVICES!
EASTBOUND ON I-80 NORTH AROUND THE QUAD-CITIES.
EASTBOUND ON I-280 SOUTH AROUND THE QUAD-CITIES.
The "Quad-Cities" area includes Davenport & Bettendorf, Iowa and Rock Island & Moline, Illinois. Find your Quad-Cities map on your state map.

ALTERNATE EASTBOUND ROUTE

SOUTH & EAST AROUND THE QUAD CITIES ON I-280: Avoids downtown Davenport to meet with I-80 across the border in Illinois.
CAMPGROUNDS: "Lakeside Manor Park": Private. Milepost 6 exit of I-280. West .5 mile on US 61. Campfires, playground. RVs/tents. $7-$14.
"West Lake County Park": Milepost 6 exit of I-280. West .5 mile on US 61, to CR Y48. North 1 mile. 32 foot max RV. Several lakes and Campgrounds. Paddleboat rentals, electricity, showers, campfires, playground. Lake fish, swim, boat. $5-$7. Campers go to Gate #5.

292 NORTHWEST BLVD, DAVENPORT/IA 130:

WACKY WATERS: North of I-80. 30 acre water park plus dune buggies, canoes, golf, swim, 10-7pm daily.
FUEL: Citco, Amoco.
FOOD: South to Iowa Machine Shed. They pride themselves in using fresh and home-baked foods and pork dishes.
MOTEL: Comfort Inn.

295 BRADY STREET, DAVENPORT/US 61:

NORTH HAS NO NEAR SERVICES. SOUTH TO DOWNTOWN DAVENPORT.
NORTH PARK MALL: Further South on US 61.
ANTIQUES OF AMERICA: South on US 61. Take first Right turn and immediate right again back toward the freeway, past Best Western.
FUEL: South to Amoco, Shell, Standard.
FOOD: South to Bonanza, Country Kitchen, River City Cafe, Village Inn, Hardees.
MOTELS: South to Motel 6*, Ramada, Best Western, Village Inn, Super 8*.

DAVENPORT

This is one of four cities that developed around "Rock Island", a peninsula formed by the Mississippi & Rock Rivers. It was an early trading center with the Natives. The Black Hawk Treaty opened up Eastern Iowa for settlement and Colonal George Davenport, a fur trader, bought a large tract on which he founded Davenport.
HAPPY JOE'S CHILDREN'S CURIOSITY CORNER: 201 North 50th Street, Davenport. Hands-on exhibits from 35 local businesses. Children can learn to milk a cow, operate a crane and saddle a horse. Daily 11-9pm.
VANDE VEER PARK AND CONSERVATORY: 214 West Central Park. Floral beds and rose gardens with 1800 varieties. Daily 10-4pm. Free.
DAVENPORT MUSEUM OF ART: 1737 West 12th Street. Collection of GRANT WOOD plus other American, European old masters, Mexican and Haitian works. Tues-Sat 10-4:30pm. Sun 1-4:30pm. Free.

PUTNAM MUSEUM: 1717 West 12th Street. Exhibits on history, archeology, natural history, minerals and art. The "Riverboat Gallery" has paintings of early river transportation. Tues-Sat 9-5pm. Sun 1-5pm. Adult $2.

VILLAGE OF EAST DAVENPORT: 2215 East 12th Street. Historic village has brick-paved streets and small shops dating back to 1851.

INTERNATIONAL FIRE MUSEUM: Same area. Tells the story of fire service around the world. In September they have the "Civil War Muster and Mercantile Exposition" with Civil War reinactments at the riverfront park.

PRESIDENT RIVERBOAT CASINO: 130 West River Drive. South on US 61 to the river. Four cruises Mon-Sat 8:30am-9pm. Sun 10-6pm. Five decks, children's area. Call for reservations: 1-800-BOAT-711.

EASTBOUND ALTERNATE ROUTE
NORTH TO BUFFALO BILL HOMESTEAD:

LONG GROVE CHURCH GRAVEYARD: 6 miles North on US 61 to First and Oak Streets, Long Grove. Buffalo Bill's brother Samuel is buried here. Ask for a tour map of Buffalo Bill Cody Historical sights to guide you on.

SCOTT COUNTY PARK: From Long Grove go East & North to this large nature preserve. Camping, picnicking, playground, swimming pool, nature center, petting farm, trails, lake and the village below.

WALNUT GROVE PIONEER VILLAGE: At the North end of the Park. Three acres of 14 historic buildings from an old blacksmith shop to the schoolhouse with its slate blackboards and geography maps. This area was a crossroads settlement in the early days. April-Oct daily 8-dusk. Free.

BUFFALO BILL HOMESTEAD: A couple miles further East to the Homestead with limestone building and walnut floors and trim. Bison and long-horns graze nearby. April-Oct 9-6pm. Donations. Continue South and East to US 67, Le Claire, Iowa and the Buffalo Bill Museum. South on US 67 to I-80 at Milepost 306.

298 **DOWNTOWN BETTENDORF/I-74:** NO NEAR SERVICES! HOSPITAL.

THE CHILDREN'S MUSEUM: 533 16th Street. Near junction with US 67. Hands-on exhibits for children, closed-circuit TV station, a trip down a rabbit hole, a place for making bubbles, and a "disassembly line" where children can take apart machines. There is also history here, ethnic cultures, and information on the local onion industry. Top "Tourism Attraction Award". Tues-Sat 10-4:30pm. Sun 1-4:30pm. Donation.

STEAMBOAT CASINO RIVER CRUISES: At foot of I-74 Bridge on the Iowa side of the Mississippi River. Call for changing information and tours: 1-800-448-7450. The Casino company is planning an RV park on the site.

MILEPOST 300 REST AREAS: WESTBOUND has trailer dump station.

301 **MIDDLE ROAD, BETTENDORF:** ELEVATION: 565 FEET.
FUEL: North to Standard.

Bettendorf began as "Gilbert", a quiet rural village. Then the "Bettendorf Axle and Wagon Company" came in 1903. This became the biggest railroad car shop west of the Mississippi.

306 **LE CLAIR/US 67:** LAST EXIT FOR IOWA! DON'T MISS IT!

MISSISSIPPI VALLEY WELCOME CENTER: WESTBOUND get your Iowa maps here! This is a MUST exit for everyone! Follow the signs North .5 mile and up a bluff to a great Visitor Center and a marvelous view of the Mississippi River. You will look down at the Rock Island Rapids, that used to be the most dangerous rapids on the river before the locks and dams were built. You can watch the barges on the river from the upstairs balcony. Read about the problems with the river in the "Illinois" chapter. Open daily 8-8:30pm.

BUFFALO BILL MUSEUM: Two miles North on US 67 to Right on Jones Street, to 200 North River Drive. Turn back time and look at the life of Le Claire's native, Bill Cody. The museum also tells the history of the area from the Indians to the first aircraft flight recorder. The last working wooden steamboat is docked outside. May-Oct daily 9-5pm. Adult $1. Child $.50

ROBERT'S RIVER RIDES: One mile North on US 67. Near the Buffalo Bill Museum. 1.5 hour sightseeing trip on the "Quad City Queen". May-Oct daily at 2:30pm. Adult $8. Child $5. Also lunch & dinner cruises. Call: 1-800-457-9975.

MISSISSIPPI BELLE II: Board at Clinton, Iowa, 23 miles North of I-80 on US 67. One way and round-trip rides on a floating casino with or without Brunch or Dinner. Trips are from 10am to 10pm. Call: 1-800-457-9975 for reservations.

MISSISSIPPI VALLEY WELCOME CENTER
Photo credit: Bob Coyle. Iowa Department of Economic Development

WESTBOUND ALTERNATE ROUTE

TO THE BUFFALO BILL HOMESTEAD: The museum will give you a tour map and you can follow the trail of Cody homes Westward to Long Grove, and South on US 61 to I-80 at Milepost 295. You'll see the Buffalo Bill 1847 Homestead with bison, burros and long horns grazing nearby. Also a Pioneer Village with 14 historic buildings. Campground too. Read Milepost 295.

EASTBOUND: Say "Goodby" to beautiful rolling Iowa. You're headed for flat prairies now.

WESTBOUND: You'll love the rolling hills of Iowa! Don't miss this Visitor Center exit!

STEAMBOATS CRUISE the MISSISSIPPI
Photo credit: Robert's River Rides

IOWA I 80 MILEPOSTS

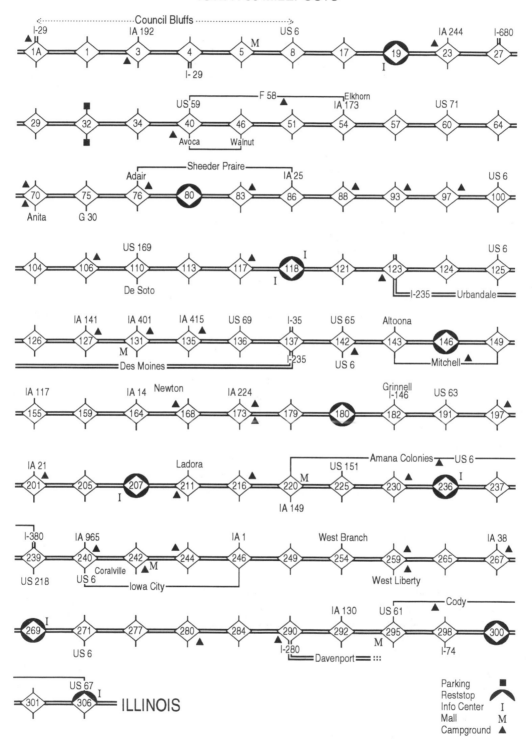

Illinois

The Prairie State

Illinois citizens feel a strong love of their prairie state. Carl Sandburg expressed his feelings for this expansive meadowland that the French baptized, "Prairie".

"Oh prairie mother, I am one of your boys.

I have loved the prairie as a man. With a heart shot full of pain over love."

The "Wisconsin Drift", an ice sheet of the Pleistocene era, covered the Eastern prairie of Indiana and Illinois leaving a pure black loam, 3-5 feet deep. The prairie grasses grew so tall that early explorers told how it could completely hide a horse and rider. One wrote that it could be knotted over the saddle. It billowed like a sea of grass touched with the rainbow colors of the wildflowers. Early travelers marveled at these miles of grass broken only by occasional clumps of trees or scrub along a stream.

Illinois covers about the same area as Iowa, 56,400 square miles, it's just more elongated. Remember how Iowa's population, almost 3 million, is twice that of Nebraska's? Well, in Illinois, we triple Iowa's population to 11,430,602. The capital is at Springfield, the city almost synonymous with Abraham Lincoln, its most prominent citizen, and is often called, "The Land of Lincoln". Illinois also gave us the political oratory of Adlai Stevenson, Everett Dirksen, and William Jennings Bryan. Bryan, born and educated in Illinois, said, "The humblest citizen of all the land, when clad in the armor of a righteous cause is stronger than all the hosts of error".

Illinois is a comparatively level state with most of its rivers draining Southwestward to the Mississippi on its Western border. With a series of locks and dams, Illinois links the Great Lakes waterway with the Mississippi River and the Gulf making it a transportation mecca. With ready transportation, manufacturing plants have flourished making Illinois the third greatest manufacturer in the nation.

The early white settlers could not use their plows in the Illinois soil until John Deere, the blacksmith, designed a new plow that would cut through and turn over the heavy soil. Visit the John Deere Company at Milepost 4. Today's top field-crops are soy beans and corn. What else? That's all you're seeing! Adding to all of this the hog-raising, coal mining, oil and natural gas resources makes Illinois one of our richest states.

ILLINOIS HISTORY

The early Illini Natives grew corn, melons, beans, squash and fruit of fine quality and size. They had permanent villages and lodges/ wegiwas and hunted in the summer. The first Europeans to explore this state were Louis Joliet and Fr. Marquette. (Read Iowa history.) On their way back up the Mississippi they turned up the Illinois River just North of St. Louis and came up to Princeton, Illinois and East to Joliet. (I-80 follows part of this route Milepost 56-133.) They went up the Des Plaines River and made a portage (at Summit) to the Chicago River that flowed into Lake Michigan (at Chicago).

In 1675, Sieur de La Salle saw the value of a fur-trading empire between the Great Lakes and the Gulf. He began to build a series of Forts along the lakes and down the rivers. Six years later he traveled down the Illinois River and the Mississippi to the Gulf. On his way back he built Fort Louis on the natural fortress of "Starved Rock" near Peru-La Salle, Milepost 81. La Salle developed a prosperous fur-trading business with the Illini. He returned to France to propose colonization of the mouth of the Mississippi. He was

Violet

given 4 ships and 400 men but they failed to find it. One ship returned to France and the other three were wrecked. He tried an overland trek but his men rebelled and killed him. He thought himself a failure but his explorations gave France a claim to the Mississippi area. Later many more French forts were established on his routes.

The French were respected by the Indians because they traded fairly, sold them good implements and weapons made of iron and did not disrupt the land. The British lacked respect for the Indians and sold them inferior goods at inflated prices. Americans came not just to trade but to settle on Indian lands, cut down trees, and plow up the land. They were wasteful of the wild life. This was sinful to the Natives who cherished the earth and all its creatures and wanted to preserve it in its natural state.

Under Thomas Jefferson's orders in 1803 to remove the Native Americans from Illinois so that it could be settled, William Henry Harrison, Governor of Indiana Territory (including Illinois) was an ardent disciple. He bribed the Kaskaskia Indian nation into giving up most of Illinois from the Southern tip to the Rock River. Then a big migration of settlers came from the Southern states and Kentucky and Tennessee, up the Mississippi and Illinois Rivers and settled here.

Western Illinois was next. Harrison got his agents to locate five bribeable lesser Sauk and Fox Chiefs (only two of whom had any authority) from the Missouri River area, and get them to St. Louis to a Treaty Session. Harrison drew up a Treaty taking 51 million acres of Sauk and Fox land between the Mississippi and the Wisconsin, Rock and Fox Rivers. This is ALL of Western Illinois through which you pass on I-80! The 5 chiefs got $2200 for signing while the Tribes got only $1,000 for their land. One chief was reluctant to sign until he was offered the life of a jailed relative accused of murder. President Jefferson was asked to grant a pardon, but meanwhile the man "was shot while trying to escape". Those 5 chiefs fled the wrath of the Illini tribes whose land they had given away. Three were never seen again. According to the terms of the Treaty, the tribes could live and hunt on the land only until it was settled. A tribe would return from a summer hunting trip to find their village and fields occupied and guns pointed at them. Chief Keokuk led his tribe across the Mississippi but old Black Hawk refused to go. Read "Iowa History" to learn the story of his fate.

The infancy of the state of Illinois was as a separate territory in 1809 and a state in 1818 with a population of just 18,000.

THE RIVERS AND THE CANALS

The Native Americans and the early explorers traveled the rivers in canoes. The French fur traders were next with their larger "pirogues" and "bateau" to which they could attach a sail. As settlers followed the explorers west their route was still the rivers because the land was too overgrown with either forests or tall grasses to lend easy passage. In the 1760's the early settlers poled keelboats with all their earthly possessions including their stock. Or they used flatboats, rafts and scows. One raft found aground with its owners dead, had a pen with 4 cows, a pig and 8 piglets. A covered structure was for the family with furniture, clothing, food, tools and other equipment. It even had a harpsichord!

Joliet was the first to propose a canal over the Portage, "by cutting through but half a league of prairie to pass from the foot of Lake Michigan to the Des Plaines". The traders and settlers agitated for a canal. In 1816 the Potawatomi gave 10 miles on each side of the Des Plaines and the Illinois Rivers to be used for a canal, but the young country did not have the funds for it until 1836. Now began the great era of canal building to connect the rivers and even make them flow backwards. The State of Illinois was transformed by its canals so vital were they to its history.

Illinois canals can be equated with Papa Bear, Mama Bear and Baby Bear. They began with Joilet's vision, the "Illinois and Michigan Canal", the Baby Bear. It was completed in 1848, with 15 locks connecting Lake Michigan with the Illinois River via the old portage between the Chicago and the Des Plaines Rivers. You will follow much of this route today from Peru-La Salle to Joliet Milepost 77-133. The "I & M" canal carried boats up to 17 feet wide and 108 feet long with a draft of 4.5 feet. Men walked the bank driving horses or mules to pull their crafts. With the canal functioning, Chicago expanded 600 per cent. The canal brought the settlers to Illinois and Missouri and on to the Great Migration Westward. The I & M opened up large scale farming in the rich soil of Illinois as it enabled the farmers to transport their crops to the

HENNEPIN CANAL (Mama Bear)
Photo credit: Illinois Department of Conservation

Eastern market where they could secure higher prices. Little Baby Bear I & M started Chicago on its way to becoming our nation's largest inland port.

By 1860 the canal boats were steam powered. There were 288 boats on the canal in 1865. When the railroads began taking the passenger service and then the freight service, the I & M dwindled out of use. By 1900 it was abandoned. The route of the I & M Canal is now called the "National Heritage Corridor". You may first visit it at Milepost 77 where the canal has water and is most intact, or take the Alternate Route between Mileposts 81 & 90. Visit it again at Milepost 112, and/or at the old town of Lockport at Milepost 133. The Rest Area at Milepost 117 has pictures of the canal. A quick exit to walk the levee of the canal is at Ottawa, Milepost 90. Just South of I-80 .5 mile, stop at Oogies Restaurant, and walk up the bank of the canal.

Even before the I & M was completed, men began agitating for a new canal to connect it to the Mississippi River from Rock Island to Hennepin. You will follow this route from Milepost 7-45. This was Mama Bear! And a whopper of a Boondoggle for the taxpayers and the Corp of Engineers! The Hennepin Canal could carry a boat 34 feet wide and 140 feet long in its 7 feet of water. It was not approved by Congress until 1890 by which time the railroads were operating and the I& M Canal was dwindling into obsolescence, too small to carry sufficient tonnage to compete. In order to utilize the Hennepin Canal's capacity, at its Eastern terminus they had to transfer the cargo from the larger ships to the I & M's smaller barges. This of course took time and manpower and was not profitable.

The two canals just didn't fit! Thus the Hennepin was only used for short hauls between local points, to supply its own operation, and for recreational purposes. In July 1951 it was abandoned without even paying for its upkeep, let alone its cost. Today both of these canals are for recreational use only. They offer boating, camping, fishing, hiking, nature centers and Visitor Centers. Eastbound you will follow the Hennepin Canal and cross it twice today. Exit at Milepost 7 to visit it, cross it at Milepost 8, ride alongside it on I-80 to view it from Mileposts 30-31 and visit it at Milepost 33. The Visitor Center is at Milepost 45. Then you'll parallel the I & M and cross it also. Relax from your driving and enjoy some of these great recreation areas along I-80.

The Papa Bear of Illinois Canals is the "Illinois Waterway" which is in use today. The fuel you purchase for your vehicle today may have come up river from Louisiana or Texas as crude petroleum in a barge and up this waterway. You can best observe the canal's activity as tow boats with strings of barges go through the Starved Rock lock near Milepost 81. This canal was begun by the state in 1920 and completed by the U.S. Corp of Engineers in 1933. It has a 9 foot channel depth and 8 navigation dams and locks. An Illinois Waterway lock can hold 8 barges plus a tow boat. Each barge can carry 1400 tons, the same as 60 semi-truck loads. In the fall luxury cruisers from the Great Lakes go down the waterway on their way to the Gulf of Mexico for the winter. The Canal is operational 24 hours a day, 12 months a year. Although there are 4 locks along I-80, the one at Starved Rock near Utica, Milepost 81, has the only Visitor Center.

TAMING THE MIGHTY MISSISSIPPI

In ancient times the Mississippi flowed Eastward from Clinton, Iowa to the Illinois River near Princeton, IL and then South with the Illinois. This ancient streambed is visible today from the air. Both the railroad and the Hennepin Canal were built through this natural depression. When the glaciers finished their work on this area, the new and present streambed carried the Mississippi. The river had difficulty eroding the glacial debris on this new route and the hard dolomite limestone outcroppings remained. There was never a thought of deep-draft boats on the Mississippi because of the shallows, submerged rocks, and rapids (especially during droughts). Storms brought more hazards like new sandbars and fallen trees. Most dangerous of all were the Rock Island Rapids on the Mississippi that extended from Davenport and Rock Island for 13.75 miles upstream. It had long spears of rock reaching out from both sides of the river. The I-80 bridge crosses the Mississippi in this area. Your best view of the former rapids is from Iowa's Milepost 306 at the Mississippi Valley Welcome Center. Knowing the importance of this river to the settlement of the west, the government tried to improve it by removing snags, shoals and sandbars and dynamiting rock hazards.

The grand era of the romantic steam-powered paddlewheel with its shallow draft began in 1830. It became the major transportation for raw and manufactured goods and for passengers. Pilots who specialized in the Rock Island rapids guided the boats between Rock Island and Rapid City, working only between those two points. Steamboats on the Mississippi and the Illinois often went aground or were wrecked. Some lasted no more than 18 months. Steamboat rides are available in Moline, Milepost 4, or on the Iowa side at Mileposts 295, 298 and 306.

Robert E. Lee surveyed the rapids in 1837 but no real improvement was made until after 1866 when a 4 foot deep channel was authorized by Congress. Coffer dams were then built and the rocks were blasted away. The steamboat's days were numbered toward the end of the century with the advent of the train and roads. River travel faded so that by the first quarter of the 20th Century only a fishing boat or a pleasure boat was seen on the river.

In 1907 a 6 foot channel was authorized by Congress. New ideas emerged on lock and dam building and diesel powered boats were developed. In 1930 Congress authorized a 9 foot deep channel. Today there is a series of 29 locks from Minneapolis, MN to St. Louis, MO. This makes it possible for tows pushing strings of 12-15 barges carrying 20,000 tons of cargo to navigate the Mississippi.

Watch as you cross the Mississippi and remember that "Old Man River" was not always so deep and placid here. Even a few summers ago during a drought year the barges backed up along the river waiting for rain and a deeper channel. You can visit Locks 14 & 15 on the Illinois side and watch the tows go through the locks. Exit Milepost 4 and go South to "Arsenal Island" and the "Mississippi River Visitor Center" to view the action.

The barges navigating today's rivers, canals, and locks, carry tons of petroleum products up from the South, and coal from Southern Illinois and Western Kentucky. Downstream go the grains, scrap iron and manufactured products. Where the largest cargo on an old river steamboat was 239 tons, today's towboat pushes 12-15 barges of 20,000 tons of cargo each. These little boats have every comfort of home from air conditioning to TV, radio-telephones and radar. Some barges have foot-thick linings of specially treated balsa wood and carry liquified methane gas at a temperature of minus 250 degrees. Others are huge vacumn bottles that carry molten sulfur at 300-350 degrees. Some barges carry bulk cement mixed with air which is pumped into and out of barges eliminating the need for bags.

ILLINOIS I-80 MILEPOSTS

ILLINOIS EMERGENCY NUMBER: Dial 911.
ROAD CONDITIONS: 708-705-4613.
NATIONAL TRAVEL ADVISORY: 708-298-1413.
RADIO FOR WEATHER AND NEWS: 78 AM OR CALL 312-944-6000.
ILLINOIS TOURIST INFORMATION: 1-800-223-0121.

EASTBOUND: You are now crossing the Mississippi River at the Rock Island Rapids. Prepare to take Milepost 1A to Illinois' "Mississippi Rapids Rest Area". You'll need to get your Illinois and Chicago maps and information here as there is NO other information center on I-80 in Illinois. Expect Illinois campgrounds from Peru East to be very expensive. In Indiana the prices return to normal.

WESTBOUND: As you cross the Mississippi, prepare to take the first exit to Iowa's Welcome Center. It is about 1/2 mile North of I-80 on a hill and has the very best view of the Rock Island Rapids and the tows operating on the Mississippi. (A towboat pushing barges is a "tow".)

MILEPOSTS:

1   MOLINE/IL 84:
FOOD: "Luciana's" on the River Road.
CAMPGROUND: "Illinewek Forest Preserve": Public. South one mile on IL 84. Showers, shelters, playground, level parking area, campfires. Mississippi River fishing, boating.

1A   MISSISSIPPI RAPIDS REST AREA:
EASTBOUND: Follow the exit road uphill to a park and Visitor Center. The Mississippi is barely visible from here. Signs say "No vehicles over 30 feet. A car and 22 foot trailer are OK. Oversized parallel parking spaces are available for motor homes and trailers. If you want to see the Quad City sights, ask for a local map here. Get your maps and information on Illinois and Chicago. You will want to know your exact exits in Eastern Illinois because driving I-80 in that part of the state can be very hairy. Exits are close together with multiple lanes and hundreds of trucks barreling down. It is easy to take the wrong exit and end up on another interstate whose nearest exit is 15 miles out. If you are visiting the Chicago area you should decide your campground or motel now. Plan your route or public transportation into the city.

4   JOHN DEERE ROAD, MOLINE/IL 5/I-88/IL 92:
MOTEL: South to Super 8 on Colona Road.
FOOD: South to Red Apple on Colona Road.

CAMPGROUND: "Lundeen's Landing": Private. West one mile on IL 5 to first Left exit. The signs will take you South 2 miles paralleling I-80, and then East 1 mile under a **12 FOOT 2" UNDERPASS** onto Barstow Road, East Left to the campground along the Rock River. It would be better to continue on IL 5 for 2 miles to Barstow Road. Then turn Left/East for 2 miles to the campground. Ideal site on the Rock River with level spaces under large trees. Boating on the river. $10-$13.

SIDETRIP INTO MOLINE AND ROCK ISLAND

FIND YOUR QUAD CITIES MAP ON THE BACK OF YOUR STATE MAP! South on IL 5 & John Deere Road to the sights listed below.

QUAD CITY DOWNS: 2 miles West on IL 5/IL 92. Harness Racing Track. April-Oct Wed-Sat 5:30pm. Sun 12:30pm. Pari-mutuel betting. Dining area with Sunday brunch. They have a Newcomer Window for first time guests, and green-coated information hostesses to assist you. The Clubhouse is $3, Grandstand $2. Call for info: 1-800-747-3696.

M O L I N E

Moline calls itself, "The Farm Implement Capital of the World". Until the middle of the 19th Century, 90 percent of Americans were farmers supplying themselves with food and through laborious work producing just a bit more to sell to the other 10 percent of Americans. Therefore of great significance to the development of farming on the prairie was the ingenuity of John Deere. He was a blacksmith from Vermont who came to the Northwest Territories in 1836 and set up shop on the Rock River Northeast of here. He was confronted with the problems that the farmers were having trying to plow the heavy black soil of the prairie. The soil stuck to the wood and iron moldboards of the plow and had to be continually scraped off. Farmers were quitting in despair. Their plows had been fine in the East where the soil was light and sandy. John Deere experimented with different shapes of plows and various materials until in 1837 he made a steel plow that cleaned itself of the heavy soil.

Demand for the new plows increased and he imported special steel first from England, then from Pittsburgh, PA. He moved to Moline for water power and for better transportation. He improved his plow over and over until it was pulled by three then four horses, then a steam engine. The company eventually developed the modern air-conditioned tractor. Where the 1830's farmer could rarely plow one acre a day, today a man can plow 10 acres an hour. The development of transportation along first the rivers and then the railroads brought this bountiful harvest to the rest of the country and the world, changing the whole economy of the country. The farmer can feed the world and make a comfortable living if he isn't eaten up by the costs of equipment, fertilizers and insecticides.

DEERE & COMPANY ADMINISTRATIVE CENTER

Six miles West and South down IL 5/John Deere Road. Open Mon-Fri 9am-5:30pm. Tours are at 10:30am & 1:30pm.

WEST OFFICE BUILDING: Great indoor garden, 2.5 stories high with trees, walkways, flowers. Also outdoor gardens with a large pond and deer.

PRODUCT DISPLAY BUILDING (museum): John Deere equipment displayed. Of special interest is the famous 3-D historical mural meticulously designed by Alexander Girard, architect and artist. He used 2000 items from 1837-1918 with everything from posters to pitchforks to, as John Kouwenhoven said, "...to express the exuberant energies of the pioneer farm community in which the John Deere enterprize grew up".

OTHER SIGHTS IN AND AROUND MOLINE, IL:

SCHADLER'S RIVER ADVENTURES: 2501 River Drive, Moline. Take IL 92 West from IL 5 to just East of where I-74 crosses the river. Ride the "Queen of Hearts Showboat" in a 1-hour sightseeing tour. Apr-Oct 2pm. Adult $6 in 1992. Or enjoy other cruises. Call for reservations: In IL 1-800-521-3346. From out of state: 1-800-227-9967. "Jubilee Restaurant" is nearby with moderate to high prices and a nice view.

The newly authorized gambling on the Mississippi River has boomed and reservations are required far ahead. As a result, former tour boats are being refitted as gambling boats. Also new Casino steamboats are being built and docks are being moved and improved so check ahead for all cruises. One is being developed off I-74 on the Iowa side of the river. The Visitor Centers and museums should have this information.

BUTTERWORTH CENTER: 1105 8th Street. & 11th Avenue. Just West of I-74 in Moline. Estate and gardens of John Deere's granddaughter built in 1892. A National Registry site. Of special interest are the 16th Century Italian painted ceilings. Tours by appointment.

DEERE-WIMMAN HOUSE: 817 11th Avenue. This one has a garage with a turntable. Summer tours 1-4pm on the hour. Both free.

ROCK ISLAND COUNTY HISTORICAL MUSEUM: 822 11th Avenue, Moline. Across the street from

Deere Wimman House. Built in 1879, furnished in 19th Century style and on the National Registry. It has Illinois history, schoolroom, dentist office, quilts, clothing, carriages, and Lincoln memorabilia. Summers: Thurs 9-4:30pm. Sun 1:30-4:30pm. Free. Call: 309-764-8590.

CENTER FOR BELGIAN CULTURE: 712 18th Street. Moline was settled by Belgians who knew how to make fine lace. The name "Moline" comes from the French word for "mill". Wed & Sat 1-4pm. Free.

MOLINE'S OLDE TOWN AREA: 7th Street and 18th Avenue. An authentic Belgian neighborhood with many shops. The Belgian Village Restaurant has home-made bread and huge sandwiches. Stop here on off-hours as it is usually crowded.

CASE IH (J.I. Case bought out International Harvester): First Street, East Moline. World's largest farm implement plant where they make big combines and corn-planters. Tours available.

RIVERSIDE RIVERSLIDE: 3300 5th Avenue, Moline. Large municipal pool with a 40 foot water slide. Summers Sun-Thurs noon-7pm. Fri-Sat Noon-5pm.

ARSENAL ISLAND

From IL 92 West of I-74, take the bridge to Arsenal Island:

TRAM TOUR OF ARSENAL ISLAND: From IL 92 just West of I-74, turn Right/North on 17th Street and go to the river. A 2-hour tram tour takes you around the island. Adult $7.

ROCK ISLAND ARSENAL: An active US Army facility. Shows history of the island plus a collection of military arms. Daily 10-4pm.

COLONEL DAVENPORT HOME: On the North shore. Built in 1833 it's the oldest home in the Quad Cities area. May-Oct Tues-Sun 10-4pm. Adult $2.

MISSISSIPPI RIVER VISITOR CENTER: West end of the island. Army Corp of Engineers facility overlooks Lock and Dam #15. Describes man's efforts to control the Mississippi.

NATIONAL AND CONFEDERATE CEMETERIES: East end of island. Includes 1864 graves of Confederates who died in the island's prison camp during the Civil War.

ROCK ISLAND SIGHTS

From I-80, 12 miles West on 92. Or Milepost 15 on I-280. North on US 67.

AUGUSTA COLLEGE'S "FRYXELL GEOLOGY MUSEUM": Yellow brick Science Building. Has a systematic display of fossils comparable to larger museums. Aug-May Mon-Fri 8-5pm. Sat-Sun 1-4pm. Free.

JOHN DEERE PLANETARIUM: On campus East of parking lot. Collection of meteorites includes a 556 pounder. Tours by appointment.

BLACK HAWK STATE HISTORIC SITE: On IL 5/John Deere Road, 16 miles West of I-80. If you're on I-280, Milepost 15 takes you up 11th Street. to East on IL 5. If you are at Augusta College or Arsenal Island, go South to IL 5.

This park marks the home of Chief Black Hawk who had been driven across the Mississippi in 1831 but returned in 1832 to try to regain his land from the settlers. Read about it in the History of Iowa. The Treaty after Black Hawk's defeat gave not only this Western Illinois land, but also the first Iowa lands to the U.S. government. Today you may hike and picnic in this nature preserve. Open sunrise to 10pm. Free.

HAUBERG INDIAN MUSEUM: On Black Hawk Road up on a bluff overlooking Rock River. This museum depicts the lives of Sauk and Fox/Mesquakie Indians between 1750 and 1832. Daily 8:30-noon & 1pm-4:30pm. Free.

> **MILEPOST 7:** I-80 crosses the Rock River. The Natives called it the "Sinnissippi" River. The campground you see to the East on the North side of the river is "Lundeen's Landing" assessable from Milepost 4A. It was on the North bank of the Rock River that the Sauk village was established in 1730. Named Saukenuk, this village and its extended suburbs was home to 3,000-7,000 Sauk and Fox Indians. It's fertile land was coveted by the whites. Read the stories of Black Hawk in the Iowa and Illinois Histories.

7 COLONA/GREEN ROCK:

FUEL: East to Sunoco.

HENNEPIN CANAL PARK AND PLAYGROUND, LOCK 28: Just West of the freeway. Relax, picnic. Let the kids play on the equipment and view the old Lock #28. This is Eastbound's 1st view of "Mama Bear" canal. Canals had always been constructed of stone, but in 1891 this canal marks the beginning in America of the use of concrete in canal construction. They found it to be less than half the price of stone masonry. This set the pattern for the Panama Canal. They were so enamored with cement that the overseers' homes had cement sidewalks, clothesline poles, and flower pots. The canal was lined with 750 pound concrete telephone poles.

MILEPOST 8: Here I-80 crosses the 104 mile Hennepin Canal.

9   **US 6 (Parallels I-80):**

NIABI ZOO: 6 miles West on US 6. This is a rural zoo with a miniature railroad, a petting zoo and large animals. April-Oct Daily 9:30-5pm. Winter weekdays 9-5pm. Adult $2. Senior $1. Child $.75.

10   <h1 style="text-align:center">M A J O R   I N T E R C H A N G E !</h1>

EASTBOUND I-80 does a big loop here. Watch the signs.

WESTBOUND I-80 loops North and West around the Quad Cities.

WESTBOUND I-280 Beltway to the West & South around the Quad Cities.

WESTBOUND I-74 Freeway West through the center of the Quad Cities.

WESTBOUND: You are entering the quad cities area. Check the back of your Illinois state map for a map of the Quad Cities. These cities are Moline and Rock Island, IL, and Davenport and Bettendorf, IA. Read Milepost 4 for sights in Moline and Rock Island. Read Iowa Mileposts 290, 295, 298, 301 and 306 to help you decide the route you will want to take through this Quad Cities area. You will also note that you can exit I-280 at Milepost 18 to get to the Moline, Rock Island, Bettendorf and Davenport sights.

19   **GENESEO/IL 82:** WALMART to North.

FUEL: North to Phillips Truck Stop, Deck Truck Stop, Amoco.

FOOD: South to Kentucky Fried. North to Deck Coffee Shop, Pizza, Hardees, DQ, Eagle Food Store.

MOTELS: North to Deck Plaza, Oakwood and Royal.

CAMPGROUND: "Geneseo CG": Private. North 4 miles on IL 82. **(RIGS OVER 10 FEET HIGH TAKE THE TRUCK ROUTE AROUND THE RAILROAD VIADUCT.)** Campfires, fishing, playground.

GENESEO HISTORICAL MUSEUM: 216 South State Street. 2 miles North of I-80. Displays include the ethnic heritage of the pioneers of Geneseo, a country store, old schoolhouse, Victorian parlor, and the largest arrowhead collection and Indian exhibit in Illinois. Sat-Sun 2-5pm but the Librarian next door may let you in at other times. Donation.

JOHNSON 1910 FARM: 4 miles East on US 6. Farmhouse, barn, school, old equipment, tools, hiking and picnicking. Fee.

SIDETRIP TO "BISHOP'S HILL"

A 42-mile round trip for someone who has a day to spare. About 15 miles South on IL 82. East 3.8 miles on CR 4. South 2 miles on CR 39. This area was settled in 1846 by Swedish Lutheran dissidents led by Erik Jansson, who disliked the rigid control by the clergy. Many died on the way there during the winter in cold Erie Canal barge cabins and some died of sickness and cholera after they arrived. However, Jansson and others were autocratic in enforcing THEIR precepts. Many rebelled against the new rules on marriage and celibacy. The climax came when John Root was denied permission to leave with his wife, Jansson's niece. So Root killed Jansson. The colony then dissolved just 15 years after it began.

America welcomed many dissident religious groups in her growing years. But the new Americans, cherishing their recently acquired freedoms, often rebelled against strict church authority. Little by little parishioners demanded democracy within the churches, leading to our parish councils and church boards of today.

Today Bishop's Hill has been restored with 15 of the original buildings, several 2-3 stories, including a church and the "Steeple Building". The latter was a hotel and is now a historical museum with a film presentation. Open from 9-5pm. The town has two other museums, "Bishop Hill" & "Henry County", plus shops and restaurants all within a few blocks. Swedish food is served at "The Red Oak", Johnson's, Olson's and Valkommen Inn. There's a B&B at "Holden's Guest House" and at "Country Hills". Crafts include pottery, broommaking, cross stitching, quilting, and woodworking. They have Swedish imports and special events May to Sept & Christmas.

27   ATKINSON:
FUEL: North to Texaco, Casey's, Shell.
FOOD: North to Grandma's, Casey's General Store.
MOTEL: North to motel.
    MILEPOST 30-31: Just 100 yards to the North of I-80 the Hennepin Canal, the Mama Bear of canals, is paralleling you. Look for an old high bridge over it at this point. The Canal is still full of water because of its Feeder Canal.

33   ANNAWAN/IL 78:
FUEL: South to Phillips, Amoco.
FOOD: South to Maid Rite.
CAMPGROUNDS: JOHNSON SAUK TRAIL STATE PARK: South about 6 miles on IL 78. Camping but no showers. Waterfowl viewing area, scenic drive, round barn, fishing, hiking, playground, picnicking. $6 + $2 for electricity. I-80 is following the Great Sauk Trail through Illinois that went from the Mississippi to Lake Michigan and was used by fur traders and trappers. The British agitated the Natives to form an alliance to keep the settlers out of all land West of the Ohio River. Black Hawk assisted the British in the War of 1812, and used this trail to go to Ft. Malden, Ontario to get pay for his services. Thus the name. The Hennepin Canal is North a very short distance with picnicking, hiking, boat launching and a primitive camping site.
    MILEPOST 44: I-80 crosses the Hennepin Canal.

45   SHEFFIELD/IL 88:
FUEL: North to Sonoco Truck Stop, Amoco.
FOOD: North to Country Farm House.
MOTEL: North to Sheffield Motor Lodge.

HENNEPIN CANAL PARKWAY VISITOR CENTER: Exit South one mile on IL 88. West .25 mile. You will cross over the Hennepin Canal for a good look at it. The 400 acre site includes wildlife displays, models of how the canal functioned, photos, restrooms, hiking trail, waterfowl observation area, boat launch ramp, picnic areas, playground, a canal truss bridge and an emergency gate. At the Visitor Center you can get a map to guide you to other features of the canal plus several primitive camping areas. Primitive campground $4. Visitor Center: Weekdays 8-4pm. Sat-Sun 10-4pm.
    SHEFFIELD HISTORICAL SOCIETY MUSEUM: South 5 miles to 2 blocks past US 6 at Washington Street. 12-room museum of artifacts. May-Nov daily 12-4pm. Winters Thurs 12-4pm. Free.
    ST PETER'S DANISH LUTHERAN CHURCH: Across the street from Museum. Built in 1880, it is the Oldest Danish Lutheran congregation in America. It has an old pot-bellied stove and kerosene lanterns. Ask at the museum for entrance to it.
    RONALD REAGON BIRTHPLACE: 36 miles North.
    MILEPOSTS 51-52 REST AREAS: Stop here and read about the famous "Great Sauk Trail" from Rock Island to Lake Michigan and Detroit, almost the same route as I-80 again. This trail was used by settlers after the Erie Canal was built. Trailer Dump Station.

56   PRINCETON/IL 26:
FUEL: North to Phillips Truck Stop. South to Standard, Shell.
FOOD: North to Phillips Restaurant. South to Sullivan's foods, Pizza, Taco Bell, Wendy's, McDonald's, Lincoln Inn. One mile South to Kristi Jean's in the Windchimer. Two miles South to Homestead Restaurant, New Imperial Inn.
MOTELS: South to Lincoln Inn, Days Inn, Princeton Motor Lodge.
    RED COVERED BRIDGE: .75 mile North on IL 26. West one mile to bridge. Built in 1863, one of two remaining covered bridges in Illinois. A sign tells you to drive only 12 animals through at a time. Free.
    THE WINDCHIMER: South one mile to Princeton. An old grain elevator renovated into antique and specialty shops. Northern Princeton is known for its antique shops.
    BUREAU COUNTY HISTORICAL SOCIETY: South 2 miles on IL 26 to South Princeton.

One block West to Pleasant and Park Avenue West. On the Right side of Courthouse Square. Collection of wedding gowns, portraits, and photos. Wed-Mon 1-5pm. Donation.

OWEN LOVEJOY HOMESTEAD: South on IL 26 two miles to US 6. Then East one mile. Built in 1838 this was the most famous of the Underground Railroad stations and is on the National Registry. Home of Owen Lovejoy, abolitionist, friend of Lincoln, preacher and legislator who introduced bill for Emancipation Proclamation. There is also an old school and a log cabin on the grounds. May-Oct Sat-Sun 1-4:30pm. Adult $1. Child $.50.

THE FUGITIVE SLAVE LAW

The U.S. Constitution included a clause that slaves fleeing to the North had to be returned to their owners. It was referred to as the "Fugitive Slave Clause". Some Northerners and law-enforcement agencies were complying. Quakers and men and women of conscience like Owen and Elijah Lovejoy, and John Hossack and William Reddick of Ottawa,IL, risked their lives to protect run-a-way slaves. In 1837 Lovejoy's brother Elijah, an anti-slavery editor in Alton, Ill. was murdered and his press destroyed after he wrote an abolitionist editorial. His martyrdom further fired up the North against slavery.

The South wanted the Fugitive Slave Law enforced. Some Northern Congressmen wanted all new states to be slave-free as the first step in the eventual freedom of the slaves, and to open up the West for the Transcontinental Railroad. Overall Congress was more concerned politically with a balance of "Slave" versus "Free" States than morally and socially dedicated to the emancipation of the slaves. So in 1850 a compromise bill was passed admitting California as one of the "Free" states and promising enforcement of the Fugitive Slave Law.

The Southern Congressmen pushed hard for this bill. But the North was appalled and increased their defense of the slaves. They provided more "Safe Houses", more stations on the "Underground RR". The British champion of the poor, Charles Dickens wrote a compilation of run-a-way slave ads that vividly portrayed the lot of the slave. Then when Elijah Lovejoy's friend, Harriet Beecher Stowe wrote "Uncle Tom's Cabin" in 1852 and sold over a million copies, slavery was doomed.

COMMEMORATIVE ROCK IN BRYANT WOODS: Further South on Main Street. This is where Abraham Lincoln delivered his Emancipation Proclamation on July 4th, 1863. This might have been more political than humanitarian since Congress had already passed laws freeing the slaves of all those fighting against the U.S, but not those in Union states.

61 **I-180 SOUTH:** NO NEAR SERVICES!

70 **LADD/IL 89:** HOSPITAL.
   FOOD: South to Hardees.
   MOTEL: South to Riviera.
   Note the mounds of red earth just North of Ladd from a 50-year old coal mine. Plantings are almost covering it now.

73 **PLANK ROAD:**
   FUEL: North to Sapp Bros Truck Stop, Citco.
   FOOD: Coffee Pot.
   MOTELS: Super 8, Howard Johnson.
   CAMPGROUND: "Barney's Camp": Private. North .8 to Frontage. West .5 mile.

75 **PERU/IL 251 NORTH TO MENDOTA:**
   FUEL: North to Shell, Phillips, Tiki Diesel Truck Stop, Amoco, '76 Truck Stop.
   FOOD: Pine Cone, Hamiltons. North to Arbys, Hardees, McDonalds, '76 Restaurant, Howard Johnson. South to Wendy's, Red Door Inn, by river with relaxed dining.
   MOTELS: Sandman, Comfort Inn. North to Days Inn, Motel 6*, Super 8, Tiki.

77 **LASALLE/IL 351:** STATE POLICE.
   FUEL: Amoco.
   MOTEL: Daniels.
   ILLINOIS & MICHIGAN CANAL, LOCK #14: South about 4 miles on IL 351. West just before the bridge. If you have crossed the river, you have gone too far. West just a block before

you turn South into a parking lot. A stairway leads to the lock built of stone and the canal that contains water as in its prime. This is #14 of 15 locks on the old canal and is representative of the mid 19th Century canal locks. It is also I-80's first encounter with the Baby Bear, the 100 mile "I & M Canal" that carried so many settlers West the middle of the 19th Century and created the boom in commerce between Chicago and St. Louis. It was dug by Irish immigrants who had escaped the great famine of 1840 and were brought from New York. Today the area along the canal is designated as "The National Heritage Corridor", a nature and recreation pre-serve with 11 state parks, 37 nature preserves and 200 historic sites. You can fish, hike and bicycle along this corridor for 40 miles from La Salle to Marseilles, mostly on the old tow path where mules trod.

I & M CANAL near LaSALLE (Baby Bear)
Photo credit: Heritage Corridor Visitors Bureau

LITTLE VERMILION AQUEDUCT (part of the I & M Canal): Take IL 351 South to East on the Canal Road. Then watch for this old aqueduct over the canal just before you get to US 39. Now you can go East to Split Rock, just East of US 39. (One railroad track goes through the railroad tunnel, the other around it.) From here you can take either US 6 or IL 71 to Utica and Starved Rock. In the hayday of the river, steamboats used to come up the Illinois River as far as LaSalle. In 1918 one of the last steamboats on the river, the Columbia, ran aground here and sank taking the lives of 87 people.

79   M A J O R   I N T E R C H A N G E !
LASALLE/I-39/US 51 NORTH:
NORTH TO ROCHELLE AND ROCKFORD.
SOUTH TO CENTRALIA AND BLOOMINGTON.
WILD BILL HICKOK STATE MEMORIAL: 7 miles North on I-39.

81   **UTICA/IL 178:** RADIO 530: Information on National Heritage Corridor.
FUEL: South to Amoco.
FOOD: South to Country Corner Restaurant.
MOTEL: South to Gateway.
CAMPGROUNDS: "KOA": Private. North for 1.5 mile to North 3150 Road. West .5 mile. Pool, playground, children's fishing creek. $15-$20.
    "White Oak Camping Resort": Private. South 1 mile. On the West side of IL 178 across from Starved Rock State Park. $18-$26.
    STARVED ROCK STATE PARK CG: South 4 miles to IL 71. East one mile. Follow signs. Electricity, showers, campfires, playground. Boating nearby. $7 + $2 electricity.

EASTBOUND ALTERNATE ROUTE

TO STARVED ROCK STATE PARK & LOCK AND DAM: South on IL 178 to the park. East on Dee Bennett Road to the lock, North to Ottawa and Milepost 90. A MUST STOP! Even if you feel that you have no time for an extensive stop along the National Heritage Corridor, at least make this loop from here to Ottawa.

There is so much to see and do here that you might first want to find a motel or campground and then go sightseeing and hiking. Do this early as the facilities fill up quickly.

FATHER MARQUETTE MEMORIAL: From IL 178 in Utica turn West on Johnson Street to St. Mary's Church. This commemorates the first non-Indian service celebrated April 14, 1675 by Fr. Marquette near Starved Rock.

LASALLE COUNTY HISTORICAL SOCIETY MUSEUM: On IL 178 on the old I & M Canal. Go slowly and you'll see it to your Left. Built in 1848 this stone building was a warehouse and general store that served the needs of residents and travelers on the old canal. It houses the carriage that carried Lincoln to the debate with Douglas in Ottawa, Indian artifacts from the old Kaskaskia Indian village just East of here, and also pioneer exhibits. April-Oct Wed-Fri 10-4pm. Sat-Sun noon-4pm. Nov-March Fri 10-4pm. Weekends noon-4pm. Fee.

STARVED ROCK STATE PARK: Continue South across the old Baby Bear/I & M Canal and across the Illinois River. Watch for the sign that will take you Left into the part of Starved Rock State Park where the "Rock" is. This is an impressive park beside the Illinois River with tall trees. Stop and picnic, stretch your legs and let the kids run a bit. There are 20 miles of trails much of it high on bluffs with great views. There are 18 canyons carved by water, a hardwood forest and waterfalls and pools in the canyons in rainy weather. Ask for a trail guide at the Visitor Center in the park just West of the "Rock". It is open weekends from May to Oct.

Go down to the river and walk around the large rock overlook on which La Salle built his "Ft. Louis" in 1682. It was abandoned after his death. Then in 1769, as the sign and literature will tell you, a group of Indians retreated to this rock for protection. They were safe from their enemies but died of starvation. Thus the park's name, "Starved Rock". But that is too abbreviated a story. The fascination in history is in the details, not in the bare essentials.

When the British won the French and Indian War in 1762 they were granted the land West to the Mississippi. They moved into the Northwest taking over the French Forts, claimed the Indian lands and treated the tribes with arrogance. Settlers also came into the Fort areas to establish farms. There was much fear of the Native Americans, encouraged by the French of course, that the British would increase their expansion into the lands of the Northwest.

An Ottawa Indian Chief, Pontiac, was able to unite the tribes of the Great Lakes and the Ohio into a confederation to resist the British. In 1763 he laid siege to Detroit for 153 days while the Shawnees and Delawares attacked Fort Pitt/Pittsburgh, Pennsylvania and other tribes combined to capture 9 of the 10 British forts. They never did capture Detroit but they killed 2,000 British to 80 Indians lost. The British rallied, counterattacked, and defeated Pontiac at the Battle of Bushy Run, near Pittsburgh.

Pontiac moved West to the lands of the Illini. He had a large following and some whites say that he was urging the tribes to join his Confederacy and try again to defeat the British. The rest of the story of Pontiac is usually that he signed a treaty with the British in 1766 and was killed by an Indian in Illinois in 1769. Allen W. Eckert tells a much more fascinating story in "Gateway to Empire". He tells of a Chief Makachatinga of the Peorie tribe of the Illini who carried a scar inflicted by Pontiac and called on his nephew to avenge him.

When the deed was done, Pontiac's Confederacy of 5-6,000 warriors converged on Illinois and slaughtered everyone they could find. One of the last remnants of the Illini, 150 warriors, retreated to this large rock outcropping on the Illinois River where they could defend themselves. They had water from the crevices in the rock, but no food. The attackers laid siege as Pontiac had taught them and waited. The Illini held out for weeks and then decided they'd rather fight their way out than starve. Not one escaped!

Meanwhile, the murderer was hunted not only by Pontiac's warriors, but by his own people who wanted to relinquish him to the enemy, along with some presents, in order to stop the destruction of their people. It's a fascinating story as Eckert tells it but you'll have to read the book to know the rest of the story.

ST LOUIS CANYON: Just South of the main park entrance on IL 178 turn Left. There is a 60 foot waterfall in this box canyon. It is fed by a spring and flows all summer. Park and hike in. To get to the State Park campground, you must get back on IL 178 and go further South to a Left on IL 71.

MATTHIESEN STATE PARK: A couple miles further South. No camping but locals say its canyons and waterfalls are more beautiful and safer than Starved Rock.

DEE BENNETT ROAD: Get back onto IL 178 and go North again back across the Illinois River. Turn Right/East onto Dee Bennett Road before you get to the I & M Canal. This road takes you through to Ottawa between the old I & M Canal and the Illinois River. There are several things to see on this road:

STARVED ROCK LOCK AND DAM, ILLINOIS WATERWAY VISITOR CENTER: 1.5 miles East of Utica off Dee Bennett Road. Today the old I & M Canal is obsolete, but the Illinois Waterway/

STARVED ROCK LOCK & DAM (Papa Bear)
Photo credit: John A. Kost

Papa Bear, takes its place and nurses large ships and barges through the locks. Here at Starved Rock you can watch from two different levels as the barges go through the locks with the tow boats pushing them. This is one of the 8 locks along the 327-mile Illinois Waterway and the ONLY one with a Visitor Center. Allow an hour to see the lock in action and view the history and displays. Open daily. Free.

OLD KASKASKIA VILLAGE SITE: 4 miles West of Ottawa on Dee Bennett Road. This was an important Indian village during the latter part of the 17th Century. Joliet recorded 74 wegiwas/dwellings here when he passed through. In 1675 a priest noted that 7 Illinois tribes were in 460 houses. He said that they were long and covered with mats so tightly woven that the elements could not penetrate. Natives had been in this area since 8,000 BC. There were 3 archeological digs here in 1969-71. Artifacts are in the La Salle County Museum on IL 178 in Utica.

HALF WAY HOUSE: About a mile East of the Locks. Four-story building now privately owned that once housed the Sulphur Springs Hotel. Well-noted because it was also a stage stop half-way between Chicago and Peoria. It has 16 fireplaces and a ball-room on the top floor. "Lincoln slept here."

BUFFALO ROCK STATE PARK: 2 miles West of Ottawa on Dee Bennett Road. A large rock there resembles a sleeping bison. A recreation area with "Effigy Tumuli", earth sculptures modeled in the tradition of mound-building representing a giant water spider, frog, catfish, turtle and snake. They call this the largest outdoor sculpture in the world. It began as an acidic tailings pile left-over from coal mining in 1942. In 1985 they neutralized and reclaimed the area, built the sculptures and reseeded it. Park in the West side of the lot near the live bison and hike a 2-mile trail to see the effigies overlooking the Illinois River. Picnic area and playground.

Continue East on Dee Bennett Road into Ottawa. Complete your tour by visiting the Ottawa sights listed below on Milepost 90. IL 23 will take you North to I-80.

90   OTTAWA/IL 23: WALMART

    FUEL: South to Amoco, Shell. South .5 mile into town to several stations with less expensive fuel. Mini Mart and Clark are on Columbus Street, the Northbound Street.

    FOOD: South to McDonalds, Hardees, Dunkin Donuts, Ponderosa Steak House, & Kentucky Fried. Or South .5 mile into town to Oogies where many townspeople eat. It's between the North and Southbound streets with a large parking lot. Enjoy a good meal and look out on the old I & M Canal. Walk the levee where once mules trod pulling barges. Now it is a hiking and biking trail. The old TOLL HOUSE still stands by the canal at Northbound 1217 Columbus Street.

    MOTELS: South to Ottawa Inn, Super 8. South .5 mile to Surrey. South 1.5 mile to Sands.

SIDETRIP THROUGH OTTAWA

After your stop at Oogies, continue South on Southbound La Salle Street to a Left on Lafayette Street to the 3 story Italianate red brick Reddick Mansion & Chamber of Commerce on your Left at the next corner.

REDDICK MANSION: Corner Lafayette & Columbus. Built in 1856 this is an elaborate mansion for the time. It is known for its marble fireplaces, woodwork and ceiling cornices. Reddick made his money in real estate and organized the free public school system. From his home here he crossed the street to Washington park to sit on the platform while Abraham Lincoln and Stephen Douglas had their first debate in 1858. As you look at the old furnishings in the parlor, you might visualize Lincoln sitting there. Tours by appointment, but the Chamber of Commerce ladies may let you stroll through. Ask for a map of Ottawa. They have an "Auto Tour" which is more extensive than the one outlined herein.

SITE OF 1ST LINCOLN-DOUGLAS DEBATE: Washington Park at Columbus Street. Here 10,000 people came by canal boat, horseback, carriage and wagon to hear Abraham Lincoln debate the slavery issue with Stephen Douglas. A trainload of 18 cars came from Chicago! It was a dry year and they say the air was thick with clouds of dust. Picture this scene with the 5'4" portly, self-confident Douglas and the tall, gangly, awkward Lincoln. But when Lincoln spoke, the fire of his integrity and magnetism arose. The two men were running for the U.S. Senate. Lincoln lost! Two years later these same two men ran for President. Guess who won? The circle of gas lights in the park are a memorial to W.D. Boyce, founder of Boy Scouts of America.

THE FOX RIVER AQUADUCT: Go North on Columbus (by the mansion) to a Right on Superior Street for 7 blocks to a Left on Champlain Street. Ahead of you is a 12 FOOT CLEARANCE! Overhead is the Aquaduct, an early engineering marvel that carried the waters of the old I & M canal over the Fox River. It was built of solid rock and was once considered the 8th wonder of the world.

Continue North to a Left on Michigan Street. At La Salle Street/IL 23 go South again across the Illinois River bridge. (Settlers fleeing during the Black Hawk War of 1832 sought refuge here at Old Ft. Ottawa/Ft. Johnson.) Straight ahead on IL 23 a couple blocks to a Right on Prospect.

JOHN HOSSACK HOUSE, an Underground RR Station: 210 Prospect. Beautiful home on National Registry. Hossack hid fleeing slaves in his house until they could be safely moved to another "station". Illinois "Black Laws" forbade blacks to live in Illinois. Humanitarians protecting slaves were in jeopardy from Federal Fugitive Slave Act.

OVERLOOK OF SILICA COMPANY: North again on IL 23 to Left on Main Street. When you come to the end, go Left/South to the overlook. This is a 190 acre quarry that has yielded 40 million tons of high grade silica used in glass manufacture. Now you can return to Columbus Street and North back to I-80. Or continue South on Boyce Memorial Drive to West on Ottawa Avenue. This will get you onto Dee Bennett Road, the Alternate Route, and the sights listed in Milepost 81, reversed.

WESTBOUND ALTERNATE ROUTE

TO STARVED ROCK LOCK & DAM AND STATE PARK: South on IL 23 to West on Main. South on Clay and West on Ottawa Avenue. A MUST STOP! You will pass through the village of NAPLATE named for the former National Plate Glass Company. This is the home of Libbey-Owens-Ford Glass Company. They make plate glass windshields and side lights. This road becomes Dee Bennett Road taking you past the sights listed in Milepost 81 on the way to Utica and Starved Rock. North on IL 178 to Milepost 81 on I-80. Even if you stop for nothing else along the National Heritage Corridor, you should at least make this loop from Ottawa to Utica. Read Milepost 81 for descriptions. You'll be seeing them in reverse.

93   **OTTAWA/IL 71:** HOSPITAL South 2 miles.
FUEL: North to Shell Oasis Truck Stop, J & L Truck Stop.
FOOD: McDonalds. North to Oasis Restaurant. South to Montes, New Cham's Chinese Food. One mile South to Hanks.

97   **MARSEILLES:**
FOOD: Hank's Italian Restaurant. South to Almac Family.
CAMPGROUNDS: "Glenwood RV Resort": Private. South 3 miles to Bluff Street. East .8 mile to La Salle Street. North 2 blocks. Pool, campfires, playground.
    "Whispering Pines CG & Resort": Private. South .25 mile to 30th Road. East 1.75 miles to East 2575th Road. South 2 miles to North 28th Road. East .5 mile to East 2625th Road. South .2 mile. Campfires, pool, playground.
    ILLINI STATE PARK: South 4 miles across the river. Electricity and toilets but no showers or swimming listed. Campfires, boating, playground. Picnic and hike and watch the barges pass. $6 + $2 for electricity.
    "Troll Hollow": 1.75 miles South of State Park on IL 15. Left .5 mile on gravel road. Playground. No further information.
    NORWEGIAN SETTLERS STATE MEMORIAL: 8 miles North on IL 71. In Norway, IL there is **THE NORSK MUSEUM** and **NORWAY STORE**. If you have Norsk roots, you may want to check these out.

105   **SENECA:** NO NEAR SERVICES!

112   **MORRIS/IL 47:** WALMART & SUPER MARKET.
RADIO 530 AM, for information on National Heritage Corridor.
FUEL: South to '76, Shell, Clark, Super gas. North to Amoco, Standard Truck Stop. Sav-Mor Auto Supply.
FOOD: South to McDonalds, Taco Bell, Ice Cream Churn, Eagle Food Store, Wendys, Golden Flame, Dairy Queen, Hardees, Burger King, The Neighborhood Place, Kentucky Fried. North .5 mile to R-Place, Family Eatery. "Rockwell Inn" South to US 6, West about 4 miles on Right. Rockwell pictures line the walls. A special dinner at moderate price.
MOTELS: South to Morris Garden, Park, Super 8. North to Comfort.
CAMPGROUND: "Waupecan Valley CG": Private. 4 miles South on IL 47 across Illinois River. Right on Southmore. 2 miles to CG. Quiet woods site. $26. Needs another water system and new restrooms.
NATURAL RECREATION AREAS (Without camping.):

M. G. STRATTON STATE PARK: South 3 miles on IL 47. Picnic ground by the Illinois River.

GOOSE LAKE PRAIRIE: South on IL 47. Across the Illinois River. East 7 miles to 5010 North Jugtown Road. Largest tract of tall grass prairie left. Visitor Center open 10-4pm daily. Free.

AUX SABLE AQUEDUCT: IL 47 South. Turn East just before the Illinois River. Go about 5 miles to I & M Canal's restored locktenders house, locks and aqueduct, one of the nicest.

NETTLE CREEK AQUEDUCT: IL 47 South. Turn West just before Illinois River. On I & M Canal. Visitor Center.

I & M CANAL STATE TRAIL/GEBHARD WOODS ACCESS: IL 47 South to West just before the Illinois River. West of Nettle Creek Aqueduct. State trail headquarters. Restored canal towpath hiking and biking. The largest tree in Illinois is a cottonwood 120 feet tall, 32 feet in circumference. It's on the South side of the canal. You might have to walk a bit to get to it.

MILEPOST 117 REST AREAS: Stop to see the photos and maps of the canals in this area.

122 MINOOKA:
FUEL: South to Casey, '76. Amoco. North to Citco.
FOOD: South to Dairy Queen, .5 mile to Minooka Family Restaurant.
After the Illinois Confederacy was slaughtered in 1769, the Potowatamies moved in from the North and gave Minooka its name.
NOTE: "A" EXITS ARE USUALLY SOUTH, "B" EXITS ARE USUALLY NORTH!

126   M A J O R   I N T E R C H A N G E !
I-55 NORTH TO CHICAGO, SOUTH TO ST LOUIS: NO NEAR SERVICES!

130 LARKIN AVENUE, JOLIET/IL 7: HOSPITAL, to North.
COLLEGE OF ST. FRANCIS to North.
FUEL: Shell, Standard, Clark, Mobile, Marathon.
FOOD: Bob Evans, Wendys, White Castle, Family Table, Western Sizzler.
MOTELS: Red Roof Inn*, Fenton, Comfort. North to Motel 6* and Super 8.

131 CENTER STREET/MEADOW AVENUE, JOLIET: NO NEAR SERVICES!
Crossing the Des Plaines River which flows South to the Illinois River. The canal locks connect it to the Chicago River which originally flowed into Lake Michigan, but now flows backwards into the Des Plaines.

132 JOLIET/US 52/IL 53: NO NEAR SERVICES!

133 RICHARD'S STREET, JOLIET/CHICAGO STREET SOUTH/IL 171:
LEWIS UNIVERSITY.
SLOVENIAN HERITAGE MUSEUM: North on IL 171 to 431 North Chicago Street.
LOCKPORT: 5 miles North on IL 171. Preserved canal town bounded by the I & M Canal, 7th Street, Washington Street, and 11th Street. Includes 37 historic sites and structures.
ILLINOIS STATE MUSEUM: LOCKPORT GALLERY/GAYLORD BUILDING: I & M CANAL VISITOR CENTER: 200 West 8th Street, Lockport. Just North of intersection with IL 7. On National Registry. Tues-Sun 10-5pm. Free. Restaurant.
WILL COUNTY HISTORICAL SOCIETY MUSEUM AND PIONEER SETTLEMENT: 803 South State Street, Lockport. Pioneer Settlement is open from April-Sept daily 1-4:30pm. Free.
LOCKPORT PRAIRIE: Old prairie grasses and wildflowers.
ISLE A LA CACHE: North another 5 miles to Romeo Road. West to an island in the Des Plaines River. Living History program takes you back to 17th Century French explorers and traders. Great for kids! Free.

134 BRIGGS STREET, JOLIET: HOSPITAL.
FUEL: Auto Travel Store. South to Amoco. North to Speedway Gas.
CAMPGROUND: "Martin's CG": Private. South one block on Griggs Street to New Lenox Road. East one mile. Playground. NEAR I-80.

WESTBOUND: YOU ARE NOW ENTERING THE NATIONAL HERITAGE CORRIDOR! This 98 mile park is probably the longest in the U.S. It parallels I-80 from here West, and encompasses the 1848 Illinois and Michigan Canal which today is a ribbon of recreation areas and historic sites. Note especially the Alternate Route between Milepost 90 and 81. RADIO 530 AM for information on National Heritage Corridor.

137 **MAPLE STREET, NEW LENNOX/US 30:** K MART to North.
US 30 was the paved Coast-to-Coast Highway of the 30's & '40s!
FUEL: Speedway, Auto Travel Store.
FOOD: North to McDonalds, Lenox Family, Hardees, Kentucky Fried, Lee Brothers.

EASTBOUND ALTERNATE ROUTE

Eastbound from here into Indiana, I-80's road surface is usually poor, the roughest road surface the length of I-80! It can be very congested, hazardous driving! If you want to avoid the nerve-wracking Chicago traffic and travel more in the country, take off Eastbound on US 30 into Indiana and weave your way back up to the Indiana tollroad. Check your map! Read "Westbound Alternate Route" at Indiana Milepost 107. It's mostly 4 lanes and much less hectic, but it has stopsigns and lights and is slower than I-80. Plenty of gas stations, food, campgrounds on the route. During rush hours it may be crowded in Chicago Heights also, but traffic has been delayed on I-80 for 2 hours and more. Ask a trucker how I-80 is ahead as he will be informed by his CB radio.

145 **MOKENA/US 45/96TH AVE:**
LAND'S END OUTLET: North to 159th Street.
FUEL: South to Shell Truck Stop, Gas City, Clark.
FOOD: South to McDonalds, Burger King, Wendy's.
MOTELS: South to Super 8.

148 **HARLEM AVENUE, TINLEY PARK/IL 43:**
CAMPGROUND: "Windy City CG": Private. Good Sam. South .25 on IL 43 to 191st Street. West one mile to 80th. North .2 to CG. Swim, fish, boat, playground. Lake San Lemar with sandy beach. One mile from railroad going to Chicago Loop. NEAR I-80.

151 **MAJOR INTERCHANGE!**
CICERO AVENUE/I-57: NO NEAR SERVICES!
EASTBOUND I-57 NORTH TO CHICAGO, SOUTH TO MEMPHIS:

EASTBOUND SIDETRIP

INTO CHICAGO: Exit North on I-57 and join I-94 North to about Exit 58, 18 miles. Ask locally. If you have any time at all to spend, Chicago is a very worthwhile and educational stop-off. Use your Chicago map on the back of your Illinois map and/or enquire at your hotel or campground to plan your desired exits from the freeways. Or get information on public transportation. It is suggested that you park your trailer or large rig somewhere before you go into the Chicago area. Parking is a real problem for CARS. Travel East to:
FIELD MUSEUM OF SCIENCE AND INDUSTRY: 57th Street and South Lake Shore Drive. Allow at least a half day for this! There are 75 exhibition halls on 14 acres! All the sciences are covered from medical, engineering, space, industry, chemistry, geology, etc. This is a hands-on museum, great for the kids! They'll love the Apollo 8 Command Module and the German Sub captured in WW II. Open summers daily 9:30-5:30pm. 9:30-4pm rest of year. Free.
HENRY CROWN SPACE CENTER AND OMNIMAX THEATER: At the museum. Watch a film on a 3-story high screen with 75 speakers that will give you the sensations of zooming off into space. Spectacular! Hourly from 10am. Fri-Sat Eve 7-8pm. Adult $4.
SHEDD AQUARIUM: 1200 South Lakeshore Drive to the North. You'll observe 6,000 marine and fresh-water animals and a coral reef where divers feed the reef fish at 11am, 2 and 3pm daily May to Aug. Summers daily 9-5pm. Winters 10-5pm. Adult $3. Free on Thursdays. This could take 2 hours at least.
FIELD MUSEUM OF NATURAL HISTORY: Across the street. Another large museum on 10 acres. Here you don't just look at things. You experience them. You can draw water from the Nile or walk on a Pacific beach or watch a lava flow. There are animal and bird displays, gems and minerals including a special jade exhibit,

anthropology of Native Americans, Eskimos, Egyptions, Chinese, and Tibetans. By now you have chosen one museum over another or you're on your second day. Daily 9-5pm. Adult $3.

ART INSTITUTE OF CHICAGO: Between Jackson and Michigan and Monroe Streets. North in downtown Chicago. It is IMMENSE! At least one day there! You could easily spend two. Enjoy the "room" arrangements with various period furniture and famous paintings displayed naturally. The beautiful serene Mary Cassatt portraits grace the walls not far from Abraham Lincoln's chaise lounge. See the paper weight art, the stained glass! The Thorne miniatures of 65 different rooms of many cultures and periods, complete to minute details. Mon-Sat 10:30-4:30pm. Sunday noon-5pm. $5. Free Tues.

THE ADLER PLANETARIUM: 1300 South Lake Shore Drive. On a peninsula on the lake. It has a collection of Astronomical equipment, history of space travel, and a solar telescope. Daily Mon-Thurs 9:30-4:30pm. Fri til 9pm. Sat-Sun 9:30-5pm. They have a sky show daily at 11, 1, 2, 3, and 4pm. Adult $3.

CHICAGO ACADEMY OF SCIENCES: North past downtown Chicago at Stockton and Armitage. This is like entering a wilderness. You walk through a jungle, gaze at the stars, explore an Illinois cave, and follow

CHICAGO SKYLINE from LAKE MICHIGAN, SEARS TOWER to left
Photo credit: City of Chicago/ Peter J. Schultz

animal tracks while birds look down on you from their perches.

HERE'S CHICAGO: At the **PUMPING STATION**, by the **WATER TOWER**. Chicago Avenue. (These two buildings are the only public buildings to survive the 1871 fire.) A Visitor Information Center with a multimedia production to show visitors what to see in Chicago. You'll learn some of the history of the city including the fire of 1871 and the Gangster Era.

SEARS TOWER: Jackson Blvd. downtown. It's the world's tallest building. Continuous tours up to the sky deck for an eagle's eye view of Chicago. Fee.

LINCOLN PARK and **BROOKFIELD**. Enquire locally. Two zoos. Both great with children's shows, etc. Summers daily 9:30-6pm. Winters 10-5pm. Free Tues.

JANE ADDAM'S HULL HOUSE is at the University of Illinois at 800 South Halsted. West of I-90/I-94 near Polk Street. She was a humanitarian, and social worker and the first American woman recipient of the Nobel Prize. Shows influence of Hull House on history. Mon-Fri 10-4pm. Sun noon-5pm.

FOR ARCHITECTURE

ROBIE HOUSE: (Frank Lloyd Wright's) 5757 Woodlawn Avenue at the University of Chicago. West of Museum of Science & Industry. North off 59th Street.

CHICAGO PUBLIC LIBRARY: 78 East Washington Street. Just North of the Art Institute. Italian marble and domes and Tiffany mosaics. 9-6pm weekdays. 9-5pm Sat.

ARCHICENTER: 330 Dearborn Avenue.

GLESSNER HOUSE: 1800 South Prairie Avenue.

FOR GARDENERS:

GARFIELD PARK CONSERVATORY: 4 miles West of downtown Chicago. One of the largest! At the North end of Garfield Park at Lake Street. 5,000 species and 8 halls.

GRANT PARK: On the lake at Columbia Drive & South Lakeshore Drive. Has a rose garden, formal gardens and seated statue of Lincoln by Saint-Gaudens.

LINCOLN PARK: On North Lake Shore Drive. Has the Standing Statue of Lincoln, a bird sanctuary, and a conservatory of 3.5 acres of flora.

CHICAGO BOTANIC GARDEN: Glencoe, Ill. 300 acres of flora.

ENJOY YOUR ETHNICITY AT:

POLISH MUSEUM OF AMERICA: 984 North Milwaukee Avenue just North of Chicago Avenue. Showing Polish contributions to America.

BALZEKAS MUSEUM OF LITHUANIAN CULTURE: 6500 South Pulaski Road, Southwest Chicago. Historical and ethnic articles from 800 years of Lithuanian culture.

SPERTUS MUSEUM OF JUDAICA: 618 South Michigan. Shows Jewish culture from all over the world along with the Holocaust Memorial.

DUSABLE MUSEUM OF AFRICAN AMERICAN HISTORY: 740 East 56th Place. Trace Black history in America with cultural and art collections.

SWEDISH AMERICAN MUSEUM: 5211 North Clark Street. Swedish American history.

UKRAINIAN NATIONAL MUSEUM: 2453 West Chicago Avenue. History and art.

FOR THE WORLD OF BUSINESS: Downtown near Sears Tower.

The BOARD OF TRADE: 141 West Jackson Blvd., futures exchange, commodities. Two viewing areas.

CHICAGO MERCANTILE EXCHANGE: 30 South Wacker Drive, world's leading futures exchange in the international market. Visitor center and exhibits. Free.

FOR PLATE COLLECTORS

THE BRADFORD MUSEUM : 9333 Milwaukee Avenue with 1300 limited edition plates.

MORE ART?

MUSEUM OF CONTEMPORARY ART: 237 East Ontario Street, North of Grand Avenue.

TERRA MUSEUM OF AMERICAN ART: 666 North Michigan Avenue.

THE DAVID AND ALFRED SMART MUSEUM OF ART: University of Chicago, 5550 South Greenwood Avenue. West of Museum of Science & Industry.

154 KEDZIE AVENUE: NO RETURN TO I-80!

155 MAJOR INTERCHANGE!

TRI STATE TOLLWAY/I-294: NO RETURN TO I-80!

ILLINOIS TOLLGATE: Toll 30-60 cents.

157 HALSTEAD STREET/IL 1:

FUEL: Marathon Truck Stop.

FOOD: Yellow Ribbon Restaurant, Mama's Pasta House.

MOTELS: Budget Inn*, Red Roof Inn*, Days Inn, Dixie Highway. South to Ramada and Motel 6*. North to Motel 6*.

YOU ARE PASSING OVER AN EXTENSIVE LIME PIT!

Building spanning I-80 has Burger King, Popeye and Mobile Gas.

160 MAJOR INTERCHANGE!

I-94 TO CHICAGO ON THE CALUMET EXPRESSWAY: NO NEAR SERVICES!

IL 394 SOUTH TO DANVILLE:

161 TORRANCE AVENUE/LANSING/US 6:

FOOD: Bob Evans

MOTELS: Fairfield Inn, Pioneer Motel, Red Roof Inn*.

EASTBOUND: HANG IN THERE! YOU'LL BE OUT OF THIS TRAFFIC MESS IN 25 MILES.

WESTBOUND: YOU HAVE 40 MILES MORE OF HEAVY TRAFFIC! IT ISN'T TOO LATE TO DECIDE TO SEE THE CHICAGO SIGHTS! TURN NORTH AT MILEPOST 160. READ MILEPOST 151 FOR DESCRIPTIONS OF CHICAGO.

ILLINOIS I 80 MILEPOSTS

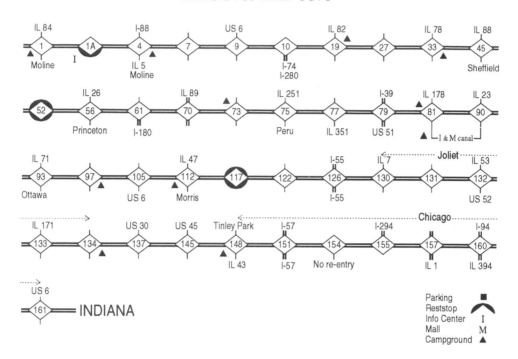

Parking ■
Reststop ⌒
Info Center I
Mall M
Campground ▲

CHICAGO SKYLINE ALONG the CHICAGO RIVER *(which was made to flow backwards)*
SEARS TOWER is at the FAR RIGHT
Photo credit: City of Chicago/Peter J. Schuts

Indiana

The Hoosier State!

What is a Hoosier? No one seems to know! It could be a derivative of a French or Indian name. Or a canal builder named Hoosier who would only hire men from one certain area. Or maybe from a settler yelling out, "Who's here?" At any rate, Indiana has used this designation for generations.

From an 11 million population in Illinois, we drop down by a half to a population of 5,544,159 in Indiana. It's smaller too with 36,291 square miles, our 38th state in size. The capital is Indianapolis, famous for the Indianapolis Speedway. Elevations in Indiana range from 320 feet on the Ohio River to 1257 feet on the Eastern and Central part of the state. I-80 crosses the very Northern tip of the state that is relatively level.

The northern half of Indiana has rich prairies and rocky moraines from that ancient ice sheet, the Wisconsin Drift. The storms of Lake Michigan spewed up vast sanddunes. Amazingly they are the highest in the world! Today they are protected in the "Indiana Dunes National Lakeshore" and "Indiana Dunes State Park". You can visit the dunes Eastbound from Milepost 16 via I-94 or Westbound from Milepost 31 via IN 49.

Indiana manages to retain its rich farms and pastoral countryside along with its enormous manufacturing output. The farms produce corn, popcorn, spearmint, peppermint, soybeans, tomatoes, tobacco, cattle, chickens and hogs. Indiana ranks 9th in the value of its agriculture and also 9th in its manufactured goods.

The factories in Hammond, Gary, East Chicago and Whiting have the largest concentration of industry. The towering smokestacks of the steel industry, and the large oil refineries are barely visible through the smog to the North of I-80. Heavy equipment, petroleum products and chemicals are manufactured. Gary, Indiana is a major steel producing area with the main plant of U.S. Steel. The mills use the iron from the North and the coal from the South. Other cities manufacture boats, trucks, mobile homes, and electrical and electronic machinery. Just South of I-80 are many RV plants. Tours are available from Milepost 101, Bristol.

Indiana has famous "sons". Knute Rockne, Notre Dames' football coach, had 5 seasons of undefeated and untied games. Ernie Pyle became famous as a World War II correspondent and wrote "Here Is Your War". Gene Stratton Porter wrote 12 novels and 7 nature books. Booth Tarkington wrote "The Magnificent Ambersons". James Whitcomb Riley's poetry is the charm of pioneer America.

"Little Orphant Annie's come to our house to stay,
An' wash the cups an' saucers an' brush the crumbs away',
An' shoo the chickens off the porch, an' dust the hearth, an' sweep,
An' make the fire, an' bake the bread, an' earn her board an' keep."

INDIANA HISTORY

Illinois and Iowa Histories describe the French explorers and fur traders who came down from the Great Lakes via the rivers. La Salle built the first fort in Indiana in 1675 at the mouth of the St. Joseph River on Lake Michigan. He named it "Ft. Miami", his French pronunciation for the Maumee Indians there. The Fox Indian Wars in 1715 forced the French traders to relinquish their portage routes in Illinois. So they built new forts on strategic waterways and portages in Indiana. One was named "Ft. Miami" again, but this time on the Maumee-Wabash portage where Ft. Wayne, Indiana stands today. From this portage the Maumee River flows into Lake Erie and the Wabash River into the Ohio River. The French also built Ft.

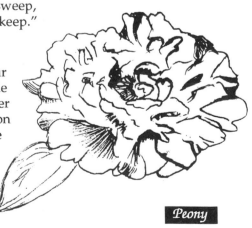

Peony

Vincennes on the Wabash River in Southwestern Indiana to control the lower Ohio River Valley.

The British, wanting a piece of the fur trade, began filtering through from the Great Lakes into the Northwest territories (Ohio, Indiana, and Illinois). This resulted in the French and Indian War from 1754 to 1763. At the Treaty of Paris in 1763, the British gained all the land East of the Mississippi River including Ft. Vincennes and Ft. Miami. They wanted the fur trade without competition from the colonists, so they issued a Proclamation in 1763 limiting Colonial settlement to East of the Appalachians. But some daring traders, explorers and settlers had already arrived via Lake Erie, the Ohio River, or the Native Warrior Paths.

Restless frontiersmen went through the Cumberland Gap into Kentucky from its discovery in 1770. There they hunted and explored all of Kentucky's rivers including the Ohio. Daniel Boone, a Pennsylvanian, especially loved to explore this area. At this time each state claimed land to the West as far as the Mississippi River, therefore Kentucky was incorporated into Virginia in 1777.

Tension between the British and the colonists increased resulting in the Revolutionary War in 1775. In 1778 Virginian Colonel George Rogers Clark went down the Ohio River to the Mississippi and defeated the British at their Fort Kaskaskia, IL on the Mississippi. The British Fort Vincennes in Southwestern Indiana then surrendered to Clark giving Virginia claim to the land Northward from the Ohio River to the Canadian border and Westward to the Mississippi. Virginia established it as "Illinois County of Virginia". Big territory for Virginia from one day's battle! Victory didn't last long though because the British pushed down from their Ft. Detroit and reclaimed Vincennes.

Travel at this time was always by the rivers. In January 1779 Clark led his Kentucky sharpshooters from Kaskaskia, Illinois to Vincennes, Indiana overland through mud and rain and retook the fort. Now the Natives, goaded and supplied by the British, were attacking settlers all over the Northwest Territories. Subsequent American war efforts in the Northwest were too feeble, and did not gain any of the territory from the British. However the Treaty of Paris in 1782-83 won much more than the battles, when all the land East of the Mississippi was given to the U.S. Read Ohio History for this story.

The Northwest Ordinance of 1787 was one of the last acts of the Continental Congress. It designated 3-5 states to be formed in the Northwest, principally Ohio, Indiana, Illinois. It provided that when each area of the Northwest had a free male population of 5,000 they could have an appointed governor and an elected legislature. When the population reached 60,000, they could petition Congress for Statehood. Slavery was prohibited. Arthur St. Clair was appointed the first governor of the Northwest Territories which at this time was over a very sparsely settled Indiana, Ohio and Illinois. In fact, the only settled parts were near the Forts although there were traders and adventurers throughout the area. The Territorial Capitol was at Vincennes, Indiana. An extensive area to oversee!

After the Battle of Fallen Timbers (Ohio History) General Anthony Wayne got the Shawnee and Delaware Nations to sign the "Treaty of Greenville" in 1795. He obtained most of Ohio, some of Eastern Indiana and 6 square miles at Dearborn/Chicago, where Ft. Dearborn was built. As settlers poured into the Ohio lands, they spilled over into Indiana and for the first time this territory knew a land rush. Mostly these settlers came up from the Southern states via Kentucky and the rivers.

In 1800 Wm Henry Harrison, became the new Northwest Territory's Delegate to Congress. He maneuvered a boundary bill through Congress separating off Ohio to form 2 Territories, Ohio and Indiana. Harrison was made the Governor of the new Western "Indiana Territory" which included Illinois. Governor Harrison was a ruthless pursuer of President Jefferson's goals of getting control of Native American land and sending the tribes to smaller reservations, notably West of the Mississippi. The Tribes would want to powwow with Harrison to protest illegal land grabs and other abuses by the settlers. Harrison would sound sympathetic and call the meeting. Then he would divide the Chiefs to deal separately with them and ply them with liquor. Then with intermittent bribes and threats he would twist and turn the proposals into "purchases" of yet more land. By 1807 he had obtained all of Southern Indiana.

TECUMSEH

Meanwhile, an intelligent educated Shawnee leader named "Tecumseh" knew what the Americans were doing. He had felt for many years that the only way that his people could ever retain any of their land was to form a Confederation of ALL the tribes. To this end, he traveled all over the Indian territories as far South as Arkansas and Florida to meet with the different Nations. He urged them to form a coalition to resist the American's demands for more and more of their territory. He tried to get them to pledge to make no more land concessions as individual tribes without the consent of the whole federation. He also urged them to stop drinking the American's "firewater" that was always the "softener" before the signing of these "Treaties". (The Native American biochemistry is very intolerant of alcohol. They are easily enslaved to it.)

Tecumseh had a one-eyed brother, "The Prophet" who was revered for his "visions". The Shawnees' main village was at Prophetstown/Lafayette, Indiana at the junction of the Wabash River and Tippecanoe Creek. (This is 81 miles South of Milepost 11 on I-65.) Tecumseh told Gov. Harrison, "Sell a country? Why not sell the air, the clouds and the great sea as well as the earth?" He fell in love with a white lady who helped him study the Bible, Shakespeare and classical history. He wanted to marry her but she insisted that he live as a white man. This was out of the question for him because he had a mission to help his brothers survive this invasion.

Harrison was at first oblivious to the negotiations going on and continued his land grabs. In 1806 he finally found out about Tecumseh's growing power and wrote a letter to the Delawares to shake their faith in the Shawnee leader. He challenged the power of "The Prophet". "If he is really a prophet ask him to cause the sun to stand still, the moon to alter its course, the rivers to cease to flow". Some historians believe that this letter came into the hands of Canadians who told Tecumseh about the eclipse of June 1806. However since the latter was already well-read he probably knew about eclipses and checked an Almanac. At any rate, word was passed through the tribes that the Prophet would blot out the sun on that date. The ruse worked and the awe and loyalty of the tribes was secured.

Tecumseh went to British Ft. Malden Northeast of Detroit and was welcomed. The British were expecting another war with the Americans over their impressment of American sailors. They were glad to obtain the cooperation of Tecumseh who got the impression that the British would help him against the Americans. Although the British had lost the Northwest in the 2nd Treaty of Paris they still didn't think the fledgling Congress would survive and they wanted the territory for fur-trading.

Gov. Harrison was a proud ambitious man. He built an enormous mansion in Vincennes, Indiana outstripping any building in or out of the Territories. He called it "Grouseland". In Sept 1809 he gathered 1100 Indians there. He played one tribe against another, bribed and threatened them. When he was through he had gained 3 million acres of Indiana for $7,000 cash and $1750 in annuities. Tecumseh was furious! He went to Grouseland and told Harrison that the Treaty was invalid, that tribe fragments could not sell land that belonged to all the Tribal Nation. He told him that the Tribes would resist the occupation of these lands. Harrison threatened force. Now Tecumseh knew what he had to do. Some attacks on the frontiers began in 1810. Tecumseh worked to contain the tribes' eagerness for war until the Confederation was ready. In the fall, 6,000 Natives went to British Ft. Malden for arms. But Tecumseh held them off. In July 1811 Tecumseh, still trying to avoid war, called on Harrison telling him that if he did not persist in occupying the land that he, Tecumseh, could restrain his tribes. Harrison replied that the surveying plans and occupation would continue. Tecumseh made the super mistake of telling Harrison that he was going South to powwow with the Creeks, Cherokee and the Choctaw. Or who knows! Maybe he just told him he'd be away trying to quiet the tribes and stop the raids. He was primarily a peacemaker!

Harrison saw his chance! In September 1811 he marched North with 1,000 troops. He stopped to build Ft. Harrison at Terre Haute and then camped 3/4 mile from Prophetstown. The Shawnee knew that they were coming. The Prophet performed his war dance that he said would render their enemy impotent. By daylight they had surrounded the sleeping Americans and charged the camp. The soldiers fought back and then the calvary charged the Shawnee from two sides. The warriors saw that they weren't invincible, lost faith in their cause and fled. Harrison destroyed Prophet's Town in this "The Battle of Tippeconoe". There were many casualties on both sides. When Tecumseh returned, Native attacks multiplied all over the Territories. Settlers fled Eastward. Harrison and others blamed it all on the British and this inflamed the War of 1812. Tecumseh's Confederation fought with the British.

The Americans who thought that they would not only defeat the British easily but take Canada as well, found themselves fighting to defend Ft. Wayne and Ft. Harrison, Indiana. At Fort Dearborn (Chicago) as the garrison was evacuating the fort, the Potawatomi attacked and everyone was either killed or taken prisoner. Read Allen Eckert's "Gateway to Empire" for a fascinating account of both Tecumseh and of Ft. Dearborn. Tecumseh was killed in 1813 at the "Battle of Thames River" near Detroit. The Native American's hope of regaining their homelands was gone forever.

THE SETTLING OF INDIANA

After the War of 1812 the next land settled was the Southern part of Indiana where there was a thick forest of hardwood trees. The early pioneers believed that a trees grew from rich soil. Being unfamiliar with the loamy soil of the prairie country to the North, they first settled the bottom lands and the forests. Families came with Conestoga wagons, and hand carts, herding their animals before them. Or floating on flatboats down the river. The continuous line of emigrants heading West came mostly from the Southern states. They were driven out by the loss of their land to the Plantation system, or their abhorrence of slavery, or the aristocratic class society that repulsed their democratic spirit. By 1816 Indiana had enough settlers and became a state.

Since the War of 1812, the government had treated the tribes with demanding authority and by 1825 the policy was removal to beyond the Mississippi. In the 1830's Central and Northern Indiana were settled by emigrants from the New England and Middle states, facilitated by the Erie Canal that opened in 1825.

INDIANA MILEPOSTS

INDIANA STATE POLICE ON TOLL ROAD: 219-234-4157.
CELLULAR PHONE EMERGENCY NUMBER: 911.
RADIO FOR WEATHER AND NEWS: NO ONE STATION. SEARCH THE DIAL.
INDIANA DEPARTMENT OF TOURISM: 1-800-289-ONIN.
INDIANA STATE PARKS: 1-800-622-4931
Rest Areas in this Indiana chapter and on the Indiana map are Plazas on the Toll Road.

EASTBOUND: I-80 AND I-94 ARE TOGETHER IN GARY.
Traffic is so congested on this stretch that unless you have an emergency it might be best to just stay on I-80 until you are through the area. Look ahead to Indiana's admirable state parks.

MILEPOSTS:

1 **CALUMET AVENUE, HAMMOND/US 41 NORTH:**
  FUEL: Martin Oil Truck Stop.

2 **WICKER BLVD., HAMMOND/US 41 SOUTH, IN 152 NORTH:**
  FOOD: Fast foods.
  MOTEL: Travellodge.

3 **KENNEDY AVENUE, HAMMOND:**
  FUEL: North to Shell.
  FOOD: North to McDonalds.

4 **INDIANAPOLIS BLVD.:**

5 **CLINE AVENUE, GARY/IN 912:**
  FUEL: Truck City.
  FOOD: South to Burger King, Bob Evans, Dennys.
  MOTELS: South to Motel 6*, Quality Inn, Super 8.

6 **BURR STREET, GARY:** RADIO: 1370 AM, NEWS/TALK.
  FUEL: North to T.A. Truck Stop, Pilot Truck Stop, Amoco.
  FOOD: North to TA Restaurant, Country Pride.
  MOTEL: North to Super 8.
  CAMPGROUND: "Gerry RV Pk": Private. Good Sam. South 1 block on Burr Street to 29th Street. West 1 block to Gerry Street. North 1 block. No tents. Self-contained only.

9 **GRANT STREET, GARY:**
  FUEL: South to Flying J, Steel City Truck Plaza.
  FOOD: South to McDonalds.

10 **BROADWAY, GARY/IN 53:** INDIANA UNIVERSITY.
  FUEL: Amoco.

12 **I-65 NORTH TO I-90, SOUTH TO INDIANAPOLIS.**

13 **CENTRAL AVENUE, GARY.**

15   RIPLEY STREET, GARY/US 6/IN 51/US 20:   LAKE STATION.

16   M A J O R   I N T E R C H A N G E !
EASTBOUND I-80 ENTERS THE INDIANA TOLLROAD WITH I-90. Ask at toll booth for
Tollroad Map and Motel/Campground lists. The Toll depends on the number of axles and the
weight and increases with each "Class". Cars are in Class 1; car and 22 foot dual-axle trailer are
in Class 2; a 26 foot 2-axle motor home is in "Class 3"; a 3-axle motor home is in Class 4. Diesel
and gas are reasonable on the tollroad.
EASTBOUND NORTHEAST ON I-94.
WESTBOUND EXIT TOLLROAD KEEPING ON I-80 WEST.

INDIANA DUNES
Photo credit: Porter County Convention & Visitor Commission

EASTBOUND ALTERNATE ROUTE

   TO INDIANA DUNES: Exit on I-94 Northeast to Milepost 26/IN 49. About 18 miles. There is a Tourist
Information Center to the Southwest of this intersection. Then go North to US 12 to the Indiana Dunes National
Lakeshore and State Park. IN 49 South takes you back to I-80 at Milepost 31.
   INDIANA DUNES NATIONAL LAKESHORE: Drive through the park on IN 12. Stop at the Visitor Center
just 3 miles East of IN 49 at Kemil Road. Open from 8-6pm. The Dunes has an unusual ecosystem with sand
deposited by the constant Northwest winds. Dunes close to the shore shift with the winds. The largest dune
is Mount Baldy which is inching away from the lake. There are hiking trails to stretch your legs. Hike the "Old
Sauk Trail" near the Joseph Bailly Homestead that is part of the Indian Trail going from the Sauk Indian tribal
grounds in Western Illinois east to Detroit. Or hike the 2-mile "Bailly-Chellberg Trail" that goes by a 19th Century
farm of Swedish immigrants. There is swimming at West Beach, Central and Kemil Beaches.
   CAMPGROUND: INDIANA DUNES STATE PARK: Hiking, showers and lake swimming. Enquire locally
and call to be sure that there is space. In this high density area, campgrounds fill up fast. $5.50-$9.

EASTBOUND ALTERNATE ROUTE

   TO SOUTH BEND: North on I-94 to Michigan. Exit Michigan Milepost 2 to US 12 East. South on US 31
to the Indiana Tollroad at Milepost 72. If you have the time, want a campground and/or prefer rural roads to
the Tollroad, try this route. You could take in the Indiana Sand Dunes too. Check your map and read above.
FUEL: At the intersection of US 12 and US 31, on the NW corner there is a service station with diesel.
CAMPGROUNDS: "Michigan City CG": Private. Exit I-94 at Milepost 34 & go South on US 421 for one mile.
The campground is on the Left/East side. Don't go too fast or you'll miss it. Pool, woods, quiet.
   There is another campground off US 12 East of Galien. It's on Bakertown Road. No further information.
   FORT JOSEPH MUSEUM: In Niles, MI. Follow signs from US 12 & US 31. This 1691 French fort was a
main stop on almost every important trade route for 150 years. The museum is located in a Victorian Carriage
House. It displays a large collection of historical and Indian artifacts.

17 **WESTBOUND EXIT ONTO I-90:**

TO DOWNTOWN CHICAGO: Stay on the tollroad which becomes I-90 Northwest. You can then exit on 63rd Street. and visit the marvelous museums and art galleries in Chicago. Read Illinois Milepost 151 for descriptions of sights.

MILEPOST 22 FIRST SERVICE PLAZA: Amoco and Hardees.

23 **PORTAGE/IN 249:**
MOTELS: North to Motel 6*, Howard Johnson's, Lee's Inn.
BURNS INTERNATIONAL WATERWAY: North on US 20 & IN 149 for about 18 miles. Indiana'a only deep-water port. Tours by appointment.

31 **CHESTERTON/IN 49:** NO NEAR SERVICES!

WESTBOUND ALTERNATE ROUTE

TO INDIANA DUNES STATE PARK: North about 18 miles on IN 49. Read Milepost 16. Return to I-80 via I-94.
CAMPGROUND: "Sand Creek CG": Private. 3.6 miles. North on IN 49 to County Road 1050 North. Right/ East to County Road 350 East. Right/South on County Road 350 East. Pool, playground, campfires, trailer sites.
MEMORIAL OPERA HOUSE & OLD JAIL MUSEUM": 9 miles South on IN 49 to Valparaiso.
WILBOR H. CUMMINGS MUSEUM OF ELECTRONICS: 15 miles South on IN 49 to Valparaiso Technical Institute, IN 130. Electronic equipment from Edison to date. The "first" machines of Philco, Crosley, etc. From wonders to antiques.
BAUMS BRIDGE: 27 miles South on IN 49, past Kouts. Both the settlers and the Pottawatomi Indians paused here on their trips down the Kankakee River.
TASSINONG HISTORICAL SITE: 27 miles South to Baum's Bridge Road. The site of the oldest settlement in Northern Indiana, this was a French Mission and Trading Post from 1663.

39 **WESTVILLE/MICHIGAN CITY/US 421:** PURDUE UNIVERSITY. OUTLET STORES
FUEL/FOOD: Trucker City.
MOTELS: Trucker City. North to Norberts, Knights Inn.
CAMPGROUND: "Michigan City CG": Private. 3 miles. North on US 421. Pool, woods, quiet.

49 **LAPORTE/IN 39:** RADIO: 96 & 102.5 FM.
MOTEL: South to Cassidy Motel.
CAMPGROUNDS: "Cassidy Motel Inc": Private. South .5 mile on IN 39. No tents. Small. 16 foot width. Playground. $11-$13.
EASTBOUND CAMPGROUND: "Rolling Timbers": Private. Exit South to IN 2. East to intersection with US 20. Right for 3/4 mile on IN 2. Lake, fish. Pool, playground, campfires. To get back onto I-80: Continue East on IN 2 to US 31. North to I-80 at Milepost 72.
"Mini Mountain CG": Private. Further East on IN 2. Campfires, lake, pool, playground.
La Porte is "The Door" to nine lakes in the area. The town's industries produce everything from baby carriages to boilers, rubber items and wine.
HESTON MONASTIC GARDENS: 10245 North 215 East. Rhododendrons and azaleas bloom from May to Oct.
KINGSBURY STATE FISH AND WILDLIFE: 6 miles South on US 35. View wildlife in natural habitat. 7-4pm.
MILEPOST 56 SERVICE PLAZA: Arbys.
MILEPOST 62 TIME CHANGE! CENTRAL TIME/EASTERN TIME.
Some of the counties along I-80 DO NOT change time. They remain the same as Chicago/Central Time (in the summer at least).

72 NILES/SOUTH BEND/US 31:

FUEL: North to diesel. Speedway Truck Stop.

WESTBOUND CAMPGROUNDS: "Mini Mountain" and "Rolling Timbers". South on US 31 to West on IN 2. Read Milepost 49.

WESTBOUND ALTERNATE ROUTE

RURAL ROUTE TO INDIANA DUNES AND I-94: North on US 31 to US 12. West to I-94. South to I-80 at Milepost 16. Nice pastoral country in this slice of Michigan. I-94 is busy but usually moves well. Campgrounds on this route. You can also visit Indiana Sand Dunes off I-94. Read Milepost 16 for "Alternate Route to the Sand Dunes", and also "Alternate Route to South Bend".

77 SOUTH BEND/US 33: NOTRE DAME UNIVERSITY.

MALL: North & West 2 miles to Mall by I-80.

FOOD: South to Bill Knapps, Wendys. North to Bob Evans, Family Smorgasbord, Bennet's Smorgasbord.

"Old Country Buffet": 5540 Grape Road. Said to be good. South on US 33 to Left/East on Douglas to Grape.

TIPPECANOE PLACE: 620 West Washington. In the Studebaker "Castle", a magnificent building! South on US 33 to a Right/West on Washington. Lunches weekdays 11:30-2pm. Dinners Mon-Fri 5-10pm. Sat 5:30-11pm. Sun Brunch 9-2pm. (Adult $9.95. Child $5.95) Dinner 4-9pm. Dinners $13+. Enjoy a gourmet meal in gentile surroundings in this 40 room 1880 mansion. Walk through the elegantly furnished rooms, admiring the ornately carved staircase, and the 20 marble fireplaces. The Studebaker family supplied the wagons for the Civil War and for the Westward Migration before they started manufacturing automobiles.

MOTELS: North to Motel 6*, Signature Inn, Randalls, Knights Inn, Best Inns, Budgeteer, Days Inn, Stephens, Ramada, Holiday Inn.

NOTRE DAME UNIVERSITY: South on US 33 just a few blocks. Left onto the campus. Founded in 1842 by Fr. Edward Sorin as a mission school for the Potawatomies. The striking Administration Building has a great golden dome crowned with a statue of the Virgin Mary. There are superb murals of Christopher Columbus created by a Vatican artist during his 17 year contract. The **GROTTO OF LOURDES** is a replica of the one in France. **A LOG CHAPEL** represents the chapel built in 1830 by Fr Stephen Badin, who was the first Roman Catholic priest ordained in the United States. There is a 12-story granite mural on the wall of the **HESBURGH LIBRARY**. The **SNITE MUSEUM OF ART** has rare religious pieces as well as great European and American Art. There are student led tours of the campus Mon-Fri during the summer.

STUDEBAKER NATIONAL MUSEUM: 525 South Main Street. South on US 33/Main Street. Displays 100 Studebakers from 1852 to the present. Includes the horsedrawn and historic carriages such as the one in which President Lincoln rode to Ford's Theater. Mon-Fri 10-4:30pm. Sat 10-4pm. Sun noon-4pm. Adult $3. Senior $2, Child $1. Family $7.

NORTHERN INDIANA HISTORICAL SOCIETY MUSEUM: 112 South Lafayette Blvd. South on US 33. West on US 20. South on Lafayette. Pioneer artifacts showing the development of farming, trades, crafts and transportation. Tues-Fri 9-5pm. Donations.

POTAWATOMI ZOO: South on US 33. 1.5 mile East on Jefferson Blvd. .25 mile South on Greenlawn. Includes a learning center and a petting zoo. Daily 10-5pm. $2.

COPSHAHOLM: 808 West Washington. South on US 33. Right/West on Washington. Two blocks West of Tippecanoe Place. On Southwest corner. Estate and 38-room

COPSHAHOLM, OLIVER MANSION MUSEUM
Photo credit: Northern Indiana Historical Society

mansion built in 1895 by Joseph Doty Oliver, founder of Oliver Chilled Plow Co, manufacturer of farm implements. Furnishings from 17th-20th Century. On National Registry. Tues-Sat 10-5pm. Sun 12-5pm. Fee.

83 **MISHAWAKA/SOUTH BEND/IN 23:**   NO NEAR SERVICES!
CAMPGROUND: "KOA": Private. 2 miles North on IN 23. Turn Left at Hardees. Pool. Nearby: Mini-golf, horseback riding, outlet stores, cafes, mall, amusement park. (It is described as a" country setting".)
MILEPOST 90: SERVICE PLAZA: Big Boy and Yogurt.

92 **ELKHART/IN 19:** MALL. K-MART.
FUEL: Yoder's Truck Stop.
FOOD: North to Shoney's, Cracker Barrel. South to Bob Evans, MCL Cafeteria, Perkins.
MOTELS: North to Knights Inn, Diplomat, Econo*, Turnpike, Comfort, Shoney's. South to Super 8, Signature, Red Roof*, Days Inn, Elkhart, Weston.
CAMPGROUND: "Elkhart CG": Private. Good Sam. North .25 mile on IN 19 to County Road 4E. East .75 mile. Pool, playground.
ELKHART was a crossroads of Indian trails but now it is noted for its small industry powered by water from the St. Joseph and Elkhart Rivers. It's special products are its musical instruments. It produces 50 percent of the nation's band instruments.
MIDWEST MUSEUM OF AMERICAN ART: 429 South Main Street. 150 years of American art including Norman Rockwell, Grandma Moses and Alexander Calder. Tues-Fri 11-5pm. Weekends 1-4pm. Adult $1.50.
RUTHMERE MUSEUM: 302 East Beardsley Avenue. .5 mile Northeast on IN 19. A Beaux-Arts mansion built in 1908 by Beardsley, of Miles Laboratories, Inc. Graced with a wrap-around marble veranda it has restorations of silk and velvet wallcoverings and decorative ceilings, Tiffany lamps and china. Tours: April-Dec Tues-Fri at 11, 1 and 3pm. Wed at 7pm. Adult $2.
AMISH ACRES: South 20 miles on IN 19 to Nappanee and one mile West/Right. An historic farm on US 6. Tour the 12-room farmhouse, "Grossdaadi Haus", and outbuildings. Watch old skills of making rugs, soap, brooms, candles. Have a buggy ride down the lanes. Restaurant Barn has "Threshers' Dinner", family style. Tour: Adult $5.50.

101 **BRISTOL/IN 15:**
CAMPGROUNDS: "Eby's Pines": Private. South to IN 120. East 3 miles. Pool, playground. $11-$15. This is a 1,000 acre preserve & tree farm. Wildlife and forestry tours. Family Restaurant.
"Scenic Hills CG": Private. Good Sam. 5 miles. South on IN 15 to cross 120 on Pearl Street to a Left/East on Elkhart Road/CR 8. Pool.
BONNEYVILLE MILL COUNTY PARK: South on IN 15 to East 2 .5 miles on IN 120. .5 mile on County Road 131. On this 223 acre park you'll see one of the first water-powered gristmills with a turbine-type wheel. Built in 1832, it still grinds corn, wheat, buckwheat and rye. Picnicking, playground, trails. Milling is done every hour on the half hour, April-Sept. 9-8pm. Spring-Fall 9-7pm. Free.
This area of Indiana is the center of the travel trailer industry. Two factory tours:
KROPF REC VEHICLES: South 6 miles on IN 15. Cross US 20 for 1.5 miles. 8-4pm, free.
ELKHART TRAVELER: South on IN 15 to US 33. West 2 miles to Greene Road. North 1 block. 9-4pm. Free.
OLD BAG FACTORY: 12 miles South on IN 15. West on US 33. Right on Indiana Avenue. Watch potters, blacksmith, doll and toy makers, egg decorators, quilters, and carpenters at work creating their crafts.

107 **MIDDLEBURY/US 131 NORTH/IN 13 SOUTH:**
FOOD: "Das Dutchman Essenhouse": South on IN 13 to US 20. West to intersection of IN 16 & US 20. Order family style or from menu. Good family Style dinner, $10+. Excellent bakery to buy food to go plus big motel and large shop. You can climb the circular staircase up to the silo observation tower above the third floor of the restaurant.
MOTELS: North to Plaza. South to Bonnet, Das Dutchman.

> CAMPGROUND: "KOA": Private. South 1.5 miles on IN 13. Campfires, lake, pool, playground, fish. $13-$19.
>
> EASTBOUND CAMPGROUND: "Twin Mills Resort": Private. South 1 mile to IN 120. East 11 miles to Campground. Return to I-80 by continuing East to IN 9 and North to I-80 at Milepost 121. Read Milepost 121.

SIDETRIP TO SHIPSHEWANA

A MENNONITE TOWN WITH AMISH FARMS AROUND: EVERYTHING CLOSES ON SUNDAY! South to IN 120. East to IN 5. South to Shipshewana. Please do not stare, take pictures of, or be rude to these beautiful people who want to live in peace with God and man. There are craft shops, restaurants, B & B, antiques, hand-crafted furniture, and a fine arts gallery.

CRAFTERS' MARKETPLACE: Watch miniature wagons being crafted. Other artisans make furniture, brassware and stained glass designs.

SHIPSHEWANA AUCTION & FLEA MARKET: With 1,000 Vendor booths and 12 auctioneers. Horse Auction on Friday. Wednesday is antiques and miscellaneous. May-Oct Tues-Wed 5:30-7pm.

MENNO-HOF MENNONITE-AMISH VISITOR CENTER: South of Shipshewana in a huge barn-like structure. Walk through the history of the Mennonite and Amish people and their religion from 1525 to the present. Gain a new understanding of this martyred sect, and their quiet faith of peace and harmony. Mon-Sat 10-5pm. Donation.

KASE HOUSE: A cheese factory just West of Shipshewana on US 20. If you're there at the right time you can watch the cheese-making.

THE OLD HOMESTEAD: .5 mile South of town on IN 5. East on County Road 200 N. This is a working Amish and Mennonite farm with the original furnishings and machinery from the 19th Century. Includes Museum, gardens, petting barn. Tues-Wed and Fri-Sat 9 to 5pm. Adult $5. Buggy rides $3.

WESTBOUND ALTERNATE ROUTE

TO AVOID CHICAGO/GARY TRAFFIC: Take a Hi-liter and mark this route on your map. South on IN 13. West on IN 4 & then IN 119. South on IN 19 to Nappanee. West on US 6. South on IN 31. West on US 30 into Illinois. US 30 is a divided highway which connects with I-80 at Illinois Milepost 137. Half of this route is country road and there are stops. Therefore it is likely to take you longer than on I-80. The difference is that it is quiet farmland except for the Western end through Merrillville and Chicago Heights. You can make several variations of this route. It may delay you more if you're there at rush hour. You will pass Amish Acres, Milepost 92, gas stations, and at least one mall. Before making your decision ask a trucker for news of the Chicago traffic.

CAMPGROUNDS: "Playmor": Private. On US 6.

"Jellystone Park CG.": Private. On US 30 West of Plymouth.

"EZ CAMP": On US 30 West of Plymouth. Nice.

"KOA": Private. East of Wanatah. Near Hanna. NEAR I-80.

POTATO CREEK STATE PARK: Northwest of US 6 & US 31 about 10 miles. Fish, hike, lake swim, showers, cabins. $9.

BASS LAKE STATE BEACH: South of US 30 on IN 23 for 12.5 miles. Showers, playground, swim beach, park. $9.

121 HOWE/LAGRANGE/IN 9: HOWE MILITARY ACADEMY.

WESTBOUND EXIT FOR SHIPSHEWANA. Read Milepost 107.

FUEL: Martin diesel.

FOOD: North to Golden Corral.

MOTELS: North to Travel Inn, Green Briar.

CAMPGROUNDS: "Twin Mills Resort": Private. South 3 miles on IN 9 to IN 120. West 2 miles. Campfires, fish, boat, pool, playground. Miniature golf has fee. Pleasant. Return to I-80 traveling West on IN 120 to IN 13 & North to Milepost 107.

"Star Mill Falls": Private. 1.5 miles. South on IN 9 to County Road 700 N. Right/West on County Road 700 N. Pool.

"Green Valley CG": Private. North on IN 9 and MI 66 to Fawn River Road. Left/West 1.5 mile. Pool.

MILEPOST 126 SERVICE PLAZA: Popeye's Chicken 'n Bisquits, Dunkin' Donuts, Amoco.

144   MAJOR INTERCHANGE!
ANGOLA/I-69: NORTH TO LANSING, MI. SOUTH TO FT WAYNE, IN.

VALLEY OUTLET CENTER: I-80 & I-69. Southwest corner. 32 shops. Name brands and food. Open 7 days a week.

FUEL: '76 Truck Stop.

FOOD: Clay's Family Restaurant. POTAWATOMI INN AT POKAGON STATE PARK: Breakfast 7-10:30am. Lunch 11:30-2pm. Dinner 5-8pm. Inexpensive.

MOTELS: North to Redwood, Lake George. South to E & L Motel, Pokagon, Red Carpet, Potawatomi Inn ($46-$50 double. Call 219-833-1077. South 1 mile on I-69 or US 27 to 1 mile West).

CAMPGROUNDS: "Cook's Happy Acre": Private. South on I-69 to Milepost 148. East 500 feet on US 20 to County Road 300 W. South one mile. Campfires, pool.

"Fawn Forest CG": South on I-69 to Milepost 150. Northwest 2.5 miles on County Road 200 W. Campfires, lake, swim, boat.

POKAGON STATE PARK: (Pronounced Po KAY gun) South 1 mile on I-69 or US 27 to 1 mile West. Max 30 foot length. Pull throughs, showers, campfires, Lake James, fish, swim, boat, trails. Perfect setting! Many activities offered by the lodge and by the Rangers. $11.

"Yogi Bear's Jellystone Park": Private. 3 miles West on IN 120. .5 mile North on County Road 300 W. Families, pool, whirlpool, boats, playground, waterslide and Miniature golf.

ANGOLA: Once a hunting ground for the Potawatomi and Miami Indians, it was settled by emigrants from the Northeastern states. Its old public square became a trading place for Natives and farmers. They call Angola "101 Lake Country".

CORD-DUISSENBURG AUTO MUSEUM: South 25 miles on I-69 to Auburn. At Milepost 129 go East/Left, and follow signs. This is the original Auburn Auto Company's ornate Showroom with original decor and a fine collection of antique and collector's cars plus other displays. Adult $6. Senior $4. Family $15.

MILEPOST 146 SERVICE PLAZA: Hardees, Fried Chicken, Amoco.

MILEPOST 165 OHIO BORDER: NO EXIT.

EASTBOUND: SAY GOODBY TO THE HOOSIER STATE.

WESTBOUND: ASK FOR THE INDIANA TOLLROAD MAP AT THE TOLL PLAZA.

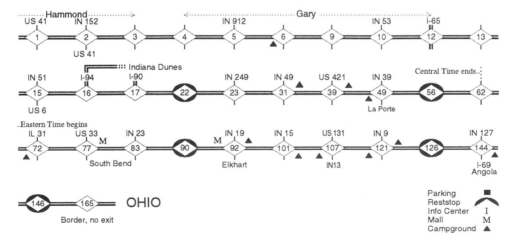

INDIANA MILEPOSTS
Rest Stops are Service Plazas

Ohio

The Buckeye State

Ohio was largely a forested state when Europeans first saw it. One of the more prolific trees popular with the natives was the "Buckeye Tree" which is in the chestnut family. They used the nut, which is larger than a chestnut and resembles the eye of a buck. With deer in abundance, the state acquired the designation of "Buckeye". Few Buckeye trees are left, but the state animal, the Eastern White Tail Deer, is so plentiful today and the highway kill so high that it was necessary to make the hunting season regulations more lenient. The state bird is the cardinal which to you Westerners means a bright red male, the female a rusty brown and both with thick bills and crests. The song is a distinctive loud sharp series of 5-7 notes. The state flower is the red carnation for Ohio's President McKinley who always wore one on his coat.

Ohio has 41,222 square miles and 10,847,115 people with many large cities heavily industrialized. Traveling old Highway 30 in the 1950's and 60's, heavy brown clouds of air pollution hung over the big cities like Toledo, Cleveland, Akron and Youngstown and left brown and black flecks on clothing and skin. Today the air is cleaner. Just South of this congested industrial area Ohio has beautiful countryside and prosperous farms. A postcard picture of Americana! Corn, hay, soybeans and wheat are leading crops, with vineyards and orchards around the shores of Lake Erie. Farm animals produce the meat for the tables and the dairy industry serves the cities with milk and prize cheeses like Liederkranz, Camembert and Swiss.

The northern part of Ohio is flat, carved by the ancient Wisconsin Drift ice sheet, with its elevation equal to Lake Erie. Ohio's lowest point is 433 feet on the Ohio River. Southern Ohio has rich glacial soil in the West and rocky terrain in the East. Besides the profitable farms, Ohio also has natural gas, coal, limestone, salt, gypsum, sandstone, clay and gravel.

Ohio's capital is Columbus at its center. They sing a song about the name of the state, "Round on the ends and high in the middle, that's O-HI-O". Shipping keeps Ohio busy with 9 Lake Erie ports serving the St. Lawrence Seaway. Amazingly the Ohio River towboats move over 80 million tons of goods a year, twice that of the Panama Canal and three times that of the St. Lawrence Seaway.

OHIO HISTORY

The dense Appalachian woodlands, twisting rivers and steep passes of Pennsylvania were a barrier against early settlement in Ohio. But some rugged and daring men followed the Native paths across the Appalachian Plateau to trade in Ohio. George Croghan was a trader from the Susquehanna valley who had several trading posts in Ohio by 1744 and supplied them via the Warriors' Paths. A few settlers came from New York via Lake Erie and stopped along Ohio's lakeshores.

The pass through the Cumberland Gap was breeched in 1770 and the Americans started moving into Kentucky and up to the Ohio River. They traveled up and down the river and began settling on the North shore in Southern Ohio, especially between Marietta and Cincinnati, Ohio. The British tried for the next 30 years to keep the settlers South of the Ohio River. It was like trying to stem the ocean tides. Although settlers were supposed to stay on the Southbank of the Ohio, and the natives were supposed to be safe from

Carnation

attack to the North, some settlers began floating down the Ohio River shooting them on sight. In Colonial America, the present states of Ohio, Indiana and Illinois were known as the Northwest Territories.

The Miamis, Potawatomies, Shawnees, and Delawares were farmers, traders, and hunters, descendants of the mound builders. The Shawnee and Delaware were displaced on the Delaware and Susquehanna Rivers by white men. Some of the Delawares who had come across the Shamokin trail from Pennsylvania had settled in Gnadenhutten, Ohio (South of Akron) under the arm of the Moravian Christian Church. In 1782, during the Revolutionary War, there were boundary disputes between Pennsylvania and Virginia. Some 300 angry Pennsylvanians who lost their lands in the dispute, came West to Ohio to find new lands. They were welcomed and entertained by the Moravian Delawares for 3 days. On the 4th the whites entered the church during services and slaughtered all 96 of the Delaware men, women and children.

Up to this time, the Ohio Delawares had remained neutral away from the intrigues of the British, the raids of the Shawnees in Southern Ohio, and the skirmishes of the Northern Miamis and Wyandots. Now they joined their brothers and the ensuing raids were awful. Colonel William Crawford was sent from the American Ft. Pitt/Pittsburgh in 1782 to destroy the Sandusky Indian Villages. On the Upper Sandusky they met Delawares and Shawnees who put them in retreat.

General Clark rallied his troops and raided Piqua and Chillicothe in Southern Ohio and this became the last campaign of the Revolutionary War in the Territories. Virginia had withdrawn all its troops from Kaskaskia, IL in 1781, so now the Americans had but scant possession of the Northwest Territories as the war ended. But even as the above battles were being fought, peace negotiations were underway. What the Americans could not gain by force, they won by diplomacy. The French had helped the Colonists (Lafayette being the most famous of the French officers who came) but they wanted to give North of the Ohio to the British and everything South of the Cumberland to Spain. So the American negotiators ignored their French allies and pursued a separate treaty with England. They gained all the land to the Mississippi without any decisive battles being fought there. So we have John Jay, John Adams and Benjamin Franklin to thank for these Northwest States. A monument to negotiations beyond war!

In the terms of the Treaty of Paris of 1783 the U.S. could not prevent the loyalists from "recovering their lawful debts" but some of the states were confiscating loyalist property. The fledgling government did not have the power over the states to enforce the treaty provisions. The British also wanted the Americans to pay pre-Revolution debts to British merchants. Therefore the British remained in their forts at Detroit, Niagara and Mackinac. They wanted to retain the trade in the Northwest and there was the possibility that the bickering States would not hold together. So British Agents manipulated the tribes to form a confederation to stand fast on their Ohio River boundary. But the tribes could not come to a complete agreement that this was worth the chance of being annihilated.

In 1785 Congress needed more land and more money to repay their war debts. They had discharged their soldiers with "Certificates of Indebtedness" with which they were to purchase public lands, and East Coast Americans whose land had been destroyed by the British needed to be relocated. So Congress passed an Ordinance to survey the Ohio lands, divide and sell it. But first they had to get the land away from the Native tribes. Several treaties were signed under duress that took Ohio from the tribes, but none held. When the tribes got home from a Treaty Session minus the firewater, they reneged. Indian lands were shrinking much too fast and game was becoming scarce. By the spring of 1786 the Indians were so incensed with the Americans that they started raiding frontier settlements all over Ohio. The British supplied them with arms.

In 1786 George Rogers Clark took 1200 men North from Ft. Steuben, Kentucky to destroy Maumee villages on the upper Maumee and the Wabash. But at the mouth of Vermillion Creek his men mutinied and returned South without one battle. The frontiersmen would fight to protect their own settlements but would not join together to fight any Northern war. In 1790 General Harmar went North to the Maumee and walked into an ambush. Then in 1791 General St Clair took 3,000 troops up the Maumee but they camped haphazardly with no security and were infiltrated by the Natives during the night. Shawnee rushed the Americans at sunrise and soon had them surrounded slaughtering them as General St Clair fled to safety. President Washington discharged St Clair and appointed General Anthony Wayne. The Tribes now carried the war to all the Middle and Northern Ohio settlements and the Americans fled South to Cincinnati and Marietta, Ohio.

Now with 2 Indian victories, in 1792 the British took the opportunity to call the tribes to a conference at the Maumee River Rapids to again persuade them to demand the Ohio River boundary. At the same time they sent George Hammond to Thomas Jefferson, Secretary of State, to demand that American settlement stop at the Ohio River in return for the British Forts and peace with the Indians. Jefferson wouldn't be budged and quoted the 1783 Treaty to them.

THE BATTLE OF FALLEN TIMBERS

President Washington felt that war was the only alternative so in the fall of 1793 he ordered General Anthony Wayne North to the attack. Wayne knew better than to have a fall campaign, so he built Ft. Greenville in Southern Indiana and wintered there training his troops. The British built a new Ft. Miami on the Maumee River (at Toledo) to protect their fort at Detroit. Lord Dorchester, expecting war with France, told the Tribal Chiefs that when war came they would fight side by side. Now with British backing and a chance of success, the united tribes prepared for war. Two thousand confident Natives waited near Ft. Miami.

Gen Wayne started North in 1794 stopping half-way to build Ft. Recovery on Ohio's Western border. The tribes attacked him there but he was able to fight them off advancing up the Au Glaize River to the Maumee. (South of Gate 2 Milepost 13.) He set up a fortification there and sent a false message through the forest that he would attack. The Tribes had chosen a defensible spot near Ft. Miami where a mass of fallen trees gave them some protection. (Five miles South of I-80 Gate 4, Milepost 60). Led by "Blue Jacket" a powerful Shawnee orator, (a Virginian adoped by the Shawnee) the warriors prepared for the coming battle by fasting. Wayne, knowing this custom, delayed for 3 days. When Wayne's troops did not arrive, 500 warriors left for Ft. Miami to get food. When Wayne attacked from two sides the Tribes held for awhile and then fled to Ft. Miami where the British locked the gates against them. In 2 hours the "Battle of Fallen Timbers" was over. Wayne then proceeded to destroy all the Native villages and all the crops for 10 miles either side of the Maumee River. Actually only 50 Natives were killed in the battle, but since the British had not helped them, they knew that their situation was hopeless. They could not turn back the tide of white men and would have to move Westward again.

Wayne strengthened Ft. Defiance (South of Gate 3, Milepost 35), built a new Fort Wayne in Indiana and in 1795 dictated the terms of the Tribal land concessions at the Treaty of Greenville of 1794. The Natives lost 2/3rds of Ohio including the Southern half of the state, all land East of Cleveland, plus 6 specific tracts within the Indian lands including that which is Chicago today. For all of this Wayne's terms amounted to one cent for each 6 acres. A windfall for Wayne, a pittance for the Natives! And some was never paid!

The British capitulated and gave up forts Miami, Detroit, and Mackinac in 1796 as the result of John Jay's Treaty . (He was Chief Justice of the US sent as special envoy to Great Britain.) The treaty retained freedom of passage for British traders and equal taxes with the Americans. With the British gone and the Indians demoralized, the Northwest was finally at peace. The Americans were overjoyed and settlers poured into Ohio. They came from Southern Ohio, Kentucky and Virginia. Some came from Pennsylvania via Forbes Road. Many came on flatboats down the Ohio. These boats only cost $30-$40 to build and could be guided by a single oarsman.

The Connecticut Land Company purchased the "Western Preserve" in Northeastern Ohio. Their agent, Moses Cleaveland, surveyed and named the city "Cleveland". One part of the Western Preserve was set aside for the people on the East Coast whose properties had been destroyed in the Revolution. Settlers came via New York and Lake Erie. In 1796 Congress authorized one of its first "highways", Zane's Trace, the first road through Ohio which joined Wheeling, West Virginia and Limestone/Maysville, Ohio. It became one of the main routes taken by emigrants.

The new settlers didn't like old Governor St Clair of the Northwest Territories nor the seat of government in far off Vincennes, Indiana. They pressured him into following the required procedure and having a census in 1798 to prove that they had over 5,000 males in Ohio and could select a legislature. Ohio selected William Henry Harrison, an army officer from the Indian Wars, as their representative to Congress.

Harrison's first push was for a new land law wherein 320 acre plots could be sold on the Frontier for $2 an acre, and men could buy it with credit! Heretofore, public land was sold on the East Coast only in large expensive parcels that were purchased by speculators and corporations.

Next Harrison was able to pass a bill forming the boundary for the new State of Ohio and another that authorized a convention to choose statehood. Harrison was appointed the governor of the new Indiana Territory to the West. In 1802 Ohioans voted for immediate admission to the U.S. and became our 17th state. Their constitution eliminated the requirement of property ownership as a prerequisite to voting. All of this in just 8 years from the Treaty of Greenville! Ten years later Ohio had a population of 250,000 and the whole Greenville Treaty area was as crowded as were all the older states.

BATTLE OF LAKE ERIE

In the War of 1812 against the British and the Native Americans, Ohio had its part. The 28 year old Oliver Hazard Perry was put in charge of the Lake Erie fleet. At Presque Isle, near Erie, Pennsylvania, 5 ships were under construction from materials that were brought from Philadelphia overland via Ft. Pitt. In August 1813 the British had taken their 6 blockading ships to Ft. Malden near Detroit, preparing for land invasion by Wm Harrison's 4500 man infantry. During their absence Perry slipped out 5 more ships from the Naval yards at Black Rock/

Buffalo and waited at Put-in-bay on Bass Island, Lake Erie. The British fleet was trapped! They accepted the challenge and attacked. The bloody Battle of Lake Erie lasted 3 hours, defeated the British, but caused 80 percent casualties of the crew of Perry's Flagship. Perry sent his famous message, scribbled on an envelope, up the Sandusky River to Harrison: "We have met the enemy and they are ours!" This victory forced the British to evacuate Ft. Malden and brought about Harrison's land victory at the ensuing Battle of the Thames. You can visit "Perry's Victory and International Peace Memorial" at Put-in-Bay, Gate 6, Milepost 92. You can also see a restoration of the ship "Niagara" at Presque Isle, North of Cleveland near Erie, PA.

OHIO MILEPOSTS

OHIO EMERGENCY HOTLINE: 1-800-525-5555.
OHIO HIGHWAY CONDITIONS: 614-466-2660.
RADIO WEATHER AND NEWS: 1100 & 1220 AM.
TRAVEL INFORMATION LINE: 1-800-BUC-KEYE. Ask about special events and accommodations.
OHIO STATE PARK LODGE AND CABIN RESERVATIONS: 800-282-7275.

OHIO CAMPGROUNDS: Call ahead. Ohio's I-80 is a high density population area and campgrounds are crowded with full-season visitors who park their RVs for the summer to stay there on weekends.

OHIO INTERCHANGES/GATES: Ohio numbers them in sequence. The Gate Number is to the Left, and the Milepost Number to the Right.

SERVICE PLAZAS: These are listed as "REST AREAS" on the map and have BP gas & diesel.

GATE: MILEPOST:

1　　　　　　　**WESTGATE TERMINAL: NORTH TO US 20.**
　　　　　　　　　MILEPOST 11: Crossing the St. Joseph River used by early fur traders. The first Fort Miami was built by La Salle at the mouth of this river.

2　　**13**　　**BRYAN-MONTPELIER INTERCHANGE/OH 15:** RADIO: 101.5 FM.
　　　　　　　MOTEL: Rainbow, Holiday Inn.
　　　　　　　CAMPGROUNDS: "Lazy River": Private. 2.5 miles. North on OH 15. West on OH 20A. Swim, boat, fish, playground.
　　　　　　　　"Shady Shores CG": Private. From US 20 & OH 49. North 3 miles on OH 49 to County Road R. East .7 mi to County Road 475. South one mile. Swim, fish, boat, playground.

EASTBOUND ALTERNATE ROUTE

TO THE SAUDER FARM AND CRAFT VILLAGE: About 20 miles. South of I-80 via Alt US 20 to OH 66. South 2 miles. Return to I-80 by going East 9 miles to Gate 3. It's 1860 here with a village of restored buildings and craftsmen dressed in period costumes. Watch the potter, the blacksmith, weaver, glassblower, broommaker, and barrel-makers. You'll see a farmhouse, barn and village museum with antique items, and a collection of early flush toilets. April-Oct Mon-Sat 9:30-5pm. Sun PM. Adult $7. Senior $6.50. Child $3.50.

FOOD: "Die Alt Sceier Restaurant" (The Old Barn): At the Gate of the Sauder Farm. Has Mennonite food served family style. 11-8pm. Sun Buffet 11-2pm.

EASTBOUND ALTERNATE ROUTE

TO DEFIANCE: South 25 miles on OH 15. Return to I-80 via US 24 & OH 108 to Gate 3. Check your map. General Anthony Wayne rebuilt Fort Defiance here in 1794 after the battle of Fallen Timbers. There are old earthworks in the Defiance City Park. Also Gen Wm Henry Harrison's Ft. Winchester built in 1812, Johnny Appleseed's nursery from 1811, the 1650 French Mission and the birthplace of the famous chief, Pontiac.

AUGLAIZE VILLAGE: 2 miles West of Defiance off US 24 on Krouse Road. A living history site where costumed villagers will guide you through 17 pioneer era buildings (1860-1920). Includes museums of historical, natural history, and archeological interest. June-Aug Sat-Sun 11-4pm. Adult $2. Student $1. Child free.

MILEPOST 21 PLAZAS & TOURIST INFORMATION CENTERS: Hardees. Westbound Trailer facilities with dump station, without showers. If you are going into any of the Ohio cities like Toledo, Cleveland, or Akron get a good city map here.

Also ask for specific directions to the sights you want to visit.

3   35   WAUSEON INTERCHANGE/ OH 108:
MOTELS: Straight ahead to Best Western. South to Arrowhead.
CAMPGROUND: "Sunny's Shady Recreation Area": Private. 5.5 miles. North on OH 108. East on County Road M. North on County Road 13. Swim, fish, playground.

WESTBOUND ALTERNATE ROUTE

TO SAUDER FARM: South on OH 108. West on OH 2. One mile South. Follow signs. Return to I-80 via Alt US 20 West and Gate 2. Read Gate 2, Milepost 13 for descriptions.

WESTBOUND ALTERNATE ROUTE

TO DEFIANCE: South on OH 108 & US 24 to Defiance. Return to I-80 via OH 15 and Gate 2. Read Gate 2, Milepost 13 for descriptions.

MILEPOST 49 PLAZAS: Charlie's General Store.

3A   53   TOLEDO AIRPORT/SWANTON:

4   60   MAUMEE-TOLEDO INTERCHANGE/US 20/I-475/OH 23:
UNIVERSITY OF TOLEDO. REYNOLDS PLAZA to the North.
FOOD: North on US 20 .5 mile to Bombay Bicycle Club and Bob Evans.
MOTELS: North to Toledo Budget, Ramada, Motel 6*. South to Country Hearth, Cross Country.
BATTLE OF FALLEN TIMBERS: Two miles South of I-80. Anthony Wayne defeated the Indians by brilliant moves. Read "Ohio History". Get directions from Toll Gate. The town of Maumee was founded in 1817. The Miami and Erie Canal with its old canal path that was finished in mid-Century, can be seen in "Side Cut Metropark" with the locks that joined the Maumee River and the canal.
OHIO BASEBALL HALL OF FAME: From Maumee: 1 mile North of US 24 on Key Street, Maumee in the "Lucas County Recreation Center". The artifacts of Cy Young, Satchel Paige and Pete Rose. Apr-Sept Mon-Fri 10-8pm. Sat-Sun noon-8pm. Rest of year Mon-Fri 10-5pm. Adult $1. Senior $.75. Child $.50.
WOLCOTT HOUSE MUSEUM COMPLEX: 1031 River Road, Maumee. Get local directions. James and Mary Wolcott's Federal-style 1836 home. Period furnishings, Indian artifacts. Also a log cabin, church, train station and saltbox farmhouse. March-Dec Tues-Sun 1-4pm. Adult $2. Child $1.
FORT MEIGS: 5 miles South on US 20. Right on OH 65 near Perrysburg. One mile Southwest of OH 25, on a bluff above the rapids of the Maumee River. Built in 1813 by Gen Wm Henry Harrison, seven blockhouses contain War of 1812 artifacts. Summers: Wed-Sat 8:30-5pm. Sun PMs. Adult $3. Senior $2.40. Child $1.
TOLEDO, LAKE ERIE AND WESTERN RAILWAY BLUEBIRD PASSENGER TRAIN: South on OH 65 to Waterville. It's a 20-mile round trip to Grand Rapids on a restored train. The view from the Maumee River Bridge is spectacular. May-Oct weekends at 12:30pm and 2:30pm. June-Sept an additional 4:30pm trip. Adult $6.50. Child $3.50.

SIDETRIP NORTH TO TOLEDO

About 10 miles North. TOLEDO is one of our largest fresh-water ports, third on the great lakes. It is at the mouth of the Maumee River, one of the largest that flows into lake Erie. This was Maumee Indian land that La Salle called "Miami". Toledo is an oil refining and glass center. It was first built as Ft. Miami/Maumee by the British to protect their Ft. Detroit. Then it was Ft. Industry in 1794 after Gen. Anthony Wayne defeated the Tribes at Fallen Timbers. There is a "Fallen Timbers" monument off Jerome Road. The "Toledo War" of 1835, a boundary dispute with Michigan, gave Toledo to Ohio and the Northern Peninsula to Michigan. Toledo was the beginning of the first railroad built West of the Alleghenies, "The Erie and Kalamazoo". They call Toledo the

"Glass Capital of the World". Check the back of your Ohio map for a city map.

TOLEDO MUSEUM OF ART: Monroe Street & Scotwood Avenue. US 20 North to OH 120. East on OH 120 and then use your Toledo map on the back of the Ohio Map. Art from Egypt to modern including Van Gogh, Rubens, El Greco, Rembrandt, Matisse, plus the world's most extensive glass collection. Tues-Sat 9-5pm. Sun 1-5pm. Free.

TOLEDO ZOOLOGICAL PARK: 3 miles Southwest of Toledo on OH 25. Get local directions. Five hundred species of animals, reptiles, fish, birds. Includes a petting zoo. April-Sept daily 10-5pm. Rest of year 10-4pm. Adult $2.50. Senior & Child $1. Parking $2.

TOLEDO BOTANICAL GARDENS: 5403 Elmer Drive. Get local directions. Azaleas, rhododendrons, roses, herbs, children's garden. April-Sept daily 8-8pm. Rest of year 8-6pm. Free.

LIBBY GLASS FACTORY OUTLET: 1205 Buckeye Street, Toledo. Off I-280 between Michigan and Central. Get local directions.

FOOD: "OLD COUNTRY BUFFET": 5301 Airport Highway. Airport Square Shopping Center. Get local directions.

> **MILEPOST 63** CROSSING THE MAUMEE RIVER FLOWING TOWARD LAKE ERIE.

4A   65   I-75 TO TOLEDO/PERRYSBURG:
> **MILEPOST 67** CHRYSLER PLANT TO NORTH.

5   72   STONYRIDGE-TOLEDO INTERCHANGE/I-280: UNIVERSITY OF TOLEDO.
BOWLING GREEN STATE UNIVERSITY: East on US 20. South on OH 105.
FUEL: South to '76 Truck Stop. Petro gas.
FOOD: TA Restaurant, McDonalds.
MOTELS: North to Charter House Inn*, Metro Inn. Lodge at Maumee Bay State Park. South to Hampton Inn & Red Roof Inn*.
CAMPGROUNDS: "Stony Ridge KOA": Private. 2 miles. South on OH 420. West on OH 163. South on Luckey Road. Swim, playground. $16-$23.
> **MAUMEE BAY STATE PARK:** As much as 20 miles North to Lake Erie. Scottish Links Golf Course, indoor & outdoor pools, racketballl, tennis, full-time recreation staff. Reserve ahead and get local directions.
> **MILEPOST 77 PLAZAS:** Hardees. Eastbound & Westbound have trailer facilities. Dump station, No showers.

6   92   FREMONT-PORT CLINTON INTERCHANGE/OH 53:
CROSSING THE SANDUSKY RIVER.
FUEL: Shell.
MOTEL: North to Best Western.
CAMPGROUNDS: "Riverfront Marina": Private. 1.5 mile. North on OH 53. Fishing, tents and trailers.
> "East Harbor State Park": Perhaps 23 miles North on OH 53. Check before you go to be sure there is room for you. Get local directions.
> "Wooded Acres": Private. 6 miles. South on OH 53. West on US 20. North on County Road 106. Swim, fish, playground.
> "Young's Camping": Private. Four miles. South on OH 53. Right on North Street. Right on Dickinson Street. Trailers only.

SIDE TRIP NORTH TO PUT-IN-BAY

North 16 miles on OH 53 to Port Clinton Jet Express ($9 per person one-way) to South Bass Island & Put-In-Bay on Lake Erie. Or further North 24 miles on OH 53 to Catawba Island and the auto ferry ($15 a car + 2 persons. Every 1/2 hour.). Bicycles are for rent. Fishing there. This is a whole day's trip! Check your map and ask locally which is best. This is a favorite vacation spot for Ohioans. Make reservations for the ferry. There is a long wait summers. Better yet take your bike across and ride it around the island.

PERRY'S VICTORY AND INTERNATIONAL PEACE MEMORIAL: At Put-in-Bay. This commemorates the "Battle of Lake Erie". Commodore Oliver Hazard Perry commanded the American Fleet during the War of

1812. This included the "Lawrence", the "Niagara" and 7 others. In a famous battle on Sept 10, 1813 he defeated the British fleet and forced them to surrender. The 352 foot high memorial is of pink Massachusetts granite. Stroll the promenade at the top and view Detroit on a clear day. National Park guides tell you the story of the Battle of Lake Erie. Daily 9-6pm. $1.

CRYSTAL CAVE: Under the Heineman Winery at Put-In-Bay. Said to have the largest strontium sulfate crystals in the world.

SIDETRIP SOUTH TO FREMONT

South 3 miles on OH 53 to Fremont. Ft. Stephenson was built here in 1813. Major George Croghan with only 150 American soldiers defeated British General Proctor with his 400 trained soldiers and 300 Indians.

HAYES PRESIDENTIAL CENTER: Hayes and Buckland Ave, Fremont. Follow the blue "Presidential Center" signs. Spiegel Grove is the estate of President Rutherford Hayes. The 6 iron gates came from the White House. This was the first Presidential Library in the U.S. Mon-Sat 9-5pm. Sun 12-5pm. Adult $3. Senior $2.50. Child $1. The Victorian mansion is $3 more.

MILEPOST 99 PLAZAS: Rax Restaurants.

7   118   SANDUSKY-NORWALK INTERCHANGE/US 250: RADIO: 1450 AM.
LAKE ERIE FACTORY OUTLET: North on US 250 & Left into the complex. RV parking is in the rear. Food available.
MOTELS: Days Inn, Super 8. South to Homestead Inn.
CAMPGROUND: "Holiday Trav-l-park": Private. 1/4 mile. North on US 250. Swim, playground.
          "Le Mar Lake Park": Private. 7 miles. South on US 250. Right on Whittlesey. Swim, fish, playground.

MILAN

Settled by emigrants from Connecticut in early 1800's. It is on a bluff over the Huron River. They built a canal and were growing well by 1840's as a wheat-shipping center. The town would not grant a right-of-way to the "Lake Shore & Michigan Southern Railroad", so the railroad went through Norwalk instead, and Milan declined. Then the area became deforested causing the river to become unnavigable. By 1870 the canal was abandoned.

MILAN GENERAL STORE: 44 Front Street. Museum/store with yesterday's merchandize hanging from walls and ceiling.

FOOD: "Homestead Inn Restaurant": On US 250. Victorian mansion with fine eating specializing in prime rib and seafood. Eat amidst gracious early furnishings. Prices "moderate". Reservations suggested.

EDISON BIRTHPLACE MUSEUM: 9 Edison Drive, Milan. Thomas A. Edison lived his first 7 years in this small brick restored cottage. It has a museum of Edisonia, including early models of famous inventions. Edison held 1093 American patents. Summers Tues-Sat 10-5pm. Feb-May Tues-Sun 1-5pm. The last tour is at 4:30pm. Adult $2. Child $1.

MILAN HISTORICAL MUSEUM: 10 Edison Drive. 2 miles South of Gate 7, Milepost 118. Several buildings including a general store, the Robert Sayles House built in 1843, Arts building, collections of pressed glass, dolls, art, china and historical items. The glass collection is nationally known. June-Aug Tues-Sun 10-5pm. Spring & Fall 1-5pm. Donations.

NORWALK: Four miles South of Milan on OH 13. New Englanders came here given land deeded them for property that was destroyed during the Revolutionary War. They called it "The Firelands". Some of the original homes still stand.

FIRELANDS MUSEUM: 4 Case Ave, Norwalk. Behind the library. 1835 federal-style house. Many pioneer and Indian artifacts. June-Sept Tues-Sun Noon to 5pm. Spring & Fall Sat-Sun 1-5pm. Adult $2. Senior $1.50. Child $1.

BELLEVUE: 11 miles West of Norwalk on US 20. An agricultural area famous for cherries has a Cherry Festival in late June.

MAD RIVER RAILROAD MUSEUM: 253 Southwest Street, Bellevue. 100 year old railroad station. June-Sept daily 1-5pm. Rest of year weekends only. Donations.

HISTORIC LYME VILLAGE: 2 miles East of Bellevue on OH 113. Early 1800 buildings with a Victorian mansion, log house, barn, museum, craft shops. Need 2 hours. June-Aug Tues-Sun 9-5pm. May & Sept Sun 1-5pm. Adult $4. Seniorr & Child $2.50.

  NATIONAL MUSEUM OF THE POSTMARK COLLECTORS CLUB: Tours Tues-Sun 1-5pm. $4.

  SENECA CAVERNS: South of Bellevue, off of OH 269. You can get to it from either exit 6 or 7. This is a natural cave formed when an earthquake split the earth. You must walk down 4 levels on primitive steps. Good walkers only!

SIDETRIP NORTH TO SANDUSKY

  North on US 250 for 10 miles. First explored by La Salle in 1679, then by George Croghan in 1760 but not settled until 1816. It has a natural harbor on Sandusky Bay and is a major coal-shipping port.

  WYANDOT COUNTY MUSEUM: 130 South 7th Street. Victorian home and furnishings. Also artifacts on Wyandot Indians who lived here in a Christian mission from 1817 to 1842 when the government forced them to go West. The old mission church is still here. Tues-Sun 1-4:30pm.

  FIRELANDS WINERY: 917 Bardshar Road, Sandusky. US 6 off US 2. Tours of winery and wine tasting, playground, herb garden, picnicking.

  CEDAR POINT: 3 miles North of Sandusky. This is a giant amusement park on 364 acres, with 55 rides,

CEDAR POINT ROLLER-COASTER, CEDAR POINT AMUSEMENT PARK
Photo credit: Dan Feicht, Cedar Point Amusement Park

wild animal shows, sea animal show, a 10-slide waterslide complex, beach, hotels and picnicking. They boast of the tallest and fastest wooden roller-coaster in the world. Opens at 9am. $21.95, includes rides. Juniors, $11.95. Lodging at "Hotel Breakers". RV's at "Camper Village".

  CAMPGROUND: "Bayshore Estates CG": 3/4 mile from Cedar Point on US 6. No further info.

  MILEPOST 132: Crossing the Vermilion River. Red clay, not red river.

  MILEPOST 139 PLAZAS: Burger King, Mrs. Field's Cookies & Yogurt. Eastbound & Westbound trailer facilities with dump stations, no showers.

8A 141 LORAIN COUNTY WEST INTERCHANGE/I-90 East/OH 2:

    MOTELS: South to Coachman, Dial, Best Western, Journey.

    CAMPGROUND: "Sommer's Mobile Home": Private. 3 miles. Northeast on I-90. East on OH 2. South on OH 57. Right on Midway Blvd. Swim, playground.

    OBERLIN COLLEGE: South about 10 miles on OH 58. Directions at Toll Gate. Founded in 1833 this is the world's first coeducational college and the first to also admit blacks. An Oberlin College graduate discovered the electrolytic process for making aluminum, and later founded Alcoa.

    ALLEN MEMORIAL ART MUSEUM: At Oberlin College, art from early Egyptians to present. Tues-Fri, 10-5pm.

SIDETRIP NORTHWEST TO VERMILION

Northwest via US 2 to Vermilion on the lake. This town is at the mouth of the Vermilion River. The Ottawa

Tribes used the clay to paint their bodies red. White settlers arrived in 1808. Today this is a fishing village and resort town. The old downtown area has restored buildings.

GREAT LAKES HISTORICAL SOCIETY MUSEUM: 480 Main Street, Vermilion. This is a Nautical Museum with ship models, paintings, and a simulated pilot house. April-Dec daily 10-5pm. Rest of year Sat-Sun 10-5pm. Adult $2. Senior $1.50. Child $.75.

8   145   LORAIN-ELYRIA INTERCHANGE/OH 57: OBERLIN COLLEGE.
MALL: May Co, Higbys, Sears, Ames.
FUEL: BP. Goodyear Truck Alignment.
FOOD: Bob Evans, Pizza, Wendys, Mountain Jack's Prime Rib. Campbell's Buffet, Burger King, 1 mile North.
MOTELS: North to Holiday Inn, Camelot, Knights Inn, Days Inn.
CASCADE PARK: North Broad Street, Elyria. Ask for directions at Toll Gate. Picnic area, waterfalls, caves, trails and rock formations.
INDIAN RIDGE MUSEUM: 2.5 miles west of Elyria on OH 113 then .5 mile South. Prehistoric Indian and Civil War artifacts.

9A   151   NORTH RIDGEVILLE-CLEVELAND INTERCHANGE/I-480 EAST:
RADIO: WEATHER & NEWS: 1100 AM & 1220 AM.
Read Gate 11, Milepost 173 for Cleveland sights.

9   152   NORTH OLMSTED-CLEVELAND INTERCHANGE/OH 10:
Read Gate 11, Milepost 173 for Cleveland sights.
MOTELS: North to Travelers, Best Budget Inn, Super 8.
CAMPGROUND: "Crystal Springs": Private. One mile South on OH 10. Left on Bagley to beyond bridge. Swim, fish, boat, playground. Tents & trailers.

10   162   STRONGSVILLE-CLEVELAND INTERCHANGE/I-71/US 42:
Read Gate 11, Milepost 173 for Cleveland sights.
MOTELS: South to Brushwood, Holiday Inn. North to Lake, Budget Host*, Summit, Cross Country Inn, Red Roof* (East on US 82), Motel 6* (North on 171 to Bagley Road, Exit 235. West one mile to Engle Road, South to motel.)
BALDWIN-WALLACE COLLEGE: Take I-71 North about 6 miles to Berea. Directions at Toll Gate. Replicas of Independence Hall and Liberty Bell. BACH LIBRARY in Merner-Pfeiffer Hall has displays on Johann Sebastian Bach. Bach Festival in late May.
HINCKLEY: About 10 miles. South off I-71, exit 226. You hear about it every March 15th when the turkey vultures return from their winter in the Smoky Mountains, as dependable as the swallows of Capistrano. If you're there between March 15th and the following Sunday you can participate in the largest birdwalk in the nation accompanied by naturalists.
MILEPOST 170 PLAZAS: McDonalds.

11   173   AKRON/CLEVELAND INTERCHANGE/I-77 VIA OH 21:
MOTEL: Knights Inn, North on I-77 to exit 149 B.
CAMPGROUND: "Dover Lake Park ": Private. Six miles North on OH 21 to Snowville Road. Turn right and follow signs. Swim, fish, playground.
HALE FARM AND VILLAGE: 2686 Oakhill Road. I-77 about 7 miles South to exit 143, Peninsula. Directions at toll gate, follow signs. This is Western Reserve Historical Society's restored village and farm of 1840 where you'll watch old skills of candlemaking, woodworking, weaving, cooking, etc. Tues-Sat 10-5pm. Sun noon to 5pm. Adult $6. Child $4.
CUYUHOGA VALLEY RAILROAD: About 7 miles South of I-80. Ride from Hale Farm to Quaker Square in Akron on Saturdays from June to October.

SIDETRIP TO CLEVELAND

North on OH 21 and West to I-77. Then North into greater Cleveland. YOU MUST HAVE A CITY MAP TO GET AROUND. From its first arrivals in 1796 Cleveland has grown to be one of the 10 largest industrial cities in the U.S. It got its first big impetus when the Erie Canal was completed in the 1820's. Then it built its own Ohio Canal of which Cleveland was its terminus in 1832. Rockefeller and Standard Oil started the major industrialization in 1870. Now it is headquarters of BP America/Standard Oil. Take I-77 to East on I-90. East on Chester, Exit 173 B to the sights below:

CASE WESTERN RESERVE UNIVERSITY:

CLEVELAND HEALTH EDUCATION MUSEUM: 8911 Euclid Ave/US 20. Chester to Right on East 89th. On Left. Shows how the human body functions with such displays as the Talking Woman and the Giant Tooth. Mon-Fri 9-4:30pm. Sat 10-5pm. Adult $3.50. Senior & Child $2.

CLEVELAND MUSEUM OF ART: 11150 East Blvd. in Wade Park. From Chester, Left on Euclid, Left on

CLEVELAND MUSEUM of ART
Photo credit: Mark Schwarts/Cleveland Convention & Visitors Bureau

East Blvd., Left into Wade Park. On Right. Displays art from early Egyptian through the Impressionists to modern art; includes Goya, Renoir, Van Gogh, El Greco, Monet, Picasso, Segal. Tues-Fri 10-5:45pm.

GARDEN CENTER OF GREATER CLEVELAND: 11030 East Boulevard. On Left just past Wade Oval.

WESTERN RESERVE HISTORICAL SOCIETY: 10825 East Blvd, Cleveland. From the Art Museum, 3-4 blocks. Crawford Auto-Aviation Museum has more than 200 vehicles, featuring the car from 1895 to 1982. Includes the Curtiss "pusher" of 1911 that was one of the first planes used on the waterfront. Observe restoration in progress and walk through an early 1900 cobblestoned street. Also clothing, furnishings and story of industrialization. Tues-Sat 10-5pm. Adult $4. Senior & Child $2.

CLEVELAND MUSEUM OF NATURAL HISTORY: Wade Oval in University Circle. From East Blvd., continue around circle to museum on Left. Prehistoric life, early man, gems, natural history including birds, fish and animals. Live animal programs on the weekends, planetarium. Mon-Sat 10-5pm. Adult $3.75. Senior & Child $1.75.

HOWARD DITTRICK MUSEUM OF HISTORICAL MEDICINE: 11000 Euclid Avenue. From Euclid go past East Blvd. Past Adelbert on the Right.

U.S.S. COD: A WW II submarine on the waterfront. I-77 to North on I-90, North on East 9th Street to pier.

CLEVELAND METROPARKS ZOO: 3900 Brookside Park Drive. Off I-71, Exit South on Fulton, Left into park. Over 3100 birds, mammals, fishes. Mon-Sat 9-5pm. Adult $3.50. Child $1.50.

CLEVELAND ARCADE: From I-90 take Euclid West. Cross 9th Street, past East 4th Blvd. On Right. A 19th Century exposition hall with a domed skylight has been transformed into a shopping village. If you happen to be in the Cleveland area the third weekend in Aug, you'll want to experience the **SLAVIC VILLAGE HARVEST FESTIVAL** with its famous Kielbasa cookoff.

MILEPOST 177: Crossing the Cuyahoga River. This was a boundary line for several of the Indian "Treaties".

12   180   AKRON INTERCHANGE/OH 8:
MOTELS: North to Regency, Motel 6*, Holiday.
CAMPGROUND: "Tamsin Park Camp": Private. 3.5 miles. South on OH 8. Swim, fish, playground. Tents/trailers.
DOVER LAKE PARK: West Highland Road, Northfield. North on OH 8 about 10 miles to Northfield. Get local directions. Large waterride complex in 240 acres of woods. A ski lift takes you to the top of the highest. Summers only. Admission charge.
NORTHFIELD HARNESS RACING: 10705 Northfield Road. About 10 miles North. Closed Sundays. Admission charge.

SIDETRIP SOUTH TO AKRON

South on OH 8 about 15 miles. The rubber capital: Mohawk, Goodyear, Goodrich, Firestone, and General. Plastics and rubber research are the objects of the "Firestone and Goodyear Laboratories". Akron's Institute of Polymer Science does original research and is famous for its work in molecular chemistry.

GOODYEAR WORLD OF RUBBER: 1201 East Market Street, Akron. Shows history and process of rubber from the rubber plantation to tires. Mon-Fri 8:30-4:30pm. Guided tour at 1pm. Free.

HOWER HOUSE: At Fir Hill & Forge Streets. On University of Akron campus. 28-room 1871 Victorian mansion 2nd Empire Italianate style with octagonal rooms, black walnut woodwork, oak parquet floors and furnishings from around the world. Wed, Fri & Sun 12:30-3:30pm. Adult $3. Senior & Child $2.

PERKINS MANSION: Copley Road and South Portage Path, Akron. Built in 1837 in Greek Revival style with period pieces. Also a home across the street where John Brown, the abolitionist lived for 2 years. Tues-Sun 1-5pm. Adult $2. Senior & Child $1.50.

QUAKER SQUARE: 120 East Mill Street, Akron. The old factory of Quaker Oats Company. Shops, hotel, murals, historical displays. Mon-Sat 11-11pm. Free.

STAN HYWET HALL & GARDENS: 714 North Portage Path, Akron. Tudor Revival 65-room house with lovely oak, walnut and sandalwood paneling. Also stained-glass, molded ceilings, leaded windows. Home of the Sieberling family. Fifty minute guided tour but you'll need more time to see the rest. Gardens and Shakespeare on the Terrace the end of July. Tues-Sat 10-4pm. Sun 1-4pm. Need 2-3 hours. Adult $5. Senior $4.50. Child $2.

FOOD IN AKRON:
Bob Evans in Cuyahoga Falls on OH 8 at Howe Road.
Country Manor in Cuyahoga Falls at 1886 State Road.
Strickland's Frozen Custard: 1809 Triplett Blvd. Akronites say its the best with a different flavor every few days.
Parasson's Italian Restaurant: 3983 Darrow Road, Stowe. Known for its budget-priced family meals. Also in Akron and in Barberton to the South.
Old Country Buffet: Chapel Hill Square. 1930 Buchholzer Blvd.

PRO FOOTBALL HALL OF FAME: About 35 miles further South of Akron to Canton. 2121 George Halas Dr, Canton. Near the Fawcett Stadium.

13   187   STREETSBORO INTERCHANGE/I-480/OH 14/OH 43:
KENT STATE UNIVERSITY.
MOTELS: South to Palms. South on OH 43 to Days Inn. North to Comfort Inn.
CAMPGROUNDS: "Woodside Lake ": Private. 4.5 miles. North on I-480. East on Frost Road. Swim, fish, playground. Tents and trailers.
"Valleyview Lake ": Private. Good Sam. 3 miles. South on OH 14. Right on OH 43. Right on Seasons Road. Left on Ferguson Road. Swim, boat, fish, playground. Tents and trailers.
"Mar-Lynn Lake": Private. 3 miles. South on OH 14. Sharp Right on OH 303. Swim, fish, playground. Tents OK.
GEAUGA LAKE AMUSEMENT PARK: Ask at the gate for directions to OH 43 North about 12 miles. Roller coasters, other rides, picnic area and water slides.

SEAWORLD: North about 12 miles on OH 43. Sea animal shows by trained whales, seals and otters. Great day with the kids! Daily 9-6. Adult $16. Child $12.

MILEPOST 197 PLAZAS: Popeyes & Dunkin' Donuts. Eastbound has trailer facilities but no showers.

14   209   WARREN INTERCHANGE/OH 5:   WEST PIKE PLAZA.

MOTEL: North to Budget Lodge.

CAMPGROUNDS: "Ridge Ranch": Private. 4 miles. Good Sam. West on OH 5. North on OH 534. West on OH 82. Southwest on OH 303. Swim, fish, playground. Tents OK.

"Pin-Oak Acres": Private. 5 miles. West on OH 5. North on Newton Falls-Braceville Road. East on Eagle Road. Tents OK.

"West Branch State Park": Public. About 6 miles South on OH 5. Check locally.

GARRETTS MILL: 8148 Main Street, Garrettsville. Northwest 10-12 miles on OH 82. The 1804 mill with 1850 French milling stones, grinds 1,000 pounds of flour per hour. Guided tours and home-made ice cream. Mon-Sat 10-8pm. Admission to the mill is free but the tours cost $2.50.

NELSON KENNEDY LEDGES STATE PARK: 12-14 miles Northwest on OH 305. Get directions from Tollbooth. Unusual geologic formations, picnicking. Daily 6-sunset. Free.

WARREN: Steel manufacturing town 5-7 miles East of I-80.

BUICK-OLDSMOBILE-CADILLAC GROUP LORDSTOWN COMPLEX: East of I-80. Ask at tollgate for directions. Plant tours Mon-Fri at 12 noon. Mon-Thurs at 6:30pm. Must have reservations. Free.

15   219   M A J O R   I N T E R C H A N G E !

NILES-YOUNGSTOWN INTERCHANGE:

EASTBOUND I-80 EXITS OHIO TURNPIKE: FOLLOW THE SIGNS.

EASTBOUND TO PHILADELPHIA, STAY ON THE OHIO TURNPIKE TO PENNSYLVANIA TURNPIKE/I-76.

WESTBOUND I-80 ENTERS THE OHIO TURNPIKE.

MILEPOST 221 : CROSSING MEANDER CREEK RESERVOIR.

223   NILES/OH 46:

FUEL: South to '76 Auto/Truck Plaza, BP, Speedway & Fuel Mart.

FOOD: South to Perkins, Dutch Pantry, McDonalds, Arbys. North to Bob Evans, Burger King, Country Kitchen.

MOTELS: North to Quality Inn, Budget Luxury. South to Knights Inn, Best Western, Super 8 Motel, Econo lodge*.

CAMPGROUND: "Ridge Lake Camp": North one mile on OH 46 to Depot Street. West .25 mile to Edwards Street. South .2 mile. Swim, campfire, playground.

NATIONAL MCKINLEY BIRTHPLACE MEMORIAL: North 5 miles on OH 46 to Niles at 40 North Main Street, Niles. A library, a museum and a marble monument to this 25th president.

224   M A J O R   I N T E R C H A N G E !

CANFIELD/OH 11 SOUTH: NO NEAR SERVICES!

WESTBOUND STAY IN RIGHT LANE FOR I-80 AND THE OHIO TURNPIKE.

226   SOUTHWEST TO I-680, BELTWAY THROUGH YOUNGSTOWN: NO NEAR SERVICES!

MILL CREEK PARK: 816 Glenwood Avenue, Youngstown. Take I-680

South. Exit on Mahoning Avenue & go South. Park with trails, 6-mile long gorge, falls, lakes, gardens of roses, views, gristmill, historic museum, picnicking, nature center, reptiles. Daily dawn-dusk. Free.

PEACOCK HAVEN EDUCATIONAL MUSEUM: 771 Old Furnace Road, Youngstown. South side of Mill Creek Park. Peacocks done in various art media. Mon-Sat noon-8:30pm. By appointment. $3.

226A   SALT SPRINGS ROAD:
FUEL: South to Petro Pilot Truck Stop
FOOD: South to Iron Skillet at Petro, Arbys

227   STATE STREET, GIRARD/YOUNGSTOWN/US 422:
YOUNGSTOWN STATE UNIVERSITY: South on US 422.
FUEL: North to BP, Amoco, Shell.
FOOD: North to Burger King. North 4 miles to Eastwood Mall. Enroute are Nichollinis, Albertinis, Bombay Bicycle Club, Dennys, Red Lobster, Aloha (Chinese) and Bob Evans at the Mall.

YOUNGSTOWN: As with Cleveland, Youngstown was named by its surveyor, John Young in 1797. This part of Ohio belonged to Connecticut at the time. As with other industrial towns, it didn't "take off" until the first industry, a smelter, was established, in 1802. Youngstown is the 4th largest processor of pig iron and steel in the U.S.

BUTLER INSTITUTE OF AMERICAN ART: 524 Wick Avenue, Youngstown. South on US 422 to Wick. North on Wick. American art from colonial days through modern. Remington, West, Copley, Gottlieb, Homer, Bierstadt, Warhol, Eakins, Sheeler and Cassatt. Tues-Sat 11-4pm. Free.

THE ARMS MUSEUM: 648 Wick Avenue, Youngstown. Historical Society Museum in the "Greystones" home of Wilford Arms. Lovely period furnishings on the first floor. Lower level has pioneer implements, utensils, relics, and a gun collection. Second Floor has the history of the county seen through the people who worked and lived here.

228   OH 11 NORTH: NO NEAR SERVICES!

229   BELMONT AVENUE, YOUNGSTOWN/OH 193:
FUEL: North to Mobile, Amoco.
FOOD: South on OH 193 to Bob Evans, McDonald's, Pizza Hut, 2.5 miles South to Ambrosio's.
MOTELS: South to Econo Lodge*. North to Motel 6*, Ramada Inn, Comfort Inn, Days Inn, Holiday Inn Metroplex, Howard Johnson.

234   SHARON/HUBBARD/OH 7/OH 62:
FUEL: North to Shell, Goodyear, Truck World.
FOOD: North to Arbys, McDonalds, Truck World Restaurant.
MOTEL: Motel/Restaurant.
CAMPGROUNDS: "Lorel's Lake CG": 6486 Chestnut Ridge Road, Hubbard. South on OH 7. No further information.

"Homestead": 1436 Brookfield Road. North 2 miles on OH 7. Pool, playground.

MILEPOST 236 OHIO REST AREA: WESTBOUND TOURIST IN-FORMATION CENTER. Welcome to Ohio! Manned welcome center. Stop here to get all the maps and brochures you'll need in Ohio. If you're exiting to any city, get those city maps now plus more specific directions to the sights.

237 **PENNSYLVANIA BORDER:** ELEVATION: 500 FEET.

EASTBOUND: Say "Goodby" to flatlands! Prepare for the wonderful Appalachian Plateau.

WESTBOUND: Welcome to the farms and cities of Ohio. Get off the Tollroad at least once, see some of the museums, art galleries, and historical sights, and experience some of Ohio's pastoral countryside.

OHIO I-80 MILEPOSTS
Rest Areas are Plazas

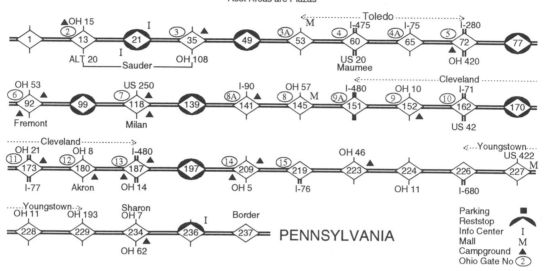

AERIAL VIEW of CEDAR POINT, CEDAR AMUSEMENT PARK
Photo credit: Dan Feicht, Cedar Point Amusement Park

Pennsylvania

The Keystone State

In the original 13 colonies, Pennsylvania was centered between the New England States (New York & North), and the Southern States (Maryland & South). With the Continental Congress meeting in Philadelphia, Pennsylvania was the "Keystone" to the fledgling United States.

Pennsylvania's I-80 has been designated as "The Keystone Shortway" by the Legislature. Completed in 1970, it took 12 years to construct its 313 miles. It follows some of the early Indian Paths through the notches of the Appalachians in almost a straight line across the state. Pennsylvania has a population of 11,881,643 in 45,136 square miles. The state flower is the Mountain Laurel, a large shrub that with the rhododendron grows very high and thick and was a barrier to travel along the Indian trails. The state tree is the hemlock that used to dominate the virgin forests along with the white pine, and provided the tannic acid for the leather industry in the early years.

The Appalachian Range covers almost 75 percent of Pennsylvania with the Western half distinctly separated into the Appalachian Plateau. With the Allegheny River draining the far Western side of the state, this area is often referred to as the Allegheny Mountains. Throughout the Appalachians the tortuous rivers have carved deeply, forming narrow valleys and leaving a series of ridges running from Southwest to Northeast in an arc across the state. In the West you begin climbing from flat Ohio at 500 feet up onto the Plateau as you proceed Eastward into Pennsylvania. From Snowshoe to Milesburg you'll travel DOWN over the Allegheny Front off the plateau into Bald Eagle Valley where US 220, the Appalachian Thruway, lines the Eastern terminus of the Plateau. Passes over the Plateau range from 1600 feet to 2250 feet which may not seem high to Westerners, but you're often climbing 1,000-1,200 feet in just a few miles. The Laurel Ridge Southeast of Pittsburgh is the highest ridge in Pennsylvania with Mount Davis, just South of there, the highest point at 3213 feet. You can't travel more than a few miles in most of Pennsylvania without climbing over yet another ridge to the next valley.

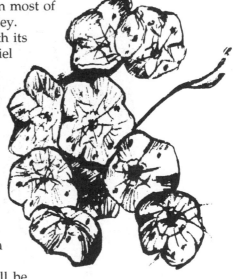

The Appalachian Plateau was a barrier to early settlement with its dense forests, twisting rivers, wicked winters and high passes. Daniel Boone, though born in Pennsylvania had to go South to the Cumberland Gap in Virginia to find his way West. Even after the highways were paved, travel in Pennsylvania was very slow until 1940 when the Pennsylvania Turnpike, the first modern tollroad, was built across the Southern part of the state. All the other roads were so windy, narrow and crowded that in 1960 with the inevitable 5 slow trucks in front, it could take 12 hours to go 350 miles. I-80 cutting straight across the state in 1970 was therefore a tremendous boon to travelers.

I-80 has its own mini Continental Divide near Clearfield, Milepost 111, with a pass at 2250. The rivers to the West flow westward into the Allegheny and Monongahalia Rivers, the Ohio, the Mississippi and the Gulf of Mexico. The rivers East of this pass flow into the Susquehana to the Chesapeake Bay and the Atlantic Ocean.

East of Milesburg and Bald Eagle Valley, Milepost 157, you'll be traveling over a different kind of mountainous terrain known as the Ridge and Valley area. Look at your map and you'll recognize the arc of ridges defined by the roads running up the valleys either side of them. This area is of the same origin

Mountain Laurel

as the Appalachian Plateau, but it was lifted and tilted vertically and then the soft material eroded away to leave rocky ridges and deep valleys.

Eastbound you are about to travel over one of the most beautiful stretches of I-80, remaining in the mountains all the way across the state. Construction was an engineering achievement bridging deep gorges and cutting through the rocky hills. As you cross those high bridges, see if you can see the river far below. The Highway Department frosted this prize with Crown Vetch (a pink-flowering ground cover), between the lanes and up the banks. Enjoy this highway in the spring and summer with its forever greenness and the masses of pink and white laurel and rhododendrons, white and yellow daisies, golden rod and giant orange and yellow day lilies. Then enjoy it again in September and October with the flaming reds, oranges and yellows of the hardwood trees. Vermont brags about her fall colors, but Pennsylvania surpasses all. Cottontail rabbits, groundhogs, turtles, deer and birds love this natural environment. Even black bears and flocks of turkeys are often seen. Watch for deer! A hit will damage your front end and possibly send you out of control. Pennsylvania has never solved the problem of the deer trails that still cross the highways. The "pick-up count" of the road-kill is 45,000 deer a year, so the Fish and Game Department estimate the total number of deer actually hit is closer to 100,000 a year! Another caution is for the slippery, icy winter roads at below-zero temperatures. This area often registers as the coldest in the nation. Traveling Eastward you'll cross over the bituminous (soft) coal beds of the Plateau, then the limestone and iron ore of the ridge and valley area, and the rich anthracite (hard) coal beds near Wilkes Barre.

Pennsylvania has many firsts to its credit including the first subscription library started by Benjamin Franklin and the first state to require motorists to drive on the right side of the road. The first hard-surfaced turnpike was built in 1795 and reached from Philadelphia to Lancaster, and the first tuneled super-highway in the U.S. was the Pennsylvania Turnpike. Pennsylvania became our second member state in the infant United States when it ratified the Constitution on December 12, 1787.

PENNSYLVANIA HISTORY

Before Europeans came to America, the Eastern valleys along the Delaware River were settled by 10,000 Lenni Lenape Natives who had migrated here from East of the Mississippi. The British named the bay, the river and the Natives, "Delaware", after Sir Thomas West, the third Lord De La War, the first Governor of Virginia. Susquehannocks were along the Susquehanna River, while Shawnee and Nanicoke also peopled the state. The Appalachians were covered with dense forests with trees up to 6-7 feet in diameter and 100-200 feet tall. They were white pine, hemlock, and white and red oak. With close underbrush of shrubs including thorny blackberry, wild roses, high laurel and rhododendrons they comprised a dense impenetrable forest. Over the centuries the Indians had developed certain "Paths"/trails that traveled up the valleys and sought the easiest crossings of the Appalachians.

The Iroquois had come down from New York State and conquered the Delawares and the Susquehannocks before the white man settled here. Shamokin was the most important Indian town in Pennsylvania as it was at the intersection of the Northern and Western Indian Paths and the Lower Susquehanna Canoe Trail. (Sunbury, PA.) The West and the North Branches of the Susquehanna were too dangerous for canoes, so only the paths were used through there. The chief Iroquois ruler to oversee the Pennsylvania tribes was stationed at Shamokin. Other tribes sought refuge under the arm of the Iroquois as had the Shawnee and the Nanticoke.

The Great Shamokin Path, reached from the broad Susquehanna Valley at Shamokin (Sunbury, Milepost 212), up the West Branch of the Susquehanna to Big Island (Lock Haven, Milepost 178). Then on to Bald Eagle Creek (Milesburg, Milepost 157), and Marsh Creek, and up the mountain to Snowshoe (Milepost 147). Here it crossed Moshannon Creek and went across country to the Susquehanna again at Chinklacamoose (Clearfield, Milepost 120). The Path followed the river to Curwensville, and up the mountain by Anderson Creek Gorge for 3 miles. It continued over the hills to the Big Spring near Luthersburg, down Stump Creek to Mahoning Creek and Kittanning. From 1730-1756 Kittanning was the largest Native settlement West of Shamokin. This was the intersection of the Canoe Trail down the Allegheny River to the Ohio.

The Appalachian Plateau between Bald Eagle Valley and Kittanning was not settled by even the tribes until late in history. It lacked sun in its deep valleys, had only thin soil, bitter cold winters and deep snows. Tribes hunted and passed through, but did not stay. The Karthaus/Quehanna and the Black Moshannon areas were considered sacred lands where Warriors could hunt, purify themselves and commune with the Great Spirit. These are our recreation areas today with extensive back-packing trails!

When Henry Hudson sailed into Delaware Bay in 1609, he claimed the land for the Dutch and they established trading posts. But a group of Swedes and Finns settled on Tinicum Island in 1643 and became the first settlers of Pennsylvania. Dutch troops under Governor Peter Stuyvesant from New Amsterdam/New York captured the area in 1655 but then the British Duke of York seized the land from the Dutch in 1664.

But it was the famous Quaker, William Penn, who initiated the real settlement of Pennsylvania. He received a charter from the British Crown in 1681 in payment for the crown's debt to his father, Admiral Penn, and created a refuge of freedom of religion, and peace with the Indians. William Penn called his land "Sylvania" (woods) but the King added the "Penn" in honor of the service of Admiral Penn. One of William Penn's first acts was to meet with the Delawares and the Susquehannock tribes at Shackamaxon/Philadelphia and purchase the land from the tribes. (Voltaire said it was "the only treaty never sworn to and never broken".) A month later Penn had established a representative government and made everyone, including the recently conquered Finns and Swedes, citizens. His honest and friendly dealings kept peace with the Natives until 1737.

Philadelphia became the center of government and of commerce. To this land of guaranteed freedom came first the Quakers, then the German religious groups, the Amish, Mennonites, Moravians, and the Dunkards who settled the broad Susquehanna Valley and turned it into rich farmland. The sturdy Scotch and Irish came too late for the rich bottom land so they pushed the frontier from the Susquehanna up the Juniata River and onto the plateaus and narrow valleys. You'll notice that the farms are on TOP of the plateaus where they receive more sunshine.

Some Delawares had used the Shamokin Path in 1720 when a group migrated Westward to Ohio. When William Penn's son cheated the Delawares of their land with the "Walking Purchase Treaty" of 1737, Milepost 309, the Delawares came West. They had towns at Big Island Milepost 178, Muncy Milepost 210, and Bald Eagle's Nest Milepost 157.

The British "Purchase of 1754" caused great anger among the Iroquois and the Delaware. They felt that the land "sold" was North only as far as the Juniata River. However the British claimed the land up the West Branch of the Susquehanna. This was sacred land to the Indians and could NOT EVER be sold. The result was the Indian participation with the French in the French & Indian War 1754-1763.

In 1753-4 the French Governor of Canada in order to hold on to the lucrative fur trade and keep the American settlers out, had built several forts in Western Pennsylvania. The first was "Presqu Isle" on Lake Erie, then Fort LeBoeuf/Waterford on French Creek, Fort Machault/Franklin, Milepost 30, where French Creek enters the Allegheny, and Fort Duquesne/Pittsburgh at the forks of the Ohio. On the Pennsylvania Frontier the British built their forts along the Susquehanna and Juniata Rivers including Fort Augusta/Sunbury, Milepost 212, Fort Granville/Lewistown, and the most western one was Fort Reed/Big Island/Lock Haven, Milepost 178. The Ridges between the two lines of forts, where the Shamoken Path passed and I-80 lies today, were the frontier.

Animosities between the French and the British increased. Twice young George Washington had been sent to Ft. Duquesne to discourage the French, but he was routed. The third time a larger army under General Braddock tried to take the fort but they were defeated and the General was killed. But Lucky George escaped with holes in his coat.

The Tribes in these Northwest woods joined the French to keep the British/American settlers out, and Western Pennsylvania became a very dangerous place to be. In 1758 British Gen. John Forbes and George Washington led 1700 Regulars and 5,000 Colonials against Duquesne, conquered it and renamed it Ft. Pitt. They also built Forbes Road from Raystown/Bedford to Ft. Pitt (along the old Raystown Indian Path) to transport troops and materials more easily. This was the first road over the Appalachian Plateau. In 1760 they captured Ft. Machault, Milepost 30, and built Ft. Venango, in its place. Subsequent battles in Quebec and Montreal ended in defeat of the French in 1763.

However, peace was short lived. That same year an Ottawa prophet, Abnaki, issued an ultimatum to all the tribes: "I give you warning, that if you suffer the Englishman to swell in your midst, their diseases and their poisons shall destroy you...and you shall die". Pontiac, an Ottawa chief, took up the challenge and formed a confederation of most of the Northern tribes, including the Delawares and the Shawnees. In May 1763 he led one group on a strike of the old fort at Detroit while the other tribes struck the other forts. In six weeks they took nine of the ten British Forts. Pontiac lost 80 warriors to the British 2,000.

Later, when the Indians were defeated, the British issued a Proclamation banning American expansion west of the Appalachians. They wanted to reserve the fur trade for themselves. But the veterans of the French and Indian War had been promised lands to the west by the colonial assemblies. Also many wealthy Americans including George Washington and Benjamin Franklin had large sums invested in Western land speculation. So the British backed off and allowed Westward settlement to continue.

In 1772 the Ohio Delawares had invited a group of 240 Moravians, German Missionaries, and their converted Delawares plus 70 oxen and horses, to travel west via the Shamokin Path and live in Ohio. They were from South of Wyalusing on the North Branch of the Susquehanna. Their land title was disputed between Connecticut and the Iroquois nation so they had to move west. Bishop Ettwein, their leader and recorder, routes them to Moravia, PA. just south of New Castle, land of the Kuskuskees. This might have been called "Ohio" at the time since it was West of the Appalachians. One group of Moravians ended up in Gnadenhutten, Ohio.

Settlers now began moving westward over the ridges and valley area and over the Allegheny Front. Lumbering began along the West Branch of the Susquehanna at Williamsport and Lock Haven in 1773. Logs of Virgin white pine were cut and floated down the Susquehanna.

When the problems between the British and the American revolutionaries erupted into war, Pennsylvanians were divided. Their money was invested in British goods so they could not easily wean themselves away from the British. Then in 1778 British Major John Butler led his "Butler's Rangers" including loyalists and Senecas South to the Wyoming Valley on the East Branch of the Susquehanna, Milepost 259. The resulting "Wyoming Massacre" sent settlers from all along the Susquehanna fleeing Eastward. They called this "The Great Runaway". Now support for the Revolutionaries grew. It was not until after the Revolutionary War was won that settlers came back West and pushed further up the Susquehanna, into the West Branch area and into the mountains transversed by I-80 today.

It was difficult for settlers to find and retain a parcel of land in the early Colonial Period and in the first years of the new nation, because even the government land was only sold in large sections called "Ranges" with the sales taking place in the Eastern cities. Wealthy speculators who were able to purchase it often held onto it for a long time to get a better price. The availability of land determined "where" the settlers could go. When the lands were finally surveyed and sold, there were often disputes as to who actually owned the land. A poor settler often purchased land from one "owner" only to have another claim the land. He would either be evicted or have to pay the 2nd time. This situation continued until the Land Act of 1800. Thereafter land was sold on credit at the frontier in 320 acre plots.

Pennsylvanians were firm about freedom and in 1780 they decreed that all children born in Pennsylvania were free. The Quakers were especially active before and during the Civil War, helping slaves escape from the south via the "Underground Railroad". Pennsylvania bought a portion of land on Lake Erie from New York in order to have a port. They built 3,000 miles of turnpikes, then canals and finally railroads. The capital moved from York to Lancaster and then to Harrisburg.

After the Revolutionary War the lumber industry along the Susquehanna grew, more settlers came and towns like Lock Haven and Williamsport were laid out. The virgin white pine was valuable for ships' spars and masts, bridges, homes, barns and factories. Lumber barons bought large tracts of virgin forests all up the West Branch subcontracting the harvesting of the pine to experienced woodsmen. They built a boom in Lock Haven to stop and sort the floating logs. Lumber barons prospered and built massive mansions in the two towns. Completion of the Pennsylvania Canal in 1834 made log floating easier. In 1860 Pennsylvania was the greatest producer of lumber in the United States. There were 13 mills in Lock Haven alone yet Williamsport tripled Lock Haven's production with 300 million board feet of lumber. In 25 years the white pine was gone. The forests were so stripped that whole areas were denuded and streambeds were destroyed. In 1865 the floods began. The flood of 1889 wiped out the log boom and the Pennsylvania Canal.

There was a second era of lumbering with logging railroads when they harvested the virgin hemlock and hardwood. Bark was removed from the hemlocks and taken to tanneries where tannin was extracted and added to large vats of water where hides were soaked to process into leather. Fine furniture was made from the hardwoods. Many forest fires raged through the logging debris destroying the forest floor's organic material that had taken centuries to accumulate. The result was barren desolation in the former woods, plus erosion.

By 1950 evergreens were rare except for the replanting of White Pines by the C.C.C's. The Appalachian forest was now second growth hardwood, tall, thin saplings about 6-12" in diameter. Forty years later the trees are bigger now but it's still largely a hardwood forest.

After the Civil War there was a tremendous growth in industry and many European immigrants arrived to find work and purchase land. Coal was discovered here at the turn of the century. This brought starving European miners to Pennsylvania to the flourishing coal and iron industries. Mill and mine owners took advantage of them and these new workers soon felt the inequities between the haves and the have-nots. Miners and factory workers were maimed and killed in unsafe workplaces. The labor movement had its foundation in Pennsylvania where many bloody battles were fought. Strikers picketing peacefully for safer working conditions and better pay were faced with armed hired thugs, "Pinkerton Men". Men were killed and workers' shacks were burned. Working men and women today are indebted to these strong people who formed the early unions to stand for human rights.

PENNSYLVANIA MILEPOSTS

PENNSYLVANIA EMERGENCY: 911
ROAD CONDITIONS: 717-783-5599
PENNSYLVANIA TOURISM INFORMATION: 1-800-VISIT-PA

Exits are numbered in sequence like Ohio's. Pennsylvania has just one manned Welcome Center on I-80 and it is on the Eastbound lane just inside the Pennsylvania Border. It has 9 other rest areas with modern facilities and 4 with parking/picnicking only.

EXITS: MILEPOSTS:

MILEPOST 1 EASTBOUND WELCOME CENTER: Open year round 8-5pm. May-Sept 8-6pm. Pennsylvania's only manned welcome center on I-80. Get your Pennsylvania maps, brochures, road conditions, and your accommodation information here.

1   5   SHARON/FARRELL/HERMITAGE/NEWCASTLE/PA 18/PA 60:
FUEL: North to Sunoco.
FOOD: North to "Seafood Express Restaurant": 110 Connelly Blvd, Sharon. Reservations suggested: 412-981-6150. Choose from 3 sections: "Quaker Steak and Lube": an old service station with a 1937 Chevy still on the lube rack of the dining room. "Tully's" has ribs and a salad bar with homemade potato chips. The "Seafood Express" has gourmet dining.
"Tara": North on PA 18 to junction with PA 258. An 1854 Greek revival style country Inn decorated with antiques and art work. Tour guides are in costume. Mon-Sat 10-3pm. Sun noon-3pm. $5. Also has 3 restaurants.
MOTELS: North to Comfort Inn, Ramada, Royal (junction of PA 18 & US 62), Collins (On US 62, .75 mile East of PA 18).
AVENUE OF FLAGS: Hillcrest Memorial Park, Hermitage. Go North on PA 18 to Hermitage. Over 400 American flags line this street as a memorial to the Iranian Hostages. Free.
KRAYNAK'S SANTA'S CHRISTMAS LANE AND EASTER BUNNY LANE: North on PA 18, West .5 mile on US 62. Decorated trees for Christmas and Easter, 175 animated characters, silk flowers and a greenhouse. Sept 4-Dec 24. Feb 15-April 30. Mon-Sat 9-9pm. Sun 10-6pm.
BAVARIAN FUN FEST: For 9 days in July-Aug. North on PA 18 to Sharon. Ethnic food, music, crafts, dance with 1600 performers. Sharon started as a mill in 1802 and celebrates its ethnic heritage.

2   16   MERCER/US 19: WESTMINSTER COLLEGE. STATE POLICE.
FUEL: North to BP, John's Fuel, Citgo Tire & Service.
FOOD: North to McDonalds, Guiseppe's Italian, Iron Bridge Inn.
MOTELS: McGoffeties B&B. North to Howard Johnson.
CAMPGROUNDS: "Junction 19/80 CG": Private. Good Sam. South on US 19 to County Road. East .5 mile. Pool, playground, tents, RVs, fish, pets. $8-$14.
"Rocky Spring CG": Private. Good Sam. North 2.3 miles on US 19 to Butler Street/PA 318. Southwest 5 miles. Campfire, pool, fish, playground. $10-$14.
"MERCER GROVE KOA": Private. South on US 19. Follow signs four miles to Southeast. Tents/RVs. Pool, fish, playground, pets, campfires. $13-$18.

17   MAJOR INTERCHANGE!
I-79 NORTH TO ERIE AND SOUTH TO PITTSBURGH.
NO NEAR SERVICES!
CAMPGROUNDS: "Mercer Grove City KOA": Private. South 3 miles on I-79 to exit 31. West 100 feet on PA 208 to North 3 miles on PA 258. Fish, pool, campfire,

playground.

"Goddard Park Vacation Land": Private. North on I-79 to Exit 34. Then .25 mile West on PA 358. Follow signs 3.5 miles North. Tents/RVs, 2 pools, 2 tennis courts, playground, miniature golf, pets.

3A   24   GROVE CITY/SANDY LAKE/PA 173: NO NEAR SERVICES!
GROVE CITY COLLEGE. HOSPITAL to South.

3   30   BARKEYVILLE/PA 8: SLIPPERY ROCK UNIVERSITY.
FUEL: South to BP Truck Stop, Texaco Truck Stop. North to Exxon Truck Stop.
FOOD: South to TA Restaurant, Country Pride. North to Burger King, Friendly's Restaurant, King's Family.
MOTEL: North to Days Inn.
CAMPGROUND: "Kozy Rest CG": Private. South 5 miles on PA 8 to PA 58. East .5 mile to County Road 4014. North 2 miles. Pool, playground, campfires. $8-$10.
JENNINGS ENVIRONMENTAL EDUCATION CENTER: 16 miles South on PA 8 to junction with PA 173 and PA 528. This is a prairie ecosystem from 6,000 years ago. Wild prairie flowers with blazing-star blooming in late July. Grounds open daily sunrise to sunset. Visitor Center open Mon-Fri 8-4pm. Free.
OLD STONE HOUSE: Same area as above. Tavern and Stage Coach Stop. Built in 1822. Tours by appointment. Call 412-794-2510.

EASTBOUND ALTERNATE ROUTE!

TO FT. MACHAULT AND OIL CITY'S OIL DISCOVERY: North 16 miles on Pa 8 to 1753's Fort Machault/ Franklin and to 1860's Oil Creek! Return to I-80 via US 322. Check your map.

DEBENCE'S MUSIC MUSEUM: 1675 Pittsburgh Road. Two miles South of Franklin on PA 8. 250 musical instruments. Great collection of Music Machines from the vanity size to the Nickelodeon and the Calliope. May-Oct Tues-Sat 10-5pm. Sun 1-5pm. Adult $5. Senior $4. Child $2-3.

FORT MACHAULT/FORT VENANGO: North on PA 8 about 16 miles to Franklin, the site of the old French Fort Machault, first built in 1753 as a bullwork against the British advancement into French fur-trading territory. The British captured Machault in 1760, rebuilt it and named it Ft. Venango.

VENANGO COUNTY COURT HOUSE: Liberty Street, Franklin. Built in 1869 it has Indian artifacts. Mon-Fri 8:30-4:30pm.

VENANGO COUNTY HISTORICAL SOCIETY: 301 South Park Street. The 1865 brick Hoge-Osmer House was restored to preserve the heritage of the county. Rotating displays. Tues-Thurs & Sat 10-2pm.

WALKING TOUR OF FRANKLIN: Brochure at Historical Society. Early oil money built homes of every major architectural style from 1830-1930.

MOTELS IN FRANKLIN: Idlewood, 1.5 miles South on PA 8. The Inn at Franklin, and Franklin Motel on Liberty Street. Lamberton House B&B on Otter Street. Quo Vadis B&B on Liberty Street.

CAMPGROUND: "Two-Mile Run County Park: North of Franklin on PA 417. Camp, swim, fish, snowmobile.

ON TO OIL CITY AND TITUSVILLE: (If you want to return to I-80, take US 322 Southeast to I-80 at Milepost 71.) North 8 miles to Oil City plus 15 more to Titusville.

Petroleum had been obtained for years from oil springs or seeps. By the 1850's men were refining it and making kerosene. The demand for this new fuel increased but the supply of oil was limited. The Seneca Oil Company sent Edwin L. Drake to Titusville to try to raise the output of the company's leased oil spring.

DRAKE OIL WELL, THE FIRST OILWELL
Photo credit: Bureau of Travel Marketing

He tried digging a well, then attempted drilling. He got help from the "salt well drillers" near Pittsburgh and hired William Smith, a blacksmith to make a derrick and engine house. They still had problems until Drake decided to drive a pipe down to bedrock and drill inside of it. On Aug 27th they were successful and brought up 20 barrels of oil a day. An oil rush followed and soon wells lined the bed of the creek between Titusville and Oil City. They overproduced too fast, the price dropped and in 1862 Drake was out of business. However Quaker State Motor Oil is still based here, still producing oil.

FOOD: Hoss's: 520 Senaca St. Oil City.

MOTELS: Holiday Inn, Corbett Inn in Oil City. McMullen House B&B at 43 East Main in Titusville, and Cross Creek Resort in Titusville.

CAMPGROUNDS: "Oil Creek State Park": Public. At Petroleum Centre, a former boom town. Visitor Center, hunt, fish, hike, camp. Bike on a 10 mile paved trail to Drake Well Park.

"Oil Creek Camping": Private. North on PA 8 to North of Cherry Tree. Follow signs 1.75 miles Southeast. Tents/RVs. Pool, trails, playground, pets.

"Happy Valley": Private. One mile further North on PA 8. Tents/RVs. Pets.

VENANGO MUSEUM OF ART, SCIENCE AND INDUSTRY: 270 Senaca Street, Oil City. Variety of exhibits on oil & machinery, a 1937 Cord car, and hands-on "Scientrific". Tues-Sat 10-4pm. Sun 1-4pm. Adult $2. Senior $1. Child $.75.

DRAKE WELL MUSEUM: South of Titusville .5 mile on PA 8. World's first oil/producing drilled well. A whole complex of buildings here with some of the old equipment and a replica of the 1859 derrick on the original site. Mon-Sat 9-5pm. Sun noon-5pm. Adult $2. Senior $1.50. Child $1.

OIL COUNTY AUTO TAPE TOUR: Tape & Cassett rented at Drake Well and returned at Holiday Inn in Oil City. Narration takes you from Titusville to Oil City.

OIL CREEK AND TITUSVILLE RAILROAD: 4 miles North of Oil City on PA 8 at "Rynd Farm". Or board at Perry Street Station in Titusville at an 1893 Freight house, or at Drake Well Park. Reservations suggested: 814-676-1733. 2.5 hour narrated train trip in 1930 cars. July-Aug, Fri-Sun. Spring & Fall, Sat-Sun. Oct, Wed & Fri. Trains leave between 11:45 and 3:30pm. Adult $7.50. Senior $6.50. Child $4.

PITHOLE HISTORIC SITE: Ghost oil-boom town. Northwest of Oil City off PA 227.

EASTBOUND RETURN TO I-80: From Oil City, go South on PA 257 and US 322. Where these two intersect you'll see Cranberry Mall with Sears, Hills, Bon-Ton, and JC Penny. Continue South on US 322 to I-80 at Exit ll/Milepost 71.

MILEPOST 31 REST AREAS.

4   35   CLINTONVILLE/PA 308:
      FUEL: North to Texaco Auto/Truck Plaza.

5   37   EMLENTON/PA 38: HARDWARE STORE to North.
      FUEL: North to Exxon, Texaco Truck Plaza.
      FOOD: North to Truck Stop Restaurant.
      MOTELS: North to Motor Inn, Whippletree Inn & Farm B&B, Big Bend Road. Apple Alley B&B 214 River Avenue. Barnard House B&B 109 River Avenue.
      CAMPGROUNDS: "Gaslight CG": Private. North on PA 38 to PA 208. West .5 mile. Pool, fish, playground, pets, miniature golf. Tents/RVs. $10-$16.

      "Yogi Bear's Jellystone Camp": Private. North on PA 38. South .2 mile on PA 138 to Calico Road. .2 mile to Peaceful Valley Road. Tents and RVs. Pool, fish, trails, playground, pets.

      OLD EMLENTON MILL COMPANY: 201 Main Street. 5 floors of original machinery and artifacts from 1870's. Mill shops with handcrafted articles of wood, porcelain, watercolors, ceramics. Also Antique shop and Boutique. Mon-Sat 10-5pm. Sun 12-5pm. Mill Cafe is open 6am-8pm. Sun 9-5pm.

      WALKING TOUR OF EMLENTON: Get brochure at Staab Typographic on Main Street. Victorian millionaire homes.

      MILEPOST 45 : Crossing the Allegheny River, the Mother of the Ohio River.

6   46   EMLENTON/SAINT PETERSBURG/PA 478:

7   54   KNOX/PA 338:

COUNTRYSIDE: Crafts and quilts.
FOOD: North to Wolf's Den Restaurant.
CAMPGROUNDS: "Colewell's CG": Private. Northeast 3.6 miles on PA 338 to PA 208. East 1.6 mile to County Road 2007. South .3 mile. Campfires, playground, pool, pets. Tents/RVs. $8-$10.

"Wolf's KOA": Private. North 500 feet on PA 338. Tents, RVs, cabins. 2 pools, spa, fish, playground, campfires. Boats, bikes, pets, waterslide, miniature golf, driving range. $13-$20.

8   60   SHIPPENVILLE/PA 66 NORTH:

FUEL: Citco
FOOD: North 3 miles to Bonanza.
CAMPGROUND: "Rustic Acres": Private. North 3 miles on PA 66 to County Road & sign. West .6 miles. Campfires, playground, pets. Tents/RVs. $8-$10.

CLARION ANTIQUE MALL: Junction of US 322 & PA 66. Leaded lamps, pottery, quilts, jewelry, porcelains, rugs, paintings, glass, arts & crafts and more. Opens 10 am daily.
MILEPOST 61: Crossing the Clarion River.

9   63   CLARION/PA 68:   HOSPITAL to North.

One of the "Cook's Forest" exits. Take PA 68 to PA 36. Read Milepost 74.
FUEL: Exxon.
FOOD: Rax, Perkins, Long John Silver, Kentucky Fried, Dutch Pantry, Burger King. North .5 mile to Clarion Clipper, Holiday Inn's Timberlands Restaurant (Great Sunday brunch). 3 miles North on Main Street, Clarion to Captain Loomis Restaurant. South to Johnny B's in Days Inn. Johnny Garneau's 2 miles East on US 322.
MOTELS: South to Days Inn. North to Knights Inn, Holiday Inn.

10   65   CLARION/NEW BETHLEHEM/PA 66 SOUTH: NO NEAR SERVICES! CLARIAN UNIVERSITY.

11   71   STRATTONVILLE/US 322:

FUEL: North to Keystone '76 Truck Stop, BP.
FOOD: North to Keystone '76 Restaurant, Burger King.
MOTEL: Knights Inn.

WESTBOUND ALTERNATE ROUTE

TO OIL CITY AND FORT VENANGO: North on US 322 to Fort Venango/Franklin. Right on PA 257 to Oil City, and Titusville oil discovery site. Read Milepost 30 for descriptions of sights. Return to I-80 via PA 8 and Milepost 30.

12   74   CORSICA/PA 949:

FUEL: North to Texaco Truck Stop.
FOOD: South to Blue Top Restaurant.

EASTBOUND ALTERNATE ROUTE

TO COOK FOREST: Travel North 15-20 miles on PA 949 and PA 36. Return to I-80 by going South on PA 36 to Milepost 78, I-80. This is Pennsylvania's only Virgin Forest of the oldest and tallest trees. Visitors come from all over to see how the forests looked when Europeans first arrived. The earliest homes in Pennsylvania were built with 24-36" wide boards, 1.5-2" wide from Virgin trees. Early photos show acres of wide stumps. Some early environmentalists managed to save Cook Forest. At the turn of the century European emigrants came to work in the coal fields and factories. They bought plots of land and laboriously pulled out the stumps and planted field crops and vegetables. Then there were meadows everywhere and wide vistas. Now after 100 years with 40-50" of rain a year, the deciduous trees of the forest have grown back.

Stop at the Visitor Center and drive along the scenic roads among the virgin trees and along the winding Clarion River. Or hike, bike or horseback ride. Canoeing, a waterslide and fishing too.

FOOD: Americo's has Italian food.

CAMPGROUNDS: COOK FOREST STATE PARK: One mile to North Cooksburg. Tents/RVs. Swim, fish.

"Peer Meadow CG": North of Cooksburg on Cook Forest Road to within 3 miles of Vowinckel. Tents/ RVs. Pool, playground, pets, miniature golf.

FURNISHED CABINS: "MacBeth's Cabins Inc". Cabins sleep from 3 to 12 persons. Call for reservations: 814-744-8400.

SAWMILL CENTER FOR THE ARTS: In Cooksburg. This is a public non-profit organization with 125 classes in arts and crafts for all ages, a "Craft Market" where 200 artisans sell their work, and many special events during the season.

WET 'N' WILD ACRES: PA 36, 2.5 miles South of Cook Forest. Water ride, go-karts, mini golf course, horse trail rides, petting zoo, cabins.

13   78   SIGLE/BROOKVILLE/PA 36: HOSPITAL.

FUEL: South to Atlantic, Citco. North to BP Truckstops of America.

FOOD: American Hotel Interchange Restaurant. North to McDonald's, Kentucky Fried, Pizza Hut, Country Pride, Ernie's in Days Inn. South to Gold Eagle Inn, Rax, Burger King, Plyler's Pizza, Family Restaurant.

MOTELS: South to Ho Jo Inn, Gold Eagle, Econolodge*. North to Super 8*, Days Inn.

CAMPGROUNDS: "Big Country CG": Private. North 4 miles on PA 36 to Richardsville Road/SR 4006. East 3 miles. Pool, fish. $7-$10.

"Clear Creek State Park": Public. About 10 miles North on PA 36 to Sigel. 4 miles Northeast on PA 949. Flush toilets, swim, canoes, fish, trails.

BROOKVILLE HISTORIC DISTRICT: South on PA 36 to 90 acres of restored Victorian buildings that provide a pleasant walking and shopping experience.

COOLSPRING POWER MUSEUM: 10 miles South on PA 36. This is a national museum of American technology dedicated to preserving the history of the internal combustion stationary engines and some of the machinery they powered. Over 250 pieces of equipment on display showing the application of the technology to industry worldwide.

WESTBOUND ALTERNATE ROUTE

TO COOK FOREST: North about 15 miles on PA 36. Return to I-80 via Pa 949 to Milepost 74. Read Milepost 74.

14   82   HAZEN/BROOKVILLE/PA 28: NO NEAR SERVICES!

15   87   REYNOLDSVILLE/PA 830:

FUEL: South to Diamond J's Truck and Auto Stop.

FOOD: Diamond J's Traveler's World Restaurant.

MILEPOST 88 REST AREAS:

16   97   BROCKWAY/DUBOIS/PA 219: STATE POLICE.

FUEL: BP, Exxon. South to Sunoco.

FOOD: South to Country Kitchen, Dutch Pantry.

MOTEL: South to Holiday Inn.

EASTBOUND ALTERNATE ROUTE

THROUGH DUBOIS: South 2 miles into Dubois. Right at the light at PA 255 South/Liberty Street to restaurants and motels. Return Eastbound by turning Right onto PA 255 North to return to I-80 at Milepost 101.

FUEL: Kwik Fill.

FOOD: Hoss's, McDonalds, Pizza, Mr. Donut. Bonanza on PA 255 North.

MOTELS: DuBois Manor, Hitching Post.
MALL: On PA 255 North: K mart to Left and JC Penny, Sears to Right.

17 101 DUBOIS/PA 255: HOSPITAL.
MALL: South to K Mart, JC Penny, Sears.
FUEL: South to Sunoco and Kwik Fill. North to Amoco.
FOOD: South to Bonanza, Burger King, Zimms, Rax, Perkins, Long John Silver.
MOTELS: Ramada Inn, Best Western.

WESTBOUND ALTERNATE ROUTE

INTO DUBOIS: Follow PA 255 South one mile into Dubois for places listed under Milepost 97. Return to I-80 via US 219 to Milepost 97.

18 111 PENFIELD/PARKER DAM/TS ELLIOTT STATE PARK/PA 153:
ELEVATION: 2250 FEET.
MILEPOST 111 HIGHEST POINT ON I-80 EAST OF THE MISSISSIPPI.
You are crossing Pennsylvania's Little Continental Divide. This ridge passing southwest from here divides the Atlantic Ocean drainage (via Susquehanna and Chesapeake Bay) from the Gulf of Mexico drainage (via the Allegheny, the Ohio and the Mississippi. WATCH OUT FOR DEER!
CAMPGROUNDS: "S.B. Elliott State Park": North 1 mile on PA 153. Right .5 mile. In a forest of White Pine planted by the C.C.C's. No showers or swimming but a lovely park with a Visitor Center that is open summer weekends. Tents/RVs. Cabins, playground. No Pets. $5-$9.
PARKER DAM STATE PARK: 5 miles North on PA 153 to a Right for 3 miles to Parker Dam. Tents/RVs. Rent boats, cabins. Fish, hike, showers, playground, dump station. Picnicking, sand beach for swimming. No pets. $11. Call 765-0630 for reservations. CCC Interpretive Center is open 1-5pm summers.
"B-Bar-M": Private. North 10 miles on PA 153 over the mountain almost to Pennfield. Fish, playground.
QUEHANNA WILD AREA. This is part of the sacred recreation and hunting grounds of the Iroquois. Beautiful country! There is a 65 mile loop trail through the wilderness area. Also shorter trails. Get more information on it at Elliott or Parker Dam State Parks.
MILEPOST 116 WESTBOUND PARKING/PICNIC AREA.
NO FACILITIES.
MILEPOST 118 Note the Coal Stripping on the Hill to the South. Pink and white laurel all through these hills in June.

19 120 CLEARFIELD/PA 879: RADIO: 900 AM. 93.5 FM.
MALL: South .5 mile, Right on River Road, 2nd Right up the hill. Pharmacy, K-Mart & Super Market, Deli, Bakery.
MALL: South .5 mile, across river, & Left for Penny's, Yogurt.
FUEL: North to Best Clearfield Truck Stop. South to BP, Amoco, Keystone.
FOOD: South to Dutch Pantry, Long John Silvers, Big Wrangler, Rax, Burger King, Classic Beef, Auntie Em's Buffet. North to Best Western Corral Buffet. Captain's Table is one mile South to PA 322 then East .2 miles.
MOTELS: North to Best Western. South to Day's Inn. Captain's Table and Royal Nine South one mile, then East on PA 322.
CAMPGROUND: CURWENSVILLE DAM RECREATION AREA: South 9 miles on PA 879 to Curwensville. Left onto PA 453. South 4 miles to Lake. Tents/RVs, boat, fish, hike, swim on 700 acre lake. $8.

CLEARFIELD

Clearfield was first called "Chinklacamoose" meaning "clearing in dense woods" ("often caused by buffalo or other large game"). This was a significant camp on the Shamokin Indian Path. From here the trail went up the Susquehanna to Curwensville. But it wasn't easy! Those tall laurel bushes were a menace. In 1758 Frederick Post had to cross the river 6 times in the 7 miles to the Anderson Creek Gorge/Curwensville and Bishop Ittwein with the Moravians in 1772 crossed it 3 times in the first four miles. Three miles up the Anderson Creek Gorge the trail climbed a ridge to the West to Big Springs. From there it went south to Mahoning Creek, Punxsutawney, Kittanning the Allegheny River, and the Ohio. Or another trail turned Northward from Big Springs to Ft. Machault.

THE SUSQUEHANNA FLOWS THROUGH the APPLALACHIAN PLATEAU
Photo credit: Bureau of Travel Marketing

In 1755 an army of French and Indians from the Western French forts of Duquesne and Machault penetrated Eastward on the Shamokin Path down to the lower Susquehanna below Lewisburg. There they killed the white settlers in Penn's Creek Valley. At Fort Granville/Lewistown they caught the garrison undermanned. A young well-liked Lieutenant Edward Armstrong was in charge. The Indians burned a hole in the stockade and then fired through the hole and killed Armstrong. The Fort was surrendered and prisoners taken back to Kittanning through Chinklacamoose spending one night here. Big brother Colonel Jack Armstrong, gathered a group of stalwart frontiersmen including Hawkins Boone, Daniel Boone's uncle, and headed West for Kittanning to avenge his brother's death. He was successful in the ensuing battle getting his vengeance, but he made no attempt to rescue the captives. Vengeance on the death of a brother was more important than compassion for the captives. Hawkins Boone with others returned Eastward via the Shamokin Trail and camped their 2nd night at Black Moshannon.

In 1757 Captain Patterson from the British Fort on the Susquehanna came this far West on the Shamokin Trail to see how far the French had penetrated. They found some Indian cabins in the Clearfield area burned but the departing owners may have burned them. In 1758 Frederick Post led a party here thinking that perhaps the French had now built a fort here. They found homesteaders slaughtered and continued on West across the mountains to the French Fort Machault on the Allegheny. Another source says that he was on his way to an Indian Council at Kuskuski and that he found an Indian Village here.

In 1772 the Moravian Missionary Party came through here from Wyalusing, Pa. herding their horses and oxen. Bishop Ettwein kept notes in his diary of their experiences here. He tells of rattlesnakes disabling stock and the masses of knats driving even the animals so crazy that they would run into the campfires.

Lumbering was big business here by 1850. Logs were cut and massed into "rafts". An early lumberman, William Bigler, found sport in riding the lumber rafts on the Susquehanna from Clearfield to Harrisburg. Very dangerous! The forerunner of I-80 through here was the "Old Erie Turnpike" completed in 1822. It connected Philadelphia to Erie, Pa.

CLEARFIELD COUNTY MUSEUM: 104 East Pine and River Streets. South on PA 879. Right on US 322 keeping Right at the light. Turn Left on River Street, just before the bridge. At Pine Street, park to your Right. Cross the street to the 1880 brick Victorian with the turret-like sections on the front. William Jennings Bryan stayed here and gave speeches in Clearfield and Philipsburg to thousands who attended. This museum has everything from Indian arrowheads found in this area to old tools, a 14 person sled, furnishings, clothing, an old Edison phonograph, and a 1900 steam-fired pumper in the carriage house. The old photos are fascinating. Open May-Oct Thurs and Sun 1:30-4:30pm. Free.

MILEPOST 121: I-80's first crossing of the West Branch of the Susquehanna River in the deep canyon that it has cut. About a mile East of here on the South side of the highway, note that the cut has a layer of low-grade coal in it. The richer grades may be deeper under the ground.

20   123   WOODLAND/SHAWVILLE/PA 970:
FUEL: South to Pacific Pride.
CAMPGROUND: "7-24 CG": Private. North .6 mile on PA 970 to County Road. East .3 mile. Swim, fish, campfires, playground, pets, rental boats, hiking, mini golf, shuffleboard. Tents/RVs. Mostly pull-thrus. $10-$14. The Shamokin Path is now

parallelling I-80 for about 30 miles Eastward. The Moravians buried one of their party here at Moravian Run.

MILEPOST 126: To the North view the "Coal Strippings" where the layers of exposed earth and rock are removed to get down to the lower layers of coal. The "E" and "F" layers are nearest the surface, but the lower "D" and "C" layers are often the prime coal that is the "stripper's" goal. With an average of 40 feet between the layers the stripping process may go down 100-150 feet. The deep coal is "A" and is usually mined via shafts and tunnels. It is profitable for strippers to remove one foot of rock for every 1" of coal, making this type of mining prevalent in the Appalachian Plateau. The problem is what they leave behind. The deep mines polluted the streams with magnesium and iron solutions producing "Red Moshannon" Creek over which you will cross at Milepost 138. The strip mines leave deep impassable trenches, so today the strippers must post bond per acre disturbed. They scrape off the top 2 feet of soil and save it in a "spoil pile". When they are finished mining they refill the trench putting the "spoil pile" back on top and planting grass.

To the South is a grassy hillside. a strip mining area that has been restored to today's legal requirements. Some years ago the strippers had to replant with trees. You'll see some areas with small trees about 10 feet tall that are on top of old tailing's piles. However some strippers found it less expensive to leave the trenches and forfeit the bond so the requirement was changed to grass. The grass is better than the impassible pits and rock piles, but is a poor taxpayer/consumer exchange for the thick forests that once were here.

21   133   KYLERTOWN/PHILIPSBURG/PA 53: More strip mining to the South!
Small **MALL:** North to grocery, laundry, hardware store.
POST OFFICE: Between the mall and the truck stop.
FUEL: North to Kwikfill Auto Truck Stop. South to Exxon.
TRUCKERS MOTEL: North by Kwikfill.

Eastbound you will first cross Red Moshannon Creek, Milepost 138 and then Black Moshannon Creek about Milepost 140. These both flow North into West Branch Susquehanna and were important crossings of the Shamokin Path.

SHORT SIDETRIP:

TO OLD ST. SEVERINS CHURCH: (On the National Registry.) Go North 5 miles on PA 53. Pass the new stone St. Severins church and turn Left/West between the cemetery gates. The old church is on the far back of the property. This church is the pioneer Roman Catholic church in this area, built in 1851 by Benedictine Fathers from Latrobe. It is made of 40 foot logs, hand-hewn on 2 sides and joined with half-dovetail notching. The structure is scheduled for restoration by July 1993. It will be most difficult to restore because of the absence of the craftsmen and the fact that logs that size are no longer available in Pennsylvania forests.

EASTBOUND ALTERNATE ROUTE

THROUGH MOSHANNON STATE PARK.   LARGE MOTOR HOMES AND TRAILERS NOT ADVISED, but inquire locally. Go North one block to a sign "Moshannon State Park 13 miles". Right 2 blocks to 2nd sign "Winburne". Turn Right and go through Winburne. (Only a couple houses.) You'll cross Red Moshannon Creek and on into the National Forest. Paved road, but curvy.

CAMPGROUND: MOSHANNON STATE PARK: Watch for sign and Left turn into the Campground. Camp, lake swim, boat, and fish. No pets.

Drive on through to PA 504 and the picnic area. Turn Left over the bridge and stop for a swim on Black Moshannon Lake. This rustic lake was born and kept alive by a spring that flows through peat moss coloring the water black. Expect your bathing suit to be covered with tiny feathery bits of peat. Continue straight ahead East on PA 504 some 10 miles over the 2200 foot pass. Stop and admire the view Eastward over the ridges. Note the Notch on the ridge ahead through which both the Shamokin Path and I-80 pass. It's a steep grade down the Allegheny Front to Bald Eagle Valley, Elevation 700 feet. In June, blooming pink to white masses of Mountain Laurel line the road over the mountain. Do stop and take a close look at the blossoms of tiny cups and buds like minute Chinese lanterns. In July there will be the trumpet-shaped rhododendron blossoms with larger shiny leaves. Left on US 220 for 2 miles to get back on I-80 at MILEPOST 157.

MILEPOST 146 REST AREAS.

22   147   SNOWSHOE/PA 144: MEDICAL CENTER. TOWN SWIMMING POOL.
FUEL: North to Citco Auto Truck Stop to Right. Exxon Truck Stop, Auto/Truck repair, straight ahead.
FOOD: North and straight ahead to Snow Shoe Restaurant. IGA Grocery & Deli, Bakery, North and to Left.
CAMPGROUND: "Snowshoe Park CG": Private. North and West .3 mile on PA 144. Pool, playground, campfires. $4-$7.
OLD TOWN OF SNOWSHOE: North and Turn Left/West on PA 144 over the hill to the stop sign. Right a couple blocks to old "Lion House", a 100 year old home. A block or so more, turn Right onto 4th Street to 210 4th, the Lion's Club's "David House". This is a typical coal-miner's home that they are restoring to mark that era. It should be open in 1993.

The Shamokin Path had an historic Native "Sleeping Place" (campsite) here. One member of the Moravian group that migrated through here in 1772 was buried here. In 1773 the state paid the Penn family for this land and the first survey was made along the Shamokin Path by Thomas Smith. When the warrants were drawn up locations stated: "on the path about one mile from the sleeping place" or "a quarter of a mile West of the sleeping place." The map returned to the land office marked the Shamokin Path and the Sleeping Place near the spring. Smith found an old Native snow shoe here, so he called it the "Snow Shoe Survey." "Snow Shoe Pike" was an old Toll Road on the Path/I-80's route. In 1815 Peter Karthaus improved it as part of his road from Karthaus to Milesburg, In 1819 coal was discovered at Snowshoe, the first in this county.
EASTBOUND: I-80 now follows the trail down the Allegheny Front to Bald Eagle Valley. The trail went through the Lucas farm laid out in 1801. Mr. Lucas said that the dead trunks of apple trees there were planted by Johnny Appleseed on his way West. Say "Goodby" to the Appalachian Plateau.

23   157   MILESBURG/BELLEFONTE/BALD EAGLE VALLEY/PA 150 NORTH/ US 220 SOUTH:
FUEL: North to Roadway Motor Plaza, Sunoco Travel Port Bald Eagle Plaza, Citco Bestway Truck Stop.
MOTELS: North to Econo Lodge*, Bestway. "Cherry Ridge Cabins" (Ask at Curtin Village, but the entrance is just across the highway. They have a rustic Finnish sauna. No pets.)

Chief Bald Eagle ("Woapalanne") of the Munsee Delawares lived with his tribe in this valley so it was known as "Bald Eagle's Nest". Spring Creek from Bellefonte joins Bald Eagle Creek here. One source claims that the Iroquois who dominated the Pennsylvania Tribes did not allow the Delawares to hunt in the sacred grounds of the Moshannon River and Quehanna Wild Area.
CURTIN VILLAGE: 3 miles North on PA 150. Curtin Village and Eagle Iron Works, 1810-1922, preserves a reminder of the feudal kingdom that existed in early industries in this country. This was a furnace complex where iron from Jacksonville and limestone from Bellefonte was made into steel. The Iron-master, Roland Curtin, had his big mansion in which he entertained other wealthy industrialists from Bellefonte. Over toward the furnace and across the creek were the log cabins of the iron workers. The iron-master provided the mid-wife, the band leader and the laying-out board for the dead. Prices were high at the village store, the only available. Today they have restored the charging house, the casting house, and the blast house along with the Federal style mansion and a log cabin. Bald Eagle canal ran behind the furnace works. Summers: Tues-Sat 10-4pm with the last tour at 3pm. Sun 1-5pm the last tour at 4pm. Fall: Sat 10-4pm. Sun 1-5pm. Adult $3 Child $1. One or two events

are featured each month in the summer. An excellent booklet "The Durable People" brings this old village back to life. You can board a train at Bellefonte station and ride here and back. See "Bellefonte" below.

WESTBOUND ALTERNATE ROUTE
THROUGH BLACK MOSHANNON STATE PARK. STEEP GRADE UP THE ALLEGHENY FRONT! NOT FOR TRAILERS OR LARGE MOTOR HOMES. Go 2 miles South on US 220 to Unionville/PA 504. Turn Right climbing up the Allegheny Front. You'll go up 1500 feet in just 4 miles. Stop for a view of the valley and ridges when you get to the top. Continue on over the mountain through the laurel and the rhododendron to Black Moshannon Lake. Lake swimming there. Then across the bridge to an immediate Right and in a couple blocks, another Right into the Campground. Read Milepost 133. To return to I-80, you'll exit the campground and keep Right following that road out through Winburne to Kylertown and Milepost 133. If you make the wrong turn, don't panic as you'll probably come out on PA 53 and a Right on that will take you to I-80.

SIDETRIP INTO BELLEFONTE:
South on PA 150 four miles to Bellefonte. As you come into town, "Spring Creek" will be on your Right. You'll note a 5-story "Gamble Mill Tavern" on your Right across Lamb Street Bridge where they serve lunches and dinners. When you come to the traffic light turn Right for one block to Talleyrand Park and the old Train Station/Chamber of Commerce on your Left where parking is provided. Larger vehicles and trailers may have difficulty parking here. Playground, picnic area, and large fish in the stream. Cross the suspension bridge to see the excellent bust of Lincoln to your Right in the garden. Then look for an opening in the fence to go closer to the road on a trail to the Left around the "Spring Building" to view the big spring, the "Beautiful Fountain" that gave Bellefonte its name. The Chamber of Commerce is open weekdays and has maps of the town and other information. Summer weekends the train picks up passengers at 1pm and 2:15pm for Curtin Village and Bald Eagle Valley. This is a 20-mile round trip. Adult $4. Child $2. Fall foliage trips are available also.

Across the street from the station is the Bush Hotel. They serve an excellent lunch on a table dressed with an old fashioned hand-worked tablecloth. Walk up the hill to Allegheny Street to view the Court House directly in front of you. On the way up you'll pass Bonfattos Restaurant, Pizza, and The Galley. Cross the street and turn around to view the fabulous 1864 Gothic Revival Brockerhoff Hotel built in 1864 on your Left and the 1872 Crider Exchange Building on your Right. The latter has the unusual fishscale tin facade. Walk just one block up Allegheny Street to the Georgian "Potter Home" on your Left at the corner of Howard Street. This was built in 1815 by the son of the founder of Milesburg and Mayor of Philadelphia. It is now the Historical Museum and Library with three rooms of memorabilia upstairs.

Now take a driving tour of some great old homes from Federal Style to Victorian to a mixture of architectural ideas. From in front of the Court house go North up Allegheny Street. On your SLOW way up watch on your Right for the massive columned "Hastings Mansion" built in 1840. It had several styles added on. Turn Right on Linn Street and view homes up to Wilson. Turn 2 Lefts to get onto Curtin. West on Curtin across Allegheny this time noting the building on the Northwest corner. A couple more blocks will bring you back onto PA 150. Right turn will take you back to Milesburg and I-80 at Milepost 157.

B&B: "Nellis House." East Linn Street, Bellefonte.

24   160   STATE COLLEGE/PA 26: PENNSYLVANIA STATE UNIVERSITY.
FUEL: South to Mobile.
CAMPGROUNDS: "Bellefont KOA": Private. North 2 miles on PA 26. Pool, playground. $18-$26.
"Twin Oaks CG": Private. North one mile on PA 26. Campfires. $9-$14.
"Bald Eagle State Park": North about 5 miles to Howard. Campground on a road to the Right there. Watch for sign. Tents/RVs. Pit toilets. No showers. Swim, fish, trails. No pets. Trailer dump.
"Fort Bellefonte CG": Private. One mile off I-80 on PA 26.

SIDETRIP TO PENN'S CAVE
South on PA 26 to Left/South 4 miles on PA 144 to Center Hall. Five miles East on PA 192. Ride a boat through a large lighted limestone cavern to a lake on the other side and back. The water dripping through the limestone formed beautiful colored columns and pillars. A nice experience! Large souvenir shop and snacks.

PENN'S CAVE
With stalactites hanging down
Photo credit: Pennsylvania Bureau of Travel Marketing

Tour includes a walk through a wildlife sanctuary. Tours on the half hour daily June-Aug 9-7pm. On the hour in Spring and fall. Adult $7.50. Senior $6.50. Child $3.50. Also you can take a 15-minute plane ride for $14 or both rides for $17.50. Free exhibit of Victorian lamps.

SIDETRIP INTO STATE COLLEGE

South on PA 26 about 15 miles to State College. Return to I-80 via the same route. This area around State College was referred to in the early days as the "Great Limestone Valley". The Susquehannocks, Kishacoquillas and other tribes met here near Rock Springs to match skills and play La Crosse. Nittany Mountain is to your Left/East.

MALL: At intersection of PA 26 and PA 150. Sears, Penny's, etc.

CENTRE FURNACE: 1001 East College Avenue on PA 26 just West of US 322 Expressway. Go SLOWLY past Puddingtown Road and Hampton Inn. Turn Right at any of the next 3 turns and park. The ironmaster's mansion, back on the hillside at the 2nd turn, is the Centre County Historical Society. Original furnishings and memorabilia, artifacts, photos. The Furnace was built in 1792, the first iron smelter in Centre County. Iron was carried to Pittsburgh by muleback. Free guided tours on Sun-Mon, Wed, & Fri 1-4pm.

PENNSYLVANIA STATE UNIVERSITY: Continue on PA 26 & East College Avenue to Bus US 322/Atherton Street. Turn Right. Penn State University was first founded in 1859 by the owners of Centre Furnace as "Farmer's High School". It became the Agricultural School of Pennsylvania in 1862, Penn State College in 1874 and achieved University status in 1955.

EARTH AND MINERAL SCIENCE MUSEUM: Pollack Street. From Atherton turn Right at the college entrance at Pollack Street and park in visitor parking space there. Walk down the street 2 blocks to the museum on the Right.

OLD MAIN ADMINISTRATION BUILDING: A couple more blocks down Pollack Street and behind the Schwab Auditorium. Inside are Frescos by Henry Varnum Poor. To the Left of this building is a sculpture of the "Nittany Lion", an extinct grey/black mountain lion that roamed this area.

PENN STATE BOOK STORE: At Pollack and Shortlidge, Southeast corner. Parking is off Shortlidge.

THE DAIRY STORE: Shortlidge Street. West on Shortlidge a few blocks to Curtin Street and a small dairy store on your Left. It will be marked by people standing around with ice cream cones. Left into the lot there or Left at the corner to more parking. The best ice cream, cream cheese, and buttermilk around.

The University also has the **FROST ENTO-MOLOGICAL MUSEUM** (Curtin Street), **PALMER MUSEUM OF ART**, the College of Agriculture's Research facilities, and the flower test gardens on Park Avenue just West of the Dairy Store.

BOALSBURG:

BOAL MANSION: Stay on Bus US 322/Atherton East to Boalsburg. From the light at Atherton and Boal Avenue go South one block to a Right into the Boal Mansion. Summers 10-5pm. Spring & Fall Wed-Mon 2-5pm. Go to the Stone Cabin first. Adult $3.50. Child $1.50. The mansion is especially known for its Christopher Columbus Chapel which was brought to the U.S. in 1919 by the

COLUMBUS CHAPEL
Photo credit: Bureau of Travel Marketing

Boals family, Columbus descendants. The mansion has 18th Century furnishings and decor. The chapel has art work dating back to 1535. It was the private chapel of the Columbus family in Spain.

BOALSBURG VILLAGE: Drive straight out from the mansion to a Right on Church Street. A couple blocks takes you to the village of old shops and B&Bs.

PENN MILITARY MUSEUM: Across US 322. A memorial to the Pennsylvania 28th Infantry Division and to soldiers of recent wars including World War II, with tanks and artillery. Large museum and a walk through a World War I battlefield with sound-effects and light-effects. Tues-Sat 9-5pm. Sun 12-5pm. Fee.

Return to I-80 via US 322 to PA 26 and to Milepost 160.

MILEPOST 171 PICNIC/PARKING AREAS. NO FACILITIES.

25 173 LAMAR/PA 64: STATE POLICE.
> **FUEL:** South to BP Truck Stop, Texaco. North to Shell, Gulf.
> **FOOD:** South to TA Country Pride. North to Cottage Restaurant.
> **MOTELS:** North to Comfort Inn and Travelers Delight.

26 178 MILL HALL/LOCK HAVEN/US 220 NORTH: ELEVATION: 1100 FEET.
> **FUEL:** South to Sunoco and Exxon.
> **FOOD:** North .5 mile to Belle Springs Restaurant.

EASTBOUND ALTERNATE ROUTE

TO LOCK HAVEN, WOOLRICH AND WILLIAMS PORT: North 7 miles on US 220. North on PA 120 into Lock Haven. Continue East on PA 150 to Woolrich Mills, and Williamsport. To return to I-80 take US 15 South to Milepost 210.

LOCK HAVEN

Exit US 220 on PA 150 North to downtown Lock Haven straight ahead to the river and East Water Street. This town was first known as "Big Island" with a large Indian settlement here when the British built Ft. Reed in 1775. Just West of the canal lock where the Fort stood is a monument. In 1778 during the Revolutionary War, the British, Tories and Indians committed the "Wyoming Massacre" near Wilkes Barre. Then they came on South and overran this area attacking American settlers. The latter evacuated and fled Eastward in what was called "The Great Runaway". After the war was over settlers returned, lumbering increased and Ft. Reed became a port on the "Pennsylvania Canal".

The town of Lock Haven was founded in 1833. This was the time of the lumber barons who logged the hundreds of acres of virgin timber on the hills to the North. The town was founded by Jerry Church and named for the Pennsylvania canal lock and the haven that it was for the logging companies, who floated their logs here to be sorted. In 1847 a 24 foot flood devastated Lock Haven. In 1849 a large boom was erected to facilitate the sorting of the logs. The boom survived a 25 foot flood in 1865. But they continued to overlog, clear-cutting whole hillsides until there was nothing Left to hold the water back. Finally the 29 foot flood of 1889 destroyed both the boom and the canal and brought an end to the days of massive lumbering. Jerry Church was a land speculator whose home was flooded. Legend is that he climbed up into a tree house with his violin and played it until he was rescued. His violin was on display in the museum but was lost in the last big flood in 1972.

Lock Haven became a town of many industries. Besides the lumber mills there were a paper mill, silk mill, wire mill, chair factory, tannery, clothing factories, and the Piper Cub airplane plant. Most are gone today to cheaper labor in the south, the Caribbean, and Southeast Asia.

HEISEY MUSEUM: 362 East Water Street. Turn Right/East along the river to the museum. It's a Victorian mansion built in 1831 and once owned by Jerry Church who had a tavern there. Being by the river it has endured many floods. After the last big flood of 1972 the mansion was beautifully restored to its mid-century look. They give you a guide-sheet describing the furnishings in each room. A rosewood piano was donated by William Raymond, the well-loved black singer who was a native of Lock Haven. An excellent museum! Tues-Fri 10-4pm. Adult $2. Child $1.

WALKING TOUR: Walk or drive up Water Street along the River. At the S Street Bridge note the Court House on the Left corner with its 2 silver towers and its clock. Between the bridge and the courthouse is a Stone Marker. A sign says: "Last outpost on Frontier to protect settlers...Site of ungrateful murder—the shooting of a friendly Indian who came to warn Lock Haven that a band of warriors were planning to attack."

The YMCA is nearby with a swimming beach.

B&B: Hoffman's Victorian B&B. 402 East Water Street, on the river.

There are many large old Victorian mansions along Water Street. If you want more details, go to the library at 3rd and Main and they will lend you a tape and a guide to the old homes. If you cross the bridge at "S Street" and go East on the other side of the river for .5 mile you'll come to the site of old Ft. Reed and the remains of the Pennsylvania Canal with the Toll-Keeper's house. Straight ahead on this road takes you directly to PA 150. Go Left/East.

WOOLRICH MILLS: PA 150 travels alongside the old Pennsylvania Canal that becomes a swimming hole in the summer and ice skating rink in the winter. At a stop sign you'll go Left to Woolrich. This lovely mill town established in 1830 is known for producing high quality outdoor wear. The "Company Houses" are proud homes under tall trees, a model for any company town. At the mill store you can shop for bargains in outdoor clothing. Seamstresses like the mill ends that you can buy by the pound. They show films narrated by Orson Welles and have an "Outdoor Hall of Fame". Mon-Fri 9-5pm.

WILLIAMSPORT

From Woolrich, go straight out across PA 150 to US 220 and go East to Williamsport. Take the Business Route Exit into town on West 4th Street. Check your speedometer as it is about 4 miles to the Tourist and Convention Center and museum at Maynard Street. Fourth street was the route of the Delawares on the Great Shamokin Path as it headed toward "Big Island".

LYCOMING COUNTY HISTORICAL MUSEUM: 858 West 4th Street. Displays of frontier to Victorian rooms, Indian culture, the lumber industry, and the Shempp Toy Train Collection of 337 complete trains. Tues-Sat 9:30-4pm. Sun 1:30-4pm. Adult $3. Senior $2.50. Child $1.

HERDIC TROLLEY: Ask at the Tourist Center/Museum for departure times. This trolley takes you down Millionaire's Row by the big Victorian mansions built by the lumber barons and to other Williamsport highlights. May-Oct Thursday & Sat. Adult $1.50. Child $.75. Or just drive up and down 4th Street and view them yourself.

OLD JAIL CENTER: Continue into Williamsport on 4th Street. Turn right on William Street. The jail will be on your Left. Have an unusual experience shopping amidst artists and craftsmen in a 100 year old jail converted into an artsy shopping center.

HIAWATHA: Susquehanna State Park on the river. Go back West on 4th Street to two blocks West of US 15. Left/South on Arch Street. Just before the bridge you'll see a sign to "Hiawatha". Turn right. Cruise the Susquehanna River on the old Paddlewheel. May-Oct Tues-Sat 10am, 11:30am, 1pm, 2:30pm, 4pm. Sun 1pm, 2:30pm, 4pm. Tuesday evenings at 6pm there is an 1.5 hour family cruise. Adult $5. Senior $4.50. Child $3.

LITTLE LEAGUE BASEBALL MUSEUM: South 1.5 miles on US 15. Little League began here as a 3 Team League in 1939. It now has 2.4 million participants in 39 countries. The Annual World Series is held here each year. The museum has the history and memorabilia of Little League plus a Drug Education Room. The children can bat and pitch and see an instant replay of their form. Summers Mon-Sat 9-7pm. Sun noon-7pm. Rest of year they close at 5pm. Adult $4. Senior $2. Child $1.

FOOD & MOTELS IN WILLIAMSPORT: You will find several as you drive between the various places of interest, but there is a greater concentration of them in the Faxon area. From US 15 just North of the river, go East on US 220. Take the Faxon exit and turn Right at the light, Washington Blvd. Here you'll find:

MALL: Shops including K mart.

FOOD: Hoss's, Elbys, Arbys, McDonalds, Pizza Hut, Long John Silvers, Rax, Kentucky Fried, Hardees, China Queen, Hickory Smoked. Go West on Washington Blvd. to Bonanza.

MOTELS: Colonial Motor Lodge & Econo Lodge*. (Bings is 3 miles North from Jct US 15/US 220.)

RETURN TO I-80: Continue South on I-15 to Milepost 210. On the way you'll pass over gigantic cuts through the mountain's maroon rock.

MOTELS SOUTH ON US 15: .5 mile South to Kings Inn. 1.5 mile South to City View. South 8 miles to Northwood.

27   185   LOGANTON/PA 477:
FUEL: South to Mobile. North to Gulf.
FOOD: South to Scoff's.
CAMPGROUND: "Holiday Pines": Private. Good Sam. North .2 miles on PA 477 to Rockey Road. East 2 miles. Tents/RVs. Campfires, pool, playground, pets. $10-$13.

28 **192** **JERSEY SHORE/PA 880:** HOSPITAL.
FUEL: South to BP. North to Mobile Travel Port Pit Stop.
FOOD: South to Pit Stop.
CAMPGROUND: "Ravensburg State Park": Five miles North on PA 880. Tents only. Pit toilets. No showers. Fish, playground, hike. No pets.

MILEPOST 194 REST AREAS.

29 **199** **MILE RUN:** NO NEAR SERVICES!

30 **210** **WILLIAMSPORT/LEWISBURG/US 15:** HOSPITAL.
SOUTH to BUCKNELL UNIVERSITY and WESTERN PENN PENITENTIARY.
FUEL: South to Shell. RV service & repair 3 miles South.
FOOD: South to Bonanza.
MOTELS: Comfort Inn South 1 mile to First exit.
CAMPGROUNDS: "Nittany Mountain CG": Private. South .25 mile on US 15 to New Columbia Road. Northwest 4.5 miles to Millers Bottom Road. West .5 mile. Pool, campfires, playground. $10-$13.
  "Willow Lake CG": Private. Good Sam. South .25 mile on US 15 to New Columbia Road. Northwest 2 miles to Gray Hill Road. North 1.5 miles to #10 Buck Road. East .5 mile. Pool, campfire, fish, playground. $8-$14.

SIDETRIP SOUTH TO LEWISBURG

South on US 15 to Lewisburg. Return via the same route.
MILTON STATE PARK: 2 miles South of I-80. No further information.
COUNTRY CUPBOARD: 5 miles South on US 15 on the West side of the highway. An indoor shopping center with craft and gift shops, restaurant, greenhouse garden center, bakery, candy shop. Behind it is a Best Western motel. People come here from all around. Food is said to be good. You might pick up an area map here. There is a "Delta Place Station" train ride on the opposite side of the highway.
SLIFER HOUSE: Just North of Lewisburg. Sign might say, "United Methodist Home". A National Registry 1860 Victorian home with period furnishings, and a hat and fan collection upstairs. It has a columned wrap-a-round porch with a charming cupola on the back. A popular setting for weddings and concerts. Architect was Samuel Sloan of Philadelphia.
CHAMBER OF COMMERCE: 418 Market Street Lewisburg. Ask for a map of the area. They have a self-guiding tour of the many Federal Style homes built in 1820's and renovated to Revival-style with taller windows and porches. You may just drive East on Market Street/PA 45 where they line the streets for 3-4 blocks between 3rd and Water Streets. Then turn around to come back on Market. This time go South/Left on 2nd Street and Right again on 3rd Street back to Market. This route takes you past 35 historic homes.
LEWISBURG ANTIQUE CENTER: 517 St. Mary Street. On the East side of US 15 across from Perkins Pancake House/Days Inn. Turn Left on St Mary's one block. A 5-story red feed mill with a large collection of antiques, glassware, furniture, and china. Daily 10-5pm.
PACKWOOD HOUSE MUSEUM: 15 North Water Street. Turn Left/East on PA 45. This old hotel grew from a log house in 1796 to serve river boats and grew to a huge 3-story building to serve canal and highway travelers. Now it is a museum with a display of Americana. Tours only beginning at the tour center. Tues-Fri 10-5pm. Sat 1-5. Sun 2-5pm. Adult $4. Senior $3.50. Child $1.75.
BROOKPARK FARM: 1 mile West of US 15. An old farm with 9 renovated buildings and a barn built with hand-hewed 2-foot square timbers. B&B and shops.
MOTELS IN LEWISBURG: Days Inn at St. Mary's Street. Lewisburg Hotel-Motel on PA 45 one half mile East of US 15.

MILEPOST 211: Crossing the West Branch of the Susquehanna River. The great Shamokin Path began South of here where the Susquehanna River Branches. It went North up the East side of the river. The Munsee tribe of the Delawares lived just North of here. This was also the site of the 1763 battle of Muncy Hills, part of Pontiac's War when over 100 men from Paxton were defeated by the Delawares.

31   212   MILTON/I-180/PA 147: NO NEAR SERVICES! STATE POLICE.
  CAMPGROUND: "Fort Boone CG": Private. North .75 mile on I-180 to Watsontown exit. West 1.2 miles to PA 405. South .3 mile. Campfires, fish, boat, playground. $12.

SUNBURY

South about 14 miles. This town was "Shamokin," one of the largest Native villages at the intersection of the Canoe Trail of the lower Susquehanna, and the land trails of the East and West Branches of the Susquehanna. The Shamokin Path began here and went Westward along much of I-80 through Clearfield. Since the Iroquois from the North had conquered the Susquehannock and Delawares residents of this area, an Iroquois-appointed chief resided here to keep control.
  FORT AUGUSTA: South on PA 147 to Sunbury. At junction of the Susquehanna River and Shamokin Creek was the largest Frontier British Fort before the French & Indian War. The powder magazine from 1756 is still there.
  HUNTER HOUSE: 1150 North Front Street. Historical exhibits on the Fort.
  BLUE BIRD GARDENS: South 2nd Street. March to May it has lovely azaleas and rhododendrons.
  JOSEPH PRIESTLY HOUSE: No further information.
  SHIKELLAMY: No further information.

32   215   LIMESTONEVILLE/PA 254:
  FUEL: North to Sunoco, Milton 32 Truck Plaza. South to All American Auto/Truck Plaza, Texaco, Shell.
  FOOD: South to All American. North to Flo's 32 Restaurant.

MILEPOST 218 REST AREAS:

33   223   DANVILLE/PA 54: SHOPPING MALL one mile South.
  HOSPITAL: GEISINGER MEDICAL CENTER HOSPITAL 3 miles South.
  FUEL: Citco, Shell, Amoco, Texaco Country Corner Market.
  FOOD: South to Dutch Pantry, Perkins, McDonalds, Kentucky Fried and Friendlys.
  MOTELS: North to Howard Johnson. South to Best Western, Red Roof*.
  CAMPGROUND: "Yogi on the River": Private. South on PA 54 to West on US 11 to 2.5 miles North of Northumberland. Tents/RVs. Pool, rental boats, bikes, fish, miniature golf, pets.
    MONTOUR PRESERVE: Public. North 8 miles on PA 54. Nature preserve on Lake Chillisquaque. Picnic, boat, fish, hike, trails. Free.
    VISITOR CENTER OF NATURAL HISTORY:. Mon-Fri 9-4pm. Summers Sat-Sun 2-5pm. Free.

34   231   BUCKHORN/BLOOMSBURG/PA 42/PA 44: ELEVATION: 484 FEET.
  MALL: North to Sears, JC Penny, Hills, BonTon.
  FUEL: Amoco. North to Mobile.
  FOOD: North to Buckhorn, Kentucky Fried, Perko, Western Sizzler, Wendy's. South to Hotel Magee (Sunday Brunch).
  MOTELS: Quality Inn. South on US 11 to Budget Host, Hotel Magee. North to Econo Lodge* and Roadway.
  CAMPGROUNDS: "Indian Head Recreation CG": Private. Good Sam. South 2.3 miles on PA 42 to Jackson Street/Reading Street. East .5 mile. Near a covered bridge. Campfires, swim, fish, playground, bike, pets. Tents/RVs. $8-$10.
    "Turner's Highview Camping": Private. North .5 mile on PA 42 to Creek Road. South .3 mile to County Road 4. Southeast 2 miles. Follow signs. Campfires, playground, pets. On hilltop with scenic view. $9-$10.
    "Knoebels Grove Amusement Resort & CG": Private. 5 miles South on PA 42. 8 miles South on PA 487. Tents/RVs. Amusement park. Pool, pets, waterslide, playground, miniature golf.

35   **235**   LIGHTSTREET/BLOOMSBURG/PA 487: BLOOMSBURG UNIVERSITY.
FUEL: Exxon. South to Texaco.
FOOD: Elby's Heritage House. North to Lightstreet Restaurant.
MOTELS: South 1.75 miles to Tenny Town Motel.
CAMPGROUND: "Deihl's Camping Resort": Private. Good Sam. North 3.5 miles on PA 487 to County Road. West .5 mile to County Road. Southwest .25 mile to County Road. North .8 mile. Pool, fish, playground, campfires. $10.

36   **239**   MIFFLINVILLE/LIME RIDGE/BERWICK: STATE POLICE.
FUEL: North to Best, Mobile Truck Stop.
FOOD: South to Hamlets.
MOTEL: Budget Host.
        MILEPOST 241: Crossing the East Branch of the Susquehanna River that flows South from Wilkes Barre.

37   **242**   BERWICK/PA 339:
FUEL: North to Shell A/T Plaza. South to Citco A/T Stop.
FOOD: North to Brennans, Pancake House, McDonalds, Tuggy's.
MOTEL: North to Motel 8.

MILEPOST 246 REST AREAS:

38   **256**   CONYNGHAM/HAZELTON/PA 93: HOSPITAL.
FUEL: South to Texaco. North to Sunoco, Pilot.
FOOD: Tona Kitchen. Library Lounge Restaurant 4 miles at PA 93/I-81.
MOTELS: South to Super 8. North 1.25 miles to Lookout Motor Lodge. Hazelton Motor Lodge 4 miles South at PA 93/I-81.

38A   **259**   MAJOR INTERCHANGE!
I-81, WILKES-BARRE & HAZELTON: ELEVATION: 1624 FEET. NO NEAR SERVICES!
CAMPGROUND: "Hazelton/Wilkes-Barre KOA": Private. North .5 mile on I-81 to exit 42. Tents/RVs. Pool, playground, pets. $17-$25.

SIDETRIP TO WILKES-BARRE

North 17 miles on I-81. Wilkes-Barre was first laid out in 1770 by Connecticut settlers on land that belonged to their state. The Susquehanna River here flows through a broad valley known by its Delaware name of "Wyoming", meaning "a wide plain". With its rich riverbottom soil it became an important source of grain on the frontier. Thus during the Revolutionary War in 1778 British Major John Butler was ordered to secure the Wyoming Valley. He led his Butler's Rangers of 1200 British Tories and Senecas down the river to capture Wintermoot's Fort and Jenkins Fort. The settlers of fighting age had joined the Continental Army and left the valley. So the old and the young men gathered at "Forty-Fort" to form a local militia. They marched North to present day 4th Street in the town of Wyoming. The British concealed themselves behind a fence, with the Senecas hiding in the swamps. In less than an hour over 300 Americans were killed. Legend has it that the Seneca's "Queen Esther" slaughtered the captured men upon a rock now known as "Queen Esther's Rock. American Colonel Denison surrendered the Valley to the British. The Indians were then allowed to loot the valley and burn the homes while most of the settlers fled Eastward.

Although local history says that the Indians didn't "slaughter" the settlers, the incident became known as "The Wyoming Massacre". It caused settlers all down the East Branch of the Susquehanna to flee. It incited the Americans to Revolutionary fever. Perhaps it was contrived that way as it was hard to get frontiersmen to join the revolution. The next year General Washington sent Gen. John Sullivan here with an army of 3500 men. They marched from Wilkes-Barre to upper New York and back destroying 40 Native towns, burning their corn, their fields, and drove them out of the valley forever. "Queen Esther" was killed at the Battle of Newtown. There is a monument in Wyoming commemorating the battle and behind it is the famous "Queen Esther Rock".

The next battles in the area were small and known as the Yankee/Pennamite Wars fought along the waterfront of Wilkes-Barre from 1769 to 1784. This was between the early Connecticut settlers and the Pennsylvanians coming North and wanting this territory to be part of THEIR state. Wilkes-Barre prospered from its extensive deposit of anthracite/hard coal. On Franklin, Ross and River Streets there are many large mansions built by the mine owners.

HISTORICAL SOCIETY MUSEUM: Behind the library at 69 South Franklin Street. Exhibits on Native Americans and mining. There is a striking old photo of 10-year old boys seated on boards leaning over their task of picking out rocks from the belt of coal. A man is behind them with a stick. An old coal miner said that he was one of those boys. If he looked up or stopped his task he would get a wack on the back with that stick. Tues-Fri 12-4pm. Sat 10-4pm.

SWETLAND HOMESTEAD: 885 Wyoming Avenue, Wyoming. On National Registry. 1797 cabin that was expanded into a large home. See a settlers kitchen and a Victorian parlor of the 1860's. Summers Thurs-Sun 12-4pm. Adult $2. Child $1.

39   262   MOUNTAIN TOP/HAZELTON/PA 309:
  FUEL: North to Texaco. South to Gulf.
  FOOD: John's Restaurant.
  MOTELS: Best Western. North to Friendship Inn, Stage Coach Inn.
    ECKLEY MINER'S VILLAGE: About 8 miles. South on PA 309 to East on PA 940. Follow signs East to Eckley. A living history museum of a 19th Century anthracite coal mining town. Visitor Center and 50 buildings depicting the lives of the miners and their families. Mon-Sat 9-5pm. Sun noon-5pm. Adult $2. Senior $1.50. Child $1.

40   272   WHITE HAVEN/PA 940/PA 437:
  FUEL: Shell. North to Mobile.
  CAMPGROUND: "Sandy Valley CG": Private. West .3 mile on PA 940 to Weatherly-White Haven Road. South .3 mile to County Road. 2.8 miles to fork. Straight ahead one mile. Follow signs. Fish, pool, boat, playground, pets, hike on trails. $14.
    LEHIGH GORGE STATE PARK: About 8 miles South near Rockport. No further information.
    WHITEWATER CHALLENGERS RAFT TOURS: South 6 miles off Weatherly-White Haven Road. Raft trips on Lehigh River. Reservations: 717-443-9532.
    MILEPOST 273: Crossing the Lehigh River.

41   274   HICKORY RUN STATE PARK/PA 534:
  FUEL: Sunoco Bandit Truck Stop. Northwest to Hickory Run Truck Plaza.
  CAMPGROUNDS: HICKORY RUN STATE PARK: Public. East 6 miles on PA 534. Follow signs. Showers, campfires, lake, fish, swim, playground, flush toilets. $6.
    "Lehigh Gorge CG": Private. North .5 mile on PA 534 to PA 940. West .2 mile. Campfires, pool, playground. $12-$15.

MILEPOST 275 EASTBOUND REST AREA.

42   276   MAJOR INTERCHANGE!
WILKES-BARRE/ALLENTOWN/PA 9 TOLL ROAD:
  Follow signs toward the Toll road to PA 940 for services:
  FUEL: Shell.
  FOOD: McDonalds, Arbys, Burger King.
  MOTELS: Pocono Mountain Lodge, Ramada Inn, Day's Stop,

43   283   BLAKESLEE/LAKE HARMONY/PA 115: STATE POLICE.
  FUEL: Exxon. South to Sunoco.
  FOOD: "Edelweiss German Restaurant" North to Blakeslee & East on PA 940. Blue Heron Inn on Big Boulder Lake, (6 miles) South on PA 115. Southwest 3 miles on PA

903. Fresh seafood and home baked foods.

CAMPGROUNDS: "Fern Ridge CG": North .2 mile on PA 115. Campfires, pool, playground. Tents/RVs. $14-$15.

"Jack & Jill CG": Private. Good Sam. South 3/4 mile on PA 115 to Long Pond Road. East 2.2 miles to Clearview Road. South .5 mile. Fish, boat, swim, playground.

"WT Family Camping": Private. 5.5 miles South on PA 115. Tents/RVs. Trails, pets.

POCONO INTERNATIONAL RACEWAY: South on PA 115. Follow signs. If you're into racing, check ahead for events scheduled here at this famous raceway.

BETWEEN HERE AND THE DELAWARE RIVER, I-80 PASSES THROUGH THE POCONO MOUNTAINS. This is New York and New Jersey's Mountain vacationland. The Poconos were first settled in the middle of the 19th Century by Welch emigrees who worked in the slate quarries. Today the Pokonos are known for their views, rivers, lakes, waterfalls, fishing, hunting, and skiing.

43A   293

MAJOR INTERCHANGE!
I-380 NORTH TO SCRANTON: ELEVATION: 1600 FEET.
MILEPOST 294 EASTBOUND REST AREA.

44   298   POKONOS/PA 611: ELEVATION: 1658 FEET.

Both North and South on PA 611 there are several motels, restaurants, gas stations and shops.

CAMPGROUND: "Pocono Mountains Four Season CG": Private. North 1.2 miles on PA 611 to Scotrun Avenue. Northwest .5 mile to Babbling Brook Road. West .75 mile. Campfires, fish, pool, playground. $15-$17.

45   299   TANNERSVILLE/PA 715:

In the 19th Century the bark of the giant hemlocks of the Poconos was used to obtain tannic acid to tan leather.

POCONO PEDDLER'S VILLAGE: North to PA 611 & Stadden Road. 21 Store shopping complex. Also an Antique and Flea Market on Sat-Sun 9-5pm.

FUEL: North to Mobile. South to Exxon, Amoco.

MOTELS: Pocono Lodge. South to Best Western.

CAMPGROUND: "Four Seasons": Private. North .25 mile on PA 715. North 1.5 miles on PA 611. One mile West. Follow signs. Tents/RVs. Pool, tennis, playground, pets. $15-$17.

CHRISTMAS BARN WAREHOUSE OUTLET: Features Christmas all year with ornaments, decor, figurines, etc. Mon-Sat 10-5. Sun 12-5pm.

CAMELBACK ALPINE SLIDE AND WATERSLIDE: Northwest 3.5 miles. Follow signs. Amusement park includes chair lift, pool, batting cage. Summers daily 10-5pm.

46   302   BARTONSVILLE/US 209 SOUTH/PA 33: ELEVATION: 420 FEET.

FUEL: North to '76 Truck Stop, Citgo Truck Stop.

FOOD: North to '76. Right on 611 to Ribs & More.

MOTELS: North & Left on 611 to Comfort Inn, Heritage Motel.

47   304   9TH STREET, STROUDSBURG/ NORTH TO US 611:

FOOD: McDonald's, Ponderosa.

48   305   MAIN STREET, STROUDSBURG/BUS 209:

North through downtown Stroudsburg connects with US 209 NORTH.

FACTORY OUTLETS: One half mile up Main Street. Right at 9th or 10th Street for one block. 35 shops.

FUEL: South to Sunoco.

MOTEL: Best Western.

CAMPGROUND: "Pocono Vacation Park": Private. South 2 miles on Bus US 209 to Shafer's Schoolhouse Road. West .5 mile. Campfires, pool, playground. $14-$16.

STROUD MANSION: Right on Main Street to 9th & Main on the Northwest corner. Built in 1795 by Col. Jacob Stroud for his son, it is now the Historical Society of Monroe County. In 1755 Fort Hamilton was built behind this building at the direction of Benjamin Franklin. Fort Penn later replaced it. Refugees came here from the Wyoming Massacre.

QUIET VALLEY LIVING HISTORY FARM: About 4.5 miles South on Bus 209. Follow Signs. Historical Society's German farm built in 1765 and brought to life by costumed volunteers. Visit 14 buildings in rural woods setting. Self-sufficient farm life of the 18th-19th Centuries. Children may pet the animals & jump in the hay in the barn. Summer tours. Mon-Sat 9:30-5:30pm. Sun 1-5:30pm. Adult $5. Senior $4. Child $2.50.

49   306   WESTBOUND EXIT ONLY TO DREHER AVENUE, STROUDSBURG/ US 209 SOUTH:

50   307   WESTBOUND BROAD STREET, DOWNTOWN STROUDSBURG:
RADIO: 93.5 FM. 840 AM.
EASTBOUND PARK AVENUE, DOWNTOWN STROUDSBURG:
US 611 EAST AND WEST.
FOOD: McDonalds, Bailey's at 5th & Sarah.

51   308   EAST STROUDSBURG: EAST STROUDSBURG UNIVERSITY.
MOTEL: South to Budget.

52   309   MARSHALL'S CREEK/MILFORD/SHAWNEE/US 209 NORTH/PA 447:
MALL: BUGLE BOY OUTLET.
FOOD: Peppi's one mile East at Mall.
CAMPGROUNDS: "Cranberry Run CG": Private. North 4.6 miles on PA 447 to PA 191. South .3 mile to Pinebrook Road. West .5 mile to Hallet Road. North .5 mile. Campfire, fish, playground. $8-$10.

"Delaware Water Gap KOA": Private. Northeast 6.4 miles on US 209 to Hollow Road. East one mile. Campfires, pool, playground. $20-$26.

"Mountain Vista CG": Private. Good Sam. North 3.75 mile on US 209 to Bus US 209. Southwest .5 mile to Craigs Meadow Road. West one mile to Taylor Drive. South 100 yards. Campfires, pool playground. $16-$17.

"Otter Lake Camp Resort": Private. North on US 209 to PA 402. North 7.2 miles. Tents/Rvs. 2 pools, sauna, boats, fish, tennis courts, playground, pets.

EASTBOUND ALTERNATE ROUTE!

THROUGH THE DELAWARE WATER GAP: 24 miles North on US 209 to the Toll Bridge at Dingman's Ferry. South about 24 miles on the New Jersey side of the river and back to I-80. This is a National Recreation Area on both sides of the Delaware River. You will need a Delaware Water Gap map. If you didn't get one in Stroudsburg, watch for signs to "Park Headquarters" on the East side of the highway. The sign is poor! It's a mile or 2 East through a golf course complex. Back on US 209 travel Northward.

DOLL & TOY MUSEUM: On the East side of US 209 near Bushkill. Private. A collection of 125 dolls, toys and miniatures.

INDIAN MUSEUM: Across the street from the Doll Museum. Private. This is a small family museum but it is very well done and more informative than most large museums. It tells the story of the 10,000 Lenni Lenape (Delaware) whom the white man first met here. You are given a tape and recorder that explains each display. The collection was started in 1784 by Mr. Treible. His descendants have researched and preserved his artifacts.

William Penn's son, Thomas, made a treaty with the Lenni Lenapes in 1737 to purchase the land that could be walked in 1.5 days. From past agreements with other tribes the Lenni Lenape thought this meant about 25,000

BUSHKILLS FALLS
Photo credit: Pennsylvannia Bureau of Travel Marketing

acres. They trusted him as they had found his father to be trustworthy. Instead Thomas Penn brought a long distance runner who ran 65 miles. Penn then calculated a wider range from that and ended up with 500,000 acres. ALL their land! The tribe was forced to move West along the I-80 corridor. As you travel West their story will go with you. The last full-blooded member of the tribe who retained and cherished the old customs and language was Nora Thompson Dean, "Touching Leaves", from the last of the Delawares who were finally forced to go to Oklahoma. She visited here in 1976 and has since passed away. She was an herbalist so there is an extensive collection of herbs here. 9:30-5:30pm. Adult $2.50. Senior $2. Child $1.

BUSHKILL FALLS: 2 miles North of Bushkill. This is another family endeavor that is very well done. A pleasant stop. The first trail and bridge was built in 1904 to the 100 foot main falls. Most tourists can make it this far. According to your agility and endurance you may hike to 7 more cascades and falls. It varies from a 45 minute walk to a 2.5 mile hike up and down stairs. If rainfall has been plentiful the falls are more generous and beautiful. (Rubber soles are good for walking on wet paths and steps.) As you enter there is a good exhibit of mounted animals. Picnic Area and snacks. April-Nov daily 9-dusk. Adult $4.50. Senior $3.75. Child $1.50.

CAMPGROUND: "Dingman's CG": Concession in National Recreation Area. Tents/RVs. Flush toilet, showers, fish, hike, swim, boat. Ranger conducted programs. Tents $11+. RVs $13+. Reservations recommended: 717-828-2266.

DINGMAN'S FALLS: Park Visitor Center open May-Oct. Film, displays, and a 20 minute trail to Dingman's and Silver Thread waterfalls. Child's Picnic Area is a 4-mile hike on trails and bridges to views of 5 waterfalls.

DINGMAN'S FERRY: The only privately owned toll bridge across the Delaware River. Cross the river and take the first road to the Right to go South. On the New Jersey side you'll want to stop at:

PETER'S VALLEY CRAFT VILLAGE.

VAN CAMPEN INN: 1746 stone house. July-Aug Sat-Sun 1-5pm.

WALPACK CENTER: A village.

MILLBROOK VILLAGE: A restored village of 1800's with craft demonstrations on weekends. Continue South to I-80.

53   310   RIVER ROAD/DELAWARE WATER GAP/PA 611 SOUTH: VACATION BUREAU INFORMATION CENTER !

WESTBOUND: Stop to get Pennsylvania and Delaware Water Gap maps.
EASTBOUND: Get Pocono and Delaware Water Gap Information here.

SIDETRIP UP THE DELAWARE RIVER

First pick up a Delaware Water Gap map at the Information Center. It's a pleasant drive up the River Road. You might enjoy the little "Streamside Cafe" before you get to Shawnee. You'll find **SHAWNEE STABLES** for scenic trail rides (hourly 9-3pm) and **SHAWNEE PLACE** a water park. You'll drive through the woods and find picnic grounds, boating, and swimming at Smithfield Beach and connect with US 209. Just before that you'll come to the Park Information Center. To continue the ride up the Delaware on US 209, read Milepost 309.

EASTBOUND: CROSSING THE DELAWARE RIVER ON A TOLL BRIDGE. YOU ARE ON THE LAST LAP OF YOUR CROSS COUNTRY TOUR! CONGRATULATIONS!

WESTBOUND: YOU JUST CROSSED THE BRIDGE INTO PENNSYLVANIA. PAY $1 FOR THE PRIVILEGE AND SAY "HELLO" TO THE BEAUTIFUL MOUNTAINS OF PENNSYLVANIA!

PENNSYLVANIA I 80 MILEPOSTS

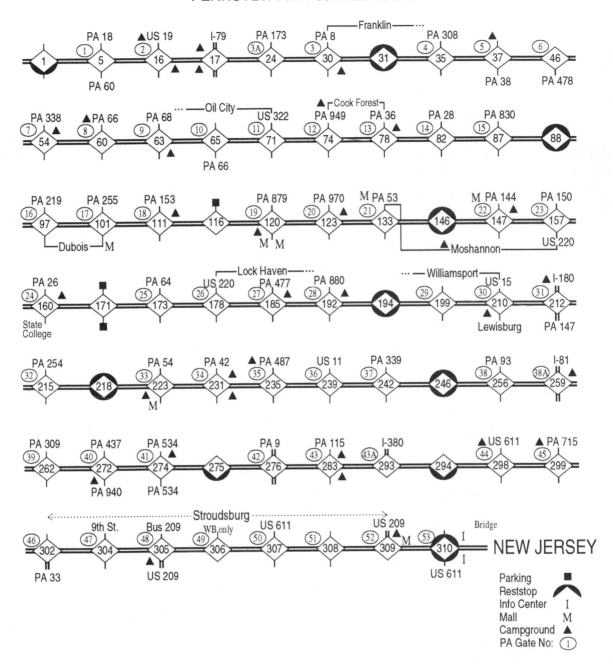

Franklin

PA 18	▲US 19	I-79	PA 173	PA 8		PA 308		
①	②		③A	③		④	⑤▲	⑥
1	5	16	17	24	30	31	35	37	46
	PA 60				▲		PA 38	PA 478

Oil City · · ·   ▲ Cook Forest

PA 338	▲PA 66	PA 68		US 322	PA 949	PA 36	PA 28	PA 830	
⑦	⑧	⑨	⑩	⑪	⑫	⑬	⑭	⑮	
54	60	63	65	71	74	78	82	87	88
▲		▲	PA 66			▲		

PA 219	PA 255	PA 153	■	PA 879	PA 970	M PA 53		M PA 144	PA 150
⑯	⑰	⑱		⑲	⑳	㉑		㉒	㉓
97	101	111	116	120	123	133	146	147	157
Dubois M				M M	▲		▲ Moshannon	US 220

Lock Haven · · ·   · · · Williamsport

PA 26	■	PA 64	US 220	PA 477	PA 880		US 15	▲I-180
㉔		㉕	㉖	㉗	㉘	㉙	㉚	㉛
160	171	173	178	185	192	194	199	210	212
State College	■			▲	▲		▲ Lewisburg	PA 147

PA 254		PA 54	PA 42	▲ PA 487	US 11	PA 339		PA 93	I-81
㉜		㉝	㉞	㉟	㊱	㊲		㊳	㊳A
215	218	223	231	235	239	242	246	256	259▲
		M	▲					

PA 309	PA 437	PA 534		PA 9	PA 115	I-380		▲US 611	▲PA 715
㊳9	㊵	㊶		㊷	㊸	㊸A		㊹	㊺
262	272	274	275	276	283	293	294	298	299
	▲ PA 940	PA 534			▲			

< · · · · · · · · · · · · Stroudsburg · · · · · · · · · · · · >

	9th St.	Bus 209	WB only	US 611		US 209	Bridge
㊻	㊼	㊽	㊾	㊿	51	52	53	I
302	304	305	306	307	308	309	310	**NEW JERSEY**
PA 33		US 209				US 611	I

US 611

Parking   ■
Reststop
Info Center   I
Mall   M
Campground   ▲
PA Gate No: ①

DELAWARE WATER GAP,
DIVIDES PENNSYLVANNIA from NEW JERSEY
Photo credit: New Jersey Division of Travel & Tourism

New Jersey

The Garden State

New Jersey has rich farmlands down the middle of the state and along the coast, producing vegetables and fruits that dress the tables of New Jersey and New York. The flavor of this produce is outstanding giving the state its title of "The Garden State".

New Jersey is the smallest state on I-80, our 46th state in size, 7836 square miles, but has the eighth largest population, 7,730,188! This population density in a small area makes New Jersey's portion of I-80 the widest, wildest and most congested as it nears New York City. In addition, I-80 is bisected by more limited-access highways (10) than in any other state. All of this in only 68 miles! I-95 reaches from Florida to Maine, and (as the New Jersey Turnpike) intersects with I-80, traveling East into New York City and then North to Maine. Therefore I-80 ends at Milepost 68, as I-95 enters, with a big sign across the freeway just 3 miles from the George Washington Bridge and The Big Apple.

New Jersey's I-80 begins in the West with 4 lanes of traffic but quickly changes to 6-8 lanes. Then I-80 Eastbound divides with the inside/Left lanes going ONLY to the George Washington Bridge. NO EXITS! Once you keep Left for that you are committed all the way to New York City. So if you want to exit ANYWHERE keep in the Right/outside lanes. It becomes very hectic! PLAN YOUR EXITS FAR AHEAD!

Except for a short connection with New York State, most of New Jersey is bordered by water: the Delaware River, Hudson River, New York Bay, and the Atlantic Ocean. Much of New Jersey is sea level or of gradual elevation as the Hudson River and the Delaware River flow serenely to the sea. Yet it does have a "High Point" of 1803 feet in its small share of the Appalachians at its far Northwestern tip where it cradles a portion of the famous Appalachian Trail. In North Jersey ancient glaciers left a line of rocky moraines with pockets of lakes. New Jersey has 127 miles of seacoast, its famous "Jersey Shore", with resorts like Atlantic City and Cape May.

The Eastern end of I-80 is a massive industrial complex centering on Paterson, Passaic, Newark, and Jersey City. Southern New Jersey has industrial centers around Trenton, the state capital, and Camden. A greater variety of goods is manufactured in New Jersey than in any other state.

Violet

New Jersey is proud of its many wildlife management areas, especially its "Pinelands National Reserve" just North of Atlantic City, an area of pines, swamps, wildflowers, and 25 varieties of native orchids. Dubbed the "Pine Barrens" for its inability to grow the normal field crops, it produces 25% of the state's agricultural products, notably cranberries and blueberries.

New Jersey has produced some of our greatest scientists including Thomas Edison, Albert Einstein and Samuel F.B. Morse. You can visit Edison's Laboratory and home from Milepost 46 in Orange, NJ. The Great Falls of the Passaic, Milepost 56, is one of America's natural wonders, and is the 2nd highest waterfall East of the Mississippi.

NEW JERSEY HISTORY

The Lenni Lenape Indians were the inhabitants of present-day New Jersey when in 1524 Giovanni de Verrazano stopped in. (You can read more about this tribe in "Pennsylvania History".) Henry Hudson sailed up the Hudson River, and claimed the land for Holland so that in 1623 this was "New Netherlands". Trading first began along the rivers in 1630 in Pavonia/Jersey

City and by 1660 the Dutch had built Bergen, New Jersey. England won the area from the Dutch in 1664 but King Charles II gave it to his brother, the Duke of York. So you know how New York got its name. But the Duke gave the land between the Delaware and Hudson Rivers to John Berkeley and George Carteret. Since the latter was former governor of the Isle of Jersey in England, he named the area, "New Jersey". They sold the land to colonists at low prices giving them religious and political freedom. Quakers headed by Edward Byllynge bought Berkeley's share of New Jersey and made West Jersey the first Quaker colony. When Carteret died another Quaker group, "The 24 Proprietors"' bought East Jersey in 1682. By 1760 there were 100,000 people in New Jersey.

The settlers, in conflict with the trade restrictions of the British and with their British governor, had their own "Tea Party" opposing British taxation at Greenwich, near Salem in 1774. That same year their "Provincial Congress" appointed delegates to the Continental Congress in Philadelphia. The last British governor was evicted July 2, 1776 when they adopted their first constitution, but it was 1845 before they had their first elected Governor.

THE CRADLE OF OUR FREEDOM!

Little New Jersey was the base of 100 battles of the Revolutionary War and the site of two winters of extreme duress by our Continental soldiers. Here men suffered and died that we might become a free nation, while businesses and farmers (unsure of Continental dollars) withheld the goods to save them.

In 1775 the British had hoped to quell the Colonists rebellion in small battles, mostly from the sea, but found the rebels too determined. By June 1776 the British had changed their strategy and the largest British Armada ever assembled anchored off Staten Island with 32,000 well-trained professional soldiers. Led by General Howe they planned to take New York City, control the Hudson River and cut through New Jersey to divide the New England Colonies from the Southern Colonies. This done they could conquer those rebellious Colonists.

Opposing this army, George Washington had 19,000 raw untrained men, poorly armed and supplied and led by amateurs. They came for only one season or even for one battle near their homes. On July 4th, 1776 Congress approved the Declaration of Independence and Washington read it to his troops in New York City on July 9th. In August, British General Howe inflicted 1500 casualties on the Colonists in Brooklyn. To preserve his army from annilation, Washington used a fishing fleet to cross the East River to Manhattan and retreated Northward. He fortified Fort Washington on the East side of the Hudson (George Washington Bridge), and Fort Lee on the Palisades on the Western Shore in New Jersey.

When General Howe's army approached, Washington (wanting to save his men and supplies) advised General Greene to evacuate Fort Washington. Green reneged. Washington fought Howe again at White Plains, N.Y. Then General Howe changed his tactics and attacked Fort Washington (as George had feared) capturing another 2800 men of the rebels small army. Cornwallis crossed the Hudson and took Fort Lee, Milepost 72, and the supplies there. Washington consolidated his devastated forces at Hackensack, Milepost 66, and retreated across New Jersey with Cornwallis close on his heels. When Washington crossed the Delaware North of Trenton on December 7th, seizing or destroying all boats, the British gave up the chase for the winter. They retreated to New York, leaving a base at Trenton and supplies at New Brunswick.

Washington had managed to preserve his small army in spite of the strength of the British and this tired, cold, rag tag-army was the Rebels only hope of winning their freedom from England. But disease was rampant, desertions high, supplies dangerously low, their morale even lower. Americans were not all rebels, up to a third were loyal to England. Benjamin Franklin's own son was a Tory. Thousands fled to Canada to the bosom of the British while others avoided the war by traveling West across the Appalachians. Many of those who stayed were more interested in profit than freedom and would not sell supplies to the rebels for Continental dollars, but traded with the British for their gold. Others waited to see which side was winning before deciding their loyalty. Washington wrote: "The conduct of the Jerseys has been most infamous. Instead of turning out to defend their country, and affording aid to our army, they are making their submissions as fast as they can. If they had given us any support, we might have made a stand at Hackensack and after that at Brunswick, but the few militia that were in arms, disbanded themselves...and left the poor remains of our army to make the best we could of it."

On hearing this, in December 1776 Thomas Paine wrote: "These are the times that try men's souls. The summer soldier and the sunshine patriot will, in this crisis, shrink from the service of their country; but he that stands it now deserves the love and thanks of man and woman."

Washington had to do something to restore morale and save the cause of liberty. So on the night of December 26th in a vicious snow storm he led 2400 men back across the icy Delaware River and defeated the British force in Trenton. The Colonials were overjoyed and enlistments rose. Howe sent Cornwallis after the Rebels but wiley George stole around him and routed another British force. Cornwallis had to retreat to New Brunswick.

Washington led his exhausted men to Morristown, Milepost 43, to rest. His army was in a better position here protected by lookouts on the hills to the East. He also had pig iron for cannonballs and Jacob Ford's Powder Mill that supplied most of the powder for the war. But food, clothing, and blankets were scarce and his men were hungry and cold.

The next year with the British in Philadelphia, Washington's troops spent that terrible winter in Valley Forge. But in the winter of 1779-1780 he again brought his troops to Morristown. This was the worst winter of the war! More so than Valley Forge! There was 4 feet of snow on the ground and many of the men had no shoes or stockings, only one blanket each and a bed of straw. Men were freezing to death or dying of diseases, especially small pox. Washington could not get supplies from the young government, but this time the local people came to his aid with food and blankets. Morristown churches became hospitals where people cared for the army invalids. Visit Morristown via Milepost 43 and hear the rest of the story.

NEW JERSEY MILEPOSTS:

NEW JERSEY STATE POLICE: 201-785-9419.
ROAD CONDITIONS: 609-530-3710.
RADIO STATIONS WITH NEWS & WEATHER EVERY 10 MINUTES: 880 & 1010 AM.
TOURIST CAMPING INFORMATION: 609-292-2470.
NEW JERSEY TRAVEL AND TOURISM: 800-JERSEY 7.

WATCH EXIT SIGNS VERY CAREFULLY! Many exits are Eastbound or Westbound only and often have NO Reentry. New Jersey Department of Transportation maps, information from the State Troopers, highway maps and actual highway signs are difficult to coordinate. Good Luck!

NEW JERSEY MOTELS: THIS IS AN AREA OF HIGH PRICED MOTELS/HOTELS. Prices seem to start at $50 for two. Motel chain prices, compared with other states, seem to vary from a $20 increase to a 100% increase.

EASTBOUND: I-80 enters New Jersey over the Delaware Water Gap Bridge. Toll $1 Westbound only. Here the famous 2,144 mile Appalachian Trail crosses the Delaware River on the sidewalk of the bridge. It was established in the 1920's-30's and follows the ridgelines of the Appalachian Mountains from Maine to Georgia.

WESTBOUND: Say "Good By" to New Jersey. You're on your way across the country!

MILEPOSTS:

0.3 **DELAWARE WATER GAP NATIONAL RECREATION AREA**
KITTATINNY POINT VISITOR CENTER:

EASTBOUND EXIT: IMMEDIATELY EAST OF THE TOLL PLAZA: Small blue sign will say, "National Recreation Area Information". If you miss this exit, take the next one to the Visitor Center.

WESTBOUND EXIT: For Visitor Center and for Alternate Route exit where sign says: "Millbrook & Flatbrookville". To get to the Information Center follow the exit road around under I-80 to the South side of the highway. To go North through the Delaware Water Gap just continue North on the River Road.

KITTATINNY POINT VISITOR CENTER: Programs and literature about the area. They have short talks on the geology of the area and hikes to Mt. Tammany and Sunfish Pond. Enquire here about traveling North through the New Jersey side of the Delaware Water Gap National Recreation Area. April-Nov daily 9-7pm.

The Delaware River flows through the Kittatinny Ridge of the Appalachians. The Tammany and Minsi Mountains are 1200 feet above the river while the river has a depth of 90 feet.

WESTBOUND SCENIC ALTERNATE ROUTE

Read Pennsylvania Milepost 52 and reverse the "Scenic Alternate Route" going North on the River Road to Millbrook Village, Walpack Center, etc. to cross to Pennsylvania at Dingman's Ferry, and so South to Bushkill Falls and the Indian Museum. Get your map at the Visitor Center.

CAMPGROUNDS: "Dingman's Ferry CG". Read Pennsylvania Milepost 52.

"Worthington State Forest CG": 4 miles North on the River Road to West on Old Mine Road (Flatbrookville). Pit toilets. No showers. Boat ramp. Fish. Tents/RV's.

MILEPOST 0.8 PARKING: Still within the Park you'll note exits for "Dunnfield Parking

Area" for the hikers on the Appalachian Trail.

4   COLUMBIA,NJ/PORTLAND,PA/NJ 94/PORTLAND TOLL BRIDGE/US 46:
FUEL: North to BP T.S. of America, Shell Rt 46 Truck Stop, Gulf Truck Stop, ACI Truck Stop.
FOOD: Country Pride Restaurant.
MOTEL: North to Days Inn.
CAMPGROUNDS: "Delaware River Camping Resort": Private. East 3.5 miles on US 46. Summers, swim, boat, playground. $18-$20.
     "Shady Acres CG": 1.5 miles North of Portland Toll Bridge. Ask for more information on it at the Kittatinny Point Visitor Center.
     SLATEFORD FARM: Cross the Delaware West to Portland and go up the river on PA 611 about 3 miles. This is an old slate quarry where on weekends you can observe the old skill of slate splitting. Costumed Rangers lead tours of the 1800's farm. Summers Wed-Sun 12-5pm.

MILEPOST 7 REST AREAS:

12   BLAIRSTOWN/HOPE/NJ 521: NO NEAR SERVICES!
CAMPGROUNDS: "Triplebrook CG": Private. South .5 mile on NJ 521 to County Road 609. West 3.2 miles to Nightingale Road. North .5 mile to sign. East .5 mile. Campfires, swim, boat, fish, 2 pools, playground. No pets. Whirlpool. $20-24.
     JENNY JUMP STATE FOREST: 3-4 miles. South on NJ 521 to Hope. East on NJ 519. South on NJ 611. Tents/RVs. Pit toilets, no showers, playground. An old legend is told of an attack by Lenni Lenapi wherein a little girl's father told her, "Jenny Jump" to escape them. Find the Rest of the Story here.
     HOPE MORAVIAN VILLAGE: South one mile to Hope. Walk through the town settled in 1774 by Moravians from Bethlehem, Pennsylvania. Several of their buildings remain. During the Revolution Moravians would not fight in the Army, but they cared for the sick and the wounded. A smallpox epidemic decimated them and those that survived went West to Pennsylvania in 1808. Hope also has shopping at "The Village Shops of Sunrise Farms". South of Hope you might want to try "The Inn at Millrace Pond".
     LAND OF MAKE BELIEVE: One mile South to Hope. East on NJ 519. South on NJ 611. Follow signs. Amusement park for children with a haunted house, a Christmas village, a maze, "Old McDonald's Farm", rides and picnicking. June-Sept daily 10-5pm. Adult $7. Child $8.25. (Includes all rides.)
     EASTBOUND: Enjoy these first 30 miles of New Jersey. as you cruise peacefully through the Appalachian Ridges with its lovely woodlands, lakes, and state parks. Soon you'll be in the piedmont of industrial cities and an Urban raceway through Passaic, Paterson, Newark and Hackensack leading into New York City.

19   HACKETTSTOWN/ANDOVER/ALLAMUCHY/NJ 517:
CAMPGROUNDS: "ALLAMUCHY STATE PARK": South on NJ 517 to 2 miles North on Willow Glen/Waterloo Road. Tents/Rvs. Fish, hike, playground, picnic. No showers.
     "Tranquility CG": Private. North 2.5 miles on PA 517 to PA 611. Northwest one mile to Quaker Road. Southwest .2 mile. Campfires, swim, playground, pets. Tents/RVs. $18-$24.
     MILEPOST 20 EASTBOUND SCENIC OVERLOOK: (NO TRUCKS)

MILEPOST 21 REST AREAS:

25   NETCONG/STANHOPE/US 206/NJ 183:
FOOD: "Barcone's Lockwood Tavern", Italian, North 2 miles on NJ 206 to Byram. "Morris Canal Ristorante", 2 Walnut Place, Stanhope. Italian food on Lake Musconetcong. Ask directions to: "Porky's", claimed to be the largest BBQ Restaurant in New Jersey. Also ask about "Chequers", Old English style.
CAMPGROUNDS: "Columbia Valley CG": Private. North 3 miles on US 206 to Lackawanna Drive/County Road 607. East 3.5 mile. Pool, fish. $10-$12.

"Panther Lake Family Camping": Private. North 4.6 miles on US 206. Campfires, fish, swim, boat, playground. $18-$26.

HOPATCONG STATE PARK: About 3 miles. Follow signs or enquire locally. Picnicking, hiking, swimming, fishing and winter sports.

STANHOPE: North to Revolutionary village and Sussex Iron Works. Ironworkers' company houses here look like French cottages. In 1821 the first anthracite furnace was built here.

WATERLOO VILLAGE: North .75 mile on US 206. Two miles Southwest via Waterloo Road. Village of "Andover Forge" was settled in 1760 and renamed in 1815. The forests were depleted and the town died, but revived again when the Morris Canal was built. Restored buildings are an inn, a church, carriage house, and blacksmith shop. The canal structures are scheduled to be restored. Craft demonstrations of candle dipping, broommaking, thrown pottery April 11-Dec Tues-Sun. Fee. They have weekend concerts in the summer.

26 **BUDD LAKE/US 46/WESTBOUND EXIT ONLY:**
CHEROKEE TRADING POST: Indian crafts & jewelry, western wear and 50 styles of moccasins.

27 **NETCONG/US 206/NJ 183 NORTH:**
FUEL: Circle Gulf Truck Stop at NJ 183 & US 46. Exxon Truck Stop. US 206 NORTH to US 46 EAST.
MOTEL: Days Inn, 2 miles North on US 46 East.
CAMPGROUND: "Fla-Net Park": Private. South .25 mile on US 206 to Old Ledgewood Road. West .7 mile to Flanders-Netcong Road. South 2 blocks. Campfires, pool, pets, fish, playground. Tents/RVs. $12-$20.
MUSCONETCONG & HOPATCONG STATE PARKS: About 3 miles to North.

29 **LEDGEWOOD/LAKE HOPATCONG/NJ 10:** ROXBURY MALL on NJ 10.
FUEL: Vantage Truck Stop, Sunoco, Exxon.
FOOD: Fireside Diner on 46 East.
MOTEL: South to Days Inn.

30 **HOWARD BLVD., MT. ARLINGTON/NJ 615:**
BERKSHIRE VALLEY WILDLIFE MANAGEMENT AREA.
FUEL: North to Exxon.

MILEPOST 32 REST AREAS:

33 **WESTBOUND EXIT TO MT. HOPE:**

34 **DOVER/WHARTON/NJ 15:**
FOOD: South on NJ 15 to Townsquare Diner.
FAIRY TALE FOREST: About 12 miles North on NJ 15 to Berkshire Valley Road & Oak Ridge Road. Mother Goose reigns here with life-sized animated characters plus a carousel, toy circus, and train rides. Summers daily 10-5pm.

35 **MOUNT HOPE/DOVER/NJ 661:** HOSPITAL. URGENT CARE CENTER.
MALLS: "ACME SHOPPING CENTERS". "ROCK-AWAY TOWN SQUARE MALL": Penny's, Lord & Taylor, Macy's, Sears, etc.
FOOD: South to Sizzler. South to US 46 West 2 miles to Travelers Diner.

37 **EASTBOUND EXIT ONLY/HIBERNIA/ROCKAWAY/NJ 513:**
FUEL: North to Shell. I-80 West Exxon Truck Stop.
FOOD: North on 513 to Hibernia Diner.

38 **EASTBOUND EXIT ONLY/DENVILLE/US 46 EAST:** HOSPITAL.
Denville was a hot springs resort. Today it has many craft shops and boutiques.

FUEL: Sunoco.
FOOD: Burger King, Charlie Brown's.

39 WESTBOUND EXIT ONLY/PARSIPPANY/NJ 53/US 46:
MOTELS: Hilton. Envoy Inn at 625 US 46 East.

42 MORRIS PLAINS/US 202/NJ 654:
Take US 202 North to US 46 East to Services:
FUEL: .5 mile to Gulf, Sunoco.
FOOD: .75 mile to Bennigans. One mile to Red Lobster, Burger King. 1.75 mile to House of Pancakes.
MOTELS: Days Inn .5 mile East on US 46. One mile to Budget Inn Motel.

43 MORRISTOWN/BOONTON/I 287/US 46:
BOONTON: North on I-287 to exit 40A. Historic Main Street has 15 antique shops open Tues-Sat 11-5pm. Some are open Sun-Mon. This town also has "New Jersey Firemens' Home & Museum" and historic homes.
CAMPGROUND: "Brookwood Swim & Tennis Club CG": Private. East on US 46, Pool. Bus to New York City twice hourly. $14-$17.

SIDETRIP TO MORRISTOWN

South 3 miles on I-287. Exit 32 to Morris Avenue. This town produced iron and most of the powder for the Revolutionary War. Washington found the town defensible against the British who tried several times to take it. If you're there in mid-March you might see the reenactment of the "Winter Encampment" of 1777-78 & 1779-80.

MORRISTOWN NATIONAL HISTORICAL PARK: Follow signs to Washington Headquarters. First you'll make a Right, and then several Lefts around in a circle past Washington's Headquarters to the parking area. Now you are behind the Headquarters Building and in front of the Museum.

HISTORICAL MUSEUM AND LIBRARY: Up the stairs from the Parking Lot. Interesting historical displays of the encampment, and letters of the Revolution. Film shown every half hour. From here you will sign up for a tour of the Headquarters Building. Get your Morristown Map here. May-Oct daily 9-5pm.

WASHINGTON'S HEADQUARTERS: 230 Morris Street. The colonial home of the Ford family, built in 1772 became the Headquarters of the Revolutionary Army. General and Mrs. Washington lived here during the winter of 1779-80. A fascinating building with fireplaces in every room, folding beds and chairs and period furnishings.

USE YOUR MORRISTOWN MAP AND PARK SERVICE PERSONNEL TO FIND THE FOLLOWING PLACES OF INTEREST:

FORT NONSENSE: West of Washington's Headquarters. This fort was built in 1777 to defend the supplies stored in the village. But it was really never used so the soldiers dubbed it "Fort Nonsense".

JOCKEY HOLLOW: 5 miles Southwest of Morristown. Visitor Center and the sites of the Continental Army's "Soldiers' Huts". The staff are costumed in a living history drama. Reconstructed huts are on the site of the former Pennsylvania troop Quarters. The tattered Revolutionary Army was stationed here for two terrible winters of freezing cold, disease, starvation and poor sanitation! Medicine was in such infancy

FORD MANSION
WASHINGTON HEADQUARTERS
Photo credit: New Jersey Division of Travel & Tourism

that some of the cures killed the men. The Surgeon General of the Continental Army said that the diseases and the hospitals "robbed the U.S. of more citizens than the sword". In 1776, 10,000 died from illness while only 1,000 were killed and 1200 wounded in battle.

WICK HOUSE: The restored farmhouse of Major Gen. Arthur St Clair in 1779.

HISTORIC SPEEDWELL: 333 Speedwell Avenue. Speedwell Iron Works was built in 1800's. In 1818, Stephen Vail made the engine for the "Savannah", the first steamship to cross the Atlantic. In 1837 his son Alfred and Samuel F.B. Morse demonstrated the function of the telegraph here. On display are engineering items, five farm buildings and 3 homes. May-Oct Thurs-Fri noon-4pm. Sat-Sun 1-5pm. $2.

THE MORRIS MUSEUM: 2.5 miles East on NJ 510. Earth sciences, fossils, minerals, animals, North American Indians, fine arts and

GLENMONT, THOMAS A. EDISON MANSION
Photo credit: New Jersey Division of Travel & Tourism

history with a five-senses section for small children. Mon-Sat 10-5pm. $2.

FRELINGHUYSEN ARBORETUM: 3 miles East on Morris Avenue, North on Ridgedale. East to 53 East Hanover Avenue. Self-guided trail has both formal gardens and natural woodlands with trees and shrubs labeled. Daily 9-4:30pm. Free.

MADISON: South 3 miles from Morristown on NJ 24. Settled in 1685 and called "Bottle Hill" after a local tavern. Later renamed in 1834 after President James Madison. Drew University is here with tours available.

NEW JERSEY SHAKESPEARE FESTIVAL: At Drew University. Performances June-Dec.

MUSEUM OF EARLY TRADES AND CRAFTS: Main Street and Green Village Road. The tools of the artisans are displayed to show the early lifestyle. June-Sept Tues-Sat 10-5pm. $1.

You might also want to ask about:

FOSTERFIELD'S LIVING HISTORICAL FARM: Agriculture from 1880-1910.

WILLOWS GOTHIC REVIVAL MANSION: Built by Paul Revere's grandson.

45 EASTBOUND EXIT ONLY/LAKE HIAWATHA/WHIPPANY/NJ 637:
WHIPPANY SHOPPING CENTER.

MOTELS: Red Roof Inn* Eastbound: East .5 mile on US 46. Econo Lodge* Eastbound: 1 mile East on US 46 East.

46 EASTBOUND SOUTH ON I-280 TO ORANGE/US 46 SOUTH:
WESTBOUND WEST ON US 46 NORTH:

MOTELS: Red Roof Inn* on US 46 West of I-80. Econo Lodge* Westbound, West of I-80.

EDISON NATIONAL HISTORICAL SITE: Main Street and Lakeside Avenue, West Orange. Take I-280 South 12 miles to Main Street Exit at West Orange. Go to the Visitor Center first to see film and exhibits. Tours depart from there. Daily 9-5pm. Tours are 9:30-3:30pm. Adult $2.

THE LABORATORY COMPLEX: Built in 1887 with its different shops and special rooms. This is where the phonograph and the movie camera were born.

GLENMONT: Ask at the Laboratory, for directions to Glenmont, a mile away. Edison's spacious and colorful 23 room mansion.

47 US 46 SOUTH TO CALDWELL:
FUEL: South to Mobile.

GROVER CLEVELAND BIRTHPLACE STATE HISTORIC SITE: 207 Bloomfield Avenue. South 5 miles on US 46. Then South on NJ 506 to Caldwell. A restoration. Wed-Sat 9-12 noon & 1-5pm. Free.

48 WESTBOUND EXIT ONLY: HOOK MOUNTAIN ROAD/PINEBROOK ROAD.

52 PASSAIC AVENUE/FAIRFIELD ROAD:
   FUEL: Sam's Service Station.

53 WAYNE/LINCOLN TUNNEL/NJ 23/US 46: WILLOWBROOK MALL: East on US 46.
   FUEL: Sunoco.
   FOOD: Red Lobster, Wendys.
   MOTEL: Holiday Inn.

54 WESTBOUND EXIT ONLY: MINNISINK ROAD, TOTOWA/LITTLE FALLS:
   Bradley's "Child's World".

55 WESTBOUND EXIT ONLY UNION BLVD., TOTOWA:
   MILEPOST 56: YOU ARE NOW CROSSING THE PASSAIC RIVER.

56 EASTBOUND ONLY/SQUIRRELWOOD ROAD, WEST PATERSON:
   GREAT FALLS OF THE PASSAIC: McBride & Wayne Avenue, Paterson, in the middle of town. Go to the Overlook Park on McBride Avenue. Explorers discovered these falls in 1669. They are the second highest waterfall East of the Mississippi. Ancient glaciers blocked the original Passaic River Channel and sent the river roaring over the 77 foot high rock wall in a spectacular plunge that is especially dramatic in the winter. Alexander Hamilton saw the possibilities of power from these falls and organized the "Society for Establishing Useful Manufactures". Paterson was planned as America's first industrial city. Pierre L'Enfant of Washington D.C. designed the raceway to harness the falls. This gave water power to run the mills and foundries that lined the banks of the river. Thus Paterson became the locomotive capital, the silk capital, and the textile center. Samuel Colt's father assisted in establishing the hydropower, and the son designed the Colt revolver in 1836 in his workshop by this river. Now this area has been restored and preserved as a historic district. Get a self-guiding tour book from the "Great Falls Tour Office", 65 McBride Avenue. Weekdays 9:30-4pm. Summer Sun 12-4pm.

57 CLIFTON/NJ 20 SOUTH/DOWNTOWN PATERSON:

58 CLIFTON/MADISON AVENUE, PATERSON:
   AMERICAN LABOR MUSEUM: 83 Norwood Street, Haledon. The "Botto House" built in 1908 was the home of an Italian weaver. Rooms show the lifestyle of the immigrant laborers and their families, and the history of the labor union in the U.S. Wed-Sun, 1-4pm, Adult $1.50.
   Haledon's socialist mayor let Paterson silk factory strikers meet here in Botto's home in 1913. Upton Sinclair met with them here.

59 MARKET STREET, PATERSON/CLIFTON/"LAMBERT CASTLE":
   LAMBERT CASTLE: The stone castle on the mountain overlooking the city. Built in 1892 by a rich silk manufacturer, it's the Passaic County Historical Society Museum. Period rooms, costumes, history, decorative and folk art, textiles. They have a 5400 piece spoon collection. Wed-Sun, 1-4pm. Adult $1.50.
   ROGERS MILL/PATTERSON MUSEUM: 2 Market Street. Collections of minerals, rocks and archeological findings plus history, the silk industry and the hulls of the first two submarines. The work of J.P. Holland of Paterson. Tues-Fri 12:30-4:30pm. Adult $1.

60 HAWTHORN/PASSAIC/NJ 20 NORTH:
   MILEPOST 60: CROSSING THE PASSAIC RIVER AGAIN!

61 ELMWOOD PARK/NJ 507:

62 SADDLEBROOK/NJ 19/GARDEN STATE PARKWAY:

BERGEN MUSEUM OF ART AND SCIENCE: Ridgewood and Farview Avenue, Paramus. Take Garden State Parkway North to Paramus. The Hackensack mastodon skeleton is here with a collection of science and art. Tues-Sat 10-5pm. Donations.

63 SADDLE RIVER ROAD.

64 ROCHELLE PARK/HACKENSACK/NJ 17 NORTH/US 46:

Hackensack began as New Barbados when it was founded by the Dutch and some of its Dutch flavor still remains. The name was changed in 1921. When Washington retreated from Ft. Lee, he stopped here. Take a look at "The Green" at the South end of Main Street that was the center of the town. The church, one of the oldest in the state, was built in 1696. It has been reconstructed several times in its Dutch Colonial architecture.

The tidal-lands south of Hackensack, known as the Meadowlands, was drained and now holds the Giants Stadium and the Meadowlands Racecourse. Go South on NJ 17 if headed for a major event here.

SUBMARINE USS LING: 150 River Street. Tours daily 10-4pm. Adult $3.

MILEPOST 64 WESTBOUND REST AREA:

65 SUMMIT AVENUE, HACKENSACK/NJ 17 SOUTH/GREEN STREET, TETERBORO:

AVIATION HALL OF FAME & MUSEUM: South on NJ 17, East off US 46 to Teterboro Airport. Museum of Aviation, the history of flight with aeronautical memorabilia. Daily 10-9pm. Adult $3. Senior and Child $2.

66 HUDSON STREET, HACKENSACK/LITTLE FERRY:

STUBEN HOUSE STATE HISTORIC SITE: 1209 Main Street, River Edge. North on NJ 503, West to Main Street. Cross NJ 4. Built in 1713, the house was Washington's headquarters in 1780. New Jersey gave it to General Von Steuben for his services in the War. Historical Society displays and Dutch furnishings from 1650-1850. Wed-Sat 10-12 noon. 1-5pm. Free.

MILEPOST 67: CROSSING THE HACKENSACK RIVER.

67 WESTBOUND ONLY, BOGATA/RIDGE FIELD PARK:

WESTBOUND HO! You have the privilege of reliving your country's history in its sequence from the Revolutionary War in New Jersey, through expansion across the Allegheny Mountains, the War of 1812, and the "Great Migration" on the Oregon and California Trails. Read the introduction and history of each state before you enter it. Each city will have the description of its sights at one of the Western entrances, so you'll have to read that ahead also. Happy Trails!

68 I-80 ENDS.

I-95 ENTERS FROM THE SOUTH AS THE NEW JERSEY TURNPIKE.

POOR I-80 WAS NOT ALLOWED TO TOUCH NEW YORK! BUT WE WON'T LEAVE YOU HANGING HERE IN MID FREEWAY LIKE THE SIGN. WE'LL TAKE YOU ON TO THE BRIDGE. I-95, Florida to Maine, intersects I-80 at this point. I-95 goes into New York City and then turns North to Maine. If you're going to Philadelphia get on I-95 South/New Jersey Turnpike.

69 TEANECK ROAD/FORT LEE ROAD, LEONIA:

LAST FULL INTERCHANGE IN NEW JERSEY!

FORT LEE HISTORIC PARK: South of George Washington Bridge in **PALISADES INTERSTATE PARK.** Go East on Fort Lee Road. There is a museum here with gun batteries overlooking the Hudson River. The Visitor Center has a film, artifacts, and miniature scenes. March-December. Wed-Sun 10-5pm. Free, but $2.50 parking.

"The Palisades of New Jersey" are a 13 mile, 500 foot tall, 750-1000 foot thick layer of black basaltic cliff that lines the Western bank of the Hudson from Fort Lee to Sparkill, New York. It is a Triassic lava flow that cooled and formed "columnar jointing" much as is seen in the Sierras and the Basin Range areas. But this massave layer was also metamorphosed to produce quartz, feldspar, magnetite and hornblende. There is much more to this complicated geological story including the glaciating of the rocks and, of course, the river action. The "Palisades Interstate Park" lines the river here to preserve this National Natural Landmark.

Fort Lee was built by George Washington in 1776 to defend New York and the Hudson River from the British. But Cornwallis crossed the Hudson and mounting his artillery on the Palisades, attacked and took Fort Lee. Washington and his troops gathered at Hackensack just West of here and then retreated Southwest across New Jersey with Cornwallis right behind him. Visiting these Revolutionary sites makes you appreciate the courage and the tenacity of our Rebel forebears, and the brilliant leadership of George Washington.

Today, restored battlements overlook the river and you can see the New York skyline across the river. Could Washington have ever imagined such a sight? Fort Lee and the Palisades had another day of fame when it was the silent film capital from 1907 to the 1920's. Exploring this new art here were Samuel Goldwyn, Charlie Chaplin, Rudolph Valentino, Theda Bara and Mary Pickford. The Palisades played a part as the backdrop for "The Perils of Pauline", a famous silent movie. Just South of here at Weehawken, Aaron Burr, the U.S. Vice President, had a duel with and killed Alexander Hamilton.

70   EASTBOUND EXIT ONLY/BROAD AVENUE, ENGLEWOOD:
ELIZABETH CADY STANTON HOUSE: 135 Highwood Avenue, Tenafly. Take Broad Avenue North to Englewood. Then North on NJ 501 to Tenafly. Stanton was THE leader of Women's Suffrage since 1848. All American women are indebted to her not only for the right to vote, but for the right to buy and sell property, conduct a business, control their own monies and have custody of their own children. All of which we take for granted today. Her home is an 1868 Victorian with a spiraling open staircase, slate roof and 11 gabled dormers.

71   WESTBOUND EXITS ONLY TO NJ 4 NORTH/US 1 & 9 SOUTH:

72   PALISADES INTERSTATE PARKWAY, NORTH ONLY:
GEORGE WASHINGTON BRIDGE: TOLL! CROSS THE HUDSON RIVER TO NEW YORK!

S o ends the story of interstate 80, its illustrustrios trek across the continent completed. You journeyed through United States history in reverse. You traveled with I-80 from the Pacific almost to the Atlantic, across a wondrous country whose terrain is as varied as all of us emigrants who have chosen it and claim it for our own.

NEW JERSEY I 80 MILEPOSTS

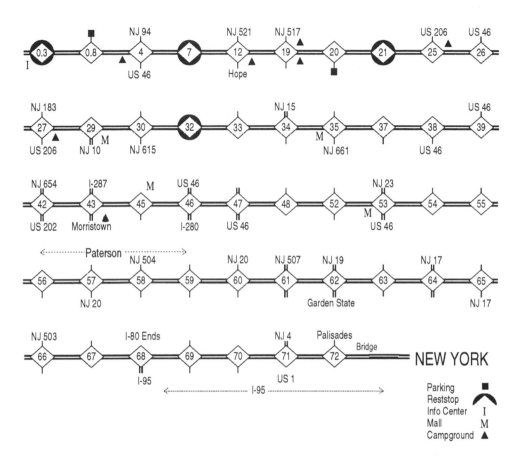

Parking ■
Reststop ⌃
Info Center I
Mall M
Campground ▲